CULTURE
and
BIOLOGICAL
MAN

Explorations in
Behavioral Anthropology

CULTURE
and
BIOLOGICAL
MAN

Explorations in
Behavioral Anthropology

Eliot D. Chapple
Rockland State Hospital
Orangeburg, N. Y.
and Cornell University
Ithaca, N. Y.

HOLT, RINEHART and WINSTON, Inc.
New York · Chicago · San Francisco · Atlanta
Dallas · Montreal · Toronto · London · Sydney

Preface

This book is intended to provide a framework within which anthropology can be understood as providing a systematic and general science of the human condition. Anthropology ranges over so many subjects and includes such great masses of information that it is often hard to determine if any unifying threads exist. Can order be brought into what seems an overwhelming concern with *everything* that is known about the biological and cultural properties of *every* people at *all* periods in history?

If anthropological knowledge is to be reduced to manageable proportions, one needs a few yardsticks to organize its mass of facts. To accomplish this in a not too lengthy book, calculated omissions are a necessity. I here include only that which bears directly on an understanding of the behavior of man as it is biologically and culturally shaped. Thus culture, vast and almost completely possessing the individual, is viewed from the ways in which it serves to constrain the animal which is man and brings about the complexities which we call civilization.

The action of culture—its modes of operation—is often taken for granted; its definition is still a subject of controversy. I here suggest that culture is reducible to a few basic dimensions (or categories) which combine, through the interplay of environment, technology, and the necessity to relate to one's fellows, to produce its apparent complexities.

This book begins with and is grounded upon biology, or what is coming to be known as behavioral biology—which includes genetics, physiology, ethology, and ecology. Traditionally, a concern with biology has been an important element in anthropology. In recent years, however, its relevance is no longer seen solely as a way of explaining the descriptive and taxonomic differences between people—stature, skin and eye color, and head form. Any lingering tendency to limit physical anthropology (human biology) to the factors which help determine such physical differences—and more generally, to sole concern with human evolution—is disappearing with the rapid growth of field studies of apes, monkeys, and the lower animals.

Behavior, like culture, is another word with a multitude of meanings. Here, its use is restricted to observable acts of individuals and their coordinate elements internal to the organism. These latter are identifiable by different techniques—electrophysiological, biochemical, and others—but the evidence indicates that they are not to be regarded as separate phenomena, but parts of single configurations. Only linguistic tradition interferes with our using a single common term for the manifest and covert aspects of specific behavioral action patterns.

Sophistication in looking at the cultural process has been spearheaded by present research in communication—based on linguistic studies, but going far beyond. Elements of culture are amenable to logical analysis; they enable one to utilize the findings of psychology, the science of learning. Inquiries into the components of communication have spread rapidly within anthropology. Their justifiable popularity, focused on defining their logics from the point of view of those possessing the culture—the native speakers—has often seemed to bury that other and equally important part of the anthropologist's field of study—the ways in which people feel and behave towards one another. I have tried to show not only the essential independence of the two areas, but also that, *after* separating them, culture and behavior (biologically considered) can be understood *conjointly*.

In subtitling the book *Explorations in Behavioral Anthropology,* and defining the field which this represents, I have not tried to ignore the logics of culture. On the contrary, one separates the two only to understand better their mutual relationships. The first part of the book deals with the properties of man and lower animals which affect and are basic to everyone at all times and in all conditions; in the second part of the book, I am concerned with the nature of culture and the biological mechanisms through which it modifies the behavior and relationships of men.

Behavioral anthropology is not all of anthropology. It is one of two parts of the total field. It can, however, be studied by itself. One can make observations and conduct experiments provided one controls the cultural constraints affecting the subjects of investigation. "To control" here means to specify and, within definable limits, to make comparable or uniform. In the same way, one can carry on studies of the cultural process—of communication and the process of symbolization, or how technology and spatial factors can order and affect the relationships of people. In so doing, one must be equally careful to control on the behavioral side. Individuals whose patterns of interactional behavior differ widely (even within the same cultural setting) will produce very different cultural results.

To repeat, what this book is intended to do is to make explicit the existence and the properties of what I have called behavioral anthropology. It then goes on to show how culture (and the cultural process) modifies the behavior of individuals through mechanisms which have a biological foundation. The book also makes clear that each of these two interdependent areas has its own logics.

Behavioral anthropology, as part of biology, is a natural science. I outline, on the basis of present knowledge, how it is constituted and how quantitative measurements can be obtained.

Culture has a two-fold aspect. Its investigation might properly be called cultural anthropology, or for that matter, social anthropology if these terms are considered equivalent—as they are *not*, in England, for example— provided its area of concern is distinguished from behavioral anthropology as here defined. First, it is built upon a systematic use of the science of learning, dependent to a large extent, but by no means limited, by what psychology has so far contributed. Second, it concentrates on the logical systems special to each of the cultural dimensions into which culture can be divided. These logical systems are based on other criteria than those of the natural sciences. The assumptions—and the logical combinations which result—may be economic or mechanical, or both in the case of the technology of the work flow; they may be perceptual and architectural in the case of space. In communication, there are a variety of these logical systems, some based on color and form, some on properties of sound and rhythm, some on symbolic logic or visual concordance.

Combining these two main areas of inquiry, cultural anthropology can then explicitly concern itself with the constraints within which the human animal lives, constraints which can no more be excluded from the behavioral side than one can study a fish as a functioning organism and ignore the ocean within which he swims.

Although the term behavioral anthropology is relatively new, the point of view was first presented in anthropology over twenty-five years ago by the author in collaboration with C. S. Coon, *Principles of Anthropology* (Chapple & Coon 1942). Since that time a remarkable growth has taken place both in behavioral biology and in the knowledge of human interaction based on the measurement of its temporal properties. Moreover, a parallel development has taken place in the investigations of culture and its biological foundations. It is now possible to sketch the properties of both more precisely and to examine the nature of the constraints which they impose on human behavior.

By way of preface it may be helpful to mention briefly the advances in biology and anthropology over the last twenty-five years which have contributed so much to the formulation of a consistent and integrated approach to human behavior and to culture.

Before doing so it should be emphasized that the present book in no way assumes that all the evidence is in. Further, it has often been necessary to make reasonable extrapolations from animal studies to humans. Sometimes insufficient work on man has been done or cannot properly be done within ethical limitations. The use of such evidence derives from the fundamental assumption that there is a continuity of process across species, however much there may be significant differences in detail. Man, as animal, must, therefore, be put into his proper place as a biological organism. Provided one is careful to establish where the similarities as well as the differences exist, extrapolations can be a fruitful guide to hypotheses which can be experimentally tested. Without so doing, the science of man will progress much more slowly since even the questions to be asked (and answered) often depend upon the clues which animal studies have afforded us.

Influences from Behavioral Biology

A)   Primate Studies

Closest to anthropological tradition are the field studies of apes and monkeys, and other lower primates like the lemurs. These have become common only in the last decade, and are increasing at a fantastic rate. C.R. Carpenter's classic work on the howler monkey, published in 1934, was the first on any species of primates and, apart from a few others which he himself conducted, no comparable systematic field investigations occurred until the middle 1950's. Since then, a surprising number of studies have been made by zoologists, psychologists, and anthropologists of various persuasions. Although they stem from such different backgrounds, the discipline of observing animals in the field has brought about a high level of comparability in their accounts.

B)   Ethology

A parallel growth has taken place in studies of lower animals, particularly in the identification and investigation of innate behavior patterns. Konrad Lorenz (1950 and before) in Austria, now in Germany, together with Niko Tinbergen (1951 and before) in Holland, now at Oxford, began in the late 1930's what they called ethological studies—ethos meaning character or custom—primarily with birds, fish, and even some species of insects. Studies by field naturalists have been supplemented, again mainly in the last decade, by laboratory research on animals in free-ranging situations, the purpose being to gain a greater understanding of behavior patterns seen in the field under more controlled observational conditions. This work has involved both lower animals and primates, with a considerable emphasis by such investigators as Harlow (1962) and Jensen (1964) on experiments designed to find out the effects of maternal behavior, or deprivations thereof, on the maturation process in infant animals.

C)   Behavior Genetics

Interest in the study of what are presumably innate behavior patterns proved to be an important counterbalance to the environmentalists who long believed that the new-born animal was a blank sheet upon which the learning process wrote out its own formulas. Particularly important in the early period of American psychology, this point of view was held long after the remarkable development of genetic theory should have suggested that behavior itself might be equally amenable to genetic investigation. Actually, it was not until 1960 that the first book on behavior genetics appeared (Fuller and Thompson 1960). Only two years before, at the Genetic Congress in Montreal, it had been impossible to arrange a symposium in the field because of lack of material.

Apart from a few individual investigators, the climate of inquiry in psychology, and even zoology, was definitely unfavorable to work in behavior genetics. This was partly due to the strong influence of stimulus-response theories, but far more important was the implied stigma of "inherited" differences which many people could not accept. Most of the early evidence was derived from clinical medicine. The occasional studies of genetic patterns of activity, aggression, and other aspects of behavior in various strains of a single species, usually laboratory animals like rats and mice, were carried on in an academic wilderness. Again, in little more than five years, a major shift has taken place; a discipline which has come to be called behavior genetics is now regarded as fundamental in understanding man as well as the lower animals.

D)   Circadian Rhythms

In botany, zoology, and general physiology, an extremely important series of investigations on the fundamental rhythms underlying all types of biological phenomena has been conducted. These rhythms are often referred to as "biological clocks," but usually emphasize the diurnal or circadian rhythms (circadian being constructed from the Latin *circa,* around, *dies,* the day). Interest in this field, at the beginning confined to botany, has a long history. It could be said to have begun in 1729 when an astronomer, deMarian, carried on experiments demonstrating that movements of the leaves of plants maintained in constant darkness varied regularly over a twenty-four hour period (Bunning 1960).

Even though a variety of people, including Charles Darwin, were interested in these phenomena, systematic studies, particularly on animals, have been largely a matter of the last thirty years. It has been shown that almost all of the fundamental, physiological and biochemical processes in all types of living forms are governed by endogenous, that is, internally controlled, rhythms, which can be modified only to a limited degree by external influences. Their wide-spread implications for the human condition are illustrated by the many popular discussions of the temporary but serious disorientations of their biological clocks (Strughold 1962) which travelers in space or in intercontinental air-travel suffer.

In addition, the study of biological rhythms has been extended to include the very fast rhythms—brain waves, muscle fibre firing, heart and respiration rates, as well as the longer rhythms—the menstrual cycle, or the migration patterns, which organize time spans of activity (and physiological function) up to the period of a year, at least.

E)   Territoriality

In the last twenty years, the fundamental significance of the possession of personal space and territory by animals at every level of complexity has been clearly demonstrated. These studies have been well described by Robert Ardrey in two books, *African Genesis* (1961) and *The Territorial Imperative* (1966). It is now accepted that the dynamics of population growth are controlled by the ways in which crowding—resulting in territorial conflicts—influences the endocrine system and the proper physiological functioning of the organism. Under natural as well as laboratory-designed experimental situations, the interindividual stresses produced by extreme crowding can bring about death in the animal, either directly or by increased susceptibility to disease through the weakening of the body defenses.

A large number of studies, collected in Wynne-Edwards' monumental book, *Animal Dispersion in Relation to Social Behavior* (1962), demonstrates that territorial behavior is fundamental in establishing social relations and in maintaining the stability of a group, both internally and externally. As Ardrey takes pleasure in pointing out, recognition of the crucial part played by the struggle for personal space has relegated to oblivion the idea that sexual relations are the cement of society.

Work in neurophysiology and physiological psychology (actually started many years ago) has begun to make explicit the biological foundations of spacing. Extensive inquiries by Berlyne (1964) and many others have shown how the reticular formation of the brain is central in controlling the orientation process of one animal towards another.

F)   Physiological Bases of Emotion

Another major thread in understanding the biological basis of human societies and their culture lies in studies of the "emotions," that is, the physiological and biochemical systems whose adaptive or maladaptive changes are an integral part of all behavior patterns. Walter B. Cannon's classic book *Bodily Changes in Fear, Hunger, Pain and Rage* (1929), brought together what was then known about the ways in which humans and animals react to stress. Since his day, the broad area of what is called the autonomic nervous system, which controls the patterns of these reactions, has been intensively investigated, with major support from the American Government because of its implications for both mental and physical disease. The field has become so vast, however, that no single person has appeared to integrate the knowledge of today as Cannon earlier did.

G)   Interaction Measurement

Methods of studying the dynamics of the relations between individuals, within a biological framework, came into being with Chapple's development of interaction measurement in the late 1930's (Chapple 1940). This method, based on measuring the time durations of actions and inactions and their frequencies, made feasible a description of the individual personality in interaction with others. The same system of measurement describes all types of group situations, in any one of which each personality has to adjust to others under the constraints of culture. Increasingly, these techniques are being applied to other animals; in fact, precise observation makes them almost inevitable. They provide a common method for studying how biological influences in animals and men must be taken into account in a scientific inquiry into man's behavior.

H)   Learning in Comparative Psychology

Inquiries into the learning process are being extended to include its biological properties. Learning theory has been one of the vital areas of study in psychology. Its investigators number in the thousands. Because of the different points of view of many of the participants, it has often been difficult to identify the various elements which can be combined in a biological formulation: no single person since Pavlov's time dominates the field. However, the rigid and often mechanical process initially postulated by some learning theorists has been significantly modified by the recognition that physiological states, as well as the various stages of development of the young animal, influence the results.

I)   Sensory Physiology or Physiological Psychology

Inquiry into the neurophysiological processes through which sensory information is received from the outside and transmitted and processed by the central nervous system is one of the oldest subjects in physiology. Though related to learning studies, comparative studies of sight, hearing, touch, taste, smell, and movement are clearly of importance in examining the constraints within which animals adapt to their environment. Apart from the importance of sensory physiology in medicine (and the medical specialties developed around them), the senses impose obvious limitations on the perceptual process in different species. They also are fundamental in mediating relationships with other animals of the same species. A great virtue of physiological psychology to many investigators is its susceptibility to precise scientific experiments and mathematical formulations of the results. It also provides the foundation for central nervous system inquiry— following the course of the signals received from internal or external sources. Our understanding of the brain and its operation has to begin with such phenomena; many aspects of animal behavior have been related to areas in the brain not previously understood—in particular, the reticular formation.

J)   The Biology of Language

Linguistics, both as a subject of its own and in psychology and anthropology, has been intensively studied as a cultural process. Yet the biological foundations of language were brought together in usable form by Lenneberg only in 1967, although many investigators have contributed to this formulation. Here the greatest influence, originally at least, was from neurology. Medicine has always had a concern with speech and language disorders due to brain damage or to hearing loss; there are a wide variety of pathological states requiring differential diagnosis and treatment. In addition, the ways language is learned are of obvious importance to educationalists. How is this learning accomplished and what are its biological prerequisites? This must include such factors as the influence of respiration, of central nervous system controls, and of the neuroanatomical apparatus without which speech becomes impossible.

Contributions from Cultural Studies

A)   The Ethnography of Communication

In the United States, and less explicitly in other parts of the world, communication has become the shibboleth not only of the advertising man, but also of the professional educator, the personnel manager, and investigators in various academic fields. Edward Sapir (1921), an anthropologist and linguist, was the first to formulate what he considered to be a coherent discipline. Only recently, however, have linguists, social anthropologists, sociologists, psychologists, and zoologists come to study communication as a unified phenomenon within a group whose boundaries are defined by the possibility of exchanging messages. Many terms—semantics, semiotics, semiology, or physics-derived labels like communication theory or cybernetics, even such mundane and traditional phrases as ethnography or social anthropology—have been borrowed to describe the subject being investigated (Hymes 1964). Whatever label is used, a variety of academic fields have become concerned with what, in this book, we shall call communication.

Typically, "communicationists" are interested in working out the logics of the system which appear to control the patterns of communication. They try to develop a model of cognitive (thinking) processes to predict what particular combinations of words and gestures individuals will use in a particular setting. In general, they begin with the data of the terminological structures with which various languages describe the formal relationships of individuals within a kinship system. From these, they look for logical principles to help explain the particular combinations of sounds, or alternatively of kinship terms, which they encounter. By carefully recording all the nuances of gesture, posture, and sound, as well as vocabulary, which make up the total situation in which the messages occur, they hope to be able to define a logic of meanings which will characterize the thinking processes of the particular individuals in a particular cultural setting.

B)   Information Theory

Communication or information theory was developed by Shannon and Weaver (1949) to deal with the problem of sending messages over telephone or radio channels. By analogy, the basic principles for estimating the degree of clarity of a given message, and the conditions under which maximum "communication" with minimum noise can be achieved, have been used as a means of analysis of the linguistic material itself. Much effort is devoted to estimating the probabilities that particular words and gestures in particular orders will be used by a specific individual in a particular situation. Presumably, understanding the logics will aid in making statistical predictions about linguistic usage.

C)   Cultural Influence of Space

Parallel to the concern with communication (and clearly related to it) have been the beginnings of studies on how cultures utilize space to control the relationships of individuals. Hall (1959) was one of the earliest writers in the field. He was interested both in extending the idea of territoriality in animals to the ways in which humans manage the distance between themselves as a communication medium, and also in how culture modified space in architecture, landscaping, and urban design. Increasing attention has been paid to spatial and aesthetic influences on interaction, with considerable emphasis on such problems as the design of mental hospitals (Osmond 1957), pediatric hospitals (Kennedy 1965) and, from the point of view of the technology of the work flow, in countless engineering studies prefatory to the design of factories or office buildings.

D)   Work Flow Engineering

Work flows, not only at the highly technical level of the assembly line, but in the development of systems engineering as an outgrowth of time and motion studies, have been a fertile source for understanding the influences of technology on human relationships. Like architecture, most of the writing has been done by practitioners—in this case by engineers. Investigations of the impact of work flows on people have been carried out largely by industrial anthropologists and sociologists as a consequence of the pioneering studies at the Hawthorne Plant of the Western Electric Company (Roethlisberger and Dickson 1939).

Almost all such investigations have been made in the United States and Great Britain. We are only beginning to obtain reports on the effects of technological factors in other cultures, published, for example, in such journals as *Human Organization,* by the Society for Applied Anthropology. However, these are almost entirely limited to modern industrial technology. One has to rely on occasional ethnographic reports for the description of nonindustrial work flow which can be used for comparative purposes.

This brief summary illustrates the many developments of the past few years on both the cultural and biological sides which require inclusion in this book. One might also mention some of the contributions of new approaches in statistics and mathematics, in particular, in such quasi-fields as cybernetics and systems theory, since they have assisted many investigators to find concepts explaining relationships within their data. Since this book is not intended to be mathematical, it does not need such levels of sophisticated description.

In this sense, it is an introductory or preliminary book, though it is not an "introduction to" in the formal textbook sense. Nor is it a textbook. Rather, as the subtitle indicates, it is intended truly as an exploration of the factors influencing human relationships. It represents an attempt to present in simple form the foundations of what can be (and have been) outlined much more systematically and abstractly in ways which can then lead to mathematical treatment (Chapple 1969a). To try to discuss in detail all the evidence which this book refers to and draws upon would require an intermediate and lengthy treatise. This book is then both a preface and introduction to a larger field of investigation.

Acknowledgment

In the writing of a book, particularly one which endeavours to bring together and restate concerns with which the author has been working for more than thirty years, it is hard to single out individuals whose contributions to it, knowingly or not, have had a preponderant influence. In addition, the sources called upon, identified in the Preface, are so widely separate that it would be improper to imply that the ways in which they rub elbows with one another here are anything other than the author's doing and for which he must take the responsibility. To all those who have played some part in what here follows, the author can only repeat the Latin encomium, *Qui palman meruit, ferat!*

As exceptions to the above, however, I need explicitly to thank Richard Sheldon who patiently read the first draft and, with remarkable patience, took the trouble to point out the assorted snares and confusions in the text which I hope have been eliminated to his satisfaction. Also, Alfred G. Smith of the University of Oregon read the same draft (among others) for the publishers and with diligence and care summarized the problems which he found from the point of view of potential readers.

Lastly, I cannot thank Kathleen Bussey sufficiently for her patience in typing successive drafts, not simply on the typewriter, but using and mastering the computer system which remarkably speeds up the rewriting and editing process. Her efforts, conjoined with those of Margaret Jones, who devoted herself to what is often the most thankless job in bringing out a book—preparing the references and the index and assisting in the editing—made this author's job of simply doing the writing almost, if not quite, a pleasurable and exciting experience.

Acknowledgments for permissions to quote must be made to:
Ethel M. Albert, " 'Rhetoric', 'Logic', and 'Poetics' in Burundi," reproduced
by permission of the American Anthropology Association from *American Anthropologist,* vol. 66, pt. 2, pp. 35–54, 1964.
Raymond Firth, *We, the Tikopia.* London: George Allen and Unwin, Ltd., 2nd ed., 1957.
Konrad Lorenz, *On Aggression.* New York: Harcourt, Brace and World, 1966 (English translation).
Sir Peter Medawar, "A Biological Retrospect," *Nature,* vol. 207, pp. 1327–1330, 1965.

E.D. Chapple

Orangeburg, N.Y.
January 1970

Contents

Part I

THE DIMENSIONS
OF BEHAVIOR

Chapter 1

Biology
and Anthropology

To begin a consideration of man and all his works by way of biology may seem a somewhat arbitrary point of departure. The reader may be prepared to accept the biological basis of human behavior abstractly as a kind of first principle, an act of faith. Yet somehow, pursuing the daily course, the people making up the world may not seem to fit one's notions of what biology is all about. By definition, biology is the science of life; it thus includes anthropology, the science of man. Remembering introductory courses in botany and zoology in high school or college, how does one jump from monocotyledenous plants or jelly fish to the *me* of personal and autonomous experience?

If physiology still sticks in the mind, it probably is remembered as the circulation of the blood or the process of digestion, as in those grade school hygiene courses of early memory. Hormones, endocrines—fear, anger, love—the patterning of behavior publicly evidenced, the complex controls of the central nervous system, are likely to have been ignored or dismissed in school as too complex or "psychological" for serious attention. Even someone majoring in biology only occasionally encounters the human being as a biological organism. If the student is premedical, man is first expected to appear at medical school—on the dissecting table. Otherwise, he clutters up the lecturer's neat packaging of molecular biology and cell physiology.

In spite of this abdication within the curriculum, the biology of man is a subject of intensive investigation. As noted in the Preface, remarkable progress has been made in unraveling the springs of human behavior. Through studies of the lower animals and the lower primates—monkeys and apes—the continuities across species are being more and more systematically explored. But this implies acceptance of the existence of the continuum. Surprisingly, even those most concerned with the emotional dynamics of man often avoid looking too closely at emotions as biological processes.

Unwillingness in research to accept and utilize the continuity of all living things seems largely the result of deeply felt beliefs that many human beings have about themselves—a consequence of cultural patterning. Man's remarkable achievements in technology and his development of an elaborate language make it easy to believe in his essential difference from the rest of the animal kingdom. A major tenet of faith for many is that a clean break can be demonstrated between man as Sapiens, and the un-Sapiens others. "Look at my works, ye Mighty," as Shelley so ironically pointed out.

Yet every human being is tightly under the control of biological processes. Very little of what man does is independent of the Old Adam. Neither atomic energy nor the conquest of space enables one's reactions to others to be conducted by abstract logical reasoning. People still love and hate, feel frightened or aggressive. The elementary forces still rule, even though there are numberless ways to rationalize one's feelings and actions. In freedom from biological needs, man has no cause to feel superior to apes or timber wolves. If commiseration there be, it can only be proffered for *their* ineptness in verbal camouflage and, of course, in lack of technological triumph.

The Revolution in Biology

The change in point of view in biology and in many other fields has been remarkably accelerated by the acceptance of what is now called ethology. Though little different from the field methods which many anthropologists like Malinowski (1922) and Chapple (1940) have advocated, essentially it involves recording happenings in their actual order and separating observation from interpretation. Sir Peter Medawar, F.R.S., Director of the National Institute for Mental Research in Great Britain, described (1966) this revolution well:

> In the early 1930's, we had also learnt finally, and I hope forever, the methodological lesson of behaviourism: that statements about what an animal feels or is conscious of, and what its motives are, belong to an altogether different class from statements about what it does and how it acts. I say the "methodological" lesson of behaviourism, because that word also stands for a certain psychological theory, namely, that the phenomenology of behaviour is the

whole of behaviour—a theory which I shall only say that, in my opinion, it is not nearly as silly as it sounds. Even the methodology of behaviourism seemed cruelly austere to a generation not yet weaned from the doctrine of privileged insight through introspection. But what comparable revolution of thought ushered in the study of animal behaviour in the style of Lorenz and Tinbergen and led to the foundation of flourishing schools of behaviour in Oxford, here in Cambridge, and throughout the world? [Beginning roughly in 1950, author's note]. I believe the following extremely simple answer to be the right one. In the thirties it did not seem to us that there *was* any way of studying behaviour "scientifically" except through some kind of experimental intervention—except by confronting the subject of our observations with a "situation" or with a nicely contrived stimulus and then recording what the animal did. The situation would then be varied in some way that seemed appropriate, whereupon the animal's behaviour would also vary. Even poking an animal would surely be better than just looking at it: that would lead to anecdotalism: that was what bird watchers did. Yet it was also what the pioneers of ethology did. They studied natural behaviour instead of contrived behaviour, and were thus able for the first time to discern natural behaviour structures or episodes—a style of analysis helped very greatly by the comparative approach, for the occurrence of the same or similar behavioural sequences in members of related species reinforced the idea that there was a certain natural connectedness between its various terms, as if they represented the playing out of a certain instinctual programme. Then, and only then, was it possible to start to obtain significant information from the study of contrived behaviour—from the application or withholding of stimuli—for it is not informative to study variations of behaviour unless we know beforehand the norm from which the variants depart.

The Fixed Action Patterns

What the ethologists discovered, a discovery long predating Lorenz and Tinbergen, was that animals performed basic behavioral sequences which they had had no opportunity to learn. Although preceded by a number of observers at the beginning of the 18th century, Charles Darwin, in his classic book *The Expression of Emotions in Man and Animals* (1872), written from an evolutionary point of view, pointed out the many patterns of behavior that occurred (automatically) either across species—like the erection of the hair in man, monkeys, cats, dogs, birds, horses, and cattle—or where a dog, raised on a hard floor, still tried to scratch nonexistent earth before lying down to sleep.

In the first formal approach to the definition of these spontaneous and inherent patterns, Jennings (1906) emphasized the importance of the identification of the animal's action system—its "characteristic set of movements."

Today, these are called the fixed action patterns. They consist of sequences of coordinated motor actions which do not have to be learned. They are *not* mere reflexes or chains of reflexes; these are becoming less and less important as we shall later see.

Obvious examples of such fixed action patterns are those of walking and speaking. These have been chosen deliberately to indicate that in the higher animals, these patterns are both fixed yet modifiable through feedback from the central nervous system. The skeletal-muscular movements in both are clearly not sequenced by deliberate decision as to which muscles are to be used in what order. The fixed aspect of the pattern means that the underlying structure of movement occurs spontaneously. How many muscles are involved in locomotion, I do not know; in speech, however, Lenneberg (1967) said there were approximately 100. Where the central nervous system (and learning) comes in is in the feedback control through which individuals learn to vary the *timing* of the contractions and relaxations of the muscle systems involved—to run, to dance, to speak one language rather than another, or to sing.

Each species has a repertoire of such fixed patterns, the totality of which the ethologists call the ethogram, the action system of Jennings. The first step, therefore, in studying a species is to identify these patterns, recognizing, in the higher animals at least, that variations can be introduced in their quantitative components but not in the sequences they follow once set in motion. This distinction should be emphasized since, in the original definition of fixed action patterns, it was assumed that they were independent of external control. To illustrate, in a much simpler animal than a mammal, it has been shown that for the locust external factors can alter the frequency of the rhythm with which it moves its wings, but the wing-stroke sequence is unaltered.

The Ethogram

No one as yet has prepared a description of the human ethogram, although a great deal of data is available, particularly from studies of infants and children. Too often, the fixed action patterns are lost sight of because of variations due either to environmental modifications (the locomotive process in water, on the side of a hill, climbing a tree), or to the temporal differentiations by which each segment of the sequence can be altered in its duration and frequency. Marler and Hamilton (1966) made the point that variations in fixed action patterns (defined as sequences) were usually grouped around a series of modes (central forms) with little continuous gradation between them. This makes it easy to recognize them, although precise definition of exactly what the sequence consists of is much more difficult.

A Scottish zoologist, Frazer Darling (1937) studied the behavior of the red deer in the Highlands. His advice to the individual seeking to establish fixed action patterns is worth quoting, particularly since, even with humans, both their cultural modifications or those distortions of behavior introduced by disease (Chapple *et al.* 1963) require just this kind of concentrated observation:

> It takes time for the eye to become accustomed to recognize differences, and once that has occurred the nature of the differences has to be defined in the mind by careful self-interrogation if the matter is to be set down on paper. . . . The fact remains that an observer has to go through a period of conditioning of a most subtle kind. . . . The observer must empty his mind and be receptive only of the deer and the signs of the country. This is quite severe discipline, calling for time and practice. . . . It is necessary intellectually to soak in the environmental complex of the animal to be studied until you have a facility with it which keeps you as it were one move ahead. You must become intimate with the animal. . . . In this state the observer learns more than he realizes.

For primates—man, apes, and the monkeys—Stuart Altmann (1962) has made the most thorough attempt to develop an ethogram for the rhesus macaque. He limited his inquiry to the patterns which made up the total communication repertoire, but included every type of physical movement as well as sounds. These monkeys were located on Cayo Santiago, a macaque colony established by C. R. Carpenter in 1938 on a small island off the east coast of Puerto Rico. Altmann was able to establish 59 elemental patterns, many of which consisted of postural positions, gestures, or forms of physical contact. Others were recognizable patterns of vocalization. From observation, he found that some of these, up to as many as four, combined into compound patterns because they took place simultaneously. A monkey could bob his head, open his jaw wide, and stare, each of these at separate times. Thus, each constituted an elemental pattern. On the other hand, all three might occur at the same time; presumably they had a different "meaning" together than when they occurred separately. For the macaque, Altmann arrived at a total of 123 communicative patterns seen in two years of continuous field work.

As he watched the interactions of the members of the several groups of rhesus on the island, he recorded the sequence of patterns manifested by each animal from the beginning to the end of the contact with one or more others. Each elemental pattern was established by a drawing or photograph so that the muscular combinations could easily be identified. Only the vocalizations caused difficulty since it was not possible to make sound spectrographs in the field. Yet their beginnings and endings and general characteristics could be roughly determined. Once he had his catalogue of rhesus communicative patterns, he then investigated the degree to which he could estimate the probabilities that one particular sequence would occur rather than another—that what a monkey did at a particular time would or would not be influenced by what had previously occurred, either immediately or some time earlier. Though aware of the importance of the differential length of time which a given pattern or sequence might take, he only recorded its frequency due to field problems. Some patterns, for example, when one animal grooms another, may last for many minutes; hitting another animal takes a fraction of a second.

Although Altmann's work is perhaps the most systematic (except for spectrographic descriptions of vocalizations which other investigators, notably Andrew (1963), Marler (1965), and Struthsaker (1967) have carried out for various primate species), there have been many similar studies on apes, monkeys, and the lower animals. If the same procedures were carried out for man, ignoring for the moment cultural elaboration, the fixed action patterns would probably approximate those of the chimpanzee. Andrew (1963) has pointed out that there is very little difference between these species in their repertoires, at least as far as their basic facial expressions and natural calls are concerned. No wonder the egocentric human thinks chimpanzees are such appealing performers!

Measurement of Fixed Action Patterns

To distinguish one fixed action pattern from another necessarily requires criteria by which to separate them. Altmann (1967) called the process sequential demarcation. He emphasized the difficulties, which everyone encounters, of determining where the cutting off point should be. Should one regard a variant on a motor pattern as just that, or as a separate category? So much attention in the literature has been devoted to the latter problem as part of the investigation into the linguistic repertoire of the animals (if linguistics be taken to include all communicative patterns) that the relative ease with which beginnings and endings can be identified has often been overlooked (Chapple 1940, 1948, and so on).

Here we can rely on observation of the muscle systems making up the pattern. Everyone knows that muscles (and muscle systems) alternate between contraction and relaxation. When a muscle system is activated, its constituent muscles keep contracting and relaxing while the pattern continues to be manifested. Its ending is marked by a relaxation of all its components or their beginning use in another different pattern. Beginning, therefore, means the start of contraction of the muscle *system,* ending, its relaxation. In interaction or communication between individuals, not only in man and his primate relatives but in the lower animals, beginnings and endings of interaction patterns are determined from changes in muscular patterns, often accompanied by sound, which is also produced by a muscular pattern.

An animal screeching at another, ends his noise, the face muscles relax; he then turns and walks away. Watching the primate face, or the human in particular, contractions are evidenced in the muscles around the mouth and eyes, in vertical or horizontal movements of the head, or by gestures of the upper body. They also can occur in the lower body when, for example, one person kicks another, or a male monkey mounts a female and begins sexual intercourse. When sound or movement of the particular muscle system involved in the action sequence ceases, relaxation occurs. Much interaction may involve a continuing sequence of such patterns and the muscle systems activating them so that the beginning and ending points are determined when a noninteraction pattern precedes or follows an interactional sequence.

If one can determine that a fixed action pattern is occurring—if criteria for recognition are objectively spelled out—its occurrence can be counted. Then, as Altmann did, its frequency can be calculated for any period of observation. If one can also identify beginnings and endings with extremely high reliability (assuming that the underbrush does not get in the way and sounds can be heard), one can measure the length of each action and the time interval between its ending and the beginning of the next.

Similar criteria, enabling time measurements to be made, can be used across the animal kingdom, assuming an ethogram has been worked out for each species to be compared. The question then arises: Yes, durations of actions, inactions, and interactions can be measured in all species, but what can we learn if we do so? The answer to this question will become clear in the chapters following. Its kernel can only be commented on here.

Utility of Measurement

Lord Kelvin, a famous physicist, best known for his work in thermodynamics, is often quoted for a statement he once made about the uses of measurements:

> I often say that when you can measure what you are speaking about, and express it in numbers, you know something about it; when you cannot measure it, when you cannot express it in numbers, your knowledge is of a meagre

and unsatisfactory kind; it may be the beginning of knowledge, but you have scarcely, in your thoughts, advanced to the stage of science, whatever the matter may be.

Thus simply stated, the significance of being able to use numbers is inadequately expressed. Kelvin was taking a good deal for granted as a physicist and mathematician. The literature dealing with living things is full of intuitive hunches, firmly held, with no quantitative data to support them. Merely to assign numbers without something more in view is also hardly sufficient if the science of man (or any science) is to advance. What one tries to ascertain is whether there is some meaningful relationship between the entities being measured.

In mathematical terms, what we require is reasonable evidence that what we are interested in understanding—in this case, the relationships of living individuals—exhibits the properties of functional dependence, that is, that some aspect which we can identify varies as a function of another. These aspects, when precisely defined, are called variables. Everyone is familiar with the simple statement, $y = f(x)$, that there is some systematic relationship such that values of y vary as a function of x.

It is clear that one person's behavior affects another's. The problem is to identify *what* aspect of the behavior is doing the influencing and *what*, in turn, is the behavioral element being affected. If we can begin to make such judgments, we can then turn naturally and easily to quantitative distinctions. "How much did he do? How long did it last? How often has he"?— the kinds of inquiry which come naturally to all of us as we try to understand an emotional upset at home, between friends, or at work. It is here that Kelvin's prescription is most apt. In spite of natural laziness, we do know that we are better off in estimating the severity of a reaction and its possible carry-over to ourselves if we can classify it by using some kind of numerical difference.

We also realize that some elements of the behavior, aspects of the fixed action patterns or their cultural (at least, central nervous system) elaborations, are only the surface characteristics of the variables we need to define with precision. What these are depends on the nature of the problems to which we have set ourselves. The neuroanatomist's interest in a fixed action pattern is doubtless concerned with the infinite detail of the mutual arrangements of each muscle bundle or even its constituent muscle fibers. Altmann's analysis of rhesus monkey communication treated each of the 123 patterns which he identified as a variable. For humans, the extraordinary cultural development of language and expressive movements would necessitate an analysis with hundreds of thousands of such variables.

Despite modern high-speed computers with built-in memories for enormous quantities of data and techniques for reducing the number of variables by statistical manipulations, the questions this book will try to answer are very different. For behavioral anthropology is concerned with understanding the properties of the factors controlling the adjustments (emotional and otherwise) of human beings to one another. In effect, this is the study of the interaction sequences—the manifestation in each individual of a complex patterning of physiological and behavioral elements. The apparent dichotomy is artificial. The skeletal-muscle components of the fixed action patterns and their variations are integral parts of the internal "emotional" events of the central nervous system.

The Biological Framework of Behavior

The foundations of behavioral anthropology are not so much the fixed action patterns; these are only the surface phenomena which can be directly observed. Underlying them are the all-pervasive biological rhythms whose multiple beats at very fast and slow frequencies shape the action and inter-action patterns of every animal. The best known of these biological clocks is that which controls the daily cycle, through which each individual's adaptation to its environment and its expenditure of activity is controlled.

These rhythms are found in all biological processes—biochemical, electrophysiological and endocrine. They include the rhythms of brain and heart and respiration, as well as such longer cycles as that of menstruation and the triggering off of migration or hibernation. Their significance lies in the fact that they provide what might be called the engines which drive behavior and its physiological components; they are the source of the spontaneity which the need to respond to the external environment may tend to conceal.

From the individual cell and its metabolic processes, its synthesis of DNA and RNA, to man as the total organism, the biological rhythms are the controlling factor. They are integral to the nervous system and endocrine mechanisms, which regulate the internal state and ready the individual for attack or flight and maintain metabolic and sexual balance. These major patterns of response to external stimuli are the primary emotional states on which much more complex variants are elaborated.

But the rhythms themselves, though differing for species, are the elements on which individuality is built, not only in man but in the lower animals. The most striking finding of studies of biological rhythms from a philosophical point of view is the consistency with which they express themselves quantitatively within the individual, though one individual may differ considerably from another within a species. This individuality, as the rhythms become transformed into interaction, is the starting point and groundwork of personality, since personality manifests itself in relationships with others. So too, reactions to changes in the external environment set off emotional–behavioral patterns in the individual. These too are personal, and are functions of the personality. They repeat themselves in characteristic ways and differ from individual to individual.

Though these will be discussed in the chapters following, they are mentioned here to make the point that measurements of the fixed action patterns through which they are expressed enable us to treat their quantitative properties within the framework of functional dependence. In this sense, the dimensions of behavior, in particular as they manifest themselves in the interaction variables, can be regarded as deterministic; that is to say, causality, if defined simply as one value occurring after another uniformly, can be ascribed to the phenomena. Epistemologically, one can, of course, argue that all phenomena are probabilistic. One never "knows" if someone falls out the window whether he will continue dropping until he hits the ground or rise against gravity to the sky.

But behavioral anthropology is a long way away from the sophistications of nuclear physics. At its present level, it is convenient to regard the behavioral dimensions as deterministic and the cultural dimensions as probabilistic. The distinction helps exposition. It emphasizes the point that predictability is high in the first situation, because it is based on physiology. Within culture, on the other hand, chance plays a far more important role; its dimensions can merely provide estimates of how often out of so many trials X may happen, providing nothing interferes.

In Part I of this book, this biological–behavioral system will be discussed, as well as the ways in which the interaction patterns of which they are the overt evidence are shaped through human physiology. In Part II, we shall be concerned with culture, the total context of the learned elements of human living, its biological foundations, and the way in which it influences the relationships of people. By way of introduction to it, and to the point of view of this book, some further discussion of the framework of anthropology may prove useful.

The Cultural Universe of Anthropology

The scope of anthropology is almost unbelievable to anyone who first encounters it. Turning over the program of the annual meeting of the American Anthropological Association (even more than scanning the courses listed at a large university), it is apparent that "everything" having to do with man is included. Of course, this is not quite an accurate judgement. Nevertheless, apart from such "traditional" topics as physical anthropology, including primate studies, archeology and large portions of human history, linguistics and communication, ethnology, social or cultural anthropology, there are a host of secondary topics discussed—technology and material culture, economics, political science, psychology, culture and personality as a variant on the latter, religion, applied anthropology (largely devoted to present day society), community studies, medical anthropology—this list is by no means intended to be complete.

In the old days, before anthropologists became sufficiently sophisticated from a public relations point of view to be preoccupied with labels, many of these subjects had the prefix "primitive" attached to them. Now this has ended. Anthropologists knew, even then, that small, isolated, technologically simple groups by no means were to be ranked at the bottom of some cultural totem pole with these United States, "God's Country," perched on top. No adequate substitute for the term, primitive, properly sterilized, has yet been found, but there is no doubt that it is on such groups that most anthropologists concentrate their studies.

In all these areas (excluding parts of physical anthropology), the overwhelming concern is with culture, a term used by some to differentiate anthropologists from sociologists (who presumably avoid it) and psychologists (who concentrate on the individual, except when they are social psychologists). In fact, this attempt to parcel out aspects of human society between academic disciplines is unworkable. Perhaps what one can say is that most anthropologists largely concern themselves with the influences of the learned habits special to a group and try to compare the uniformities of one group with others. Although the human being brings basic biological properties with him into the world (including the capacity to learn), culture in the anthropological sense provides the environment through which his patterns of behavior, derived from his biological states, are shaped.

The Domain of Culture

The subjects which anthropologists talk about at their meetings provide a shorthand statement of what the term "culture" includes. What is not apparent, however, in such a listing is the specificity of the detail observed and recorded. This is another way to differentiate the field. If time, money, and the limitations which human energy put in the way of perfection were not at issue, the ideal ethnography—the basic record of what goes on in any group selected for study—would consist of continuous sound motion pictures of each individual each day with all the variations in activities and interactions which the yearly round brings forth. This would be supplemented by careful coding of all the environmental factors which film omits, as well as all the material objects used by each person. Beyond this, the ethnographer would try to supplement his data with interviews to ascertain what was unexpressed in what he has recorded in personal or group history, belief, and explanation of custom.

No one person, not even a team, could possibly do this for a whole society, even a small one. Yet the history of ethnography shows that very carefully described data can be obtained on major aspects of a culture. Such care in collecting what often seem like minutiae has been a source of criticism in some nonanthropological quarters. It is, however, exactly comparable to what is now done in zoology and ecology as a consequence of the "ethological revolution." Clearly, such collection does depend on what it is being collected for, but if it can be shown that such specifics do alter the consequences in the analysis, then there is no alternative.

If culture is regarded as the totality of the learned environment within which a particular group of human beings adapts, it of course begins with the individual. From the moment of birth, and throughout his life, his behaviors are shaped by the conditioning process which others in the group provide. He learns to interact, to adapt his vocalizations and movements to the patterns of others. Given his cortical complexity, it is possible for him to discriminate contexts and situations external to him in the finest detail and to learn to associate these with the language of his group. Through similar processes, he acquires all types of patterned movements. He learns to manage spatial distance from others and to follow a prescribed order in performing various activities. Some of these patterns facilitate technical performance, others are expressive forms (including language) through which he carries out particular sequences of adjustment to others.

Each of these cultural configurations has its emotional components. As these repeat themselves and become stabilized, we call the product the structure of organizations or institutions—the family, the factory, the church, the school, the political unit, or the secret society. The ways in which the individual personality varies these configurations provide the bridge between culture and behavior, and the structural differences or organizations in which they interact, for personalities can only occur within a cultural framework. On the other hand, the interplay is not a one way street. Cultural patterns do shift as a consequence of individual and group dynamics.

There has been a tendency in anthropology, sometimes emotionally maintained, to try to limit the field (and the analysis) to one part only of the totality. Thus, cultural anthropologists were once distinguished from social anthropologists because the latter tried (in theory) to minimize the influence of cultural patterning while the former complicated our understanding of institutions unnecessarily. Whatever justifications might have existed for the argument in the past, they are long since irrelevant. Perhaps only the individual, and individuality, needs to be rescued as an integral part of the system, as Opler (1964) so cogently pointed out.

The Ethnography of Communication

Today, the predominant theme in anthropological inquiry derives from the remarkable advances in the analysis of language to which ethnologists, linguists, psychologists—even mathematicians—are contributing. The reasons are not merely to put language into a logical system (the term here is intended to include the entire repertoire of speech and expressive movement, both verbal *and* nonverbal aspects of communication). Underneath, there is the hope, not always made explicit, that the systematic examination of the ways languages are constructed out of culture, and used within it by individuals and by groups, will provide the means of getting at how the process of thinking takes place within the brain. Analysis of these cognitive processes which language facilitates (even if it may not be absolutely indispensable to it) might then make an approach to the operation of the human cortex possible. It is even plausible to hold that communication could then become the basis for a model of the thinking process, perhaps to be computerized in the *ultimate* future. The emphasis on "ultimate" is to caution those who overestimate computer potentials after listening to their devotees.

At the moment, the available models—the mathematical formulations of thinking processes—are based on very simple parallels between the neurones—the nerve cells—and electrical circuits. Essentially, such models assume a switching system, as in a present-day computer, based on binary states like the electrical switch which is either off or on. Though this ultimate aim is not always an explicit consideration, the attempt to use communication theory (in the broadest sense) to organize cultural phenomena is widespread and popular. It is worth commenting on briefly to contrast it with behavioral anthropology.

In what Hymes (1964) called the "Ethnography of Communication," and Sturtevant (1964) called "Ethnoscience" (there are many other titles), and beginning with the work of Goodenough (1956), there has arisen an attempt to relate linguistics, broadly defined, with the classical ethnographic interest in kinship terminology. By explaining the logics by which terms are used in various contexts to refer to one's relatives, one might then extend this kind of logical analysis to all of culture. The underlying thesis assumes that it may be possible to isolate a limited number of components, essentially classificatory principles, enabling one to predict what terms a native speaker would use in referring to his kinfolk (or any other cultural situation). Although there is some disagreement as to ultimate ends (Pospisil 1965), the general position of most of those working in this area of endeavor is, as Goodenough put it (1957), that any description should enable anyone (the anthropologists, of course, in particular) to act appropriately as a member of the culture in question. Frake (1964) said the model of an ethnographic statement should be stated in such a way that "if a person is in situation X, performance Y will be judged appropriate by native actors." Yet even the specialists realize that this may not be all of communication. Goffman (1964), after discussing various situational aspects of communication, commented:

> At one level of analysis, then, the study of writable statements and the study of speaking are different things. At one level of analysis, the study of turns at talking and things said during one's turn are part of the study of face-to-face interaction. Face-to-face interaction has its own regulations; it has its own processes and its own structure, and these don't seem to be intrinsically linguistic in character, however often expressed through a linguistic medium.

Though the quotation, probably not intentionally, omits the nonverbal patterns of behavior from "speaking," the distinction is an important one to keep in mind. In Goffman's phrase, the study of face-to-face interaction is the area with which behavioral anthropology is concerned.

The value of differentiating the communication field from the behavioral (in the biological sense) lies in the fact that each describes and analyzes the emotional aspects of the patterns (linguistic on the one hand, actions and interactions on the other) in very different ways. In communication this is done by semantic analysis, that is, by trying to establish the phenomena to which the symbols used by the speaker refer; in interaction investigations, autonomic and skeletal muscle nervous systems (the autonomic controlling the hormones, endocrines, and so on, which produce the various emotional states) are the "emotions" themselves. To talk about this area, one has to use awkward phrases like emotional–behavioral or emotional–interactional or, for that matter, autonomic–interactional. The purpose of so doing is to make clear the physiological reality that overt and observable patterns of action and reaction are not mere surface phenomena, unrelated to the overall functioning of the organism as a biological system.

Interaction and Communication

In these brief comments on the ethnography of communication, the key words are those which define its goal as mastering the logics of a language so that the "performance . . . will be judged appropriate by native actors." Not only is this a different problem, as Goffman suggested, but it is probably not one susceptible to the kinds of prediction which physiological phenomena make possible. If the field of behavioral anthropology is defined as one which is concerned with predicting how the behavior of one individual (animal or human) changes as a consequence of the behavior of another, we are dealing with a state of functional dependence in the mathematical sense.

For this assumption to have validity, we have to be able to demonstrate not only that the changes occur, but that they take place lawfully—that a mathematical function will describe them. In other words, if one animal becomes increasingly aggressive towards another, even to attacking him, then knowing the properties of both individuals' interactional states, we can predict the nature of the reactions and their intensity. Moreover, our explanations have to work consistently. Hence, deviations must be shown to be a function of states altered by prior interaction. As this book suggests, these functional relationships do exist between individuals and are predictable. They do so, of course, because they depend for their lawfulness on the internal mechanisms of the body. Just as the heart beat, the respiration rate, and other functions follow lawful patterns, so do the interaction patterns with which, in fact, they are physiologically interrelated.

Words or communicative messages also influence the actions of men. They differ in that the only ultimate test of their influence is through observation of the resulting actions. The same message may produce one result now, a different result at a later time, or no result at all. Its meaning, in other words, can vary remarkably, even for the same person at different times. When one tries to move from one person to the next, even within a single cultural unit, problems of establishing "meaning" become almost insurmountable. George Schaller, in his charming book *The Year of the Gorilla* (1964), told of a female gorilla who sounded the alarm call when she saw him. Since none of her group showed any sign of concern by changing their behavior, it was obvious to him that in spite of conveying a message identical in form to that which other gorillas use, she had probably called "wolf" too often.

From the point of view of behavioral biology, "meaning" depends on whether the action is followed by a change in the behavior of other animals or, as in this case, nothing happened in consequence. Thus, one defines the nature of the relationships of individuals by the patterns of response. From the biological and physiological point of view, the appearance of responses, followed by other responses, brings about in each individual a series of adjustments which fit or do not fit the previously continuing patterns of behavior. Hence, the validation of the message is always *after the fact*. In obtaining a statement of probabilities in the behavioral case, the functional relation requires a predictable response, not an estimate that it might or might not occur.

This emphasis on communication as a logical system through which cultural phenomena may be organized is important in that other aspects of culture can be included within its framework. Since spatial relations (vertical or horizontal distance apart) and the order or sequence in which actions are performed in all types of the division of labor affect the probabilities that interaction will or will not occur, it should be pointed out that they, singly or in combination, can also be subsumed under the logic of communication. Preserving the proper distance or following the prescribed sequence in a ritual of greeting can be considered communication. Alternatively, other logics—of efficiency, of the mechanics of building construction—might be utilized. When they are regarded from the point of view of behavioral anthropology, they too, with communication, become dimensional; that is, they provide a group of scales by which one can estimate the probability that a response will or will not be elicited.

Dimensions of Behavior and Culture

In the table of contents, I have described the first part of this book as concerned with the dimensions of behavior; the second, the dimensions of culture. For the reader, the idea of dimensions in connection with behavior is probably not hard to understand since, as described at the beginning of this chapter, we are to be concerned with the measurement of the fixed action patterns in interaction. Since these measurements are temporal, the implications of which will begin to be evident in the chapter following, it is not hard to understand that the time durations of actions and inactions not only can be measured but also are dimensional in the dictionary sense.

On the other hand, the use of the word, dimension, in conjunction with culture may appear arbitrary or a perversion of meaning. It is meant to be taken literally, however, not always as a continuous measurement but as an ordered array of response-eliciting potentials. It thus provides a way of estimating probabilities. In other words, Part II of this book will be concerned with isolating those elements of culture which can be treated as separate dimensions. It will show that their operative effects are biologically based and that their dimensional characteristics are probabilistic. What this means is that each such dimension gives us a scale along which we can assign the probabilities of the response occurring. In some cultural situations, this probability may be very high (almost 1.00, roughly equivalent to 100 percent), as in rituals and ceremonies; in others, it can be extremely low but still consistent.

If one focuses on the biological organism—in this case, on the human—one can predict with reasonable accuracy what his behavior will be, how he will react, what changes we can expect in his interaction patterns (including their component emotional states) given specific (measurable) patterns on the part of others. But he carries on these interactions within the cultural settings of his group, and this has indefinite consequences. We can assume (and under certain circumstances demonstrate) that if his environment could be tightly controlled, as if the world were a laboratory, the task of prediction would be infinitely simplified. In theory, every moment of his daily round could be prescribed and programmed. Then the classic simplicity which nonscientists impute to experiments in physics would be immediately at hand.

Unfortunately, the world, even of monkeys and apes, is remarkably complex in the erratic way in which happenings occur, and experimental influences build up for any given individual. For the human, even at the simplest cultural level, the complexities of environment, technology, and symbolic apparatus appear to be so diverse that it might seem too difficult to break them down into separate categories. Yet this can be done as Part II will illustrate. To indicate the nature of the argument, a few comments here may be helpful in understanding what follows.

One obvious category with dimensional properties clearly affecting the probabilities that two people will or will not interact and what form or pattern that interaction will take is provided by spatial distance. Hall (1966) has pointed out that the geometrical distance separating two people does influence these probabilities and has suggested that the perceptual limitations of the human anatomy and nervous system are at work. We would expect that people who are very close (or touching one another) are much more likely to interact than if they are 50 feet away. This does not mean that they *will* interact; one can lie next to someone without interacting, but one can estimate the probabilities on a reasonable (biological) basis.

Another category with dimensional properties is the order or sequence in which actions and interactions occur. When an Eskimo fashions a harpoon head out of walrus ivory, the technology prescribes the order of actions and no other person need necessarily be involved. But most cultural sequences require some kind of division of labor, whether in the preparation of a meal, carrying out a ritual or ceremony, or in the kind of work flow to be seen in assembly line operations in modern industrial plants. These cultural sequences or flows of actions increase the probability that some interaction will occur between people who are next to each other in the sequence. The actions making up the interaction may, however, be limited to such nonverbal activities as passing a partly finished object to the next worker in the line. Again, interaction does not have to occur. One can put the object beside the person who is to work on it without his responding in any way, but the chances are markedly increased either for conversation or technological or ritual movement.

Utility of the Dimensional Approach

Like the movie producer in the good old days of the weekly perils of Pearl White, I reserve the right to make you wait for an explanation of the uses of cultural dimensions until the next episode. This will take place when you read Part II. Yet one of the consequences of trying to reduce culture to dimensional form is that one has to make a reasonable attempt to define dimensions in such a way that one can, in theory, construct a culture from them, at least sort its elements into the categories chosen. After concluding the book, the reader may believe that other dimensions should be added. At least, I think, he will find that what is outlined here is an essential beginning.

For what these dimensions do is to provide a means of estimating the probabilities that specific cultural settings or elements will modify or constrain the interaction, interaction which is the output of individuals and, therefore, idiosyncratic within their biological states. To say that the influence of culture is extremely powerful is not enough. One has to take into account the precise nature of the interplay of the cultural dimensions and the interaction patterns of the individual if either are to be accurately predicted.

Apart from its utility in estimating the probabilities of constraints affecting the ongoing interaction of individuals in varying cultural situations, the value of this approach lies in developing an alternate view of culture itself. Culture is commonly looked at in terms of the logics of its various segments—the logics of communication, esthetics, technology—each representing a universe where general principles can be derived from certain underlying uniformities. But culture also needs to be considered for its direct impact on human beings in managing their relationships to one another. With this at hand, it becomes possible to use cultural analysis to develop a set of probabilistic constraints to accomplish a wide variety of purposes and test the effectiveness of the prescription by measurable results.

Although this book separates out behavioral anthropology from its cultural counterpart, it does this first to define the mode of operation and uniformities of each. Having so done, they can be put together and their mutual relationships can then indeed be understood. Since one cannot manage human interaction outside a cultural framework—any more than one can conduct chemical experiments without test tubes, beakers, and glass linkages to control the rates at which chemical processes occur—the practical as well as scientific implications for this approach should prove useful.

Returning to behavioral anthropology (though this comment applies to culture also), its isolation as an independent field provides remarkable opportunities for research studies which can be conducted by very simple techniques of measurement. In reading this book, it will become obvious how many fundamental experiments (or observations of ongoing situations) can be made with little more required than a stop watch, a counter, and a pad of paper. Later, more sophisticated methods of measurement can be used, but these are only aids to greater precision.

It is not often realized how enormous an advantage observers have when animals (and humans) are the subject of investigation. For all the difficulties, the experimenter is not trying to peer into the heart of the atom or the cell using highly complicated instrumentation. To accept the results of so many indirect measuring processes, necessitated by the very small (or large), demands a considerable act of faith. In behavioral biology, the observer is in the middle of, and of the same magnitude, as the phenomena he studies. Watching a fight between two gorillas presents little instrumental difficulty (except for personal safety). Contrast the physicist's problem in trying to deduce from photographs that two different types of particles encountered one another in a bubble chamber. (Disturbances introduced by the observer, a popular subject in epistemological discussion, are by no means more serious in the animal (or human) case than in physics.)

A further virtue, perhaps (at least a necessity), is that this book is built on evidence from a wide variety of fields, briefly commented on in the preface. There has been a fashion, hopefully vanishing, that science can only be advanced if specialists from many disciplines come together with man disarticulated under an interdisciplinary microscope. By contrast, although no one knows better than the author the inadequacies of his knowledge in some of the areas which contribute to this book's point of view, on the other hand, he cannot too strongly urge the reader to take the contrary path, to make himself as multidisciplinary as he can.

Only the investigator knows what might prove useful to him. In consequence, he should feel free to pick and choose, making sure that he exposes himself to as wide a variety of influences as possible. Through assiduous sampling, he can select how *he* wants to be interdisciplinary or multidisciplinary, assuming its utility for his investigations. As an extra dividend, he will also truly experience the (emotional *and* cognitive) esthetic rewards of his efforts and no longer feel he must accept the claim of the humanistic studies that they are the sole source and provider of the arts of creativity (and scientific investigation).

Chapter 2

Biological Clocks— The Natural Rhythms of Behavior Patterns

The occurrence of fixed action patterns in the behavior of animals and men has elicited relatively little curiosity on the part of most investigators except for the ethologists. Since the beginnings and endings of such sequences can be defined with reasonable confidence and thereby observed and measured, one would have supposed that all types, short or long, would have been the subject of study.

Considering the amount of time and energy devoted by men to acting and interacting, it is surprising how rarely anyone has asked whether what can be seen and heard might be grounded in the essential nature of the biological organism. Human speech began to be of interest to the Greeks before Aristotle. Since then, from the rise of the grammarians and philologists, and the parallel concern with rhetoric, most linguistic inquiry, until today, has been limited to the formal properties of speech (Marx 1967). A few students, (Goldman–Eisler 1954, Hudgins and Stetson 1937, Peterson and Lehiste 1960, the first influenced by her previous work in interaction measurement), have measured the durations and frequencies of speech elements. Only Huggins (1963) and Lenneberg (1967) have realized that these durations have rhythmic properties and a biological foundation.

Time-study engineers, from Frederick Taylor's day on, routinely measure how long the various actions used to perform a job will take in order to set production standards. Their measurements are usually on the order of seconds. Whitehead (1938) and Abruzzi (1952) are the only ones who tried to study their occurrence over time. Most investigations of regularities in behavior patterns have been carried on by zoologists and physiological psychologists. They were interested in the alternations between intervals of activity and inactivity (or sleep and waking) over successive 24-hour periods or, alternatively, in short-term counts of the frequencies of response activities after a stimulus.

To a large extent, the scattered nature of the evidence and the relatively episodic character of the investigations stem from the predominant interest in studying the effects of a stimulus in producing a response from the organism. Such studies yield quantitative data. Their point of view was based upon the fundamental, though often implicit assumption, that all actions should more properly be regarded as "reactions"—as response to a stimulus, both singular and plural. Life itself, that is the decision as to whether an animal is alive or dead, was determined—and often defined—by trying to elicit this reactivity.

Where intervals of action occurred when no external stimulus could be detected, the organism was considered to be reacting to an *internal* stimulus. It has long been known, for example, that the pangs of hunger set up contractions in the gut—and movement in the animal. Thus, *all* animal activity could theoretically be described with this simple model of stimulus and response.

Since periods of activity are necessarily followed by periods of inactivity, the conception of a static animal, waiting for the stimulus, was consciously or unconsciously adopted. The schools of psychology responsible for this kind of thinking were unfamiliar with studies by biologists (and rare psychologists) of what was then called "spontaneous" activity. If external and, in the traditional sense, internal stimuli are controlled and, if possible, eliminated, animals persist in starting to act, act for an appreciable period, and then stop and become inactive. Though one can still talk about internal "forces" in the central nervous system or elsewhere, they are hardly equivalent to stimuli in the classical sense.

Yet stimulus–response psychology had developed such a strong hold on behavioral studies that even extended sequences of actions and inactions were explained in terms of this "reaction" philosophy. So much is the United States the center of learning theory that its pervasive prominence may be cultural—another evidence of the American's belief that learning is the cultural road to social success. Many distinguished psychologists have reacted against this emphasis (Koch *et al.* 1959—see particularly Koch, Vol. III, and Tolman, Vol. II), but this hardly explains the meagre evidence on spontaneity in such an enormous outpouring of literature. Even Hinde, an outstanding English ethologist, in his 1966 volume *Animal Behavior,* where he attempts to synthesize ethology and comparative psychology, touches on this problem only tangentially.

The Organizing Principle of Rhythmicity

In his *Biological Foundations of Language* (1967), Lenneberg refers to rhythm as the organizing principle of speech and language. He points out that the human capacity to discriminate between pattern (or order in time) and randomness (or disorder) depends on the pulse or beat. He uses the analogy of an underlying carrier pulse (the beat or rhythm) and refers to work which shows that one can "eliminate variations in pitch, loudness, or timbre and still recognize the melody, but if we destroy the internal temporal relationships without distorting the other variables, the melody becomes at once unrecognizable."

Though I shall return to the points he makes with regard to articulation and syllabic (or phonemic) rates of production, it is worth considering the organizing power of rhythms much more broadly. If biology is to be brought to bear on the materials with which anthropology is primarily concerned, one needs a working hypothesis on which to predicate the existence of regularities in the scientific sense. Since biological studies have shown that such rhythms are omnipresent and range from very fast ones, on the order of ten a second, to those associated with annual migrations (birds, in particular), grounds for a hypothesis do exist. Many of the rhythms studied in biology are electrophysiological or biochemical; others consist of sequences of behavior patterns at all ranges of frequency, and are thus directly observable. They may or may not be coincident with other rhythms. Since the late thirties, I have been working out the nature of the underlying properties of interaction—a major class of such rhythms. In their communicative aspects, the variations in the patterns utilized are similar to those melodic qualities of sound which, Lenneberg emphasizes, are determined by the pulse (Chapple 1970a).

Our focus, therefore, in this chapter, is on the various rhythms which exist, their properties and the ways in which they can be said, by hypothesis, to act as the organizing principles for human (and animal) activities and interaction. This enables us to make certain experimentally verifiable assumptions about the nature of interaction and to relate it to the whole universe of physiology and biology generally. A quantitative analysis, in the scientific sense (since rhythm is by necessity quantitative), depends for its fruitfulness on its organizing principles. One can, of course, count almost anything, provided the "things" counted can be separated by some kind of discriminations. Counting, in itself, however, is not primary even if the counting is given more operational reality by the prior measurement or identification of potentially measurable durations. What is looked for is the demonstrable existence of a state of functional dependence in the regularities we can quantitatively describe. And here the rationale, the organizing principles which provide the foundation for investigation, are the biological rhythms themselves.

The casual observer, the field naturalist, or the anthropologist is unlikely to identify these rhythms even when he is looking for them, without the deliberate use of devices to measure the timing characteristics of behavior. Gross features of the daily cycle can, of course, be noted—periods of sleep or inactivity contrasted with intervals of sustained activity. But so many situations do arise, serving as stimuli, in which intervals of response (interactional or otherwise) are elicited, that these serve to mask the underlying rhythms by displacing them from their repetitive regularity. These displacements result in compensatory intervals of activity or inactivity. As we shall see, they are lawful consequences of the interferences to the timing pattern. To observe and record such environmental (interpersonal) shifts is often very difficult. Without the aid of accurate measurement, quantitative uniformities become hard to isolate.

The Universality of Circadian Rhythms

Daily rhythms are the easiest to observe and the most widely studied. Called circadian by Halberg (1960) to indicate that their period is approximately, but often not exactly, 24 hours in length, the term has replaced diurnal, a word now reserved for rhythms where the animal is active during the day, while nocturnal is applied to the activity cycles of mice or rats. Circadian rhythms are of remarkable interest because they have been identified in the simplest, single cell animals like Amoeba and Paramecium (and in single cells taken from multicellular species). They are to be found, not merely in the more familiar laboratory species—fruitflies (Drosophila), mice, cockroaches, hamsters, and that ubiquitous experimental animal, Homo sapiens—but in all animals and, probably, in all plants. They are thus universal to living things.

Directly observable are the activity rhythms, that is, the occurrence of physical activity (whatever its species-limited forms); its onsets, durations, and cutoffs of periods of activity and inactivity appear with surprising uniformity.

Not merely is activity characterized by its rhythmic occurrence, so too are the major physiological and biochemical functions of the body. After a few experiences with a clinical thermometer, one learns that body temperature follows a circadian path, higher in midday and lower in the morning and at night. Halberg (1960) reported that circadian rhythms have been identified for blood sugar, liver glycogen, eosinophil count (roughly a leucocyte or white corpuscle), adrenal activity, RNA and DNA synthesis, cell division, and drug-specific sensitivities, to name only a few. As Pittendrigh (1960) pointed out, the list has been limited only by available assay methods and the time invested.

Not only are circadian rhythms clearly demonstrable in the single cell isolated from the body, but there are significant differences in these rhythms between species *and* between individuals within species. The most striking finding is that, no matter what the species, individuals show the highest consistency in the regularities with which their rhythms manifest themselves. In other words, individual differences lie at the very heart of the cellular constitution.

Given such universality and the constant properties of the rhythms themselves wherever the investigator turns, it seems reasonable to assume that the total amount of activity and inactivity manifested during the 24-hour day is constant for the individual animal. Of the three elements of total activity—the durations of activity and inactivity, their periodicity, and their amplitude—Aschoff (1960) pointed out that the first two were constant and under the control of remarkably accurate biological clocks. Amplitude, in man exemplified by the rapidity or excursive violence of his muscular movements or the loudness of his voice, appeared to be directly related (perhaps proportional) to the duration of the activity. In other words, the greater the amplitude, the longer the activity and, probably, the longer the inactivity. (See Chapters 4, 5, and 6 for further discussions on this point.)

If the amounts of activity and inactivity may thus be regarded as fundamentally constant, it follows, and has been shown experimentally, that when the animal is prevented from expending this activity, compensatory increases need to be taken to restore the balance; if forced to exceed this amount, compensatory reductions are in order. Since activity is the total sum of which interaction is a part—the proportion varying for the individual and his situation—then a similar hypothesis can be tentatively advanced and tested for interaction. If the interaction rhythm demonstrates such constants, a wide variety of test areas follow—in studies of isolation and deprivation, in bereavement and similar losses of interpersonal outlet, in effects of social or territorial mobility—the types of natural and controlled experiments which can be made (or observed) are almost infinite.

Properties of Circadian Rhythms

In studying mice, rats, or hamsters (even the proverbial squirrel), a common laboratory method of measuring activity is to place the animal on a running wheel in a cage. Visitors to such a laboratory see each animal busily engaged in turning the wheel, often for very long periods of time, yet stopping at times to eat or to rest. Day after day, if not interfered with, each animal turns out his daily quota, set by internal clocks; if delays are interposed, he struggles with extra effort to make up for lost time. Though running wheels are by no means the best method of measuring activity, they symbolize the predicament of all living things. Each plant or animal, and therefore each human being, has to expend activity at various periodicities in the amounts characteristic for him. The clock strikes (internally) and he begins to act; it (or another clock) strikes to bring the action to an end.

Clearly, the utility of biological clocks for survival requires little elaboration; some adaptive process is necessary since the organism has to synchronize to the changing properties of his environment. If habituated to hunt by day, with all the physiological and anatomical specialization this can involve, an animal would quickly become a castoff or a victim if he suddenly began to sleep through the sun. Since the length of the day and the onset of dawn and sunset vary throughout the year, the animal needs to be able to shift its circadian rhythms to remain in phase (that is, to be synchronized, or in time as in music). It does this, with individual idiosyncrasies, quite consistently. If this were all, one would have to assume that these rhythms were purely matters of adjustment to external environmental changes.

In fact, however, extensive experiments in which the animal is consistently in the dark (or light) have demonstrated that the clock-setting mechanism is separate from the clock itself; in other words, circadian rhythms are innate and repetitive. The animal, accustomed to an approximately 12-hour period of light during which he is active, followed by one of darkness and inactivity, maintains this rhythm when the lights stay on for 24 hours. Under these or similar conditions, when environmental influences are held constant, the rhythm is called free running. For an individual animal, it shows a remarkably small variance (a statistical index of variability) in its periods.

In addition, the length of period for any animal is not often exactly 24 hours. This is further evidence against the idea that the external periodicities of the sun (controlled by the period of the earth's rotations) are the sole determining factor. The intensity of the light (the level of illumination) shortens the period in diurnal (light-active) animals and lengthens it in nocturnal (dark-active) animals. Aschoff (1965), who first pointed out this general rule and for whom it is named, has shown that it applies to humans in experiments done in soundproof underground observation rooms. These findings have been supplemented by various enthusiasts who have lived in caves for long periods of time and carefully recorded, or had recorded, their patterns of sleeping and waking.

One might argue, as a few investigators have, that an external or exogenous rhythm would be sufficient to enable all living things to adapt to the changing environment. One would not then need to postulate an innate or endogenous rhythm as the master clock. But the arguments, both experimentally and rationally, are all on the other side. As Aschoff (1965) so aptly phrased it, all organisms live and must adapt to a "temporally programmed world." Although one should not pursue the computer analogy too far, observation of all forms of life demonstrates the remarkable dependence on timing of the actions and the adaptive changes of plants and animals. Through its own endogenous rhythms, the organism anticipates each stage of adaptation; it begins to react in advance in terms of its own internal organization. It is always prepared and this prevision (almost literally) enables it to survive.

But given these rhythms, both of activity and its associated physiological functions, there must be a way of setting each clock to the external environment with its own solar system rhythms. Biologists use the term "entrainment" to describe the process, and the particular synchronizer or cue is commonly referred to by the German word, "Zeitgeber." Though this word, translatable as synchronizer, is used in technical literature, the English term with similar implications will be used in this text.

There are three synchronizers whose effects on circadian rhythms have been established:

(1)   Light is the primary clock-setting mechanism. As far as is known, it affects all species. Thus, most investigations of the entrainment process have used it as the experimental variable.

(2)   Temperature acts as a synchronizer for some species, but most circadian rhythms are temperature-compensated; significant alterations take place only when thermo-equilibrium limits are broken through.

(3)   Only one other synchronizer has been shown to trigger the entrainment process; unfortunately, too little work has been done on how it works. This is the interaction rhythm of animals; what they are doing can significantly change the circadian rhythms, presumably for most species, though this has not been adequately established.

Aschoff (1960) reported that a Japanese investigator, Dr. Fujimoto, introduced a highly aggressive male mouse into a group of mice, all of whom were active in the dark. As a consequence of his attacks and constant victories, though he remained dark-active, his victims shifted their phases to become preponderantly light-active.

Less dramatic are such studies as that of Halberg et al. (1960) who housed blinded rats with normal rats. He found that the period of the blinded rats became synchronized with and shifted to that of the normal ones after a three-month period (behavioral cues apparently being the synchronizers). Sometimes only the amplitude of the rhythm will vary. Stephens (1962) isolated a fiddler crab and found that it became less and less active. Adding another animal to the container brought the crab's level back to its former state. In the human, entraining to the rhythms of a particular culture appear to be easily demonstrable. Everyone is aware that people learn to adjust their rhythms to abnormal routines, like working on the night shift. But as Lobban's (1960) data suggest, patterns of sleeping and waking are much more easily shifted than some of the other physiological functions.

Lobban, an English physiologist, was able to make systematic observations with groups of students taken to the Arctic environment of Spitzbergen. Her primary concern was with the shifts in various metabolic processes during periods when the sun shone for 24 hours or when it absented itself for equal periods of time. She supplemented this work with studies on Arctic Indians. Entrainment by the light synchronizer did not occur for all rhythms at once. For both groups, body temperature and activity level shifted as a function of the all-dark or all-light period, but such rhythmic processes as that of potassium excretion were clearly disassociated from that of sodium and lagged behind.

Actually, for these excretory functions, the overriding factor was whether people were living in light or darkness. In the winter, Arctic Indians follow a regular routine. In the summer, their routines are very irregular both for children and adults. Yet excretion of potassium, and so on, remains out of phase in the winter, even though sleeping and waking and the manifestation of activity shift to the cycles to be expected of a light-dependent animal. Thus light, rather than group interactional routines, was predominant.

Coordination (or Coupling) of Individual Circadian Rhythms

Since the evidence indicates that even the single cell has its fundamental rhythms, whether as a part of a multicellular organism or in an independent form, and a wide variety of the living body processes exhibit similar regularities, some way of synchronizing or coupling all these rhythms together is clearly necessary. If this did not happen, the organism's ability to survive, dependent upon its being able to function as an organizational system, would be markedly reduced. Not only are the body's clocks synchronized, experiments have shown that they can also be desynchronized (the Arctic example illustrates this). To supplement Lobban's work, Aschoff (1965) described one human subject whose activity cycle lengthened, while living in isolation with no time cues, to 32.6 hours which was paralleled by his calcium excretion cycle. On the other hand, his rhythms of body temperature and excretion of water and potassium had a 24.7-hour period.

Although there has been much debate about the location of the coupling mechanism, for light, at least, the answer appears at hand. The pineal body, believed for many years to be a functionless organ like the appendix, translates the energy of light into a fundamental secretion, melanin, which has biochemical impact on the whole regulatory or autonomic nervous system. It also acts directly on the hypothalamus, the autonomic coordinating center. The pineal body thus maintains the body's rhythms in phase with one another through the hypothalamus. Light appears to be the primary coupling mechanism, though other neural and endocrine functions play a part (Wurtman and Axelrod 1965). The endocrines, and more particularly those secretions arising from adrenal function, have clearly defined influences on mammalian activity and metabolism. Nevertheless, they do not act as the master clock; the independence of these rhythms in cells and tissue indicates they couple or synchronize the rhythms in conjunction with the pineal body (and hypothalamus) so that they stay in phase with one another.

If circadian rhythms are not coupled to the external environment, serious damage can happen to the individual. Animal or human well-being is directly affected by dysphasias (when the rhythms are out of synchronization). This damage is both biochemical and physiological, and can become organic; rapid growth of tumors occurs, extreme susceptibility to disease is endemic and, for some species subjected to radical shifts—such as Arctic mice placed in continuous light—death can occur in a week to ten days. Such deaths are consequent on a radical disorganization of endocrine activity. Susceptibility differs. It is a function of genetic (inherited) factors modified by differences between individuals in experiencing environmental stresses during the early periods of their lives.

Interest in the pathological effects of shifting circadian rhythms out of phase has markedly increased due to physiological research on man's capacity to adapt to travel in space. The jet airplane has already produced incontrovertible evidence on the upsets to "health" after flying in a few hours from New York to Moscow or from California to Paris. Reports of not "feeling right," of being unable to function normally, have been shown to have scientific reality. Not only does one "feel" abnormal under these conditions, but the rhythms of behavior and body functioning undergo measurable shifts as the system endeavours to readjust. Today, the crews of jet liners have their lay-over patterns scheduled so that transient dysphasic effects can be alleviated. Present advice to the jet traveler on business or political mission is to avoid serious negotiations until the body's system has adapted and reset its cycles to the new synchronizer.

Transients—Changes Consequent on Entrainment

The changes in the values of circadian rhythms during the process of entrainment are called "transients," borrowing a term from electronics. Initially, they were regarded as temporary states between one phase of the rhythm and the new one, though they may be evidence for permanent disorganization. "Temporary" has to be regarded as a matter of definition since transients may continue for weeks. More important, the term implies that there are quantitative relationships between the initial and final states such that the shifts show definite and reproducible regularities; they are not, in other words, simply random occurrences. If one is measuring a periodic function, that is, a regular repetition of a rhythm like a sine curve in trigonometry, the occurrence of a synchronizer out of phase with the beat sets up a disturbance in the quantitative regularities of the curve. Depending on its magnitude and the point at which it is applied, damping or resonance may occur. Typically, a series of values will show exponential (logarithmic) increases or decreases before the new rhythm is established. Thus, transients are directly measurable. Their properties and the magnitude of their effects can be determined.

A great many experiments have been carried on to try to shift circadian rhythms and to examine the transients produced in so doing. Changes in the relative proportions of light and dark and the time at which the periods begin are the best studied and easily understood by the weary jet traveler. Equally important has been the introduction of nonperiodic signals, for example, lights which flash briefly or stay on for intervals of 10 to 15 minutes or longer. Clearly defined shifts occur when this is done, with the transients plainly evident. Their quantitative properties (equations) depend on the position in the periodic circadian cycle where the light signal occurred. One can advance or delay the curve's onset by the placement and length of time elapsing before one introduces the signal.

In interaction, the entrainment process and the quantitative properties of the ways in which transients are set in motion can be clearly demonstrated. Though one cannot, of course, argue that the effects of light on the circadian rhythms and their phase relationships are part of a process identical with interactional adjustment, experimental data show remarkable similarities (Chapple 1970b). Since one can assume and demonstrate a basic periodicity in free-running interaction situations, changes brought about in this interaction pattern by the need to adjust to another person set up clearly defined transient patterns. It is probable that these transients can alter the circadian rhythm and definitely modify the faster rhythms which make up its components. The other persons act as synchronizers, thus setting the clocks, as will be discussed in the chapter following.

Development of Rhythms in the Young

It might be expected that the newly born would exhibit full-fledged circadian rhythms if, as the evidence on adults suggests, these rhythms are endogenous, that is, built into the organism. This assumption, however, is complicated by the fact that, in infant mammals at least, the various centers involved in the production of circadian rhythms are by no means fully developed. From the evolutionary point of view, such delays are understandable, since the infant animal is dependent upon its mother for existence. A considerable period of time, varying for species, could easily elapse before the inherited potentialities are given full expression.

Where animals can be raised in constant conditions without the presence of older animals, for example, with chickens and lizards who emerge from the egg and can survive independently, clearly defined periodicities can be established. With mammals, if the mothers nurse their offspring, one might suspect the maternal rhythm would influence theirs, yet the evidence hardly supports such an interpretation.

Hellbrugge, in Germany (1960 and 1964), has reported very extensive studies of children, from birth until they become about 15 years old, demonstrating the differential rates at which various body functions achieve full periodicity. Before birth, about the only physiological activity that can be (or at least has been) measured is the heart rate. Hellbrugge found that the fetal heart sounds were constant throughout the whole period although the mothers showed a typical 24-hour rhythm. This stability (or lack of periodicity) persists after birth. Not until about the sixth week do differences between night and day rates begin to appear. A clearly defined rhythm similar to the adult (though not quite so well marked) does not take over until the latter part of the first year of life. A similar course is followed by measures of body temperature.

For both of these rhythms, the low point on the curve also shifts as the child gets older. While the low for a child about two months old is at 9 P.M., at six months it has shifted to 11 P.M., and to 3 P.M. from the second to the fifth year after birth. By the time the child becomes ten years old, its low occurs at 5 A.M. and for adults, in Germany at least, the low point is at 7 in the morning. A similar shift is also recorded for the sleeping cycle.

Studies of activity or body movement and, more generally, the alternation of periods of waking and sleeping are the basis for much of the later differentiation of the individual's activity and interaction patterns. In the infant, they are complicated by the effects of hunger contractions. As anyone familiar with human babies realizes, the infant wakes, voices his dissatisfaction until fed, and then falls asleep. Hellbrugge, doing his work in an orthopedic hospital in Germany, was apparently unable to overcome the bureaucracy which fixed the times at which the babies should be fed, though it was quite evident to him that hunger activity was modifying what otherwise were controlled conditions. In the United States, Parmelee *et al.* (1961) studied newly born infants who were on a self-demand feeding schedule. In contrast to German babies who were awake much of the night because they were hungry, elimination of the feeding variable showed that the babies slept much more between 11 P.M. and 7 A.M. than during the day, even in the first three days of life.

In both these studies (and others), the length of time that the babies were awake was relatively short, usually less than an hour, but the number of alternations from being asleep to being awake was relatively high. Not until the middle of the first year does most of the continuous period of sleeping occur at night, that is, with fewer sleeping intervals during the day and only by the second year do mealtimes lose their influence. Considering the adult propensity, sometimes cultural and sometimes individual, for taking an afternoon siesta, it is worth noting that Hellbrugge reported that younger school-age children (in hospital settings) almost universally slept from 1 to 3 P.M.; in older children, up to their 15th year, he reported 40 percent still indulging.

Although body temperature, heart beat, activity and electrical resistance of the skin follow a parallel course in developing periodicities, other physiological functions take much longer periods of time to establish their circadian rhythms. It is not particularly relevant to discuss exactly which ones do, for example in rates of excretion of various chemicals important in body functioning; it is important to remember that some of these may not become fully established until the child reaches school age and later. Hellbrugge's finding that ability to concentrate in eleven-year-old children is remarkably reduced before 8 A.M., between 2 and 4 P.M., and after 8 P.M., has interesting educational portents.

The importance of maturation and, in fact, a definitive argument for the endogenous character of these rhythms, is provided by studies on premature babies. If environment were the primary agent, we would expect that premature babies (as well as babies born at full term) would develop the several rhythms at the same points in time. However, premature babies manifest these rhythms much later. It is the stage of physiological maturation and differentiation which is important, not the influence of the external environment.

Individual Differences in the New Born

Although the differences in maturation time of the circadian rhythms for activity and associated physiological functions are not too surprising, remarkable differences occur in the amount of activity and in the frequency and durations of movements in individual babies. Irwin (1930) carried out an extremely detailed study on activity in the first ten days of life in which he recorded both total body activity and the movements of individual segments. Accustomed as he was to seeing babies swaddled in clothes and inhibited in movement by bed covers, he was surprised by the amount and frequency of their movement. There was a progressive increase in activity from the first day, and babies were very different in their starting and established activity levels.

Several of his findings are worth noting:

(1)   The earliest beginnings of social behavior are derived from the total activity of the infant and its crying, the latter appearing to be an integral part of body movement. In other words, vocal sounds occur at this stage of life in conjunction with total activity.

(2)   The relative proportion of the upper body movements, including moving the arms, decreases over a ten-day period and leg movements become much more frequent.

(3)   Most of the so-called reflex patterns, which had been supposed to be present at birth, actually develop from the total activity of the baby and thus represent a kind of segregation into separate components.

His data, therefore, suggest that interaction patterns, not to mention other nonsocial patterns of muscular activity, begin as parts of total activity. This finding lends support to the hypothesis that interaction and noninteractional activity are functionally related.

Unfortunately, Irwin made his measurements with a polygraph which could only record frequency, so that there was no data on the actual durations of these motions, particularly of bursts of total activity. In addition, as he pointed out, many complications were introduced by hunger contractions.

Kleitman (1955), however, reported similar findings for human infants with the action-inaction cycle repeating itself in slightly under an hour. When the infants were on a self-demand schedule, the interfeeding intervals were multiples of these cycles.

Escalona (1965), in studies up to the 32nd week, has pointed out that one can usefully differentiate babies into those who utilize their whole body in their activity (kicking, thrashing about, and so on) and those who use gentle, part-body movements and rarely activate the entire skeletal-muscle system. These she called high- and low-activity babies, respectively. Other work by her associates indicates that the high-activity babies are also active for longer periods than their confreres. Escalona's colleague, Bridger (1966), found that infants, from two to five days old, differed significantly in the intensity with which they responded to mild stimuli. They were consistent in the degree of reactivity to each type of stimulus. There were also autonomic differences between babies with high heart rates when sleeping and high rates when awake and active and vice versa. Their research has by no means been brought to a conclusion, but it seems probable that these individual personality differences appear immediately after birth and are stable over time.

Species Differences in Activity Rhythms

Very few studies have been carried out on the patterns of duration in infant lower animals. Stier (1930), working with two highly inbred strains of mice, found that they exhibited regular, and highly repetitive, patterns. With baby mice supported in a harness (so they would not topple over) on a tambour (a drum head by which any movement is recorded by pressure changes), he found that durations of activity lasted 0.3 to 0.6 minute and, for inactivity, 1 to 3 minutes. In adult mice, his ranges for activity were between 25 and 135 minutes, for inactivity 15 to 160 minutes. Further analysis showed that periods of activity in the adult lasted for some multiple of 24 minutes plus a 25-minute constant, while inactivity lasted for some multiple of 15 minutes plus a 15-minute constant. There were quantitative differences between the two strains, with one active for longer than the other.

Such differences between strains or species, or between individuals within relatively homogeneous groups, have largely been described for adults in terms of activity level, and only secondarily in terms of the rhythms themselves. Thus, Stier established systematic differences in the frequency and durations of intervals of activity and inactivity for his two strains of mice. He then altered the body temperature of the baby mice (their temperature does not stabilize until adulthood) and found that different chemical pacemakers appeared to be controlling these rates. Rundquist (1933), later Brody (1942), in the United States, and Broadhurst (1958b) in England, picked out high- and low-activity animals from laboratory rat strains. By selective mating of high with high and low with low, they each succeeded in establishing substrains quite clearly differentiated by activity level. With mice, there have been many studies of the genetic aspects of activity levels and related factors, where strain differences are clearly demonstrated.

Since the usual method of estimating activity in small laboratory animals involves the use of running wheels, most of the research has ignored differences in the free-ranging rhythms themselves. DeCoursey (1960) reported on the striking individual differences in periodicity between the flying squirrels she observed, with a range from 22 hours and 58 minutes to 24 hours and 21 minutes but, as mentioned earlier, each individual animal was remarkably consistent within his own circadian cycle. Apparently, the same rhythm was manifested in outdoor natural surroundings and on the running wheel in the laboratory.

Little systematic study has been done with primates. Field observations indicate that there are marked differences in the daily cycles of monkeys and apes. These suggest both the possibility of differences in circadian periods and in the amount and amplitude of activity which they manifest. Schaller (1964) described the stay-a-bed characteristics of the gorillas. Not for them to get up when the rays of the sun begin to appear; an hour or so may elapse before they start on breakfast; after the two hours or so required to get their fill, a siesta is in order until mid-afternoon. It is true that some of the adults content themselves with sitting rather than lying down to sleep, but the impression is that they take long periods of rest, while the younger ones play around their semicomatose older relatives. By nightfall, actually between 6 and 7 P.M., the day is over; the gorillas have built their nests and are bedded down for the night. Carpenter (1934) reported that the howler monkeys on Barro Colorado Island in the Canal Zone were up and about for a longer period, rising between 5 and 6 A.M. and settling down for sleep between seven and eight p.m. They, too, have a long period of inactivity during the middle of the day, a pattern characteristic of other primates and many human groups.

Not only do the durations of the periods of activity and inactivity differ between groups and individuals, with the younger animals usually being active for longer periods, but the level of activity also differs. Carpenter regarded the howlers he observed as low in general activity, while Schaller's gorillas seemed to be almost slothful in comparison with the chimpanzees, their cousins, from what field studies by Goodall and Reynolds (1965) indicated. No field measurements on the circadian rhythms of men, monkeys, or apes are available, only observations such as these.

For human groups, few studies exist in which any attempt is made to describe what single individuals or the individuals making up a small group actually did from the time they rose in the morning until they went to sleep. Even with these, quantitative measures are not taken directly, though some estimates can be made when clock time is available. Roberts (1965) with three separate family groups among the Zuni, patiently recorded what each did on a minute-to-minute basis. In a few cases where a single person has been selected in American culture, chronology has been subordinated to the narrative account. The only exception to these statements is in studies of sleep patterns, but here only EEG records of the brain waves seem of interest, though one suspects activity–inactivity data are available in laboratory records.

The scope of this discussion of circadian rhythms is intended to make clear their pervasive and universal characteristics. It also suggests the framework within which shorter and longer rhythms are organized and coordinated. They differ by species, but the constancy and individualization of the rhythms special to a particular member of that species are most remarkable. For here is the foundation for the biological definition of the individuality of the individual.

From evidence available from studies of other types of rhythms, including the interactional, it seems clear that circadian rhythms provide a working model for rhythmic phenomena in general. This does not mean that the nature of the synchronizers will be the same, nor will the form of the transients, nor the periodic properties of the rhythms. But the circadian rhythms set up quantitative constraints on the manifestation of activity and inactivity by the individual organism. From the evidence which Irwin and others have obtained, the hypothesis that patterns of human interaction are built up out of overall activity appears a reasonable one, and certainly subject to empirical investigation.*

Contributions of the Shorter Rhythms

Of these, the beating of the heart and the regularity of breathing are the most conspicuous. Even in daily living, one suddenly becomes conscious of these rhythms; lying in bed at night, with a particular juxtaposition of

---

*There are many rhythms, also grounded physiologically, which take a much longer period to work themselves out and are extremely important. Perhaps the most obvious is the menstrual cycle of the female, varying in length by species. Others include the onset of biannual migrations, particularly of birds, and the hibernation of mammals when the climatic conditions begin to change.

But a wide variety of other cycles has been described, particularly in medicine, where, as Richter (1965) has shown, various types of continuing illness have characteristic periodicities, although often specific to a single individual. These include the well-known swings from over to under activity in psychiatric conditions like manic-depressive psychosis and periodic catatonic schizophrenia. Interesting as these are, they are secondary manifestations (and disturbances) of the more fundamental rhythms on which all behavior is founded

body and bedclothes, the sound of the pulse, like the "Tell-Tale Heart," is amplified. While waiting for sleep, the rhythm of inhaling and exhaling becomes a matter for serious attention as if its alteration could eliminate insomnia. Less pervasive, since intermittent, are the gripping rhythms of muscle systems when chilled. Shivers are set off at a rate of approximately ten cycles per second, far faster than the "normal" pulse rate of 72 beats per minute or respiration at about 20 breaths per minute.

Apparently, tiny contractions or vibrations are constantly going on in muscles at about the 10 cycle per second frequency, which parallels and may be associated with the "brain waves," the regular rhythms of electrical tracings from the brain which also have faster and slower components. These microvibrations appear to be the basis for temperature regulation (as in shivering) and in the rapidity with which the external activity of the animal can be altered. Other rhythms of both the heart and respiration combine these muscle action trains into longer series under the mediation of the hypothalamus, the brain's controller for the relatively independent functions of the body, which make up what is called the autonomic nervous system. This system regulates the heart, breathing, stomach, intestines, and so on. Various studies have shown that 2-minute, 7-minute, 35-minute, and 3½-hour cycles in temperature and ventilation rates can be identified.

The interdependence of these various rhythms, complicated by the longer rhythms of the circadian cycle, is still far from being thoroughly understood. They are important, however, in suggesting that the regularities in patterns of activity and interaction, that is, of the skeletal muscles, are built up out of these fundamental rhythms of which they are a part. This begins with their control of the speed of reaction time which can produce a muscular contraction. For practical purposes, one does not have to be concerned with time intervals much longer than a tenth of a second; apparently, the organism requires about this much time to activate a new pattern of behavior. Experiments have shown that with training, most people can learn to beat time at this rate; and the highly skilled are said to reach 20 per second for brief intervals. The fastest setting for the beat of a metronome is between a third and a quarter of a second; the slowest is two thirds of a second.

Biological Rhythms in Communication

In Lenneberg's discussion of the ways in which rhythm organizes speech and language, he points out that one can "hypothesize a basic periodicity of approximately six cycles a second" for motor patterns similar to those which underlie speech. This hypothesis is based on observational evidence: Hudgins and Stetson (1937) found this speed to range, in different individuals, from between 5.5 and 7.5 per second, equivalent to the rate of breath-pulse clusters. This, of course, means that the basic duration interval is 0.166 second. In addition, he points out that, apart from 10 per second alpha rhythm obtained from the cortex, Brazier (1960) has shown that there is a 7 per second rhythm which is also a fundamental one. Interestingly, children appear able to develop speech only when this rhythm is established.

Whether syllables or phonemes are examined, the evidence tends to support his idea that the speech which occurs within demarcable durations of action is controlled by these rhythms. The slower tempo of the interaction rate may be coincident with the respiration rate or with the longer intervals in multiples of minutes described earlier. In any case, they provide the time characteristics necessary for the basic rhythm of interaction pattern response. Analysis of the distributions of such intervals through interaction measurement under basal conditions show that they fall within a series of modal ranges on the frequency distribution (Chapple 1970c). Each one of these modes, around which action durations cluster, approximates the periodicity of other rhythms.

The More General Implications of Biological Rhythms

Musical rhythms and the sheer mass of rhythmical sound continuously produced by radio, television, record players, and individual performance so pervade modern culture that it is surprising so little attention has been paid to its physiological impact. Voodoo drums, the regular and driving rhythms of revivalistic ceremonies, the incessant beat of jazz or its teenage variants in rock and roll, must synchronize with the rhythms of muscular activity centered in the brain and nervous system.

Combined with the dance or with other rhythmic forms of synchronized mass movement—stamping the feet or clapping the hands over and over again—the sound and the action of responding as the tempo speeds up clearly "possess" and control the participant. The external rhythm becomes the synchronizer to set the internal clocks of these fast rhythms. In fact, in speaking of "possession," we appear to have a process of entrainment as accurate and highly synchronized as the changes in the time of sunrise and sunset are for the circadian rhythm (Sargant 1957).

Further, the entrainment is more precise since the beat, or combination of beats making up the total rhythm, is timed in terms of fractions of seconds, while circadian variations are in fractions of hours. As every musician knows, minute shifts in the beat can spoil the effect. Entrainment, and/or possession in this sense, is determined by the inevitability of regularity.

But all communication is endowed with rhythmic properties. This is obvious in theatrical performances, in preaching, or in making a public speech. Even ordinary conversation possesses these to some degree. The beat is built up from the length of each action and the interval of silence or inaction in between, the summation of which establishes the tempo (or pace) of the individual's pattern of behavior. It is further elaborated by the rise and fall of amplitude managed by modulation of voice intensity, gesture, and the total postural repertoire of the individual, and by pitch, timbre, and their nonvocal equivalents. Though these bring forth briefer responses, they also reinforce the total rhythmic structure which, as it develops in the performance, has effects on individuals. These rhythms of interactional behavior include the total pattern of action, not merely the voice, and compel responses from the listener or the audience, making all such performances equivalent to a musical form. As part of the interplay, the responders are not necessarily passive; they too may be trying to perform a role shaped by their own internal needs.

Lord Chesterfield, in describing to his son the method by which he persuaded Parliament to adopt the Gregorian calendar (1751), wrote:

> For my own part, I could just as soon have talked Celtic or Sclavonian to them, as astronomy, and they would have understood me full as well: so I resolved to do better than speak to the purpose, and to please instead of informing them. I gave them, therefore, only a historical account of calendars, from the Egyptian down to the Gregorian, amusing them now and then with little episodes; but I was particularly attentive to the choice of my words, to the harmony and roundness of my periods, to my elocution, to my action. This succeeded, and ever will succeed; they thought I informed, because I pleased them; and many of them said that I had made the whole very clear to them; when, God knows, I had not even attempted it.

The crux of Lord Chesterfield's method lay in his ability to suit the rhythm of his presentation to that of the noble lords making up his audience, eliciting responses from them by whatever means he could manage. What takes place inside the individual, why we respond to the wit, the gesture, the harmony, the well-turned phrase, the performance—these questions emphasize that there is far more to it than merely the words being used. What happens when someone hits a rhythm which is tuned to our internal clocks? Why is it that "being out of tune" has quite other interactional effects?

Chapter 3

Biological Rhythms and Personality

Although the term personality has as many meanings as authors writing about it, there is a central core on which most of them would agree. Whatever one may ascribe to personality and how one tries to get at its essential elements, it does refer to a "something" which is individual, which characterizes an individual and can be used to distinguish him from others. Most of those who use the word (although there are notable exceptions) would also be willing to go so far as to say that the "whatever it is" primarily manifests itself in the individual's relations with others. Naturally, this does not mean that it vanishes when people are not around. It is latent from an observational point of view, a way of describing certain properties of the organism.

From there on, differences of definition are easily worth at least a whole chapter in a Ph.D. dissertation. Some subsume temperament and character under the label: many regard "feeling" as primary, reflected in the person's acts. Endless discussions go on as to whether intellectual capacity—the cognitive processes through which learning and the organization of learning take place—is integral to the definition.

In this book, I am taking off from a more limited vantage point, in effect, from considerations raised in the first paragraph. What one must focus on is the observation of individuals. Only then can one deal with their behaviors in combination. Since the aim of science is to translate (or transform) observation into measurement, what is to be measured are those fixed action patterns of muscular movement comprising the repertoire, the ethogram, of the particular species being studied. But these are individualized; one does not observe a species. Its ethogram is only a kind of least common denominator of the fixed action patterns, and combinations and variations thereof, of a series of individuals. Both measurement and epistemology are grounded on individuality. Thereafter, one has to deal with constructs as individuals show evidence of some kind of mutual adjustment (or lack of it) and thus of functional dependence in the mathematical sense.

Before beginning to describe personality, it is useful to restrict the term. One must also abstract out, for reasons to become apparent in the three chapters following, the contribution of "feeling" to the definition. Feeling or emotion is a consequence of complex physiological factors. To talk about it before the process of individuation of biological rhythms into personality characteristics is outlined would be confusing. I hope that the reader will hold this aspect of experience in abeyance and regard it as minimized for the sake of clarity. Like all writers, I am insisting on my inherent right to define words in ways most convenient to me. So personality is made up of the individual's constituent biological rhythms of interaction. Feeling (or emotion) makes up what I call his temperament, those varied reactions to interactional adjustment which set physiological changes in operation.

It should be mentioned that, from the point of view of behavioral biology (and anthropology), the concept of personality used here can be applied to nonhumans wherever there is reasonable evidence that idiosyncratic or individualized interactional patterns characterize them. Its definition implies that one can distinguish, and demonstrate by objective means, the presence of intraspecies behavioral differences. Intensive field and laboratory studies have made the existence of individual differences in fiddler crabs, mice, dogs and cats, apes and monkeys hardly a matter of controversy. Such differences may be identifiable among insects, but the criterion must be that the differential behaviors isolated are individual and that each member of the same species does behave idiosyncratically.

The Basic Elements of Personality

If we return to Lenneberg's phrase and the notion of the existence of carrier pulses underlying speech and language (and I repeat that this must include the nonverbal aspects of communication sequences), the various biological rhythms are the carriers—more accurately, the carrier waves—on the surface of which muscular pattern differentiation is constantly going on. To determine how these patterns are structuralized or organized into rhythms, however varied their quantitative properties, we have to begin by recording the beat or, more specifically, the identifiable durations. This necessitates the setting up of rigorous criteria to determine their beginnings and endings. Thus the beat or the pulse, and its frequency—whether this is a matter of seconds, minutes, hours, days, or longer intervals—has been determined by (and abstracted from) continuous measurement of durations of actions and intervals between these durations (where nonaction, by operational definition, can be said to have taken place).

Studies such as those by Irwin (1960), Escalona (1965), Bridger (1966), Hellebrugge (1960) and, for the lower animals, by Stier (1930) and non-quantitatively by many others indicate that individual differences in rhythms of activity and inactivity and in "responsiveness" manifest themselves very early in life. Though individuals may have greater variability in infancy and youth, measures of this variability (the variance) show that each person (or individual) has a much lower randomness with regard to his own performance over time than when compared with another. The individual is thus "individualized" early with regard to the components of his biological rhythms, taken under basal conditions.

It is worth commenting briefly on the term "basal," since it involves certain assumptions as to the conditions under which measurements of the biological rhythms are made. By controlling the circumstances under which the animal is to be observed, one tries to achieve the situation where the external environment (and the internal environment to whatever degree is relevant) is constant. Measuring the behavior under such conditions, one can assume a basal state in a first rough approximation at least, and test how close one comes by calculating the variation in the values measured. Though one can always argue that such a constant state of the environment can never be obtained, this is a mere matter of dialectics. Such assumptions always have to be made in science. Given prior acquaintance with the animal and an adequate understanding, which can be tested experimentally, of the factors that might affect the constancy of a particular rhythm, one can proceed with some confidence.

In the brief discussion of Hellebrugge's work on babies, the hunger cycle proved a distorting influence. Consequently, demand feeding for the baby, what biological experimenters like to call *ad libitum* feeding, has to be arranged. Thus, the influence of this variable on what are essentially successive periods of muscular contraction and relaxation which make up the activity rhythm can be minimized. In measuring interaction, similar considerations have to be taken into account. Since they are directly relevant to the discussion, the means by which one approximates basal conditions will be commented on in this chapter and those following.

Observation of the Interaction Rhythm

After identifying the "communicative patterns" for each species (or culture), the observer begins his inquiry into the nature of interaction by watching his subjects—animals or people—and recording for each one the duration of each action, the duration of the following interval of inaction, and so on, continuously. In studies on humans, where much of the interaction takes the form of conversation, it is common to talk of the alternation between periods of action and inaction as response and silence. Although a way of highlighting what is being observed, these terms are extremely inaccurate. Even conversation has many action intervals—smiling, nodding the head, and grimacing occur in "silence" intervals; nonetheless, they are extremely important types of response. (And technically, by starting a conversation, the action initiating it is hardly a "response.")

Since individuals differ remarkably in how much verbal and nonverbal action they manifest in their interaction with others (and there are important differences between cultures in this regard), limiting one's observation to the presence of speech alone is highly misleading. Many researchers like to rely on tape recordings. Yet the intervals of silence which the tape reveals often are bridged by response behavior. Beyond the overt responses mentioned above, the individual can habitually hesitate between words while his mouth and face are still active. He may need to breathe and stop his speech in doing so; individuals vary in being able to produce words continuously without perceptible pauses between them. Moreover, overt nonverbal responses while the other person is talking may have "encouraging" effects on his action durations. Smiles and head nods have experimentally been shown to increase the length of the other person's talk. To speak while the other person is talking is discouraged in some cultures, including that of the United States. By contrast, even in the most vocal cultures not all individuals talk when another is doing so.

If each person is regarded for a moment as an island unto himself, in the poet's sense, and observed from morning until night, alternation of actions and inactions would go on until he went to sleep, itself an interval of inaction. But this alternating sequence of interaction takes place with other people present. Observation again tells us that, to a considerable extent, these alternating sequences are roughly synchronized. While one individual is active, the other is inactive; at least his response patterns, whether verbal or nonverbal or both, are relatively brief. This alternation, in popular accounts, is usually called the give-and-take of conversation. This is often too polite a way of referring to what actually happens; the phrase implies a kind of equality of opportunity to talk which may not be the case.

Although interaction assumes the presence of another person with whom one interacts, interactional behavior or communicative patterning may occur in isolation. Everyone has had the experience, and perhaps the satisfaction, of talking or singing to himself. In addition, there are several important types of "mental" or "emotional" disturbance or illness where interaction patterns appear without a "someone" else towards whom they are aimed. This is particularly characteristic of psychosis, in schizophrenia or organic brain damage where the patient is "hallucinating." Whatever other implications this term may have for the psychiatrist, for the recorder it simply means that he observes the patient behaving *as if* he were interacting with someone else. Various types of drugs produce similar effects, as does severe illness with high fever, where this interactional behavior is described by saying that "he is out of his head."

Thus, interactional sequences do not necessarily require the presence of another person, or at least that person's response, since the factors that control their occurrence are endogenous to the organism. Analysis of the measurements shows they follow a basic rhythm, altered, it is true, by another person being present, but only because he too has his own basic rhythm. The process of adaptation or adjustment (or lack of it), and all that that implies, systematically alters each rhythm in very specific and individualized ways.

If it were possible to isolate an individual from all external stimuli and, like the infant, provide him with "demand-responding" so that unsynchronized response contractions by another would not affect his rhythmic pattern, it can be postulated that how long he talks or how long he is silent (using these terms in the general sense to stand for actions and inactions) would be extremely regular. In consequence, his beat or tempo of starting to act would also, of course, be regular. Such conditions can be approximated in specially sound-proofed rooms or with alcohol or drugs. They can also be produced in situations where the other person provides little more than a mirror against which the individual's pattern is reflected with minimum interference.

A great deal of effort has gone into investigations of the most effective means of programming interviews in order to elicit such basal states. Some of it derives from attempts to develop techniques for more effective psychotherapy or counseling. It is well known that the therapist may unwittingly throw the subject off, altering his communication pattern by what he says when it comes his turn in the give-and-take. The classical psychoanalytic technique was intended to get the patient to "free associate." This meant he was to say anything that came into his head and let the stream of associations continue without the psychoanalyst commenting. Ideally, the analyst, seated behind the couch, might, with a voluble patient, be completely silent for the 50-minute hour. Rogers (1942) and his followers have elaborated a similar kind of program in their client-centered counseling (similar, that is, in an interactional sense). Far more than the psychoanalysts, they try to play the foil to the other person's response patterns.

All these techniques, and there are many variants, are primarily concerned with limiting the words and other types of response used by the interviewer. Their intent is primarily therapeutic. On the other hand, Chapple (1953) and his associates over many years have been engaged in developing and perfecting interview (and conversational) designs which are strictly programmed not only as to the words used (given a statement by the person being interviewed) but, most important, in the quantitative properties of the interviewer's interaction itself. Without going into detail, since the procedures are published at length elsewhere, such programming involves specifying how soon the interviewer is to respond when he detects the end of the subject's response, the duration of what he is to say (ordinarily 5 seconds), the degree to which nonverbal action (gesture, facial expression, and so forth) may be used and when, when not to respond and for how long, and so on. The procedures are also designed to elicit the basal states earlier referred to so that the natural rhythms of the individual can be determined. Transient behaviors at the beginning of a new interactional contact (interview or otherwise) are eliminated through tests of variability. The basal value looked for is regarded by definition as that sequence of the rhythm—often occurring only after 5, 10, or more minutes—where the variance became minimal.

Actually, the use of fixed action durations by the interviewer in such a program provides one with data only on action duration rhythms. Other procedures, only now beginning to be used, have to be designed to determine the inaction or "silence" component of the rhythm. By programming the interviewer to continue to act for various duration intervals, the length of action before the person listening is impelled to act and does so (even if the action is only a nonverbal response like a smile or head-nod) provides a measure of his tempo.

Another way to obtain basic values for the rhythm is to observe an individual interacting with a number of different persons. If they are different enough interactionally, they substitute for programming. However, analysis, even to establish his fundamental rhythm, is much more difficult. Like harmonics in music, a person may have several modal components for actions and silences (most people do), that is, he will have short ones (at a particular value), long ones, and some in between. Like the values which Stier obtained on his mice, the data suggest that these rhythms are multiples of one another. How they are elicited brings us to a very fundamental property of human interaction.

Definition of Complementary Personalities

Still restricting the discussion to this alternating series of actions and inactions (or of responses and nonresponses), programming interviews to try to determine the quantitative values of the basal rhythm may be much more time-consuming than chance proves necessary. For there may exist a person whose own rhythm is just the obverse of the individual in whom we are interested. When together, their give-and-take is precisely synchronized. When one acts, the other is inactive. When an action ends, he who was the listener begins with perfect synchronization (within the limits of measurement), that is, there are no overlaps. The silent person is neither a little late in responding, thus causing a measurable delay or latency, nor alternatively does the type of overlap occur where he comes in too soon and actually interrupts and cuts off the speaker.

Perfect synchronization occurs more frequently than one would suspect, though not for long exchanges. Where there are an appreciable number of synchronous sequences during interaction, the two individuals are said to be the *complement* of each other, and the state, one of *complementarity*. To achieve such a state, the beat or *tempo* of the two persons has to be identical. Hence, within the length of time from one pulse or beat to the next, the length of the action of one equals the length of the inaction of the other, and vice versa. Chapple and Lindemann (1941) showed that "normal" persons are likely to have much higher synchronization frequencies when interviewed than psychiatric patients, and Kendon (1963) demonstrated that instances of complementarity are far more frequent in close friends or married couples who "got on well" than in strangers interacting for the first time. One can roughly estimate the degree of complementarity in the relationship of two persons by seeing how often they tend to synchronize (thus making possible skeptical or cynical appraisals of how "close" they really are). However, keeping a count, or even trying to measure durations with a stop watch and writing them down, is extremely difficult to do accurately, particularly for a long period of time. Too much that goes on is lost in the interplay of two persons, even in a conversation and far more in any fast give-and-take such as children or animals playing with one another.*

For reasons suggested by the studies of Kendon, complementarity is a consummation devoutly to be sought. Its achievement is less simple. The opposite of synchronization, dysphasia or asynchrony (less accurately, but

---

*Various types of simple recording devices are available for measuring interaction. Their complexity and expense are not in the recording mechanism itself but in the degree to which data processing by a computer can be done directly from the record. All of them fall into the class of what are technically called "event recorders." Each has two or more keys which, when pressed down individually, either draw a line on a roll of paper moving at a uniform speed or put a tone on a magnetic tape. No matter how many individuals are interacting, one key is assigned to each person. When he starts to act, his key is pressed down; when he stops, it is released. The lines, or signals, are recorded on parallel channels and, since the tape is moving at uniform speed, the length of each action and inaction can be measured. By comparing channels, measures of the various intervals when the individuals are not completely synchronized are also obtained, that is, synchronization being determined where one line ends in one channel and the line in the next channel begins.

easier on the tongue, lack of adjustment), is liable to be the prevailing condition in human relationships for reasons which will be discussed in the three chapters following. The fact is that people vary in their ability to adjust their rhythms to other people and thus in their *flexibility*. Many an unwitting lover finds too late that *the* girl adjusts beautifully *to* him. She is only his complement at the limits of her secondary rhythms, which make up the full range of her flexibility. Her basal rate is a county mile away.

Awkward as such a statement seems, the point is simple. Most people try to adjust their rhythms to reach some approximation of synchronization. Since human beings differ remarkably in their basal rhythms, the looked-for complement (basally) may not be available. Think of those, whom everyone encounters, whose need to keep on talking turns into a monologue. Only the most silent, inactive person can adjust to make the perfect foil. As the speech goes on, the listener is driven by his internal clocks to act repeatedly, perhaps at his longest beat, perhaps also minimally. Then, there is the silent, taciturn figure of the New England hills, if this is his natural rhythm and not his reaction to the incursion of a stranger. Response, how often? Can one wait so long for so little to come forth? Perhaps in a poem by Robert Frost, but not in real life.

The emotional significance of complementarity will be taken up in the next three chapters so we can understand the nature of the physiological systems involved as well as those which are set in motion when asynchrony takes place. Here, we must continue to regard the other (or others) in the interaction as shadowy figures to enable us to understand how each person's rhythms appear to operate on their own. Thus, in the basal state, the train or sequence of action patterns making up the total duration of each action repeats itself, whether or not the elements of speech, gesture, or expression are the same. An interval of nonresponse action then follows; the beat is fixed when the next action starts. The first variables, then, to be identified, which are capable of measurement, are actions, inactions (or silences, a less accurate but not so awkward term if taken for both verbal and nonverbal response, that is, absence of communicative noise) and tempo—the beat, the sum of one action and one silence.

For reasons relating to the nature of the biological rhythms involved, but requiring a technical discussion, measures of this fundamental rhythm show a slight internal periodicity, a degree of variability, not random, but regular in its occurrence. It parallels what goes on in amplitude modulation, the internal beats that take place within a duration of action of any length.

Again, ignoring the other person for the moment, the degree of flexibility, a derived variable, is determined from estimates of the number and range of secondary rhythms to which the individual can shift if lack of synchronization takes place at his basal rate. Some people seem to have one rhythm only; they stick to it through thick and thin. Others are able to operate at a very fast tempo or a slow one, and possibly several in between. Fast rhythms appear to be built on respiratory rates, the slower on energy expenditure levels dependent on components of the long-term circadian rhythms which organize the overall distribution of interaction; precisely how, we still do not know. As mentioned earlier, these secondary rhythms—this repertoire available to the individual—have internal relationships. They are not random, but ratios of the fundamental rhythm.

Circadian Constraints on Interaction Rhythms

One of the major implications of the circadian rhythms of activity and inactivity for behavioral anthropology is the derived hypothesis that the total interaction manifested during a day can be regarded as constant. Empirically, the hypothesis appears to be reasonable; it would explain the differences between individuals in how much interaction they can "take." On the other hand, no one has yet measured an individual's interaction from waking to going to sleep, day after day, and combined this with measures of the noninteractional activity. Only when this is done can the precise degree of mutual dependence of these two types of activity expenditure be determined.

Analysis is complicated by the degree to which complementarity is present or absent. Each individual needs to interact for so much time, with so many people, as well as to experience intervals when he is by himself and *not* interacting. When prevented, physiological (emotional) disturbances occur. One only has to look at a small boy, cooped up in the house in the rain, hoping to be released to find "someone to play with." Partly this seems to depend on the deficit in his interaction which bad weather and solicitous parents have enforced upon him. More important is the need, not merely for any kind of interaction, but interaction of the type which produces emotional satisfactions within him.

Even if each person gets the quota of interaction which his daily rhythm requires, he also is seeking interaction with his complements. Any old interaction will not do; he needs to utilize his endogenous rhythms of action and inaction, at a *tempo* within the natural limits of his repertoire, and thus experience a maximum degree of synchronization by the other person. In other words, he wants a "listener." He looks for people who listen (or at least are inactive) when he is talking, who obligingly talk themselves only when he in turn is silent at *his* rhythm. Only a minimum effort on his part should be expended to modify his behavior to fit theirs when this begins to deviate from his endogenous values.

Primary Variables in Unsynchronized Interaction

The world, unfortunately, is rarely so well organized that complementarity is at hand when needed. What happens requires us now to take the other person out of the shadows and consider him as live (and observable) flesh and blood. Reinstating our measuring device to deal with two persons and recording the interaction for each, we find that two types of lack of synchronization occur. Either one or the other person does not respond immediately when the other stops acting or, conversely, one or the other starts to act (interrupts in the nonpurposive sense) while the other is still acting. If this were all, the identifiable variables would be relatively simple to manage.

The difficulty lies in the fact that measurement of rhythms necessitates prior measurements (otherwise one could never establish the repetitiveness of the beat needed to define its quantitative properties). Clearly, what has gone on immediately before may have a bearing on what comes after; in other words, we need to determine the state prior to the occurrence of a particular type of lack of synchronization. We cannot close our examination until its consequences in affecting the free manifestation of the rhythm are identified. Depending on which person is the point of focus, and either may be (if both, then separate calculations are necessary for each), the rule is to continue or to go back to either an action or silence interval in which the person focused upon is in the opposing state to the other person. It might be thought of as synchrony of a sort, *except* that it may not occur at the end of an action.

Remembering now the discussion of entrainment in circadian rhythms, what we encounter are the varieties of entrainment which occur in the interaction rhythm of a person when the synchronizer, setting the entrainment process in operation, is another person. The experimenter studying circadian rhythms measures the length of time the organism has been in a particular state of activity or inactivity before the stimulus is introduced. We must do the same, for reasons to be evident shortly. Of course, he (and we) then measures the duration of the stimulus and, after it has ended, how long a period of time elapsed before a change in state took place.

Given two persons interacting, two types of lack of adjustment (as has been said earlier) may occur, either a delay, with both persons being inactive, or an interruption, with both persons acting at the same time. Taking each in turn and, for convenience, calling the person on whom we are to focus individual A and the other B, the following possibilities occur.

The Nonresponse Variables

(1)   *A* is acting; *A* stops. *B* does not synchronize and both are silent. *B* then acts.

(2)   Precisely the same sequence occurs but the last act differs. *A* starts up again.

(3)   *B* is acting, stops. *A* does not respond so both are silent. *A* then acts.

(4)   Again the same sequence, except that it is concluded by *B* starting to act again.

The Interruptive Variables

(1)   *A* is acting. After an interval of time, *B* interrupts. *A* continues, *B* stops. *A* continues and finally stops.

(2)   A similar sequence, but *A* stops at some point while *B* is still acting. *B* keeps on and finally stops.

(3)   *B* is acting. *A* interrupts after an interval. *A* continues; *B* stops and *A* keeps on and finally stops.

(4)   A similar sequence, but *A* stops after interrupting, continues and finally stops. (It should be noted that two other types of situations can occur but do so very rarely in two-person interaction. In these, both can start at the same time or stop at the same time. Their complications need not concern us here.)

In each of the above sequences, there are three parts: (a) the interval before the lack of synchronization occurred (in the nonresponse case, an entire action), (b) the duration of the lack of synchronization when both persons are in the same state rather than in the opposite one as complementarity requires, and (c) the duration of the final state (again in the case of the nonresponse, a whole—and the next—action).

Note that four of these cases of lack of synchronization result in the other person losing his turn in the regular course of this alternating series which ideally makes up the interaction sequence. In (2) and (4) for the nonresponse variables, the person acting starts in again without having to wait and listen to his partner. In (2) and (3) for the interruptive variables, the interruptor takes the ball away from the speaker and prevents him from continuing to act until his own rhythms bring the action to an end.

Moving away from the abstract quality which these definitions imply, let us call them by the terms which have been current in interaction measurement literature for many years. Their classification depends on the expected state which would have occurred if the "right" person had taken or maintained his turn (as in tennis), but differing for the nonresponse and interruptive variables.

Taking the first: when either speaker stops, the interval of silence before the one whose turn it is to act finally does is called *his latency*. If after the silence goes on and the person previously speaking starts up again, the interval of nonresponse is called *his quickness*. Whichever person starts to act, whether it is his turn or not, is said to take the *initiative*, though clearly (and experimentally) these two types of initiative differ in their significance as will become apparent later on. The actions which make up the duration of the initiation have been given the apt but somewhat short-hand labels of *prods* or *nonprods*, derived from their use in diagnostic and therapeutic interviews. The prodded action occurs after an interval of *latency;* the person who has just spoken is waiting for the impact of his acting to have the appropriate results. If his rhythm is too quick to let him wait so long, *his* action is unprodded. Clearly, it occurred without the intervention of the other.

In interruption, the situation differs slightly. The interval between the time the speaker started and the occurrence of the interruption is called the *cycling* factor. In the earlier discussion of circadian rhythms, the reader will remember that the point at which the synchronizer is introduced is highly significant in its consequences. Here, the cycling factor is short, the impact is much greater than if the other person's interaction has been continuing for a considerable time, and the rhythm on its way to being well established. Alternatively, if it comes in towards the end, it can cut off the action and speed up the tempo. From the time the interruption begins until it ends by one or the other person's giving up, *persistence* is measured, literally persisting in the face of the other's competition for the floor. The person who keeps on acting, who out-acts the other and so wins the persistence bout, *dominates* and the loser is *dominated.* After *domination* has brought the interruption to an end, the length of time the dominator continues is called the *maintenance* factor. Through continuing, he maintains his control over the sequence and, in so doing, maintains or reestablishes his rhythm of actions as against the loser.

Initiative and Dominance Variables as Components of Personality

The moment we move from neatly synchronized interaction to the various types of situation which result when one or the other person, through lack of adjustment, unwittingly brings about a change in the even give-and-take, we necessarily encounter the physiological and behavioral consequences of entrainment. Unless the failure to synchronize is minimal quantitatively, there are the beginnings of the emotional–interactional reactions of temperament, a subject to be dealt with in the three chapters following. Just as entrainment to changed light–dark cycles can have serious consequences on the physiological state of the Arctic mouse, so interactional entrainment is *the* stress (or if one prefers, the stressor) to which the individual must adapt in his relations to others.

Personality factors are not derived from emotional elements. The initiative and dominance variables develop early in the maturation process, and evidence from behavior genetics indicates that they have genetic components. The difficulty with the available data is that the types of rigorous definition outlined above have been little used so far in animal studies. Words like dominant, aggressive, submissive, timid, and the like, represent rough, natural history types of labels. It is often hard, when reading research reports, to determine what the animal actually did in interaction terms.

However, using what might be called common-sense criteria, there are differences in these variables between species and between individuals. Dominant animals fight and win; timid animals give up easily and are unable to take the initiative. In humans, similar differences between individuals can be identified. Here, with the benefit of thousands of cases where interaction measurement has been used under controlled (programmed) conditions, dominance can be shown to occur in one person without observable evidence of stress, and this is also true conversely. Some people are naturally very quick and take the initiative repeatedly; others are very slow and almost always wait for the other to start them off. Such personality differences occur very early in children; there are, however, no studies over time to determine their continuity and stability in later life.

In defining the personality, one must add to the action–inaction variables at least some of the initiative and dominance variables. By determining the relative frequency of dominating or of initiating, it becomes possible to calculate cumulative percentage totals for the individual, and also for his relationships with each individual with whom he interacts over a twenty-four hour period. A wide variety of studies indicate that these percentages, for each individual, and often for each relationship, are relatively constant. Further, significant deviations in the individual's net position brings about attempts to compensate when there is a deficit, or a slacking off if he is ahead of the game. People, of course, differ widely in the percentage level they are able to maintain. Everyone has encountered persons who are at the extremes, never able to dominate or take the initiative (these two qualities are by no means correlated in the same person). There are others who must always dominate, or who initiate to all and sundry, doing their utmost to avoid having to respond to someone else's attempt to initiate to them.

But these capacities to maintain a relatively stable percentage of dominance or of initiative are dependent upon the quantitative values of the variables which compose each situation. If an individual's persistence when interrupted is brief, only if he selects persons to interact with whose persistence is even briefer has he a chance of being dominant. Humans differ remarkably in this capacity to persist. Many people stop almost instantaneously when interrupted, allowing the other to dominate them. Others keep on going against persistent opposition almost as if they were quite unaware of being interrupted. Those who give up easily may not remain out of the combat for long. Many persons characteristically cut back in and interrupt before the other person has gone very far. The faster this occurs, the greater the possibility of conflict. Tit for tat results both in lengthening persistence and accelerating the tempo as each side attempts to win.

In addition, the cycling point in the other's action where the individual tries to break in and start his interruption is extremely important. If one interrupts just as the other person gets under way, an interruption of the same duration has far greater impact than if it occurs somewhere towards the middle of the expected duration of the action. Once the full rhythm is set in motion, brief interruptions are easily managed and act to "encourage" (whether verbal or nonverbal). Under such circumstances, a much longer interval of persistent action will stop the speaker in his tracks. Finally, cutting the individual off just before he comes to the end, and doing this repeatedly, can systematically reduce his length of actions so that each time he talks he becomes shorter and the persistence duration needed to manage this can be quite short.

People vary also in how long their *latency* lasts. Each individual has his own idiosyncratic tolerance level differing from others for such intervals of silence. Some, finding the other person not responding, can wait only a few seconds before taking the initiative again. They are so quick to initiate that even a modest wait, perhaps caused by the other person being inattentive as he tries to finish some task, is too much for them. In contrast, there are others who wait for long intervals before taking the initiative. When two such persons are together, the long meditative silences produce the impression (and the measurements) of an extremely slow tempo of acting.

Initiative and Dominance Variables in Studies of Groups

Although the study of groups is more properly a consideration for Part II of this book, it is worth commenting briefly on the implications of these personality variables for group situations. Relatively few interaction measurement studies have been carried out on human face-to-face groups, and most of these are so recent that they have not yet reached the stage of publication. Some approximations to these on-going investigations have been made in the past in studies of small groups, either concerned with problem-solving or other types of cultural and cognitive questions, where the interaction, usually only who initiates and the length and frequency of verbal speech, often taken from tape recordings, is about all that is available. There are a few long-term field studies of small groups or organizational situations, perhaps the best and earliest of these being W. F. Whyte's *Street Corner Society* (1943). Most of these rely on the interpretation of interviews to try to isolate interactional factors; they are not cases where interaction measurement has been used in the sense discussed here.

Field studies of apes and monkeys are becoming more systematic. They provide one of the few sources where there is an attempt (varying in rigor, to be sure) to try to describe the interactions of groups of animals. The most useful studies are those where it is possible to identify the animals by marking them or by isolating peculiarities of their appearance. Here again, however, lack of clarity of definition of the interaction patterns makes the data hard to use. Yet when two macaques indulge in threat behavior and one attacks and keeps on fighting until the other flees or adopts a submissive posture, the dominance sequence is clearly evident.

Where obvious fighting or threat behavior is no longer present, investigators often have difficulty in deciding how to judge the situation. When the howler monkeys of Barro Colorado Island in the Panama Zone, first observed by Carpenter (1934), encounter groups of other howlers as they move through the trees where they habitually live, they howl (as their name implies) until one or the other group is outhowled and moves away. By interactional definition this is clear evidence of dominance, but primatologists are likely to state that howler monkeys do not have dominance patterns since they howl, but rarely, if ever, fight, like macaques, for example.

A chimp, like a little boy, may grab a stick and wave it in the air or shake branches. Man, though most lethal in some of the dominance actions which his technology facilitates, is far more likely to use his voice and gestures to achieve dominance over his fellows, thus putting him on a par with the howlers.

The reader interested in accounts of animal behavior and, in particular in studies of monkeys and apes, will constantly encounter confusion in the literature about the meaning of such terms as dominance and aggression. There are frequent references to "dominance hierarchies" with events cited which clearly illustrate that one animal has taken the initiative to the other. Dominance hierarchies, human or animal, are, in fact, hierarchies based on the establishment of repetitive patterns of taking the initiative. These set up the order in which the animals are ranked in terms of who acts first and who responds. Dominance provides the ultimate sanction by which one animal or human enforces his prerogative to take the initiative to another, since the final authority is force. Once he establishes his ability to dominate, or the other accepts this without a prior struggle, initiative becomes a routine aspect of the relationship.

Various primate groups differ in the frequency with which fights for dominance are reported. For many of them, patterns are established very early without fighting because of the hierarchical position of the mother and her consort (Sade 1967). In consequence, the usual pattern in such groups when two individuals come together is that one is free to take the initiative and the other waits or gets out of the way. The dominant male in a group of gorillas, as Schaller (1963) reported, had only to rise from his nap during a midday siesta and move a few hundred feet, to have all the rest of the group get up and trail him until he has settled down to resume his nap, when they did the same. Typically, for every kind of group, animal and human, the leader combines dominance and initiative in judicious amounts, using the former to make sure that there will be no question that the *group responds to his initiative.* Such interactions are technically called set or group events (Chapple 1940) and imply the occurrence of simultaneous response by the other animals. Koford (1963) commented that the leader of a group of rhesus was not the monkey who was the quickest to act aggressively towards members of another group but the one who was especially rapid in settling conflict between members of his own group by rushing to the scene and threatening one or another until they stopped. Thus, initiative in conjunction with dominance is not merely a matter of initiating to another animal; the crux of the distinction is that two or more individuals respond in unison, and are made to by force if they will not.

To initiate in set events (and to enforce this pattern by dominance) is so built into the framework of human societies that it has to be looked at within the framework of the consideration of culture in Part II of this book. However, it is hardly surprising that people vary in their capacity to get people to respond to them. The charismatic leader, be he politician, priest, or football coach, has this capacity as a major interactional component of his personality. Partly, it is related to the capacity to initiate new events after no interaction has been going on, in contrast to the initiative that occurs within an interaction sequence, and partly to the capacity to use dominance when needed. Whyte's book on street corner gangs is one of the best, and one of the few, field studies in the literature on the dynamics of set events and their relation to leadership. Yet so much is the pattern a part of our folk culture and art that there is hardly a Western film where the hero does not force the bad men or the local citizenry, usually after glorious battle, to respond when he tells them to, or else.

In essence, then, personality is built upon the basal rhythms of action–inaction sequences and the tempo at which they tend to occur. In adjusting to others, the individual tries to shift the other's rhythm as close as possible to one of his own constituent rhythms, if not to the dominant (basal) rhythm of his personality. To do so, the initiative and dominance variables facilitate this process (or make it more difficult to achieve). They, therefore, stabilize the optimal adjustment possible (which of course may be minimal). In situations where complementarity is approximated to a considerable degree, their manifestation at threshold values provides a means of estimating the range within which the basal rhythms fall.

Unfortunately, each variable making up the personality is rarely favored with an interactional situation in which its basic values are elicited and given free-running opportunities. Those quantitative properties of the personalities of others, which do not complement the individual's, produce stress as he encounters them. When this occurs, the physiology of emotion becomes manifest as it colors (and controls) the idiosyncratic temperamental reactions which have developed over time, often in the very early years of the individual's existence. As these are set in motion and superimposed upon the fabric of the basic rhythms of the personality, each person becomes even more truly an individual. Though he will be different from every other, yet he has in common the emotional–interactional patterns which make man a human being. In turn, for every animal species, these patterns make its individualities special to it, though equally differentiated.

Chapter 4

The Biological Basis of Emotional Behavior

Lack of awareness of the existence and all-pervasive quality of the biological clocks has resulted in many attempts to deal with the surfacing of behaviors derived from them by introducing explanatory concepts like "drive" or "motivation." Primarily, this has been due to limitations in stimulus—response theory. Long trains of behavior could be set off (or at least detected) in such studies, and it has become increasingly evident that the state of the organism during a given experiment affected the results.

A major finding of research on the influence of hormones has been that behavior is very directly modified by them. Obviously, the female rat in heat is in a different state of "motivation" for sexual adventure than in the nonoestrous part of her cycle. Though there are many complexities to be unraveled since hormones can have more than one effect at the same time, for example, in organs and in the central nervous system, the general tendency in elaborating stimulus-response theory has been to accept hormonal changes as motivating factors. In the same way, it is now realized that internal stimuli derived from other physiological processes also influence "motivation." Hunger contractions were an early case, and a large number of other types have been identified. Yet in spite of the mounting evidence that the basic variables are physiological, many writers, even Hinde (1966), are still loth to drop the notion of a separate factor, motivation, as an intervening variable. Though the sufficiency of physiology is well substantiated for eliminating "motivation" as an explanatory concept, the study of circadian rhythms (and others) and its implications has remained too long in a separate compartment in science, not often opened by behaviorists.

Reliance on the concept of "drives" is much more easily understood since here behavior and physiology are obviously interdependent. Sex, hunger, fear, and the like are clearly physiological and manifest themselves in overt behavior. Somehow they are thought to combine themselves into a kind of generalized drive which also sets off a series of actions by the organism. Today, biological investigation is overtaking explanatory concepts. Although it was argued that individual "drives," say the sexual drive, might well be physiological, it was still maintained that one could not explain its level of activation unless some kind of drive mechanism was postulated. In other words, one had to explain its discharge level and what factors made external stimuli sometimes set it off, and at other times not do so. This level of activation or arousal has now been shown to be a product of the operation of the reticular formation of the brain.

The fact is that biological rhythms, at their various frequencies and with their physiological properties, do enable the investigator to reduce the number of explanatory concepts to a manageable level. Moreover, they provide a straightforward basis for bringing together the patterns of action and interaction and their emotional components as part of a single physiological system, as we shall see.

One can still ask the question, in a rear-guard action, as many might do if they were familiar with the evidence, "if the fundamental rhythms of the body are so all pervasive and regular, how does it happen that they appear to be obscured in daily life?" Grant that the alternation between sleep and waking is evidence enough of the circadian cycle; the faster rhythms of behavior seem much less obvious. Such a question fails to take into account that the properties of the synchronizers which mediate changes in rhythms are determined in free-running states. To do so, the synchronizers are deliberately held constant (or eliminated) to establish the prior basal state. But interaction, which for man and his fellow animals alters rhythms in the same way that light and dark do, is going on all the time. The shorter rhythms of which it is composed, and its circadian components, are obscured by synchronizers from other people. The possibilities of the individual achieving an easily observable, free-running state are, therefore, minimal.

The natural rhythms of the body maintain the internal system in a state of equilibrium or dynamic balance, and enable the organisms to adapt to external stimuli through its constituent elements. Thus, the light synchronizer shifts the basic circadian rhythms as the sun moves on its course. It sets the clock for the whole complex of rhythms down to those of the single cell. It, therefore, imposes adaptation on the animal, and thus survival. In the same way, at a much more rapid pace, the occurrence of interactions and, of course, changes in their properties enforce changes on the organism which reciprocally set up changes with those of his fellows with whom he interacts.

This adaptive (or reactive) property of the animal takes place, not merely behaviorally, in the sense of overt, observable changes in skeletal-muscle activity, but also in bringing about coincident changes in the internal biochemical and physiological states which mediate the adaptive action. By contrast with common verbal usage, the two are integrally related. They are, in fact, parts of a single system. Each time a change in skeletal-muscle action is elicited, even at the threshold level, at least a modicum of energy is expended. The coincident changes in physiological states on which fixed action patterns are based are called "emotional reactions." If the idea seems strange that each action, and interval between, making up the essential and overt rhythms of behavior, has anything to do with emotion, this is only due to the literary traditions associated with the term. Examining how emotions actually occur, in the great dramatic sense of the word as ordinarily interpreted, will help clarify the significance of their part in the reactive properties of the organism.

Emotions and their Physiological Roots

Although the emotions have always been said to have a most powerful influence on human affairs—how predominant they are can be established by honest introspection—students of man's behavior have been surprisingly unwilling to accept the full implications of what takes place when they react emotionally to a situation. It is as if, by examining the biological basis of what they call emotion, its power or precious quality will be destroyed. Many nonbiologists, in fact, still appear to believe that emotions operate in a world independent of the human body and are not physiological.

Yet there is beginning to be an increasing sophistication as to the dependence of emotional reactions on the body processes. It is accepted that well-defined medical conditions like ulcers, ulcerative colitis, arthritis and asthma, coronary heart disease, and high blood pressure are made worse by emotion. Whether they can be produced "solely" by behavioral stress is still being debated. In any case, the emotional component of many diseases is recognized far beyond its initial limitation to the various forms of "mental" disease—the neuroses, psychoses, and the personality or character disorders. The degree of shift in attitude is well illustrated by the fact that in 1966 a three-day conference was held on the "Psychophysiological Aspects of Cancer" without causing critical comment.

There are those who hold that physiological explanations are too simple to describe the heights to which a lover rises (emotionally) in thinking of his loved one, or the hero's dedication in dying for his country. Partly this is due to the emotion being imbedded in a symbolic statement as we shall see in Part II of this book. More properly, literary usage (academic and otherwise) appears to be at the root of this type of skepticism. So many words have been written to try to describe the nuances of an emotional reaction that biology is considered alien to the symbols. Yet what are symbols if not cultural shapings of neurophysiological events?

On the research side, apart from dogma, most of the argument has come from those who have been given an injection of one of the drug substances involved in the physiology of emotion. From introspection, they have concluded that what they "feel" differs from *the* emotion which they presume it should produce. The fact, as will be shortly evident, is that the body does not deal in a single substance, but in substances and body states in combination.

Even without a textbook at hand, everyone applies specific labels to the internal feelings and moods he experiences. In addition, he supplements his description of internal states by noticing in himself and in others such physical evidences of emotion as blushing, becoming pale, perspiring, or tensing the muscles of the jaw or fist. When the emotion becomes intense, there is violent bodily movement or gesture and extreme changes in the voice—"scream with terror," "cry out in rage." The physiologist, and the physician, can make simple measurements of other criteria of emotional states—changes in heart rate, blood pressure, the contractions of the stomach or the intestines. Beyond these are more subtle measures of neurological and hormonal changes which help define the total physiological states which constitute the emotions.

Although a complete description of the biological basis of emotional behavior is highly complicated, the broad outlines are fairly straightforward. Risking the charge by specialists that this account is oversimplified, the essential factors involved can be outlined without confusing the reader—and losing the writer in a mess of anatomical and physiological detail.

The Autonomic Nervous System and Emotion

In the last analysis, all organisms try to achieve a balance between their internal (endogenous) requirements for energy expenditure, monitored and controlled by their biological clocks, and the adaptive changes which the external environment necessitates. Both types of operation are mediated by the nervous system, since the various organs making up the body would otherwise be independent and uncoordinated. A distinction used to be made between the involuntary and voluntary functions: activities like the heart beat, the digestive processes, or respiration were considered able to continue without the individual being able to influence them to any significant extent. Others, like walking, or sitting and hammering a typewriter, primarily involve the action of the skeletal muscles and were, for that reason, regarded as voluntary.

The involuntary or autonomic actions of the body were held to have achieved that status because changes—in blood pressure to increase energy or respiratory movements to make more oxygen available—had to take place automatically in order to prepare the body for survival. These could be of the emergency type when flight or fighting were required, they could be more adaptive as in the regular shift in the circadian rhythm of activity as the sun moves on its annual course. Activity—or respiration for that matter—illustrates the limitations on such definitions. The controls for autonomic and voluntary operation are obviously intermeshed. Voluntarily, one can control the frequency of one's breathing for a few breaths and, as in a medical examination, breathe deeply or shallowly, fast or slow. But shortly, autonomic influences begin to operate. After such brief evidence of "free will," compensatory changes are set in motion and breathing is taken over by involuntary forces. In the same way, our activity—even our interaction with others—has its very obvious voluntary aspects, yet inner and autonomic compulsions require one to act in spite of oneself.

Since emotions seem to occur largely involuntarily, the first thing to look at is that part of the nervous system which controls them—the autonomic (self-regulating) nervous system. As suggested above, it is concerned with the regulation of the heart and the gastrointestinal tract, the flexing of the smooth muscles of the blood vessels, bladder, bronchi, and skin, and the secretions of the various glands. It has two major subdivisions, the sympathetic and parasympathetic nervous systems. Although it is easier to understand their operation if one treats them as independent of one another, in many emotional states, particularly when they are intense, there are well-defined interrelations.

Mutual Relations of the Sympathetic and Parasympathetic Nervous Systems

Generally speaking, the sympathetic nervous system produces discharges of nervous impulses affecting the whole body, enhanced by the secretion of two major substances, adrenalin and noradrenalin (often called epinephrine and norepinephrine). The first is primarily associated with the emotion of fear, the second with anger or rage. On the other hand, the parasympathetic system controls the operation of individual organs. For example, it regulates the emptying of the bladder, the colon and the rectum (in acute stress with remarkable speed), as well as the dilation and activation of the sexual organs. It is responsible for the flow of saliva and gastric juices, the muscular contractions of the stomach and alimentary canal, and the entire process of digesting and assimilating food. Except under extreme activation, it sets in motion feelings of well-being, affection, and love.

Again, in a general way, the sympathetic and parasympathetic systems can be regarded as opposed to each other: For example, the sympathetic speeds up the heart beat and increases the blood pressure, the parasympathetic decreases them; the iris of the eye (often used as a test for autonomic activity) becomes smaller under parasympathetic influence and larger when the sympathetic takes over. Adrenalin and noradrenalin are counterbalanced by the parasympathetic substance, acetylcholine, which accelerates the activity of the various organs controlled by its system. In addition, acetylcholine is the primary chemical mediator managing the transmission of nerve impulses electrically across a synapse (junction of two neurones—nerves) in the neuronal circuits or networks of the body. Noradrenalin is also secreted by the nerve endings of the sympathetic system, while adrenalin arises in that part of the adrenal glands called the medulla (its internal part).

The "Emotional–Interactional" Complex

It is common to speak of the sympathetic system as adrenergic and the parasympathetic as cholinergic (from the choline in acetylcholine). Individuals can then be differentiated from one another in terms of the presumed preponderance of one or the other systems in their physiological reaction patterns. Thus, a cholinergic person would have low blood pressure, a slow heart rate, and breathe slowly; he would have an overactive gut with attending frequency of voiding, tend to blush since his facial blood vessels would be dilated and he would weep easily. In contrast, he who is adrenergic is liable to pallor, to sweating of the palms, has a dry mouth through reduction in saliva, and much less gastrointestinal activity; he is slow to digest his food and to evacuate; together with a faster pulse, higher blood pressure, and rapid respiration, he would have higher blood sugar. The activity level of the cholinergic individual is higher, that is, he talks in longer intervals; the adrenergic, particularly when anxious or hostile, becomes short and quick to act.

Yet this simple opposition of the two systems is inadequate to describe what happens under more complex or intense stimuli from the external environment. A point is reached in which they become interdependent, that is, where one can be said to bring the other into operation. In addition, other systems of the body, interrelated with these, begin to play their part, and all are mediated through the complex functionings of the nervous system.

Emotional Control Through the Papez Circuit

The easiest way to understand the total operation of the central, autonomic, and skeletal (somatic) nervous systems, and their associated organs insofar as emotional reactions are concerned is to simplify the anatomical complexities to a minimum. In fact, Papez (1937) postulated the existence of what is now known as the Papez circuit, a combination of anatomical structures of the lower brain constituting the limbic (border) region connected to the most important "emotional" body, the hypothalamus. Papez believed that this circuit constituted "a harmonic mechanism which may elaborate the functions of central emotion, as well as participate in emotional expression." Though modified by further work, particularly by emphasizing the role played by the neocortex—the storage and association areas of the cerebrum—in essence, his hypothesis has been substantiated.

The hypothalamus is the central element in the emotional circuit since it receives the preponderance of its neural signals from the limbic system, though also from the cortex. Directly, and through the pituitary gland, it controls the autonomic nervous system. In addition, changes in internal state are signaled to the cortex. One can regard the hypothalamus as the controller of emotion since its anterior division is the parasympathetic origin and its posterior, the sympathetic. Through its pathways, it indicates to the anterior and posterior lobes of the hypophysis (pituitary) the necessity for specific hormone secretions to begin (Hamilton 1958).

Just as the hypothalamus is the neural controller of the nervous system for emotion, though interdependent with the various higher or lower elements of that system, so the pituitary controls the state of activity of the thyroid, the adrenal cortex, and the sex glands through hormones which it secretes. Yet the pituitary is not merely concerned with these functions; it also produces ACTH, (adrenocorticotrophic hormone), the secretion through which the body adapts itself to major stress and prepares itself for fighting. ACTH is released into the blood stream and carried to the adrenal gland where, from the adrenal cortex, cortisone is released. This is the substance which was found to have such dramatic effects in treating arthritis; it affects metabolism, the circulatory system, the kidneys, and the muscular tone of the body.

Rates of Emotional Reactivity

In considering the elements of any particular emotional reaction, it is important to remember that neuronal signals are set in motion and travel much more rapidly to various parts of the body than do the hormones. Reaction of the organism to the occurrence of environmental change through the sympathetic and parasympathetic systems happens almost instantly. It depends on the speed with which the electrical signals travel along the nerve chains, with acetylcholine or noradrenalin increasing the transmission rate at the synapses. On the other hand, the hormones have to travel from their source of origin to the target organs which they affect. These hormones may, in turn, release other hormones produced by those organs. Since they are carried by the blood stream, their rate of action depends on the rate of flow through the body and the routes followed.

Once these substances are secreted into the blood stream, their effects continue until chemical processes alter their form and they are absorbed or excreted from the system (or from the organs which they activate). The rates at which these happen differ considerably. The body also produces substances which counterbalance their effects. The picture of what goes on is not simply the secretion of hormones and their gradual dissipation or chemical degradation, but also the secretion or production of enzymes which can inhibit or destroy these substances. Thus, acetylcholine maintains an uneasy balance with its enzyme, cholinesterase; insulin, also produced during autonomic reactions through parasympathetic influences on the pancreas, has recently been found to have a countereffecting enzyme, orinase, apart from its dissipation in the process of utilizing and using up blood sugar.

Such neural and hormonal changes are not simply one-shot affairs. The hypothalamus, as the coordinating center of the Papez circuit through which signals are being transmitted as they come in from the external environment, continues its directional activities as long as the situation continues. It is also receiving signals from the body itself as each change in autonomic activity takes place. This may result in messages calling for shifts in the constituent systems and their chemical interdependence. A mild alert in the sympathetic system with minimal adrenergic activity may increase in intensity. When this happens, a shift occurs, not merely from the noradrenalin of anger to the preponderance of the adrenalin of fear. As the system becomes more affected, an acute parasympathetic reaction is triggered off which combines with adrenalin to make the animal unable to move. This is the state of what one can call shock, physiologically and behaviorally.

The traditional separation of visceral or autonomic activity from the "voluntary" actions of the skeletal muscles is quite unreal once any emotional state is induced by changes in the external (or internal) environment. The sympathetic and parasympathetic systems are mobilized precisely to take over the animal's behavior patterns and to ready him for conflict, for running away, or for love. Only when stresses due to changes in the external situation impinging on the organism are not occurring can one talk about the muscle systems controlling activity and interaction as if they were under "voluntary" control.

Everyone is aware of this state of interdependence. Athletes, from ball players to golfers and billiard experts, realize too well how often their performance is affected, usually for the worse, by their emotions. The inability to control oneself and to execute the coordinated movements or thoughts which a particular sport requires are constantly to be fought against. Additional evidence is produced by those competitors whose primary (and effective) stock in trade is to get their opponent's "goat" by "oneupmanship" or any of the many ploys which can elicit emotion. Emotion is also put to the use of sport—the last ditch stand at the goal-line or the desperate efforts of the underdog. But these, too, are mediated by achieving a level of balance in which noradrenalin predominates, aided by ACTH. This balance is also a consequence of patterns of interaction which enhance and control the expression of emotion.

Neurophysiological Bases of Emotional Behavior Patterns

The surprising thing about this inattention to the omnipotent intertwining of the viscera and one's actions is that multitudes of investigators have been carrying on experiments with cats and dogs, with monkeys and even, during surgery, with humans, to establish the relationships of major patterns of behavior and their neural and chemical components. With the development of ethology and the beginnings of a systematic identification and description of the natural patterns of behavior for each species, a parallelism in effort has been underway. Neuroanatomists have been able to elicit precisely these same patterns, in whole or in part, by electrical stimulation of the areas of the brain which control them. Brown and Hunsperger (1963), for example, referred to this approach as neuroethology. They demonstrated very clearly that the behavior patterns of a cat, when threatened by another, are localized in the hypothalamus and the associated areas of the limbic system. Not that there is a one-to-one correspondence between anatomical loci and specific behavioral components. Rather, these are interrelated within the region associated with threat and flight reactions. The centers from which these two types of reactions are activated are adjacent to one another.

Thus, there are specific centers in the brain through which particular ethological patterns making up the total repertoire of the animal are set in motion. More important, the intensity of the stimulation (through frequency of the electrical signal or an increase in its voltage) may produce marked latencies in response. Alternatively, with other fixed action patterns and their locations in the brain, extreme skeletal-muscular reactions occur, needing no scientist to tell the onlooker that the cat has become furious and he had better stay out of reach of its claws.

Brown and Hunsperger emphasize that a single region is concerned with the patterns of reaction associated with threat, attack, and escape. Also, there is a gradation between them so that one does not have to postulate separate centers which inhibit one another; rather, stimulation of that part of the hypothalamus associated with escape will strengthen the activation of the threat–attack hypothalamus zone. Thus, various combinations of elemental behavior patterns (perhaps with a single locus) can be elicited as one moves from one part of the brain to another. The subtle interdependence which slightly varying interactional situations demonstrate is built up from a series of signals coming in to adjacent portions of the limbic region. As the authors referred to point out, the evidence suggests that what the other animal does can be crucial.

> The absence of fear evinced in these ("pure") attacks is specific to the opponent or the location and depends on previous establishment and stabilization of a dominant–subordinate relationship. If the opponent is slow in leaving, a mild threat may occur; and if it stays, strong threat followed by fighting often results. It would appear probable from this relationship that the more hesitant the attack and the more resistance of the opponent, the more activation of a threat system in the attacker (Brown and Hunsperger 1963).

Cues from the timing of interaction and the patterns composing it become part of the learned experience of the animal. They differentially stimulate the various emotional centers involved in the threat–attack–escape complex.

In the same way, the patterns of sexual behavior and response are associated with the limbic system and the hypothalamus. But the situation is made more complex because of the obvious and easily demonstrated influence of the hormones originating in the pituitary which liberate the sex hormones from the ovaries or testicles; there is a feedback through which these hormones sensitize the hypothalamic centers and these in turn set in motion specific skeletal muscle and autonomic patterns of reaction in the individuals. Though affection and love, as Cobb (1958) has pointed out, are associated with soft voice, color in the face, wide pupils, relaxation of the muscles and intestines, a feeling of warmth and the secretion of sexual hormones—(and in interaction terms, of complementarity) all cholinergic symptoms—the sexual act itself involves both the parasympathetic and the sympathetic nervous system, particularly when orgasm occurs.

Equally important to the organism from the point of its survival and that of its species is the requirement to eat. Once referred to as the hunger drive, the necessity to take in food is again organized through the autonomic system, in particular, through the hypothalamus and its associated components in the Papez circuit. It is as if the evolutionary process, Dame Nature if you will, regarded this activity as too important to be left to the chance operation of simple reflexes. There also appears to be a "satiety" as well as a "hunger" center in the hypothalamus. The interplay between them of positive and negative feedbacks from signals from the various organs involved in the acquisition or assimilation of food are mediated through the sympathetic and parasympathetic neurone channels.

Control of Velocity of Arousal

In each of these major emotional systems, activation (or stimulation) through the internal or external environment produces a state of increased alertness. With certain exceptions when the degree of the stress is overpowering, increased motor activity occurs. This state of arousal is brought about through the midbrain and specifically that part of it called the reticular formation. Its primary effects occur because it sends its signals diffusely to the entire cortex, signals which may come from the limbic system (of which technically it is a part) or from the nerve receptors on the surface (internal or external) of the body. Thus, information is coming into the lower centers and the cortex both through specific pathways and through diffuse ones. At the same time, neural discharges are traveling downward, that is, away from the cortex, to the spinal cord, increasing its excitability and capacity to transmit signals in both directions.

To complicate the situation further, as mentioned specifically in discussing the sexual reaction patterns, each of the fundamental emotional systems is not only a neural system whose activation is due to the transmission of electrical signals from neurone to neurone, it is also a chemical system. The various hormones carried by the blood (and nonhormonal chemical substances ranging from the metals needed for body function to the complex proteins like amino acids) become part of the tissue cells. The nerve chains are thus bathed in a highly varied liquid medium which alters or modifies what might otherwise be thought of as an essentially simple system of electrical circuits. In turn, the patterns of neural activity influence the chemical system, and the resulting product is one of almost infinite shadings.

The magnitude of the stimulation or activation of a given autonomic center, with all its inherent capacities for variation, has clearly marked differential effects. For example, mild stimulation (low frequency) of a particular portion of the hypothalamus will ordinarily produce parasympathetic responses. One can, however, obtain a shift into sympathetic responses simply by increasing the frequency. It is easy to see how mixed cholinergic and adrenergic effects can be obtained. If they are present in equal force in a single organ, they will tend to cancel each other out. But in the whole system involved in a major emotional reaction, an extremely complex pattern is operating for which the term cholinergic or adrenergic is not particularly helpful. In fact, it should be emphasized that these terms are merely ways either of describing a single reaction or, for the individual in a particular state, of the proportional rates of the various chemical and neuronal elements in his system. In extreme reactions to stress—the orgasm, the transition from fear to dejection and defeat, or from anger to violent rage—both parasympathetic and sympathetic systems are activated—in differing sequences and in different amounts depending on the stage through which the emotion is going.

The Rhythms of Emotional Patterns

The major emotional (autonomic) reaction systems are set in motion by environmental changes and may, therefore, be regarded as responses or ways of adapting to stress. Yet at the same time, it needs to be reemphasized that they also have well-defined biological rhythms, the circadian being the most all-encompassing. The mature female shows periodic changes over a longer period in the sexual organs—the menstrual cycle. Not only do sexual receptivity and time of ovulation follow a cyclical pattern, but physical activity fluctuates parallel to changes in the rates of hormone secretion.

A great many studies have shown that the hypothalamic system (and the pituitary gland) control the rhythms of the thyroid, the adrenal cortex, and the male and female sex glands. The various circadian rhythms described in Chapter 2, from RNA and DNA synthesis to metabolic rhythms, illustrated in body temperature, are coordinated or entrained by the pineal body and the adrenal–pituitary system. Though dependent on one's choice of a definition of "master clock," since even individual cells show their own rhythms, the pineal body and the hypothalamus combine in the coupling mechanisms which link all the various rhythms together by entrainment. Thought of as a clock, in that sense, they can be called the master clock since this does not prevent each clock from potentially operating on its own.

Each of the major systems responsible for emotional reactions has clearly defined circadian rhythms. There are also both shorter and longer cycles for the various components of the autonomic nervous system and, for that matter, for the cortex itself. These biological rhythms of the body represent the free-running pattern of "spontaneous" expenditure of energy. They range from 10 to 20 per second in the case of cortical (and muscle fiber) activity through the daily cycle of activity and inactivity in wakefulness and sleep, to the longer cycles—the longest being the annual migrations of birds and the hibernation of some animals. One must differentiate the spontaneous or free-running properties of biological rhythms and the changes of which they are capable when entrainment from the external environment is set in motion. The reaction patterns described are part of, and not separate from, the processes which biological rhythms represent.

Where radical changes are experimentally brought about, as by putting a nocturnal animal into continuous light, a series of autonomic changes is set in motion with concomitant behavioral and physiological disturbances before some degree of stability is achieved. If the imposed shift is too great, that is, beyond the animal's limits of tolerance, major changes in hormonal function occur, in particular in ACTH. These can rapidly lead to death as a consequence of endocrine gland destruction. Selye (1956) had labeled this enforced shift of physiological rhythms outside its limits, "the general alarm syndrome." The imposition of external stress resulting in major emotional reactions can be so severe as to deplete the system of its recuperative powers.

Although such stresses represent the extreme case, they are commonly cited as examples of the relationships of behavioral and autonomic patterns in the literature. The fact is, however, that each response of the organism which involves any part of the activity (or interaction) rhythms has its autonomic components. Though the change may be below the threshold (the point at which overt change becomes detectable), repetition of such responses can rapidly cumulate their effects. Once they pass over the threshold, a measurable change in behavior is set in motion. Since each individual has different thresholds for different situations as a consequence of the experiential influences which have made up his past, reactions can trigger changes in the rhythmic patterns of behavior remarkably rapidly.

Terminological Difficulties

A major difficulty in keeping this interrelationship clear is a question of semantics. As is so often the case, the problem is to find a word which means emotional–behavioral, emotional–interactional, or autonomic–

interactional, some conjunction of the two aspects of the organism which can be, and unfortunately have usually been, studied separately. True, the mind–body separation is presumably ended once and for all, yet people talk about psychosomatic illness, or psychosocial functions or, for that matter, psychobiology, indicating that the ghost is by no means banished.

Apart from the biological necessity of considering skeletal muscle and autonomic functions conjointly, some very useful consequences result in simplifying the number of explanatory concepts or levels required. As commented on at the beginning of the chapter, one does not have to create additional hypotheses about "drives" or "motivation". The phenomena they were intended to describe are adequately dealt with by biological variables directly grounded on studies of the organism (even if all the interrelations have by no means been worked out in detail). Though for many, these terms became a matter of common usage, they require one to think of them, independently or together, as existing in addition to the biological systems just described. To continue their use, one has to believe that living organisms have, so to speak, no continuously running internal motors modified in their rates of operation and their mutual states by external forces.

Biological rhythms are, therefore, fundamental to the organism. Their equilibrium characteristics, their capacity to respond to entrainment and to other physiological stresses, demonstrate that they are able, within limits, to return to a steady state in the process of adjustment. Their short-term variations through the reaction patterns of the autonomic are mediated, and identified, through the emotional-interactional patterns which can be observed and measured by the discriminations outlined in the preceding chapters.

The Scope of Emotional States

In this chapter, emphasis has been on the ways in which the body generates emotion as a consequence of disturbances to its physiological states. The reader should not, however, have the idea that physiology only explains emotions in their unequivocal expression. The matter is far more subtle. There are highly complex relationships between sympathetic and parasympathetic, and these are further varied by the differential thresholds by which elements of one may receive only minor activation while another may be set off much more intensely. The fact is that these appear in those fundamental ways of reacting to the world, as specific interaction patterns from others impinge on the human being. These shadings infinitely variegate the individual personality.

For how one reacts to changes in interactional states is the subject both of this book and, on a different level, of those who try through their art to reveal the true properties of human nature. One must remember, however, that in Part I of the book, we are concerned only with the dimensions of interpersonal behavior. All those feelings and emotional nuances which we associate with music and the arts, with significant symbols in the communication process, represent a further differentiation of these emotional states taking place through the cognitive, that is, through the interdependence of the cortical and autonomic. It is in this mingling that the aesthetic and affectional subtleties of our lives become evident. They are built upon and elaborated through the biological foundations with which we are here concerned.

Chapter 5

Emotional–Interactional Patterning of Temperament

The up-flowing of emotion which shapes the patterns of interaction, elaborated by intensity and visible autonomic signs, comprises the human temperament. Too often, it is bracketed with character, as if synonymous. However, the latter represents its cultural transmutation; it is the structuring of emotional-interactional patterns within the accepted constraints of a particular society. A man of rectitude may be such for different temperamental reasons—anxious, timid, or inflexible; the shadings of character depend on which temperamental foundation this characteristic has been constructed. A thief, where thieving is not the approved occupation of a special group, has temperamental tendencies which drive him towards this way of living. Though dishonesty is taken for granted, his character may include that rectitude which honor within his kind presumes exists.

Psychiatrists these days are often considered *the* specialists on human emotion, a popular belief whose grounding is little more than the trailing aura of Freud and psychoanalysis. Perhaps this relegation of the countless others similarly concerned is symbolized by psychiatric diagnostic classification; apart from obvious taxonomic anarchy, it is ironic that the individual temperament is nonexistent in their nomenclature. The reaction patterns with which we shall be concerned are now parceled out between those extreme disorders labeled "psychotic," "psychophysiological," "psychoneurotic," and lastly, "personality." All tend to be lumped together as "behavior disorders." We cannot here discuss these diagnostic vagaries other than to point out that the carrier waves of interaction patterns are inextricably confused with cultural elements in such classifications. Therefore, they are properly criticized by most psychiatrists (Redlich and Freedman 1966) even though they continue, such is the inertia of tradition, to use them. To begin to identify the primary temperamental reactions included under these varied labels would require the prior discussion of the cultural dimensions themselves, and this book is not concerned with the necessary revision which psychiatry must undergo.

But one usage of the word temperament itself should be commented upon. Commonly applied to extremes—the great diva, the Hollywood star of the good old days, the terrible tempered boss, or the wife whose impact is traumatic—temperament is not evidenced merely in repeated and disturbing outbursts. On the contrary, in this book, temperament is defined as the occurrence of observable emotional–interactional patterns, great and small, which are reactions to what some other person (or persons) is doing. They are properties of the individual, established at a very early age (so much so that they are often referred to as infantile by psychiatrists); they make up the characteristic ways in which particular personalities react to particular situations. They are repetitive and predictable. They vary in severity and staying power for a given person, depending on his initial state and the degree of asynchronous stress he encounters.

Temperamental reactions generally range from the extreme (and sudden) to the very small changes in the basal rhythms which can only just be detected by interaction measurement. Once one is set in motion, it may continue for a long period of time without further exacerbation by lack of adjustment, or it can be reinforced repeatedly, as any battling married couple well knows. Estimation of the threshold for any individual for a particular reaction depends on the magnitude of the other person's asynchrony *and* of the reaction elicited. This is a matter of experimental trial (ordinarily provided by real life contacts). It assumes that the disturbing pattern has been introduced after a period when the free-running rhythm (a state of complementarity) has occurred.

Reactions of Complementarity

Although there are many more identifiable variants on the disturbing theme where fear and anger or their different masks take over, temperamental reactions can also be beneficent or loving. These stem from the positive properties of the parasympathetic, as in the pleasures of love and eating. They are of first importance since they occur in the free-running states of the biological rhythms on which they are based.

Finding the "perfect listener," gaining that sense of relaxation from being able to talk or not talk when one "wants" to, is one of the greater pleasures. More accurately, the individual experiences a sense that *his* rhythm is being freely expressed which synchronization enhances. No matter if the complementarity which sets this in motion is forced from the other person's view, peripheral to his own, occurring when the other's preferred rates are not those he can consistently maintain. But true complementarity is not restricted to "boy-meets-girl" situations where, in the words of the best-selling German waltz of the 1920's (Zwei Herzen in Drei-zierten set takt), two hearts beating in three-quarters time. This basic underlying need for interactional satisfaction may make, on the surface, for quite incongruous friendships.

Sometimes the culture provides the framework, within special types of activities—sports of all kinds, hunting, fishing, sailing, dancing, even sewing or cooking. If their rhythms fit the timing patterns of individual personalities, special relationships can be built up and become necessary for each person. Yet they are often limited to these situations alone. A flexible person may interact at several tempos almost equally well. The interaction patterns which poker engenders can bring about and sustain the meshing of personalities, and yet this may prove to be an uncertain complementarity as players change; even the preferred dealer's choice may prove too constraining. Other relationships may create dissonance. One's old hunting partner may be the soul of complementarity; yet he will not necessarily achieve a similar pattern with one's wife.

Compatibility does imply complementarity, but it is strongly affected by cultural factors. Being compatible may merely mean that two people possess common interests though they may still fight like cats and dogs. Complementarity ignores these interests; it is limited solely to interactional synchronization. Two people may "get along beautifully" and yet appear to have "nothing in common." Far rarer is the case when cultural and interactional patterns are closely knit, where people actually appear to think and act alike and have in common similar wells of emotional feeling and outlooks on the world. Defining the full scope of complementarity and its effects is limited by our inadequate understanding of the ways in which these rhythms have immediate impact in eliciting parasympathetic reactions. That they do so is quite clear, but the literature abounds with statements like that of Cobb's previously quoted—affection and love, soft voice, color in the face, relaxation of the muscles and the gut, a feeling of warmth, and the secretion of sexual hormones are cholinergic. Apart from its laundry list quality, it ignores the quantitative description of the interaction rhythms and how they do the trick.

Complementarity can also be regarded as a consequence of other personality variables. The initiative and dominance ratios (or net positions) are elements of complementarity. They aid in eliciting and maintaining the basic rhythms and the parasympathetic patterns of which they are a part. This multivariate state is often best achieved in the pleasures of play, culturally expressed in games and sports. Within limits of skill and luck, the needed balancing out of one's initiative and dominance rates is easy in playing tennis or chess, or some equivalent in another culture. The needed action–inaction sequences of the personality and their particular tempos are also made manifest since initiative and dominance patterns are built upon them. Yet in striking contrast to the impact of lack of synchronization and the transients resulting—fear, anger, aggression—too little study has been devoted to the complementary (pleasure) states.

From empirical observation, one knows that people are constantly searching for those who will give them a satisfactory degree of complementarity. There is much literature on family problems, marital relations, industrial supervision and psychotherapy, of accounts of "human" problems and the techniques employed to try to do something about them. Perhaps only Masters and Johnson (1965) in their physiological inquiries into sexual intercourse have seriously tackled one of these problems, beginning, however, only when the pair went to bed and tactile interaction could be maximized. Throughout the literature is the assumption that routines—stable and nondisturbing patterns of interaction, continuing over time—are the essential ingredients in temperamental (emotional) stability and satisfaction. Sometimes the desired condition is symbolized by the nurturing relation of mother and child or by the model of the "expert" lovers; apart from sex physiology, the interactional patterns sought for—that state of "being well adjusted," a kind of social work psychiatric Holy Grail—has not been a subject for scientific investigation.

Its opposing face, the arousal of violent reactions as a consequence of interpersonal stress, is demonstrably disturbing and debilitating. Surprisingly, research here is on much solider ground. For reasons possibly stemming from Victorian prudery, the studies of anger, fear, and rage, brought together by Cannon in the 1920's, have had, since then, the concentrated attention of investigators. Though Cannon (1928), like Cobb (1960) after him, spoke of the pleasures of the mild arousal of the parasympathetic, it was much easier, with a New England heritage, to plumb the depths of fear and anger, the factual litany of the Puritan church. Sex can be investigated, but even today it has only been measured negatively by finding out what it is not—as Harlow has tried to do in his deprivation studies on infant monkeys.

One thing is certain by way of conclusion. When complementarity occurs and the parasympathetic becomes activated (*not* in its more extreme reactions), the individuals experiencing it try to continue its state indefinitely. The endless conversation of lovers, the interminable swapping of stories in some special sporting world, the dilemmas accompanying the playing of games, continuing as long as strength and brain hold out, are evidence enough of the satisfactions so derived.

Cybernetic Aspects of Synchronization

The popularity of cybernetics (and cybernetic terms) has meant their use as explanatory concepts without sufficient understanding that decisions as to applicability depend on measurements. Yet the idea of feedback is clearly useful. Here small amounts of the energy (or whatever it is in the particular case), constituting the output of a system, are fed back as input to compensate for changes outside the limits within which the system is intended to operate. Steering a boat, the source of the term coined from the Greek by Wiener, is a case in point. If the vessel starts to shift from her course, the helmsman compensates by a small movement of the rudder; a good helmsman on a sailing vessel, for example, can anticipate such a deviation from the "feel" of the rudder (a minor change in pressure). He then shifts the rudder minimally before the vessel actually is off course.

This is no place for a discussion of cybernetics, though it forms an important part of instrument design, of electronic circuitry, and systems analysis generally. However, the idea of feedback is useful to express the mutual dependence of a system where a trial-and-error process goes on to determine the precise amount of adjustment to be used and its direction. Today, this is a matter of formula, but the idea of hunting, of varying the feedback until the quantitative parameters of the system can be estimated, is useful in understanding complementarity.

Although each person is impelled to act by the requirements of his internal states, the interactional rhythms which these control are interfered with by the refractory or recalcitrant properties of other people. Not that this is a matter of their intent. They, too, are malleable only up to a threshold point which varies remarkably from one to the next. Even the rhythms from which they start may demand interactional characteristics widely different from those that other people can provide. Think how hard it is for a naturally "outgoing," "social," "friendly" person to try to keep from being exasperated by a stone-faced, unresponsive partner who appears to ignore each effort to strike up a conversation. Consider the bore who persists in telling you all the minutiae of his daily life until your every will to indicate attention by a smile or other signal becomes paralyzed into immobility.

Nevertheless, internally each individual's metronomes still maintain their beats. Their compulsions lie only beneath the surface. True, the rhythms of interaction for any single person are not fixed to one single fundamental beat; they consist of a set of subsidiary tempos with capacities to act or not act for given durations fixed within each tempo level. However, people do not easily shift from one state to the next along a continuous scale. The shifting is dependent upon the degree of disturbance which given amounts of lack of synchronization entail—of being dominated, or of not getting a response and having to take the initiative. In addition, individual ranges are definitely limited. Though the conventions of music enable one to write compositions over many octaves, the particular instrument selected has a limit beyond which it cannot even produce a note.

When individuals whose basic interactional personalities are quantitatively within the same general range meet and are able to manage at least a modest degree of synchronization, the process of adjustment is equivalent to the kind of process which engineers describe in cybernetics. At the first instance of lack of synchronization, there is a feedback as one person tries to alter his pattern to adjust to the other. For example, if one person talks 60 seconds, a length of time which approaches the limit at which the other can continue to remain silent, the listener may break in on the speaker (by interrupting and dominating) and cut him off. On the next speech, he might then try (usually unconsciously) to wait for longer than 60 seconds before acting; on the other hand, the speaker, finding that he has been interrupted, might shorten *his* action to 55 seconds.

With another person, at the end of the unit of action of 60 seconds, he might encounter a marked delay in response, perhaps of the order of 5 seconds. In the next action, then, he might lengthen his response while the other, for his part, might shorten his silence to fit the expected 60-second action. After a series of such interchanges, which might or might not mean that both persons hit their fundamental rates, a relative degree of adjustment (and complementarity) can be stabilized.

Two persons may differ considerably in relative complementarity, that is, in the degree to which the tempos at which they are operating, and the ratios of action and silence needed to adjust, fit their fundamental rhythms. One person may be at, or close to, this level and thus able to continue at his rate for long intervals; the other may be at his periphery and have to try to suppress *his* basic rhythms; since no one can go beyond his inherent limits, he will be unable to continue doing so for very long.

Perhaps the psychoanalyst's 50-minute hour is a reflection of this limitation for the longer rhythms. Though in theory they must be flexible and presumably able to listen, casual observation in social situations makes one suspect that often they are extremely talkative. Perhaps they need to compensate for a day-long "listening" regimen. For those who play this role, a high level of activity *with* equally long silence periods (and a slow rhythm in consequence) is a necessity. Not all psychiatrists follow such inactive procedures. Many are aware, without being fully conscious of their interaction patterns, that there is a kind of natural selection of techniques they like to use and hence in acquiring and holding patients. They are more successful with certain types (interactionally) than with others. Referrals to other therapists are often made on the basis of some kind of intuitive feeling about potential complementarity.

The process of feedback, by which individuals make adjustments in their interaction rhythms, requires that their rhythms are within reaching distance of each other's and that at least one of them is flexible enough to approach complementarity. Further, the adjustment process itself cannot be so disturbing as to set untoward reactions into being. For the fact is that lack of synchronization, often to an extremely minor quantitative degree, may have become so integrated with autonomic nervous system reactions that substantial changes are triggered off in consequence. These various types of asynchronous behavior which individuals encounter in others constitute stresses—stresses which mobilize extreme emotional (and behavioral) patterns.

To minimize their cumulative effects and achieve partial complementarity, individuals often take turns at manifesting their basic rhythms in an unconscious agreement. One person finds he is free to talk and the other to listen. Then the pattern of interaction shifts and the listener becomes the speaker. As this alternation in proportionality continues between the two partners, each, if sufficiently flexible, may be able to synchronize at the appropriate tempos while being the "listener." Often a process of exploration of the ranges within which each person can interact very obviously takes place, a cybernetic hunting for the most stable rhythm at which the other adjusts. This ability to shift one's performance, just as someone new to dancing learns to lead and follow, increases the pleasure which synchrony affords.

Properties of Asynchrony

When perfect complementarity is achieved, the person experiencing it reaches that proportionate output of activity to inactivity which is at the tempo most characteristic for him. Yet most of his interaction will be with people whose own fundamental states are unsynchronized with his; one or the other (or both) will have to shift their values to approach this complementarity. Simply to reach a pattern of alternation requires a shift in phase, that is, the action interval of one will occur during the silence interval of the other. If their basic interaction rates are not the complement of one another, adjustment has to take place, depending on the degree to which each is flexible or capable of variation. There are people whose values are so fixed that, almost literally, they are unable to adjust to others. Their initiative and dominance variables prove unvarying. Most persons adapt to some degree, though the magnitude of the adjustment will vary, depending on the potential capacity for adjustment of the other person.

The first variables to be affected in the interaction sequence will be the relative length of actions and inactions. If both people have high activity and short silences, they constantly will find they are attempting to dominate each other. Each can try to reach some midway point by shortening actions and lengthening inactions or, more radically, shift to almost complete complementarity for a period, only to reverse the pattern later in the interaction. The tempo or beat is far less likely to shift if the individual can adjust his proportions of action durations to silences for the length of time the contact continues.

Whatever type of asynchronization occurs, the basic properties of the personality elicited result from the interaction of two separate and distinct persons. The chance of encountering complementarity is fluctuating, and usually infrequent. People are thrown together by cultural processes, with little explicit or implicit consideration for their interactional limitations and requirements. Lament over one's incompatibilities with those who make up one's interpersonal world has been an old dog's tale since human history began. "The Lord gives you your relatives; at least you can choose your friends" is not an absolutely accurate rendition of the proverb, but it has the message. Yet opportunity to choose is far too often vulnerable to accidents of physical appearance, common interests, or peripheral (but momentary) complementarity. So even friendships disintegrate; only the relatives remain!

Where lack of synchronization occurs, no matter how brief, we are recording, and measuring, the durations (and frequencies derived from them) of the initiative and dominance variables. Hence, the temperamental patterns constituting each person's idiosyncratic reactions to particular types (personality variables) of asynchrony are measured as deviations from the basal or fundamental rhythms and their "harmonics," if we may borrow the term to describe those rhythms secondary to the basal or fundamental one.

Having determined the quantitative values describing the basal rhythm and its harmonics, one compares the values occurring after the interruption, the nonresponse or whatever, with those values which came before. For practical purposes, this is done by computing the ratio or proportion of the change in values in each of the constituent personality variables. However, the nature of the transient phenomena which we can measure makes it possible to use more sophisticated descriptive mathematical techniques by which the order of change can be given in an equation. For example, immediately after an instance of asynchrony, a long action value may occur, followed by successively smaller ones until the basal rhythm is restored. The trend of the values can be expressed by a linear decrease (the values decreasing in equal increments) or, for a more accurate fit, logarithmically. This method of analysis reveals nuances about the nature of the individual's reaction patterns that linear accounts do not, but cannot be dealt with in a nonmathematical book. Yet in what follows, it should be kept in mind that each fundamental emotional–interactional pattern defining a temperamental reaction can be expressed in a quantitative equation.

Returning to the discussion, these deviations from the basal values which define reaction patterns can be positive or negative. They are increases or decreases from the fundamental interaction rhythm. Each is mediated through different autonomic elements; each is repetitive and characteristic of *that* individual. Thus, if a person's reaction to instances of nonresponse (one or many) is to shift to long bursts of speech, this is idiosyncratic for him. Next time the same asynchrony occurs, he will react in the same way, not in a different direction, since the autonomic–interactional reaction system underlying the visible measurements is an essential property of his individuality.

Each reaction pattern will not always include the same variables. Whichever ones are involved, they will differentially increase or decrease (or both). One pattern might be made up of an increase in action duration, decrease in silence, and increase in persistence. When a different type of asynchrony (or stress) occurs, it is unlikely that the same directional changes in the constituent variables will take place. Someone who "can't stop talking" after nonresponse will behave in a quite different fashion when his dominance over another is at issue. Finally, the components of his fundamental rhythms as well as the constituent variables of the initiative and dominance groups may also vary independently. An increase in duration of the action response in the above instance could be accompanied by a decrease or increase in the length of the inaction or silence which accompanies it. Obviously, tempo has to be dependent on the two since it is made up of the arithmetical sum; conversely, since the beat or pulse of the biological rhythm is controlling, it imposes constraints or limits on the internal intervals making it up.

Synchronizers as Interpersonal Stresses

The term, synchronizer, derived from the study of biological clocks, has been used predominantly so far since it implies the mathematical formulation of the regularities in the way changes in rhythms take place. Yet in physiology, the integral relationships of these reaction patterns and their autonomic components are commonly referred to as responses to "stress." Stress has achieved popularity in lay and scientific writings dealing with emotion; in so doing, though we shall also use it, it has acquired those ambiguities of definition which, for the purposes of this book, need to be remedied.

Stress is defined as occurring when two or more persons come together and an instance of asynchrony takes place. The stress can be minimal, below the individual's threshold; perhaps a reaction will be produced, and only after constant repetition. On the other hand, one cannot say that a single instance will not produce a stress reaction. Some people have such low thresholds for particular temperamental states that one such occurrence may be sufficient to trigger off a violent reaction. The thresholds and the amount of stress required to overpower them are determined by observation and measurement. Accurate test procedures can be programmed into interviews (Chapple 1970b). Given this data, one can predict with confidence what will happen when stated amounts of stress are introduced in the course of interactional contacts.

Stress reactions are set in motion when lack of synchronization takes place, but they manifest themselves through changes in the values of the personality variables described in Chapter 3. Each type of asynchrony is defined by the composition of its particular interactional sequence. What stress can occur depends on the prior state where there is no asynchrony. Obviously, one cannot interrupt someone who is silent, or become latent if he is still talking. Once the asynchronous stress occurs, how severe it will be depends on its quantitative pattern and the length of time the other person continues the state which makes possible the asynchrony. Ordinarily, during the actual interval of stress, the interaction rhythm of each is shifted. The stress comes to an end when one or the other person changes his state so that synchronization can reappear, or another person intervenes and the prior interaction ends. In this stage, the stressed individual (often both of them) goes through a compensatory period of reaction, a transient state. A significant deviation from his basal rhythm, his prestress state, occurs and this may entrain repeated instances of asynchrony. In the least complicated case, however, after the transient runs its course, the individual returns to equilibrium and to his basic rhythms, that is, if there are no new stresses— due to failure to adjust—appearing in the situation. Each stress thus has the capacity to entrain the interaction rhythm to a new (if brief) state; removal of the stress ordinarily produces a transient pattern as a compensatory shift in the interaction rhythm. Only after this has run its course and no further asynchrony takes place does a stable rhythm (and equilibrium) become reestablished.

Though these are the bare bones of what happens if the transients are prolonged, it is rare that repeated stresses will not occur before they run their course and synchronous interaction is reestablished. Whatever labels might be applied to these stress situations, and often they are lumped together either as "aggressiveness," or "rejection," they are actually compound sequences. Moreover, they may include alternations between several opposing types, for example, latencies and interruptions, with one having the greater frequency and magnitude.

Emotional Components of Stresses

When reaction to any stress is quickly ended, little evidence of its carry-over into other relationships can be detected. Even if prolonged, the individual's threshold may be high enough not to set transients in motion. The British call such persons "unflappable." Neither visible nor interactionally affected by the stress, they show no apparent temperamental reactions in consequence. When the stress ends, they return to their basic patterns of interaction as if nothing had happened. Perhaps the truly unflappable are those able to adapt easily to each of the several types of interactional stress. Such individuals are far less common than those who are not disturbed by *one* particular stress pattern, that is, they are able to meet new persons easily or are not thrown off by nonresponse.

It should not be surprising, however, that temperamental reactions occur, not only *during* the stress, but *after* it has ended. Many people experience much more severe reactions once a stress is over than during the situation itself. This is a common report on soldiers after a battle, or in members of a family caring for a dying relative. During the stress period itself, the individual's characteristic reaction pattern may enable him to cope, even though the interactional changes he has had to make may be disturbing for others. Thus, some people react to nonresponse by accelerating their initiative. As each action becomes shorter and shorter, a person reacting this way can do many different things very rapidly, provided no explanation is required to persuade others of the need for action.

But when the stress ends, the emotional components of the temperamental reaction are not automatically switched off. Adrenalin or noradrenalin, acetylcholine, ACTH—whatever substances have been mobilized and pumped into the blood stream are still there—the heart rate and blood pressure do not instantly return to normal. If the reaction is severe, the whole system of the body, *including* the skeletal muscles which have altered the quantitative patterns of action and inaction in ways characteristic for that individual, is still mobilized in its response to stress.

Remembering from the preceding chapter the complexities through which the autonomic sets its operations in motion, the incidence of stress initially involves a signal (signals) traveling along its neural chains. This signal is electrophysiological and fast; it then is followed by chemical changes when hormones are liberated within organs and in the blood stream. Some of these are directly activated by the neural signal, but others, for example, substances from thyroid, gonads, adrenals and the like may be liberated only on the impact of prior hormones on these organs. Without restating the complexities of these interrelationships, the time characteristics of each of these steps in the sequence differ—not only in how long a given amount of hormonal or enzymatic secretion will continue to modify the system of the body, but also how long it will take the chemical processes of modification or destruction of the liberated hormones to run their course.

Whatever the time factors of these sequential internal changes (and their overt skeletal-muscle concomitants), they are occurring both within the period of stress and after, since it is unlikely that the homeostatic process, the internal restoration of equilibrium, will be brief. Externally, cessation of stress provides the measurable evidence of the stress's impact.

The recurrence of synchronization—say the ending of a disturbing pattern of nonresponse and the adaptations by the individual to it—for many people acts as a trigger to set off a violent reaction. Like the cork held under water, letting it go results in its rapid passage to the surface. To choose just one such example, people who are very quick and short may now be at the mercy of a long-continuing burst of speech, in the extreme case sometimes lasting for 10 to 15 minutes before stopping. The next action will be shorter. After several of them, the transient temperamental reaction comes to an end and the individual returns to his basic interaction rhythms.

During this type of acute reaction, clear evidence of a cholinergic involvement is apparent—flushing of face, tearfulness, often the full range of the activated parasympathetic system. Obviously, the individual is "upset," but like all such common words in the emotional dictionary, the behavioral criteria are very different from those that others may manifest.

Whenever a compensatory reaction takes place, and before the personality can return to the equilibrium of the unstressed state, the individual's interactional system has to go through its idiosyncratic changes. Yet not all people return to equilibrium by an overcompensatory response. An object masquerading as a cork does not always pop up from the depths of the pool and bound about before it finally comes to rest. Many underreact; the temperamental patterns which stress can trigger off are remarkably varied.

The Stress of Nonresponse (Withdrawal)

Intervals of nonresponse of varying lengths of time are followed (and brought to an end) by one or the other person taking the initiative. In the regular alternation of interaction in which one person talks while the other is silent and so to its final ending, such intervals of nonresponse may frequently occur. Efforts to synchronize by two persons with slow tempos and relatively low activity levels may produce these hesitancies. Provided they do not last too long, they may not exceed the threshold at which a reaction is triggered off. But many people who are quick to act require an immediate response; for them, the long delay before replying is very stressful. Placed with a slow, "meditative" person (or whatever label might be applied to his characteristic latencies), they cannot wait. Seeing nothing happening, they break the silence and take the initiative out of turn. In so doing, the associated indications of autonomic stress begin to operate. At this point, individual differences in temperamental reaction start to manifest themselves, each in its own characteristic way.

A large series of basic categories of reaction to nonresponse have been identified in interaction research. At the onset of stress, the personality variables begin to alter their quantitative values and shift, often dramatically, from the limits of the fundamental rhythm and its "harmonics." The stress sets off an autonomic reaction. In turn, this shifts the interaction patterns with which it is associated and interrelated—more accurately (since there is no encompassing single term) of which the interaction sequence is a part. Each category of reaction represents a combination of the component interaction variables differing remarkably from the others in its effects. It is defined in terms of the occurrence of marked decreases or increases in the values of the variables. Thus, the direction of change and the magnitude of the deviations from the basal rhythms of each variable are the means of defining each temperamental reaction pattern.

The reader may be helped to appreciate the contexts in which these reactions occur by referring from time to time to terms used in the literature. Thus, nonresponse is often referred to as withdrawal or as rejection. When used in studies of animal behavior, or psychiatry for that matter, such terms are usually imprecise since it is rarely clear whether physical or interactional withdrawal is being discussed. A mother may beat her infant to force it away and thus "rejection" may in fact consist of overt "aggressive" acts of dominance. Yet lack of response, either because no one is available or the person present does not react, produces extreme behavior reactions on its own, as is so obvious in the infant. With babies, the immediate reaction is to cry or scream and their body movements become agitated. If withdrawal or separation continues, this pattern is then followed by a sequence of changes, which become stabilized. Kaufman and Rosenblum (1967) have reviewed studies on monkeys and humans and showed how each stage of behavioral change could be based on neurophysiological processes. From such studies, it appears evident that the different temperamental reaction patterns to be described become established at specific stages in infantile (or young juvenile) interaction and then continue into adult life by repetitive reinforcement.

The Temperamental Reactions of Quickness

The need to take the initiative, even if infrequently, is a necessary accompaniment of acting. Without it, the internal rhythms would be unable to fire spontaneously. As a consequence of the development of personality, each person achieves a balance in his initiative rate which can only be maintained if he finds others who can complement his needs. Whether high or low, maintaining a balance depends on reciprocity. He must interact with people who have their own requirements; if, for whatever reason, he always tries to initiate, the chances are good that others will avoid him or be unresponsive to him.

This need for reciprocity in initiative, in which I initiate to you and you then initiate to me, is woven through the whole social and cultural fabric. It is not merely framed in codes of etiquette but in ritual, in the rules of economic exchange, as well as in games that children play with one another, or when monkeys chase each other through the trees. But delay in taking one's turn, however unintentional, becomes emotional stress and temperamental displays can very quickly be set in motion. Therefore, he who is too quick and cannot wait takes the initiative again and again. While he is disturbed by the slowness and lack of response, his opposite, finding himself under repeated pressure to respond, may equally be upset.

A)   Prefers Physical Action or to Interact Briefly

For some people, the repeated stress of not getting a response speeds up their tempo; it is adrenergic; each time they initiate more quickly than the last. Yet they are only able to act very briefly, as if throwing out a phrase or a question will somehow make the other person react more rapidly. In personality variable terms, they are trying to prod him to act. In consequence, the other person finds himself being initiated to repeatedly without being given time to respond. His rhythm of action and inaction has been broken up; he has lost, literally, the initiative. The give-and-take, adapted to his slow tempo, which did allow him to initiate at his own rhythm, is no longer reciprocal; his turn to act has gone by, not once but repeatedly.

For the initiator, however, this accelerated pattern reduces the durations of each of his actions, hence the amount of communicative information which the carrier wave (his prod) can make available. Lasting a few seconds, only a brief phrase, a command, or an exclamation can be mustered out. Small wonder that people having such a temperamental reaction have grave difficulty in explaining how situations might be met, in delegating to others—all they can do is to issue a peremptory order. Finding the world too often unresponsive, they prefer to do things themselves rather than find that others will not operate at the tempo congenial to them, and run the risk that they will become emotionally disturbed.

So strong can such a temperamental pattern be that the whole personality is colored by its presence. Quick to act, to take the initiative—in any crisis where others are too slow—the frequency and tempo of their initiative rate rise so high that others cannot compete, even if they will. Such people provide a spectacle of apparent constant energy, initiating to all and sundry, or doing everything themselves at frenzied speed. When this acute temperamental reaction is set off, they become, through the strength of the emotion possessing them, rigid, inflexible. They carry on at a tempo (and minimal action duration) affording no place for alternate interaction rhythms.

B)   Takes the Floor

But quickness to take the initiative when the other person is latent may not always result in acceleration of tempo (and initiative) with intervals of action and silence becoming shorter and shorter. Quite in contrast is the person for whom the latency serves as a compulsion to act and keep on acting. His prods continue and are unbroken, not brief intervals as above. At each repeated interval of nonresponse, he talks longer and longer, necessarily taking the initiative in order to do so. Perhaps after-dinner speakers, as a group, are characterized by this kind of temperamental reaction. The longer the silence the longer they talk. The audience's lack of response—some have compared it to the hypnotic state which a snake creates in its frightened victim—is the compulsion which makes the speaker unable to stop.

The effect on the listener can be *severe.* Not only has he lost the initiative, but the long bursts of speech force him into a silence which lengthens his tempo and shifts his preferred balance of action to inaction. His only recourse is to break in and try to dominate and cut the speaker short, as the chairman of the meeting must when he looks at his watch and sees that the assigned 30 minutes are long since past.

In the less extreme cases, such capacity to sustain an action after taking the initiative has utility unless repetition of the stress overwhelms his flexibility and creates the after-dinner image. When nonresponse occurs, varying durations are necessary to determine to what degree an approach to complementarity is possible and at what tempo and action–inaction ratio. If intervals of nonresponse repeat themselves at the beginning of the sequence, such a "hunting" process should take place; if the stress increases in intensity, and the longer intervals do not reduce the other person's latency, the characteristic temperamental reaction of the individual with longer and longer actions becomes established.

This push of speech, this need to take the floor when others have become silent, is compounded by and possibly triggered off through noradrenalin, since anger appears to be a subsidiary component. The action values manifested are not a continuation of the basal rate, they are significantly higher. In some individuals who react this way, the intervals of silence (their quickness) becomes increasingly short; in others, as long as they appear to be able to count on their partner's silence, acceleration of their quickness intervals does not occur.

C)   Suspicion: Coincident Withdrawal

Latency of response does not always operate in the ways described above; for many, not getting a response sets in motion a similar latency. Low in their capacity to take the initiative, they become even slower when the other person's response is not immediate. Whatever their intent, they wait it out until their partner finally responds. When they do initiate, each action duration tends to become increasingly brief. From physiological clues, this pattern appears to be a conjoined sympathetic reaction, both adrenalin and noradrenalin combining to produce fear and anger in association with this inhibition of action. One can call this temperamental reaction "suspiciousness"; in the severe state where it is prolonged, even after the other person's latency is reduced to a minimum, it becomes one form of what the psychiatrists call *paranoid.*

The use of terms like "suspicious," or "distrustful," or "paranoid" (commonly applied to such behavior) raises the question of the cultural aspects of the temperamental reactions. Far more than in the first two categories, such terms imply a view of life, behaviorally *and* culturally defined, which so colors the impression the individual makes in most of his interaction with others that other temperamental reactions, positive and negative, set off by stress, become almost completely obscured.

In daily life, there are many, many possibilities of nonresponse occurring. Sometimes this is simply because the other person is naturally hesitant, has a slow tempo, is inattentive, or perhaps has other temperamental reaction patterns which produce a marked latency. As a result, the suspicious individual constantly encounters what for him are highly disturbing situations. These reinforce his pattern of reaction and the intense emotion associated with it. In consequence, the general impact he has on others is to appear "suspicious" in every situation, even though he may behave quite amiably when he is not encountering nonresponse. Parenthetically, the technique of handling such individuals, even if extreme, is simply to respond immediately to each action, allowing no latency, being sure the response is more than monosyllabic, and keep it up.

In addition, though, the term assumes that what the person talks *about,* the way he rationalizes his relations to others—the words, phrases, stories, the content of what he has to say—is recognizable evidence of this suspicious or paranoid state. How this comes about will be discussed in Part II when the part played by communication in interaction will be examined. For the moment, this particular temperament reaction can serve as the type case to reinforce the point that the emotional–interactional pattern affects and shapes the cultural components of the human condition.

In each of these reaction patterns, all set in motion by the failure of the other person to take his turn—at least within the limited interval of waiting set by this property of quickness to initiate—very different quantitative values of the constituent interaction variables are encountered. In the first two types, ability to wait, to be silent, is brief; it becomes shorter with each repetition, but the duration of the actions which constitute the initiation (the prod) move in opposite directions. They represent the extremes in deviation from their fundamental rhythms. In the first, tempo accelerates and with it *both* actions and silences; in the second, tempo becomes slower, silences shorter, and actions significantly longer. Many individuals show intermediate states, with varying intervals of action, silence and tempo. Though still quick to act, the emotion is not so extreme as to override the capacity to vary the quantitative pattern to try to reestablish the alternating pattern of give-and-take. In the third type, silence increases (the limit being the cutoff point when the other person finally responds) and actions decrease; the tempo may or may not become slower. Here, too, variations occur in the regularity of change if nonresponse repeats itself.

Yet all these *quickness* reactions have in common the fact that the occurrence of nonresponse alters the values of the constituent variables making up the interaction rhythm—tempo, action, inaction. Once the initiative is taken, and comes to the end of its duration, it again becomes the other's turn to respond. Why he delays, what is at the root of his inability to act and to synchronize, and what happens when he finally does (assuming the other still waits) present a much more complicated set of patterns of reaction. To understand them, other major types of stresses need to be examined, for latency of response may occur after any of them. In combination, the temperamental (emotional–interactional) properties of the latency will differ as a consequence.

Transient Reactions to Nonresponse

So far, the discussion has dealt solely with the reaction to stress. What happens in the transient state when the stress is over but before equilibrium is restored and the basal rhythms can reestablish themselves? There are, of course, people for whom the single stress or its repetition shows little carry-over. The moment the lack of adjustment comes to an end, either with the same person or, more commonly, with someone else, the individual bounces back to his fundamental rate. Presumably, if the stress repeated itself over and over again, there would be a point at which the threshold for emotional reaction would be crossed. Even the unflappable may not be able to take too much.

Those unaffected by the repetition of the stress of nonresponse (which Chapple and his associates (1970b) administer in their programmed diag-nostic interviews) are far less common than the reactors. Yet the quantita-tive values of the stress used in such interviews are by no means large. Restricting the definition of the transients to the variables of action, inaction, and tempo only, three types can be identified. Coincident patterns of asynchrony—latency, interruptions—further differentiate these three types into a variety of subtypes, but will be discussed in the chapter following.

From quantitative measures of the primary variables, it will come as no surprise to learn that the three basic types are similar in makeup to those occurring within the period of stress. However, and this is most important, it does not follow that the temperamental pattern of reaction during this phase of transition to the basal rhythm will be identical with the pattern the individual exhibits under stress. Quite the contrary. Except for one special instance where continuity occurs, no simple correlation of reaction *during* and *after* stress is evident. Often, but by no means always, opposite trends occur.

A)   Impatience

Though the term used here to characterize this transient reaction pattern has its ambiguities (and is necessarily subjective also), the quantita-tive pattern is quite straightforward. When synchronization begins, tempo is fast, action and silences short. Individuals possessing this reaction pattern have a marked inability to slow their tempo down and increase the length of actions to a range of duration more normal for the individual. Often marked by inattention in gaze control, and measurably by inability to adapt to the slower pace of give-and-take of others, such people appear restless and quick and are often called "impatient" while this period of getting over the stress continues. They are characterized by the adrenergic side of the differential emphasis of the autonomic nervous system; such physiological signs as occur tend to justify this assumption. Although one might assume that there is a delay in the reduction of the level of sympathetic substances by contrast with other reaction pattern, it suggests that a single substance is operating in a relatively uncomplicated way. But, as has been emphasized, the interdependence of sympathetic and parasympathetic is not a simple matter of alternate modes of physiological functioning. One may trigger off the other as intensity of reaction increases.

B)   The Uncontrolled Outburst

Suitable names for temperamental reactions are remarkably difficult to find, however much one hunts through the dictionary. The notion of temper or temper tantrum which might be used to describe the uncontrollable burst of talking set off after not getting a response—being rejected, or realizing that the other person is withdrawing from interaction by nonresponse—is a case in point. Though one often thinks of the tantrum as uncontrollable, it is also an extreme reaction. Like the word temper itself, it is often used to refer to the extremeness, and not to its duration. A burst of temper may mean a single blow with the fist, a screaming curse, as well as the long-continued action reaction of the "uncontrollable" wail and tears of the desolate child. Also, if temper is used for the extreme case, the more common, medium degrees of reaction when upset by nonresponse, though characterized by long actions often lasting many minutes (but unaccompanied by such intensity and elaborations as tears or screams) do not quite seem to fit, semantically.

Whatever it be called, the press of speech set off by a period of nonresponse is a very easily recognizable temperamental trait. When associated with tears, flushing, and other cholinergic symptoms, the need to go on talking for "reassurance," that is, for responses within the action, is so much a matter of experience that folk therapy and psychiatry utilize a common strategy. Encourage the upset person by listening patiently, with repeated admonitions to "get it off your chest." After a while, patience pays off. For this time at least, the tears are dried and equilibrium reestablished.

C)   Distrustful (or Paranoid)

When one encounters someone, after the stress of nonresponse, whose tempo is slow, actions brief, and intervals of silence long, ordinarily one also finds long latencies associated with this quantitative pattern. Although the significance of latency of response as an additional temperamental variable will be discussed in the chapter following, this pattern of interaction is found only in the questioning or suspicious person whose reactions were similar during the period of stress itself. The continuation of this pattern is highly disturbing to other people. One can deal more easily with reactors by "letting them alone until they get over it" or by listening patiently and sympathetically to the "overtalkative." Not only is the pattern in itself hard to adjust to; it is supplemented by visible evidences of hostility and negativeness.

The term "distrustful" implies a greater degree of severity than "questioning" or "suspiciousness," because it is a continuation of the reaction when the stress occurred. In psychiatric diagnosis, such people are called "paranoid." The term is used here only to aid in recognition, since psychiatric classification has difficulty in differentiating between paranoid states, paranoias, paranoid schizophrenias, and the like. In addition, there is another type of "paranoid" reaction which can be identified in the dominance variables. It can too easily be confused with this one, unless interaction measures are used.

The Effects of Breaking Off Interaction

The longer relationships continue over time, the greater their stabilizing effects on the individual's total pattern of adjustment. This is true whether the interaction is one of complementarity or of stress. If ended by death or separation, a compensatory outlet is required to replace the missing interaction. It may seem surprising that this is true when the relationship has been highly stressful. Yet any quantitative deficit in the constant values of the interaction variables through which the individual maintains some kind of stable state needs to be replaced. This does not mean that another equally stressful relationship is always sought. Yet dependence on particular patterns is remarkably characteristic of humans, or, more precisely, on the repetition of sequences of patterns in which stress, and its "exciting" sequel in a specific transient reaction, turns out to be the primary means through which the personality manages an adequate outlet for interaction. The real (and literary) world provides ample evidence of the child (of either sex) never able to leave the 'castrating' mother, the husband and wife whose mutual hostility and recurrent conflict are interspersed with tearful but temporary episodes of "making up." And how often this dependence is strengthened by an increased attachment to a third family member, a mother or sister in the first case, or a child—the prize of conflict for each—in the second.

When death comes and a replacement is found, the substitute is often a picture image of the person lost. So common are relationships recreated— "making the same mistake" in choosing an equally paralyzing personality— that such situations need not be elaborated here. But it is the intensity of the emotional state which occurs when a significant emotional–interactional resource is lost which drives them to it. The need to replace it forces the individual to look for similarities (hopefully with a difference, of course) and what goes on internally rarely finds the individual consciously aware of why and what he is doing.

Though loss, in a narrow view, might be considered a kind of nonresponse comparable to what occurs in ongoing interaction, its involvements are much more complex. When the interaction is literally ended by separation or bereavement, and there is no possibility of its being reinstituted (the case of separation, even if final, is slightly different), the disturbance is more severe. The temperamental reactions evoked include *all* idiosyncratic transients. Thus, a whole series of emotional patterns are discharged, often following one another with surprising speed and, where they are very different in interactional pattern and autonomic components, their alternation becomes very difficult for the nonbereaved to adapt to. Loving, weeping and reproaching, cursing and hating tumble out one after another in bewildering order. The full repertoire of behavioral distress built on the emotions of grief and fear and anger are set in motion. Even where the relationship has involved the close complementarity of love, parting, in spite of the poet's words, is never such "sweet" sorrow. The survivor continues to experience extreme stress unless a new state of equilibrium can be established with an equal partner. On the other hand, the emotional state of loss is less complex, though equally severe, if the relationship was both intense, and long continuing, and a major source of stress. In this instance, grief and fear *and* hostility—a whole host of transients embodied in the interaction now ended—are simultaneously activated and need to be worked out.

Grief Reactions

In psychiatry in recent years, considerable attention has been paid to the "grief reactions" occurring after a crisis in the individual's relations to others. These derive from anthropological studies of the life crisis (Chapple 1940, Chapple & Coon 1942) which include the changes in interactional patterns occurring at pregnancy, birth, marriage, death, illness—in fact, any change in interactional state including transition from one institution or organizational position to another. Lindemann (1944) has emphasized that these are often so severe (and frequently repressed) that it may be necessary to force the individual to act out his grief reactions (to abreact, in psychiatric terms). Only by so doing does it become possible for him to establish effective interactional relations with others once again. To summarize him:

The picture shown by persons in acute grief is remarkably uniform. Common to all is the following syndrome: sensations of somatic distress occurring in waves lasting from 20 minutes to an hour at a time, a feeling of tightness in the throat, choking with shortness of breath, need for sighing, an empty feeling in the abdomen, lack of muscular power, and an intense subjective distress described as tension or mental pain. The patient soon learns that these waves of discomfort can be precipitated by visits, by mentioning the deceased, and by receiving sympathy. There is a tendency to avoid the syndrome at any cost, to refuse visits lest they should precipitate the reaction, and to keep deliberately from thought all references to the decreased.

The striking features are as follows.

(1) A marked tendency to sighing respiration; this respiratory disturbance was most conspicuous when the patient was made to discuss his grief.

(2) The complaint about lack of strength and exhaustion is universal and is described as follows: "It is almost impossible to climb up a stairway." "Everything I lift seems so heavy." "The slightest effort makes me feel exhausted." "I can't walk to the corner without feeling exhausted."

(3) Digestive symptoms are described thus: "The food tastes like sand." "I have no appetite at all." "I stuff the food down because I have to eat." "My abdomen feels hollow." "Everything seems slowed up in my stomach."

Another strong preoccupation is with feelings of guilt. The bereaved searches the time before the death for evidence of failure to do right by the lost one. He accuses himself of negligence and exaggerates minor omissions. After the fire disaster the central topic of discussion for a young married woman was the fact that her husband died after he left her following a quarrel, and for a young man whose wife died that he fainted too soon to save her.

In addition, there is often disconcerting loss of warmth in relationship to other people, a tendency to respond with irritability and anger, a wish not to be bothered by others at a time when friends and relatives make a special effort to keep up friendly relationships.

These feelings of hostility, surprising and quite inexplicable to the patients, disturbed them and again were often taken as signs of approaching insanity. Great efforts are made to handle them, and the result is often a formalized, stiff manner of social interaction.

The activity throughout the day of the severely bereaved person shows remarkable changes. There is no retardation of action and speech; quite to the contrary, there is a push of speech, especially when talking about the deceased. There is restlessness, inability to sit still, moving about in the aimless fashion, continually searching for something to do. There is, however, at the same time, a painful lack of capacity to initiate and maintain organized patterns of activity. What is done is done with lack of zest, as though one were going through the motions. The bereaved clings to the daily routine of prescribed activities; but these activities do not proceed in the automatic, self-sustaining fashion which characterizes normal work but have to be carried on with effort, as though each fragment of the activity became a special task. The bereaved is surprised to find how large a part of his customary activity was done in some meaningful relationship to the deceased and has now lost its significance. Especially the habits of social interaction—meeting friends, making conversation, sharing enterprises with others—seem to have been lost. This loss leads to a strong dependency on anyone who will stimulate the bereaved to activity and serve as the initiating agent.

A major test of this hypothesis occurred after the Cocoanut Grove fire in Boston in 1942 when 493 people died and the hospitals were crowded with survivors and relatives of the dead (Lindemann 1957). Sargant in England (1957), and Grinker and Spiegel (1943) in the United States, during World War II clearly showed that using drugs as emergency treatment of battle-induced psychotic reactions and employing a variety of very simple interactional patterns could aid the individual to recreate and act out the stress situation. Where this could be done early enough after the breakdown, a high percentage of the cases could be restored to effective living.

It is extremely important to emphasize how great the need is for the organism to discharge "grief" and to realize that it often is at the bottom of many types of emotional disorders. Not all psychiatric conditions are triggered off by the life crises, but many more are than is commonly recognized. In their most obvious form, they present themselves in the depressions, but often these are masked by hostility or violence, by anxiety attacks, as well as by the effects of loss in extreme personality types (as in many of the schizophrenias). Though they cannot be dealt with in this book, cultures throughout history have developed means of dealing with these "grief" reactions.

In all religions and cultures, the rituals and ceremonies associated with death or other crises in which a relationship ends, produce, or are intended to produce, similar patterns of readjustment. Though they will be discussed in more detail in Part II of this book, they consist of organized patterns of interaction and culturally derived patterns of individualized activity which the participants must follow (with the bereaved often being literally dragged through the ritual movements) enabling abreaction to take place. The complexity and duration of these rituals depend on the significance of the departed for the individuals remaining; contrast the death of the paramount chief with that of a new-born child in a small family. But such distinctions are largely due to the extent of the system of relations in which the dead person took part, hence of the cultural elaboration; they do not mirror the intensity of the bereaved one's grief.

Perhaps the most interesting studies on separation or bereavement have dealt with their effects in modifying the behavior of the very young. A great deal of evidence has been collected, not always systematically, to show that separation from the mother in the first few years of a child's life is highly disturbing and likely to establish severe temperamental reaction patterns. Bowlby (1962) has been one of the most active students in this field. He has described the behavioral sequences occurring during the crisis which may be set in motion not merely by the death of the mother, but if she leaves the child (or reduces interaction significantly) for varying intervals of time when ill, having another child, or going to the hospital. A very detailed study at the National Institute of Mental Health (Stabenau *et al.* 1966) has shown that such crises for both schizophrenic and delinquent (primary behavior disorder) children consistently occurred between six months and three years, with separation a primary factor in the first and a disturbance to the father in the second.

These patterns of reaction occur not merely in cases of complete separation, either permanent or temporal; they are set in motion also in those cases where no actual spatial separation exists, but where the parent will not respond, "no longer loves," or becomes alienated from the child— some variant of what is usually called "rejection." These crises are of obvious importance in shifting the idiosyncratic values of the personality variables at an early age, in fixating severe temperament reactions, and in creating major difficulties in adjusting to others in later life. Some factors causing their elaboration will be discussed in the chapters following.

Chapter 6

Dominance
and Other
Major Temperamental
Reaction Patterns

The shift in interaction from situations where nonresponse—briefly or forever—sets the stage for emotional–interactional stress to its opposite—conflict and the attempt to dominate—heightens the drama of observation. Although nonaction as a temperamental "outburst" can reinforce tension or grief, it is the explosive outburst of anger or rage which catches the eye and the sense of inquiry. Struggles for dominance have interested man since his literary beginnings; biochemists, physiologists, neurologists, and experimental psychologists, following Cannon, have tried to unravel the processes set in motion when an individual attacks or is attacked.

These physiological inquiries have been singularly limited on the behavioral side. One suspects that the violent all-or-none reaction is so easy to obtain that research on the effects of quantitative gradations in the amount of stress administered is unattractive. In real life, on the other hand, with animals or humans in free-ranging situations, dramatic struggles for dominance are infrequent. The interaction sequences where dominance plays a preponderant part are also complex. Attack and defense, and reactions thereto, imply a repetitive sequence of attempts by each competitor to break in and dominate the other, persisting for longer and longer periods until one or the other wins out by forcing the opponent to stop acting.

In ordinary give-and-take, dominance attempts occur intermittently, interspersed with other types of asynchrony. Provided they are within the tolerance limits of the individuals concerned, one person's frequent winning may not be disturbing. Yet when the balance in an individual's dominance rates shifts too far and interferes with his capacity to act at a satisfactory rhythm, sympathetic nervous system reactions are set in motion. Depending on the nature of each person's interactional system, temperamental reactions, differing considerably in pattern and length of time, occur.

In almost all such situations, the most striking change in interaction rhythms is the acceleration of tempo. There is a shift from the relatively slow beat of the fundamental rhythm (with rare exceptions) to very fast exchanges and reductions in the durations of both actions and silences. Yet there are rare individuals who shift from the fast beat to a slower one as the dominance attempts continue.

A) Persistence

In actual conflicts, each combatant has to persist for longer and longer intervals if he is to dominate. The increase in *persistence,* the personality variable, then becomes a temperamental reaction to the stress imposed by the other person's attempts to win. Such a progressive increase in durations of actions is ordinarily associated with an increase in the intensity (or amplitude) of muscle action movements and the sound of the voice. There is good reason to believe that the amplitude of the action and its duration are directly related, as in the case of the circadian rhythms. How dominant a person can be thus depends upon his capacity to persist for longer and longer intervals. Inability to sustain the competition through persistence guarantees that he will be a loser, at least in this encounter.

People differ remarkably in the degree to which their persistence will increase as a function of someone else's attempt to dominate. They also vary in the threshold level at which this display of increased persistence appears. Some people need only a brief amount of pressure by the other before they spring to the defense. Far more common are those for whom a considerable shift in dominance (and its restriction on their freedom to act at a regular rhythm) is necessary before the reaction is set in motion. Once it does occur, visible symptoms of anger begin to appear, the extent varying with the individual and the shift in his interactional values.

B) Competitiveness

Most people have relatively low dominance and persistence levels. This changes only under extreme stress, when a full-fledged adrenergic reaction is set off and noradrenalin, gaining primary control, mobilizes such other ingredients of the conflict system as ACTH. Not that all people are so transported; in some, fear becomes predominant and they are reduced to submission. For persistence under extreme pressure is not a typical, commonly occurring reaction pattern. More usual is an increase in acceleration of action (cycling), breaking in faster and faster and, even though domi-nated, coming back in almost immediately. This cutting back in is charac-teristic of arguments and aggressive or combative behavior.

Watch two youngsters telling each other off, or a married couple struggling to see who is going to be dominant. As the battle goes on, persistence may also increase, but the tit for tat, each interrupting the other, never letting the opposing person finish what he or she has to say, is the essential characteristic of conflict. Intensity of action increases, silences be-come shorter and shorter with latency completely vanishing, until one or the other acknowledges defeat by retreating to another room or leaving the house and slamming the door—the penultimate sequence before the battle ends perhaps having been punctuated by violence in coming to blows.

People again differ in how rapidly such behavior is set in motion. The "highly aggressive" are those who react to the slightest hint of attempted dominance, who cannot maintain adjustment without trying to break in and force the other to submit (be dominated). Where the patterns of interaction of two persons are so completely noncomplementary, even the most trivial statement or action will trigger off an aggressive response which, if one relied on interpretation of what was said, would be inexplicable on any kind of rational basis. This kind of competitive aggression is not limited to pair relationships; for some countries it appears the proper model for conducting foreign affairs. As the pace of the separate aggressive acts "escalates," warning signals go up. The only hope of preventing out-and-out conflict, both with individuals and with groups, is some kind of "cooling off period," an interval of time during which neither side initiates to the other nor runs the risk of setting off attempts to dominate.

C) Submissiveness

There are those for whom the threat of dominance is so disturbing (usually as a consequence of their early up-bringing) that they are unable to fight back. Adrenalin rather than noradrenalin takes over. They become fearful and anxious and try to avoid becoming involved in an argument or fight. Wherever possible, they move away rapidly from the scene or, as the animal researchers say, "they have a flight reaction" and bring the inter-action to an end. Yet even a successful termination does not prevent serious repercussions in their adrenergic system. Where they are unable to get away soon enough, the adrenergic (adrenalin) reaction is supplemented by a cholin-ergic one. Once this intervenes, they literally become unable to move or to respond. Their plight sets off long latencies after being dominated. In some species of animals, the adoption of a completely submissive posture results in what is called "tonic immobility." The animal lies unmoving. It can be picked up limp, unable to contract its muscles, a relaxation of complete helplessness.

The beaten animal or human cowers or lies unmoving before the victor. The dog lies on his back, his feet up in the air, belly exposed, while his conqueror pokes him tentatively a few times to see if he still has any fight left in him. In the human, such reaction patterns can be elicited both in children and adults. How overpowering the impact of being dominated proves to be can be determined by the literal inability of the loser to respond when his opponent stops acting after having won.

Transient Reactions to Dominance

As in all other types of stresses, the ending of conflict is not immediately followed by a restoration of the individual to normal functioning. His whole autonomic system has become involved in his reaction patterns. Mobilized for fighting or fleeing, it has liberated powerful biochemical substances into his blood stream and brain, the effects of which are not quickly overcome. These transient reactions have to work themselves out before the individual is able to return to a state of equilibrium and once again able to operate at his basic interaction rhythms. These temperamental reactions, occurring after encountering competition or opposition, or, more specifically, after instances of aggressive behavior and attempts by the other to dominate, may be very extreme. They include marked changes in action and inaction durations (and capacity to synchronize) and in the length of time these reactions continue.

Perhaps the most common transients are those which are quantitatively defined as underreactions. They vary widely, however, both in their patterns *and* in their effects on others. Not only has the individual undergone stress and its emotional-interactional changes, but the people he encounters afterwards may be unable to adapt to his transient reaction pattern. To meet a friend after a fight with the boss or wife is an easy illustration. However close a degree of complementarity they ordinarily achieve, adapting to a temperamental reaction after a battle may be extremely hard. Many a major fallout in relationships has occurred when one of the persons has had adjustment difficulties beforehand. One does not expect one's friend to behave "this way." Whatever the explanation, the impact of the post-conflict reaction can easily prove highly traumatic as well as unexpected.

A)   Oversensitive

Of the underreactions, the most frequently met, and to some extent the most deceptive, is that pattern in which the former combatant appears to be at his usual interaction rhythm, but in fact has not been able to reach the level where he can talk easily and freely. His actions are often just a little too short and his pace a little too fast; in consequence, adjustment by his partner is hard to manage with adequate synchronization. Astute observers, with the advantage of knowing their friends or relatives, quickly become aware that the emotional aftermath of the conflict is by no means over. If the interaction did not consist of a "mild" disagreement or argument and degenerated into out-and-out fighting, friends (or even bystanders) may regard this kind of transient pattern as evidence that the individual is too easily hurt or is oversensitive. Usually people whose emotional reactions still continue do not like to interact. "Getting over it" is often managed by avoiding acquaintances until the emotional upset has subsided.

B)   Petulance

Far more severe reactions occur when the individual is demonstrably short and terse and unwilling to interact with anyone. This can result even when he has actually been the dominant person and, in this case, when his activity and persistence during the conflict were high. By being monosyllabic and permitting only brief interaction in his transient state, he in fact discourages others from any continued contact. Commonly such reactions are associated with a very quick tempo. Not only is the response to one's comment brief, but little opportunity is provided for any extended talk.

C)   Bearing a Grudge

A less common, and more serious pattern is evidenced by very long intervals of silence between each brief action, often complicated by latency of response. Here, hostility is predominant in the emotional pattern, lasting much longer than in the former type. In clinical terms, this is another and more dangerous type of what is loosely called the paranoid reaction. Reaction to losing an argument or a fight can set off a long continued hostility (or grudge) against the opponent, resulting in attempts to damage him months or years thereafter.

D)   Impulsive

For some, the rapid tempo of the interchange in the argument or conflict continues even though adjustment by another person is taking place. Coincident with this rapid tempo is the necessity to find individuals to initiate to who are able to interact either for a brief interval or for longer periods at a rapid tempo. Where the next person encountered after the dominance situation is unable to adjust and, through his natural (basal) longer actions, threatens (unknowingly) to dominate, the contact is terminated. The excombatant then dashes off to find someone else to interact with during his continuing state of excitement. Such people react to conflict, after the fact, by a marked increase in initiative, often far above what they ordinarily require when encountering nonresponse situations. The need to initiate, to "tell the news," often involves people with whom the individual would not normally interact. The reaction can be labeled. "excitable" or "impulsive," since those possessing it cannot control the emotional consequences of their accelerated tempo.

E) Self-justification

Just as these various patterns of emotional and behavioral reaction stem from the differential effects of adrenergic elements, so there are overreactive persons for whom the ending of conflict is a signal to try to compensate for the restriction on activity which the dominance situation involves. These reactions are primarily under cholinergic influences with some adrenergic elements (adrenalin). Not only is there a push of speech and quite obvious parasympathetic signs or symptoms, but the compensatory swings which take place in this type of transient markedly exceed the normal ranges of the fundamental rhythm.

Sometimes each action lasts 10 to 15 minutes at a time, as if by continuing talking the potential threat of further attempts to dominate can be averted. Further, once the individual is able to launch into this long burst of activity without new attempts to dominate and cut him off, the occasional break-ins by the other person by way of response occur at those points in the action duration where they have minimal inhibiting effect and help to extend its length. The excombatant now is able to build up a residue of "dominances" which he has won and which are quite safe to elicit when he is in full voice. Though the outsider's impression of such performances may be that this is another instance of a "further explanation" syndrome, this protracted talk is necessary to the individual to try to stabilize his system after being dominated.

Reactions to the Stress of Encountering a New Person or Situation

The reaction of animals to new situations is often treated as an inquiry into curiosity and exploration (Berlyne 1966). Yet recent work has demonstrated that there are two aspects of the activity classified under these terms:

(1)   That activity set in motion when the animal is uncertain and disturbed by lack of information about the situation, and

(2)   that activity which slight environmental differences create by providing outlets for their endogenous activity needs.

In the second case, the variations on a common theme provide the basis for play and curiosity; in the first, the problem is how to adapt safely, making decisions on what to do.

In humans (and animals as well), stress begins with the recognition of "the stranger in our midst," but prior to actual interaction. There are many people who can begin interaction with someone new (or in a new situation) and quickly begin to adjust with minimum feedback. They show no reactions to the need to synchronize and achieve some measure of complementarity. Others, however, exhibit the full-fledged indicators of emotional stress, of anxiety (adrenergically set off) so much so that every culture has developed ritual techniques to try to establish relationships (or prevent them from occurring) and minimize the emotional disturbances which trying to adjust to an unknown person can produce.

Among too many groups, the "stranger," perhaps a traveler passing by the village, is dangerous and a potential threat of disturbance. Elaborate rituals exist among many tribes which prescribe the beginning steps in interaction and the sequence necessary if further contact is to take place. Deviations from such rituals, or the inability to get them properly started off, may result in the stranger being killed.

The anticipated stress is twofold. First, and particularly among small groups, to adapt to the newcomer requires the redistribution of interaction in existing relationships. As his interaction begins to increase with specific people, they in turn must undergo some decrease in their contacts with others. Thus in many of the rites through which acceptance into the community is finally achieved, this increase in interaction is regulated and occurs slowly, often over many months. Comparable techniques are becoming more common in the United States, with Newcomer clubs, and so on; these are often tinged with commercialism as in the Welcome Wagon hostess.

Second, the necessity to begin to interact with someone whose patterns are not familiar and thus cannot be anticipated, or to take part in a situation where the behaviors are again outside one's experience (a new job, or joining a fraternity) are immediately stressful until some degree of adjustment is made. In fact, the greater the regularity of the interaction rhythms, that is, the lower the flexibility, the more vulnerable the individual is to being disturbed. The internal rhythms control the need to interact; availability of an outlet is delayed for a few moments, sometimes for much longer, until the new interaction begins. Apart from this delay before the new "someone" is to respond, there is uncertainty as to the nature of the inter-action about to take place and its potential for emotional disturbance. Anxiety or fear is set in motion, perhaps only in a small degree, but the pattern of reaction is modified by it, in ways acquired very early in life.

A) The Shy or Bashful

In the human, the differential operation of adrenergic and cholinergic states and, in some persons, their mutual relations, is extremely obvious. The individual who would be called shy or bashful demonstrates in many ways their debilitating effects. Unable to talk for any sustained intervals, taking refuge in silence, and often not responding even to the other person's comments, he is physically awkward and tense, liable to pallor, his mouth dry, his palms sweating and his heart rate speeded up. Provided the reaction is not too acute, the sympathetic reactions begin to disappear, his actions become longer and silences shorter; gradually he begins to get over his shyness and act naturally. In the extreme case, as countless "situation com-edies" make clear, he loses control of his physical coordination, stumbling over the furniture or upsetting his cup of coffee. The variants on this theme are endless.

B) The Pretentious

In contrast are those people for whom the adrenalin triggers off an acute cholinergic reaction. They, too, if interrogated, may apply the term "shy" to themselves, but their behavior is quite the opposite from that just described. Typically, with their first action, they exhibit a push of speech which goes on and on without stopping long enough to let the other person respond. The first action may last 10 to 15 minutes, the next one somewhat less, until gradually they too get down to their basal level. Often cultural patterning of the communication is very obvious in these persons; they may tell one "funny" story after another or summarize everything that has hap-pened to them for years—in a variety of ways finding a context in which the push of speech is presumably made acceptable. This high activity, though initially triggered off by adrenalin, is definitely parasympathetic, charac-terized by long bursts of speech, flushed face, a feeling of nausea, and the need to urinate or void the bowels—common in the theatrical performer, particularly before the interaction begins.

The important element in these two types of temperamental reactions from which so many people suffer (however hard it is for the audience to see this with the overly pretentious) is that they are the transients after which the individual, if fortunate, returns to his basal rates. The stress is set off *before* the interaction begins. It is anxiety in the straightforward, physiological sense, triggered by adrenalin, which may then be elaborated by a cholinergic or even a noradrenalin reaction.

In the latter case, more common in personality or character disorders, particularly of adolescents, the anxiety when about to talk to someone new is pyramided by hostility and this takes several forms. Either the individual is monosyllabic, silent, and unresponsive, or his brief actions consist of attempts to dominate and bring the interaction to an end. The reactions are quite easy to measure and to differentiate, but the available words, such as hostility, or withdrawal, which might be applied, are so interwoven with other types of temperamental reactions that it is perhaps simpler to say that there are two other basic transients to be included in the description of reactions to this type of stress.

All four major types (and there are a variety of subtypes) are often stubborn to deal with. In other words, they may repeat themselves over and over again even where the relationship has involved daily contact for many weeks. Though everyone knows someone who finds it "very hard to meet people," an extra degree of flexibility is needed for those who are on the receiving end of the relationship. To realize, from the first moment of interaction, that the other person is unable to adjust (and clearly is undergoing severe emotional disturbances) makes the relationship immediately difficult and stressful to continue. It contrasts with other types of stress reactions where asynchrony occurs after an interval of complementarity. Once one knows this propensity, one tries to adjust from the very beginning of the contact and avoid the possibility of triggering off a temperamental outburst by careless adjustment.

Variegations in Temperamental Reactions

The temperamental reactions during and after particular types of stress involve a variety of interaction patterns. They are remarkably differentiated by the quantitative ranges of the component variables—action, inaction, or silence, tempo—since their values can vary in their component durations from fractions of seconds to many minutes each. Yet this is not all, for these basic variables are further differentiated by the initiative and dominance variables into sub-categories whose emotional impact must not be assumed to be minor. For lack of a better term to describe this process I have borrowed one from art and geology, to variegate, which means to diversify in external appearance, to dapple or streak, as with different colors.

The primary classes of these variables which variegate and further differentiate the basic temperamental patterns are the *latency reactions* and the *dominance-cycling reactions,* (There is no available word to combine the point at which an interruption begins, its duration and outcome, while latency of response is a standard term in psychology and psychiatry and far more frequently studied.)

In each, the variegation process is emotional, that is, the temperamental patterns which they color shift in their autonomic composition. Conjoined with the quantitative values of the action, silence, and tempo variables which define each reaction pattern, they become associated with the kind of symbolic configuration which psychiatrists try to use diagnostically, but these intermingle content and behavior and need not concern us here. Remember that their purpose is to interpret the patient's subjective emotional states by translating the communicative symbols which he uses. Without adequate observational criteria, they can only be suggestive for the purposes of this book.

The Latency Reactions

A latency of response during the process of adjustment may only be a consequence of the cybernetic aspects of interaction. An individual finds he is out of phase with the speaker in tempo and/or in his ratio of action to silence because his partner brought his action to an end sooner than expected. But if the attempt to synchronize on the next exchange is unsuccessful (or is not even made) and an appreciable interval of time elapses, either the tempo and A/S ratio are inflexible or temperamental reactions are occurring. By varying the rhythm, or observing whether such latencies take place only with one person or with several others, one easily determines whether they are primarily a function of the internal limits of the personality variables or of emotion. The varieties of temperamental patterns produced by latency are very large. Here we discuss only a few, chosen to help convey the significance of such variegation.

A)   Hesitancy or Uncertainty

One frequently encounters persons whose latencies of response, ordinarily between 1 and 5 seconds, occur consistently throughout their interactional contacts. If this kind of regularity is observed, though probably temperamental in origin, it usually represents a fundamental property of the personality, developed in the very early years through experiential influences. There are some investigators who regard latency as an indicator of thought and the creative process (Goldman-Eisler 1962). Even if such factors may be associated with it, consistent hesitancy before responding, whatever the other's tempo or action/silence ratios, is clear evidence of timidity or uncertainty, probably established after prior periods of intense exposure to dominance.

More commonly, latencies of response on this order of magnitude occur during and after intervals of stress. Thus, the shy or bashful person typically is also latent; values at this level of significance disappear when he reaches his basal rates. The oversensitive person, recovering from a struggle for dominance, similarly may show such latencies though, in other situations (and other stresses), they have not occurred. Therefore, the occurrence of latencies in conjunction with a particular type of stress reaction or its following transient is a reliable index of a significant increase in emotional disturbance.

B) The Longer Latencies

In many individuals, the association of latencies with a particular period of stress, or recovery after, is far more conspicuous because the latencies are no longer relatively short. Values of 10 to 15 seconds, often much longer, appear repeatedly. When they occur, the ability to respond is in itself inhibited. The latent person runs the risk of losing his turn if the other person, being too quick, takes the initiative once again. As examples, two of the most important can be cited as follows.

1) Easily Discouraged

When someone has not responded for a substantial interval of time, whether or not he or his partner finally took the initiative, the long latency is an indicator of a progressive inhibition in the individual's capacity to act. If this stress repeats itself and the latency becomes longer (and his silence with it), he becomes less and less capable of responding to a prod. The association of such long latencies with the so-called mood disturbances of depression is a useful index of the latter. However, it has to be differentiated from a similar occurrence associated with that reaction to the stress of nonresponse we have called the suspicious or questioning. Both are sympathetic in origin; they vary as a consequence of the basic personality pattern and the specific patterns of *all* the variables manifested to the stress of no response.

In fact, the "depression" is worth commenting on since, as with so many other common terms derived from psychiatric classification, it refers to a wide variety of interaction patterns whose only common element is the presumption that what the individual says indicates he is unhappy or sad. The label has to stretch from the so-called agitated depression, where the person is unable to stop acting but his voice, speech, and appearance suggest the symptoms of "unhappiness," to the endogenous or "psychotic" depression, where the individual is able to talk only for very brief intervals, is unmoving, and unresponsive, passing his days in constant inactivity. Between these polar extremes, there are many other variants and much controversy as to the differential criteria for diagnosis.

The problem is further complicated by the fact that even if latency were utilized as a more objective indicator of depression, latencies are typical of the patterns of most schizophrenics, though their action-silence rhythms are *very different.* What is required to straighten out the confusion is easily perceived if one relies on the observable and measurable. Thus, the pattern of being easily discouraged occurs in conjunction with a particular quantitative configuration of actions, inactions, tempos, and patterns of asynchrony. It differs, therefore, from another common type which can be called submissive.

2) *Submissive*

In the discussion of dominance situations and the reactions to this stress, the pattern of latency of response, submissiveness, was mentioned. Each time the individual, human or animal, is dominated, his latency, since it is now his turn to respond to the victor, increases. After the fight for dominance has concluded, in the extreme case used as an example, his posture is one of complete physical submission, lying or sitting unmoving, unable to respond. This pattern, in turn, for he who dominated is evidence of victory. No doubt one could say that "depressed" individuals are submissive, but the term loses any precise meaning if so used. Presumably they do not fight or have not; thus the prior interactional conditions and patterns of give-and-take have not been evidenced. Nevertheless, reaction to dominance by complete withdrawal and latency is also definable in autonomic and interactional terms though the conjoint mechanisms of the body's system do differ from the properties of being easily discouraged in the sense defined earlier.

Though the latency reactions cannot be covered in detail in this book, the quantitative continuum of each specific temperamental reaction pattern is such that mild states of submissiveness are identified by latency values significantly greater in duration than those manifested under basal conditions. Sometimes, they vary during the interactional day if the interactional activity available through the circadian cycle occurs at one time of the day rather than at another. They also can be a consequence of a stress which has taken place earlier in the day the effects of which are still operating on the organism.

To illustrate: There are many people whose circadian rhythms appear to be out of phase with the cultural requirements of the United States, at least, in getting up early in the morning and starting to work in high gear. By contrast, when the early riser is heading for early bed, these people are at their activity peak. So obvious is this difference that Kleitman (1963) suggested during World War II that factory workers be screened for these differential rhythms. Yet a common stereotype in psychiatric diagnosis is that such early morning problems are evidences of depression. In some cases, with more precise determination, this may be so; ordinarily, it turns out to be a morning affair—something which coffee, the morning paper, and silence at the breakfast table will quickly remedy.

The Dominance-Cycling Reactions

Again, space does not permit an extensive discussion of these bursts of attempted (or successful) dominances since they show as much variation in conjunction with the basic temperamental reactions as does latency of response. However, such major categories as aggressive behavior, hostility, and being competitive can be commented on. They are defined by those cases in which the person to whom they are attributed is the interruptor.

A)   Competitiveness

Many people, though easily dominated, react sufficiently under sympathetic (noradrenalin) activation to cut back in and interrupt the person who has just dominated them. They recycle fast after giving up. Since the other person is not too likely to be highly persistent, they are able to redress their loss and the potential deficit in their dominance ratio. To do so successfully, they must be capable of operating at a rapid tempo which the adrenergic pattern reinforces. If they had characteristically had long silences, this would make such intervention impossible.

B)   Aggressiveness

Though competitive people may also be aggressive, the reverse is not necessarily true. Aggressiveness, interactionally defined, means interrupting the other person when he starts to act in contrast to doing so *only* after being interrupted (and dominated) first. The success with which an individual manages aggressiveness depends on his tempo, that is, how fast he can get in where the chances of stopping the speaker are higher, and how persistent he is in continuing to act whether or not he finally out-acts the other person. Being aggressive does not necessarily mean that the individual has high dominance. In fact, many aggressive people are not and suffer the penalties of their temperaments when their opponents turn out to be unyielding.

C)   Persistence

Persistence, as mentioned earlier, has to be looked at from two points of view, the persistence shown when someone else interrupts, is aggressive or competitive, as opposed to the case when one starts to interrupt and tries to continue long enough to take over control of the interaction sequence. It, therefore, can be categorized under two headings, first as a personality variable whose temperamental reaction aspects are a function of the other person's lack of synchrony, and then as a *dominance-cycling reaction,* which determines the effectiveness of the aggressive act just commented on.

Temperamental Variegations of the Patterns

These patterns of variegation are differentiated in quantitative impact and emotional significance by the particular type of stress, or following transient state, which increases or decreases their frequency and magnitude. In some extreme conditions of psychotic or emotionally disturbed behavior, one finds instances in which action on the part of the patient occurs *only* when another person is talking. Thereupon, he interrupts, being aggressive to the *n*th degree, and continues only while the other person persists. When the latter stops, so does the patient; he will remain silent for long intervals of time until the same person, or someone else, starts to speak. Sometimes these patterns of reaction typically appear only after nonresponse, as in the hostile individual (not necessarily a patient) who does not respond to the first two or three initiatives (prods) and then suddenly becomes aggressive. The combinations which the temperamental patterns manifest are highly varied in the sequencing and quantitative values of the interaction variables. One can only say that the forms in which emotional behavior are channeled are remarkably diverse. Small wonder that man is indeed a "creature of infinite variety."

Time Factors in the Adjustment Process

Every temperamental reaction cumulates its effects over time. Repeated occurrences shift the threshold to reaction downwards both through the learning process (identifying the interactional cues more quickly) and by the carry-over of emotional states from previous situations. Conflict is an easy example. Though a single encounter can set off a battle, far more common is the gradual cumulative buildup of dominance situations, day after day, often year after year. Here, each instance carries with it its emotional increment. Many events may have to occur between individuals or groups before a once relatively balanced relationship begins to exhibit instability. Perhaps attempts to dominate may be too infrequent, or their impact may be compensated for by other aspects of the relationships. Intervals of complementarity, for example, can make up for the "trivial" disagreements which occasionally create moments of tension and disturbance.

The growth of marital disharmony exemplifies the cumulative process. The rite of marriage marks its onset. Ordinarily, the excitement of sex and some degree of complementarity conceal the crucial fact that the wife's biological rhythms create an intensely stressful situation for the husband, and conversely. Arguments may be infrequent at the beginning, but as the pair must readjust to their new relationship and make the necessary changes in their old ones, a series of stresses take place throughout the whole network of their interactions with others, having acute repercussions on their adjustment. Perhaps the first, the second, or the thirteenth time has little impact. Yet, as these recur and problems begin to appear in other relationships, those blessed intervals of complementarity (and even sex) become more and more infrequent. Perhaps the transitive reactions to mother-in-law or "problems at the office" contribute to the primary disturbance. But these are subsidiary in that the incompatibilities of the two personalities and their temperamental reactions minimize flexibility. As stress becomes more frequent and the reactions more severe, intervals of complementarity decrease very rapidly. If the husband's activity and tempo are such that "inadvertently" he is likely to interrupt her as she makes up for the long day alone by telling him about the household crises, if she reacts by refusing (overtly and otherwise) to talk and to respond (being "hurt" or "mad"), the consequences are immediately predictable. No amount of intellectual discussion to gain "insight" about "misunderstanding" solves the dilemma. Whatever the disagreement is about and what the course of the argument, the cumulative effect is one of emotional disturbance, so much so that their every contact becomes a potential stress.

But conflict after repeated instances of maladjustment is not solely a function of the dominance variables as this familiar marital situation illustrates. All the personality variables are necessarily involved. The dominance struggle is set off by the temperamental pattern of nonresponse after the successful attempt to dominate; but its severity is multiplied by the lack of outlet for the dominant rhythms which inadequate interactional events during the day provide. Thus, observation of this couple's interaction throughout the day, and day after day, would evidence the fluctuations, often moment to moment, in the occurrence of the particular variables and their quantitative values. The relationship is rarely limited at its beginning to the sequence—wife starts to talk, husband interrupts and dominates, wife refuses to respond when he stops to give her a turn. Usually, there is considerable variation in the patterns used. Yet as the maladjustment becomes more constant, rigidity increases. Finally, this simple pattern, and the quantitative values accompanying it, becomes so extreme and repetitive that even the minimal duration of interruption is enough to trigger off a long-continuing sulking.

On the other hand, the learning process can result in becoming "habituated" to minor degrees of stress, provided other relationships with higher complementarity are built up. Thus, one can learn to adjust and do so by spotting the cues of potential disturbance. In essence, much of psychotherapy and personnel training attempts to encourage such adaptability, ordinarily intuitively and by verbal precept. Witness the fashion for training programs on "being a good listener" which have become so fashionable in executive circles. Only in interaction therapy (based on the principles and methods herein described, Chapple 1970b) is this process carried out explicitly, so far only with psychiatric patients.

Whatever the interactional context, the adjustment problems of the individual (and group) are far more often the consequences of minor degrees of interactional stresses. Whether one is concerned with understanding international relationships or "merely" the problems of kindergarten and the family, the autonomic nervous system as the controlling agent over the emotional–interactional patterns of behavior has its sway. Logic and rational considerations of human problems are all very well; unfortunately, they are constantly overridden by the age-old and fundamental requirements of the organism. As A. N. Whitehead (1925) once said, "we cannot think first and act afterwards. From the moment of birth we are immersed in action, and can only fitfully guide it by taking thought."

Chapter 7

The Individual as an Interactional System

Though the interaction patterns making up the individual's personality and its temperamental reactions are measurable with great precision, this in no sense implies that individuality is a static thing. The fundamental biological rhythms on which the personality is built and the physiological properties through which its actions and reactions are mediated are, in themselves, *dynamic* forces. The interactional (and noninteractional) energy which they produce in measurable amounts has to find sufficient outlets in the external environment. To a large extent, this environment is made up of other individuals with their own interactional requirements.

Quite properly, one can regard each individual as a force, analogous to a physical force. This is gratifying to the ego; more important, dynamics deals with the ways in which changes in the expenditure of energy take place. Insofar as stability is achieved for the individual by arriving at a state of equilibrium, it is a balance struck between the rates for each of his constituent variables and those of the others with whom he is in contact.

The Concept of Equilibrium

Equilibrium in the human sciences is too often thought of as a static condition, as in mechanics, like the pendulum which reaches a state of rest after being set to swing. Thus, it is necessary to define how equilibrium in biological systems differs. In statics, the object is moved by external forces; in dynamics, the object is actually the force itself, for example a chemical reaction or a rate at which energy is being transformed. By impressing a small change on this rate (more generally on the total system of rates, making up a system), a change takes place (say in the action rhythm during an attempt to dominate); once the dominance attempt stops, the rate goes back to its previous level after a compensatory shift or transient has worked itself out. In a sense, the pendulum provides a partial analogy; by holding it to one side, the force has been impressed; releasing it causes it to swing back and forth in an ever-narrowing range until it comes to rest.

In biology, since Cannon invented the term, dynamic equilibrium is more commonly referred to as "homeostatis." Cannon selected the word to emphasize the self-regulating aspects of the internal environment illustrated by the way it maintains the body temperature at an approximately constant level. More properly, since homeostatis has limited application to some physiological processes, biologists refer to the organism as in a steady state. They mean by this that at any given time the system is in dynamic equilibrium. This does not imply, however, that the quantitative properties of a steady state today are the same as those one will find ten years from now. Growth, development, and inevitable decline characterize the flesh. Parallel to this, change, though not necessarily decline, occurs in the interactional domain. How much changes in personality and temperament accompany growing older (even for the child going into adolescence) is not known from longitudinal studies. All one can say, and this from common knowledge, is that it varies considerably from person to person. In general, the data suggest there are long intervals of a steady state, but not always many of them, in an individual's lifetime.

In this book, dynamic equilibrium (equilibrium for short) will be used in preference to steady state since the term can more easily imply its converse, disequilibrium, or disturbed equilibrium. But equilibrium, dynamic or otherwise, is not "good," that is, not something to be desired and to be considered as preferable to disequilibrium. Harlow's cloth or wire-raised infants have reached a state of equilibrium from which it is very hard to budge them. Neither they, nor chronic psychotic patients in a mental hospital (often referred to by psychiatrists as "adjusted to their psychosis" and, by definition, also in a state of equilibrium) can be considered to be in a condition which should be sought after or emulated.

For these individuals, and often for many others, disequilibrium is a necessary precursor of a new and more effective state—the criteria for its necessity being the inadequate degree of activity produced and the low level of complementarity in interaction with others. The schizophrenic avoids interaction, which is stressful for him (Ludwig and Marx, 1968). His interaction pattern is so erratic and arhythmic that it is very difficult for the ordinary person to interact satisfactorily with him. If he is to improve, something has to be done to jar him out of this unyielding state. Decisions as to intervention thus depend on determining whether the basal rhythms (not necessarily too high) are able to achieve any adequate outlet and what degree of complementarity is present.

Among patients, this requires seeing how much interaction is displaced in atypical action patterns—stereotypy, hallucinations, and so on. Where the individual's equilibrium is clearly nonadaptive, the need to manage the transition from one state to another must take into account the potentiality that extreme reactions can occur and even that violent swings may be inevitable before a new state can be stabilized. Thus, equilibrium in itself is no ultimate for the human being; what kind of state and how it relates to the biological necessities of individuality must be the source of ultimate decision.

There are many people, however, who are not frozen in a disabling equilibrium state yet oscillate between severe and incapacitating temperamental reactions of sufficient magnitude and duration so that they maintain a precarious equilibrium balance. Clearly, if small amounts of stress produce violent and prolonged reactions, some kind of intervention is a necessity. They too require a quantitative evaluation of their biological rhythms and their potential for complementarity. From estimates of properties of their equilibrium (disequilibrium) state, one can begin to program the amount and type of stresses in minimal amounts to be administered to habituate them to the effects of stress and reinforce their potential for complementarity. A long series of experiments has shown how shifts in interpersonal relations can be brought about through controlled retraining in interaction. These reduce the violence of the reactions (and strengthen the patterns in which adjustment does occur). Such programs (Chapple *et al.*, 1970) are being used very effectively with adolescents who "act out"— the antisocial sociopaths, as psychiatrists call them, whose reactions to minimal stress are violent and destructive.

For most persons, whatever the psychiatric label, even if the equilibrium state has been warped by almost constant states of stress over a long period of time, whether they are hostile, rejecting, or unresponsive, new and less debilitating states can be achieved. With the schizophrenics, in particular with those who are chronically ill (and have achieved a nonadaptive equilibrium) and the childhood cases whose behavior patterns are so much like Harlow's monkeys that one wonders whether interactional patterns were ever learned, the problem is far more serious. It is difficult to guess what they might be like if an equilibrium state with a marked increase in interaction could be restored.

The Impact of the Internal Rhythms

The underlying dynamics of the individual's equilibrium state, be he human or animal, are provided by the biological rhythms, the inherent property of every organism. The clocks which require him to act and interact go on ticking whatever may be happening in the external environment. Some set limits for the approximately 24 hours of circadian rhythms, while others, operating at rates whose frequencies are a matter of minutes or fractions thereof, shape their manifestations of energy within the quantitative expression of activity and interaction.

But though the clocks tick away at the rates which that particular period in the individual's maturation process has established, the external environment is not always (one might say is not often) cooperative in providing sufficient outlets for the expenditure of interactional energy. There may be simply no one available, yet ordinarily few people inhabit desert islands or their equivalents. More common is the case when the number of people with whom one can interact satisfactorily is remarkably limited. In many cultures, small family groups or even parts of such groups are alone together for long intervals of time. Whatever the group's size, it does not follow that those within it interact very frequently with every member. Though the standard formula calculates the number of possible pair relations in a group, $N(N+1)/2$ (a group of 10 individuals having 45 possible pairs), many of these pairs will have little or no observable interaction. Thus, adults (who are not parents) have little to do with small children, and juveniles with those not of their own age. This reduces the number of interacting pairs surprisingly.

Age and sex thus restrict the number of individuals in a group with whom any single individual will interact. More important, the restraining influences of personality and temperament interfere with the free manifestation of interaction. Thus, someone with low initiative may only be able to begin interaction if he is initiated to. He may also try to avoid persons who are stressful for him. He may withdraw and not respond even when someone else initiates to him. These personality and temperament characteristics have been discussed in previous chapters, but not as far as their consequences in providing outlets for the underlying biological rhythms on which they are built. Since the controlling rhythms appear to be circadian, with the faster rhythms modifying the distribution over the active period in the 24-hour cycle, each individual has a total amount of activity (and, by hypothesis, interaction) to be expended within the day. Hence at any point during the day, one can add up the amount of interaction and determine whether a person's net position is proportional to his needs or is behind or ahead of the pace he should be setting. (Since the phenomena are multivariate, the mathematical process is much more complicated, but this will illustrate the point.)

To oversimplify further and ignore the effects of emotional reactions, if circumstances are such that a person has had very little interaction for a considerable period, the need to compensate for this lack sets up internal pressures which can become very strong. The child kept in the house on a rainy day may try to make up for his loss by badgering his mother into interaction. If the rain's end doesn't bring relief to his beleaguered mother, bundling the child up and sending him off to play with a friend somewhere else is the only solution.

By contrast, involvement in too much interaction during the day (even excluding emotional situations) has an opposite and obvious effect. Assuming the individual's personality is not characterized by extremely high activity levels, overexpenditure of interactional effort requires intervals of noninteraction to balance out the net position before beginning again. Thus, the "hard day at the office" as an excuse for the husband's monosyllabic responses when he comes home and his unwillingness to go out in the evening may simply be an expression of his having expended an excess of interactional energy which can only be compensated for by avoiding interaction for an appreciable period. (Alternatively, temperamental reactions and lack of complementarity may be indicated.)

Since the evidence from circadian studies suggests that intensity of action is directly related to its duration, one can see quite clearly how intensity increases with the need for activity. The wife, staying home all day, with built-up requirements for interaction, shows much greater expressiveness and more body movements. Her tired husband may try to interact briefly, or not at all, but his intensity of movement is markedly reduced.

As indicated earlier, the net position of the interaction rhythms is rarely simple to estimate. The personality variables, and ways in which these are modified by the individual's (idiosyncratic) temperament reactions, vary the underlying needs for the interactional outlet. The individual is not simply seeking interaction *per se.* He is trying to find other persons with whom he can achieve some degree of complementarity, avoiding those who are stressful for him. The idea of net position thus becomes very much more complicated. What he (and each of us) is trying to manage is to achieve and maintain a state of equilibrium against the impact of disturbances which others create for him and, of course, he for them.

Cumulative Consequences of Daily Interaction

In consequence, each contact with another person contributes to the cumulative state of the system of interaction variables. Suppose he takes the initiative in starting the interaction, thereby helping to redress that day's negative balance in his initiative rate; yet though he obtains a response, the other person persists in doing all the talking. Each time our deficit-ridden subject tries to get a word in, he is dominated. Not only does this shift his dominance rate to lower values, but he becomes upset as he fails to win. Temperamentally, this may force him to become shorter and shorter in speech. When he finally manages to break away, the emotional carry-over makes him avoid talking to a good friend who comes along, because he does not "feel like seeing anyone just then."

Interactional sequences such as this one, with all degrees of differences in their quantitative combinations, occur throughout the day. It is unnecessary to give further examples—the reader can fill them in for himself—but such cases indicate that one must try to evaluate the events in which someone takes part in terms of the interactional and emotional components of which they consist. If any of us could record what he does interactionally during the course of the day or, more easily, measure the interaction of others, thus being more objective and precise, it becomes obvious how the effects of the interaction cumulate. Of course, its significance is more meaningful in personal terms. Try to school oneself to concentrate on one's own interaction and the emotional components of each interactional situation. Such introspection on one's own interaction (and observation of it as objectively as possible) reveals how a series of brief events with different poeple, each producing the same type of stress, caused a temperamental reaction to explode, which otherwise seemed inexplicable. For the cumulative process builds up to the point when the last of the brief stresses becomes the straw which crosses the threshold at which equilibrium will be disturbed. Schaller (1964), like many field naturalists, commented that since the gorillas "are so closely associated day and night, tempers naturally become a little frayed at times, usually for *trivial* reasons."(Italics, the author's.)

Even in small groups, whether they are gorilla females squabbling, children playing in the park, or executives holding a serious conference, interactional events are constantly shifting between one individual and the next. Two persons start to talk, a third breaks in, one or the other starters may drop out; permutations over an hour long session may be quite large. Whatever the formal or cultural rationale underlying the particular behaviors and the words and gestures used, each individual, consciously or unconsciously, is trying to maintain a stable equilibrium or to reestablish it if he has become emotionally upset. Careful observation and measurement will demonstrate that changes in the sequence of contacts between the individuals in the group and their character is mediated in large part by carryover from prior interactions.

The Transitive Character of Interactional Events

Abstractly one might think that two persons who have been interacting with varying degrees of maladjustment could easily terminate their interaction at will and cease all further contacts. Yet this is rarely manageable. Each independently may try to begin interaction with someone else in order to compensate for what has gone before. Sometimes such contacts are very brief and they fall back into the old relationship. At other times, a long chain of events may be started and the imbalance of being initiated to or dominated is remedied by doing the same to someone else.

With humans, and the higher animals generally, such simple "peck-order" sequences are inadequate. The individuals try to establish complementary relationships; if successful, continue them as long as possible. Ironically, however, they are very often the consequence of a severe reaction to a stress. The disturbed person looks for someone who will adjust to his pattern until he begins to return to equilibrium. In exposing the other to his outbursts, however, he runs the risk of setting the disturbing patterns in motion again through his reaction pattern unless his chosen partner is extremely flexible. Achieving the pleasurable emotions produced by complementary interaction is an essential factor in finally reestablishing the stability of his equilibrium state.

Most contacts set a variety of emotional reactions in motion. One person reacting against another may bring in an entire group before stability is at last restored. Here, too, each stage of an interaction sequence between antagonists may be interspersed by contacts with others, seeking adjustment and possible coalition, or by facilitating escape when losing the verbal or physical battle.

This characteristic of human (and animal) interaction is called *transitiveness,* that is, the emotional properties of a particular interaction pattern affects others in their turn, whether as a reaction to stress or in achieving a high degree of adjustment*

Such chains of interactional events, moving from one person to the next, can take place very quickly in a group. They may also proceed at a much slower pace if each event has a long duration. The contacts in the chain may be limited to two persons only and the opportunity to interact may have to be contrived. Temperamentally, not everyone is able to initiate immediately after a disturbance, and cultural factors may also intervene. Until the appropriate (and complementary) person is available, one must wait to achieve a compensatory outlet.

And such transitive chains are by no means ended at the next contact. They may lead to others until the chain doubles, triples back upon itself in bringing "influence" to bear on the two individuals originally involved.

Conspiracy and conniving, politicking and managing, are the natural consequences of the transitive quality of interaction. The springs which set them off are the internal requirements of the individual. The forms they take are shaped by the individual personalities. Where their adjustment to one another is unstable, extreme reactions are continually produced and the great chain of violence keeps on revolving. However unspecific when looked at closely, many common labels used to try to explain unstable personalities suggest their interactional character—"he has an inferiority complex," "is a social climber," "is power-mad," or "selfdestructive." Yet the labels have little value until the complex nature of the individual personality and its temperamental reactions is accurately described.

The Individual as an Interactional System in Equilibrium

In the last analysis, at any given moment in an individual's life, one has to determine the ways in which he has come to interactional terms with the environment surrounding him, made up of other personalities with all their abrasive qualities. To do this, the fundamental requirements of his basic interaction rhythms must first be identified. Do his reactions to stress and the sources of stress maintain an uneasy balance in him or, on the contrary, are they absorbed within his limits of tolerance? One cannot

---

*It should be pointed out that this is apparently only true for nonpsychotic individuals. Chronic schizophrenics, for example, appear to end the interaction in the pair relationship, even when conflict or open hostility has occurred. Otherwise as has often been pointed out, patients in a mental hospital, perhaps 75 to 125 in a ward, would be in a constant state of turmoil, revolting against each other and the few attendants responsible for their supervision. Unlike prisons, riots among schizophrenics do *not* occur. If they had not lost their capacity for transitiveness with much of the rest of their natural patterns of interaction, mental hospitals would be untenable.

regard the individual as if his reactions are a matter of chance, nor can one treat the events that happen to him as inconsequential for *his* stability, however trivial they may appear to others. The biological determinants of his basic rhythms operate day and night, shaped as they are by the autonomic properties of his interaction patterns. Since, in this view, there is constant interplay between the internal and external worlds, no interactional event is without *some* fragment of influence. This does *not* mean that only if one knows an individual's complete interactional history from the moment of birth, or before, can one understand why he behaves the way he does.

The theory that the individual constitutes a system in dynamic equilibrium means that if one's yardsticks are appropriately selected, measurements of the system at a particular time should be sufficient to predict his future behavior. The time interval cannot be instantaneous or, in anthropological terminology, at a synchronic minimum, since rates of interaction are being measured. Time is needed to measure the interaction over a sufficiently long period if one is to compute the rates and the way they change under varying situations. Where one can experimentally introduce standard amounts of stress under controlled conditions to establish the basic personality and temperament variables, the length of time required to measure them and describe the parameters of change will be less than that required by observation of ongoing contacts. In any case, the diachronic limit, as anthropologists like to term historical studies, is a matter of days or weeks.

Although the 24-hour cycle provides the quantitative framework within which the equilibrium equations can be established, one does not necessarily arrive at the end of the circadian day with all one's interactional accounts neatly balanced. But since the cycle is to begin again with the same requirements for expenditure of energy, the inactive portion of the cycle, essentially the period of sleep, appears to act to "recharge the batteries" and to eliminate much of the carry-over from the previous day. In fact, studies of sleep have shown rather conclusively that some kind of reequilibrating mechanism is at work. If the sleep pattern is seriously disturbed, behavioral (and mental) aberrations take place, perhaps as the consequence of the carry-over itself. To lend substance to the importance that man over the ages has attributed to dreams, the clearing of the traces of the daily round is said to occur during periods of dreaming which can be detected from the electrical record of the brain waves.

Long-Term Changes in the Equilibrium State

Yet not all the equilibrium disturbance is eliminated within 24 hours, partly because the emotional states often associated with inability to sleep do not follow the necessary restorative stages which sleep studies have established as necessary. It is tempting to think that violent or highly disturbed dreams are symptoms of interactional imbalance, but this can only be speculation at the present stage of our understanding. One of the important signs of mental illness, clinically, is a significantly disturbed sleeping pattern.

However this carry-over works neurophysiologically, there is no question that behavioral measures begin to show definite trends toward disequilibrium. By repeating daily observations, measurements indicate one or more of the temperamental patterns occurring more frequently, lasting for longer periods, with less and less stress required to trigger off the reaction. If these patterns continue for months, basic personality characteristics may begin to change. These are extremely noticeable in initiative and dominance variables but also may affect the basic patterns of activity and tempo. Usually what one sees is a gradual trend in the quantitative values of the variables making up the whole system, until a major crisis takes place in the interactional environment and/or in the biochemical correlates of the behavior. No one has followed the process minutely with moment-to-moment measurements to establish the uniformities by which cumulation of deficits shifts the system. Such studies might show that the biochemical cumulations associated with these stress reactions alone are enough to cause the "breakdown." On the other hand, for some fundamental system changes, a major interactional crisis clearly built upon less dramatic trends in adjustment appears necessary.

Almost any case history of what is often called, euphemistically, a "nervous breakdown" (provided attention has been given to the sequence of interaction events leading to the state) indicates a progressive, though slow change in the quantitative properties of the individual's interactional system. One almost always finds references to the fact that the patient began to see people less and less, that he spent more and more time in bed, that he became increasingly absent from school, that he no longer saw such friends as he may have had, that his adjustment to his parents became worse— changes often glossed over in case histories. Accurate chronological descriptions of life histories are infrequent.

Apparently only writers like Marcel Proust, endlessly ruminating over the events of their early years, and blessed with almost total recall, are able to construct autobiographies which strike the reader as meaningful in spite of the obvious fictional distortions. Yet the problems of obtaining useful case histories are not as serious as they might appear, providing all events are put in absolute chronology. The difficulty is that the convention of taking up different areas one at a time makes it almost impossible to know whether a particular interactional crisis in the school occurred before or after a crisis reported in the family. Taking a good case history means one has to use rigorous "archeological" approaches to be certain that the stratigraphy of events (historically and chronologically) is firmly established by skillful and patient cross examination (Saslow and Chapple 1945).

Nonlethal Shifts in Equilibrium Systems

Disequilibrium states build up over shorter or longer intervals. Crises in relationships may be so prolonged that they will alter the personality. More common, and far more frequently experienced, are those shifts in the individual's equilibrium system which change the membership of his world quite rapidly. Ronken and Lawrence (1952) described a series of changes in relationships and emotional stability in their account of the introduction of a new product in an electronics factory during the various attempts made to move from the pilot stage to mass production. In a unit consisting of two girl workers, Claire and Alice, and two industrial engineers, a very close association between the four individuals developed. There was frequent give-and-take in initiating contacts, both in connection with the work and as part of what clearly appeared to be quite complementary interaction patterns. When the product appeared to be out of the experimental pilot stage, the two engineers were transferred and a production supervisor was brought in.

Where there had been hourly, daily, and often minute to minute contacts with the engineers, the new supervisor, Lou, interacted only once or twice a day. Even when present at the work bench, he rarely talked and responded to questions only briefly. From early February, when the change was made, until May, Claire became increasingly disturbed. She began to pick fights with her former close friend Alice, who in turn began to be friendly with new girls whom Lou, the supervisor, had brought in. Finally, Alice accepted Lou as her superior and began interaction with him, leaving Claire in such complete isolation that she requested a transfer out of the department.

Crises in the adjustment of two people consequent on changes in their interaction with others (and this book has many other excellent examples) are a commonplace in every social situation, in humans and among the lower animals. Koford (1963), discussing the macaques on Cayo Santiago, commented about the ways in which individuals shifted from one group to another. Ordinarily these were the younger adult males who, constantly dominated by the older males, found it almost hopeless to acquire females.

> During every month at least one monkey changes bands. Most of these animals are peripheral males; many are orphans. A few shift frequently between the edges of two bands, so that their membership is indefinite. After a period as solitary males, some adults join bands and rise to high status. Most of the changes occur during autumn, when mating is at its height and males are most aggressive and restless. In one large band there were a dozen changes during this season.

Sometimes changes in system constituents may occur within a 24-hour period, built, it is true, upon a gradual increase in the maladjustment of an individual with others, say the members of his family, leading to a fight and dramatic break. The drama is too often restricted to the final showdown, yet it is rare that patterns of temperamental reaction do not become sequentially more severe. On every exchange, they last longer with each person continuing to exacerbate the other in ways to which he is particularly vulnerable. Everyday life is so full of such occurrences that the wonder is that human animals come back for more so often, instead of ending the stressful relationship forever. Some do, of course, by walking out, by murder, or by suicide, but most people's interaction patterns depend for reinforcement on segments of the opponent's interaction patterns if they are to maintain what from the outside appears to be a highly unstable equilibrium.

Too often the amount of initiative or dominance necessary to break off the relationship is not available in the personality except when the stress reaches unbearable dimensions and the temperamental reaction activates the necessary behavior. The problem is not, as earlier emphasized, a simple matter of single interaction variables. The emotional consequences of acting to end a relationship may be highly complex and too disturbing for the individual to experience, even in a minor degree. Managing a shift from one group to another is thus by no means easy or frequent. From the outside looking in, it is remarkable how the particular properties of an individual's state of dynamic equilibrium may be such that months, years, almost a lifetime may go by before the situation becomes so intolerable as to force the unhappy person to make a move towards freedom.

Maturation and the Crises of Life

The nature of existence, for animals as well as humans, compels each individual to change his patterns of interaction since the particular people with whom this interaction takes place come and go. Immediately after birth, a new-born infant's interaction is almost entirely limited to its mother, though the father and siblings may quickly begin to establish relationships. Until the human child is able to move about on its own, ordinarily not until after the first year, it is dependent for its emerging patterns of interaction upon the happenstance of those who come to it, either in response to its actions and its sounds, or on their own initiative. In contrast, monkeys and apes are usually able to achieve some independence by the second month of life and, by the third month, to extend their interactions to other females and infants in the band, though apes, and particularly gorillas, are about a month or two behind the monkey.

When the infant animals become increasingly mobile, they begin to break away from dependence for interaction on their mothers. Most of their contacts are then with their age mates. With humans, the institutions of a culture take over, requiring relationships with adults in which the young are subject to dominance in order to learn the skills necessary for adulthood.

It is hardly necessary to describe the entire life cycle of an individual—going to school, getting a job, marrying, having a family, the whole progression through the various stages of living—to make the point that each of these stages (and there may be many of them) constantly changes the people with whom the individual is to interact and thus the quantitative properties of his interaction. Where the change involves the loss of former interactional partners or the acquisition of new ones, with all those emotional consequences, the crisis may have serious potentials for long-term development. The life crises—death of the mother or father at an early age, marriage, maladjustment, divorce, acquisition of a new job or loss of an old, entering into new activities in new or different organizations, or having to reduce participation in one so as to increase activity in another, retirement, illness, or accident which alters the persons with whom one interacts and the pattern of the interaction—all require a new state of dynamic equilibrium to be established.

Not only is there a redistribution of interaction at each such crisis, but the degree of complementarity achieved may be threatened or lost, and the frequency and extent of stress may be magnified. Thus, changes in the individual's level of adjustment may occur at any age in his life cycle. When these take place, major trends in the nature of his adjustments are set in motion as a function of his personality requirements for interaction and his temperamental reactions to specific types of stress. Far worse, life itself is doing this for and to him, largely by chance. Life crisis is followed by life crisis, sometimes with incredible celerity. Ill luck never runs singly, says the old saw, and often the death of a parent, loss of a job, illness—the combination of possibilities is endless—may repeatedly buffet a painfully achieved stability.

The Ultimate Direction

In consequence, each person seeks, consciously or unconsciously, to increase the amount of complementary interaction he can find, or tries to escape from what disturbs him to a presumed "better" life. At the end of the rainbow, whether it be in Southern California or Majorca, or Greenwich Village, perhaps the people one believes one needs exist in comfortable numbers. At least the rainbow itself promises that one can get completely away from the frustration of one's present situation. Until this happens, life consists of trying to reduce disturbing contacts to a minimum and achieve some occasional periods when elements of complementarity provide emotional satisfactions.

From a quantitative point of view, the problem of analysis is much simpler than the decisions the individual faces when caught in the turmoil of his personal situation. The observer can determine through measurement the requirements of a personality for outlet; he can estimate the nature of the idiosyncratic patterns of adjustment or maladjustment and their emotional consequences. Thus, he can maintain a running account of how much each interactional contact contributes to stability or instability over a 24-hour period or longer. From such data, fairly reasonable estimates can be made of the nature of the interactional deficits, the kinds of situations which the individual should avoid for his own emotional good, and what he requires if he is to achieve some kind of satisfactory adjustment to life. To help him find a cultural setting within which he can become more closely attuned to his own internal needs is much more difficult. These needs may be contrary to those which others require; hence some kinds of equilibria, as in the psychotic, can be destructive of others or ultimately self-destructive. More common, the kinds of situations and personalities which can make him "fulfill" his potential may be extremely hard to find, as in cases of minority groups, the uneducated, or the unskilled.

Yet, at the last, the individual has to take responsibility for his own emancipation. Though others may be able to estimate when and if, how much, and in what ways they might intervene, all they can do is start him on the path. But he, himself, must do the acting; he must *learn* how to manage his adjustment problems; all that others can do is facilitate the process. As Ortega y Gasset has pointed out so cogently, one must seek one's vocation. What this means is that one has to differentiate between the "superficial" and immediately gratifying interpersonal events and those which make the "true" or basal personality and its potential for emotional harmony and expressiveness predominant. How does each act (interaction) contribute to achieving maximum potential for the personality in its environment, its special world, which it requires to take over primary control? The term "world" does not imply a need for many people; simply to increase interaction is not a good in-and-of-itself. Yet each personality needs to be able to minimize its temperamental reactions to stress and find those persons with whom its constituent emotional–interactional rhythms attain a meaningful and enhanced degree of complementarity.

This kind of "vocational" realization makes possible an expansion of the personality. As Suzanne Langer points out, the emotional–interactional balance achieved is the basis for creativity. Again, this is not simply saying that happiness is good. So it is, but what happiness? Not the mere evidence of achievement of cultural aspirations. Too often the constraints imposed by the cultural dimensions are incompatible with the fundamental rhythms of the individual's personality. For happiness lies in their full realization and thus is biological in the broadest sense. It may be no solitary drum, but it must be special to one's individuality.

Chapter 8

Origins of Personality and Temperament Patterns

The remarkable differences in how people think and feel and act, and thus in their personalities and temperaments, are probably the principal conversational topic of humans. Perhaps, as Konrad Lorenz suggested (1952), if King Solomon's Ring could be materialized, giving us the power to understand the language of the lower animals, they too would be found to be essentially preoccupied with what their friends and neighbors are doing and why. Personality and temperament, and character as an old-fashioned variant on these two, are the basis for an enormous literature in almost every field.

Controversial Background of Heredity and Environment in Human Studies

Until the 19th century, most people were hereditarians. Many still think this way. The various traits of personality and character were presumed to be passed down the family line. Setting a proper example was important, but a kind of predestination philosophy was at the heart of most commonly held theories, usually documented by reference to the Greeks and Romans. This type of explanation was reinforced not only by the theological vagaries of which the doctrine of infant damnation was a persistent form, but by the aristocratic nature of society, "obviously" brought about by inherited position.

Coincident with the development of Darwinian evolution, a kind of neo-Lamarckism took over the broad field of what might be called philosophical psychology. Lamarck endeavored to explain evolution by the doctrine of the inheritance of acquired characteristics. Hence, his Just So Story for the giraffe's long neck was that the more its progenitors ate the lower leaves, the longer their successors' necks needed to be if giraffes were to continue feeding at the tree top level.

Students of learning, in the United States particularly, excited by Pavlov's discoveries of what could be done with the conditioned reflex, and influenced by the egalitarian philosophy of the Republic's founders, came to believe that all individual differences were the results of environmental influences. John Locke, whose *Essay Concerning Human Understanding* had such a powerful effect on thinking at the end of the 17th century, promulgated the doctrine of the *tabula rasa*—the smoothed tablet. He held that the newborn child arrived in the world with no heritable factors and that all his experience was built on sense impressions from the environment. John B. Watson, the founder in the 1920's of what was then called behaviorism (very different from behavioral biology as it is presently evolving) described what for many years was the fundamental tenet of experimental psychology (Watson, 1925):

> Give me a dozen healthy infants, well-formed, and my own specified world to bring them up, and I'll guarantee to take any one at random and train him to become any type of specialist I might select—doctor, lawyer, artist, merchant and yes, even beggar and thief, regardless of the talents, penchants, tendencies, abilities, vocations, and race of his ancestors.

From quite different sources, the work of Freud and his followers tended to reinforce environmentalism. Psychoanalysis emphasizes the overwhelming importance of early childhood experiences in forming the personality. From these, the mental disorders appearing in later life originated. Many psychoanalysts assumed that one could ignore hereditary influences. Freud, however, was by no means so dogmatic on this subject.

Finally, one must in no way underestimate the enormous impact of racist doctrine as it manifested itself in Hitler's Germany. Germans were the Master Race, justified by their assumed Nordic characteristics (a racial category that is only infrequently found among Germans, and certainly not in Hitler nor most of his immediate subordinates, as physical anthropologists take pleasure in pointing out). This racial phantasy was the rationalization for the destruction of the Jews (and Gypsies and other "inferior" breeds) to eliminate racial impurity. The ultimate goal was to be the reduction to slavery of the rest of the non-Nordic world. The profound revulsion by many people, even by serious students of biology, against exploring how genetics might affect behavior was only natural. Implicitly, they were afraid that racism could slip in the back door.

However understandable, this attitude stems from a lack of familiarity with behavioral genetics and precisely what is involved when hereditary factors are taken into account. This prejudice is even found among geneticists who have been divorced from work in the behavioral field. When they take such linguistic and cultural constructs as I.Q. tests as having a genetic reality, they are assuming genetic determinism in ways which behavioral genetics today in no way implies.

Genetics of Behavior

Most high school biology courses make at least a passing reference to Mendel's law and to classical Mendelian genetics. They rarely suggest, however, that there are very important differences between genetic studies of the color of sweet peas, the occurrence of hemophilia (hereditary tendency to bleed) or polydactyly (having an extra, usually only a sixth finger on the hand), and measurements of behavior. Classical genetics was developed, as these examples indicate, in terms of qualitative differences in color, uncheckable bleeding, or an extra finger. Hence breeding experiments, though they have become remarkably sophisticated, are always reduced to a "yes" or "no" answer. The phenotype—literally, the mark that shows—the observable manifestations in the organism of the genotype, the gene complex, was essentially demonstrated either by its presence or absence. Minor research variations in this qualitative approach were occasionally carried out, but the essential principles were always followed.

Behavior, however, is almost never adequately described by qualitative means alone. The patterns or sequences making up the ethogram could be described merely as present or absent, but in fact they are varied enormously by quantitative differences in the durations, and so on, of their component parts. The speed of a horse and the amount of activity of a rat on a running wheel are examples. The behavioral biologist must primarily be concerned with answers to questions such as "How much? How long? How often?" within the framework of one qualitative factor, for example running (or not running).

In order to adapt Mendelian genetics to such measurements, a fundamental reformulation of its mathematical methods had to be carried out. This has been accomplished only during the last twenty years, originally by Mather (1949) and Falconer (1960) in England and by Sewell Wright (1952) and others in the United States. To do so required a new statistical approach to the whole problem of quantitative measurements, and the experimental methods to obtain them became more complex and elaborate.

Yet genetic experiments have probably been conducted by selective breeding since the very beginnings of agriculture and the domestication of animals, entirely, of course, on a trial-and-error basis. Agriculturalists and pastoralists appear to have selected desirable traits and cross-bred those possessing them to try to improve the yield of grain or its resistance to the weather, to breed both dogs and horses for speed, staying power, or hunting abilities. Until the advent of kennel clubs and the commercialization of dog shows, most varieties of dogs were bred primarily for behavioral characteristics, only secondarily for physical conformation. One has only to begin to list them—the basset hound, the collie, the retriever, the pit bulldog, the staghound, and so through most breeds—to realize the ease with which these special behavioral qualities were segregated out through selective breeding.

Though individual differences between dogs of a single breed and even of the same litter occur, strain differences are clearly inherited and usually override the individual or idiosyncratic. Fox terriers behave very differently from beagles even though one fox terrier may have a quite different personality and temperament than another. Dogs, in fact, have been the subject of one of the longest series of experiments in behavior genetics, carried out over many years by J.P. Scott and J.L. Fuller (1965) and their associates at the Jackson Laboratory in Bar Harbor, Maine. Using five breeds—fox terriers, shelties, basenjis, beagles, and cocker spaniels—they compared the behavior of the pure stock animals with cross-breeds in a wide variety of situations, showing that quantitative genetics could be used to explain what happened when particular crosses were carried out.

Among the primates, very marked behavioral differences are reported for closely related species. The rhesus macaque, the most common laboratory monkey, is noted for his aggressiveness and concentrated hostility towards experimenters. Extreme care has to be taken in handling or risk losing a finger. Stump-tail macaques, on the other hand, are described as docile, easy to handle, often anxious to be scratched or stroked by any human available, a gesture which, with the rhesus, is an invitation for mayhem (Orbach and Kling, 1964).

Pig tail and bonnet macaques, two other species, also far easier to deal with, differ strikingly in patterns of physical contact. Bonnet macaques habitually sit touching others. Four or five will crowd against each other and remain that way for quite long periods of time. Pig tails, on the contrary, sit motionless, no doubt meditating on their species-specific singularity, without touching their neighbors. They avoid any tendency to become involved in a group huddle (Rosenblum et al., 1964). It would be interesting to know what would take place if breeding experiments could be conducted among these several macaque species. Only by so doing could one see whether such a whole pattern, defined quantitatively in terms of its frequency and duration, is genetically homogeneous.

Breeding for Activity Level

The major weakness of behavioral genetics is the lack of precision in defining a phenotype which experimentally can be presumed to have a homogeneous genotype as its base. This is well illustrated in the unsystematic procedures used in defining the natural patterns of activity and interaction. Even those studies of mice and rats, which have begun with strains built up by brother and sister matings for twenty generations (the number required before one can consider the population adequately randomized genetically), have used highly arbitrary behavioral measures. Most common, of course, has been the use of the running wheel to measure activity. Yet the running wheel cage in which the animal is confined in the laboratory is far different from anything that he or his remotest ancestors ever encountered in natural surroundings. The running wheel has been of undoubted value, particularly in the study of circadian rhythms, but no one knows why rats, mice, and squirrels run on it. Individual animals vary widely in their capacity to learn to do it (at least to do it). Kavanau (1963) found with deer mice (Peromyscus) that, on a motor wheel on which they could run more freely than one on which they did all the work, once they learned to turn the motor off and on, they would run *only* when *they* turned on the motor. If the experimenter did so, they would refuse to run. Such recalcitrance in taking the initiative clearly helps to confuse the issue as to what is actually going on.

Rundquist (1933) and later Brody (1942) using the same stock, developed strains of rats of high and low activity on the running wheel which bred relatively consistently. In contrast, Broadhurst (1957) used an "open field" test for his high- and low-activity strains in which activity was reckoned by the number of squares crossed by the animal on a grid laid out on the floor of the cage. This latter type of measure is clearly different from running wheel activity and, in turn, from total time of movement. In fact, as Eayrs (1956) showed, the two measures are uncorrelated in the same animals. Others have used the time rats take to get through a maze or how long mice placed on top of a small pole take to get down on a kind of supporting mesh. All are "ingenious" procedures whose only rationale is that they provide easy ways of getting measurements to compare animals. Certainly, they are rarely built up on patterns which have been observed in free-moving or natural situations.

Explicit in genetic studies is the assumption that one can proceed backwards from the phenotype (running the wheel, climbing down the pole) to the genotype (the genetic constitution of the individual). By the use of the statistical methods of quantitative genetics, one can separate out the environmental factors which have modified the genotype into its phenotypic form. By following its procedures, one can determine whether one or several genes can be identified, whether the trait is determined by polygenic effects, and so on. Without going into the technique and the methods of analysis, it appears obvious that research, and life for the experimenter, would be much less equivocal if the phenotype represented a definable pattern of behavior manifested by the animal in its natural surroundings.

Some researchers advocate taking a wide variety of activity measures, for example, running wheels—powered or not—mazes, cage grids, whatever one can contrive, and apply them all to the same animals. By statistical brute force, some kind of factoring out of a common characteristic would hopefully result. Alternatively, one could try to see whether known genotypes, established through other types of analysis for other purposes, for example, coat color in the mouse, differentially affect behavior under genetic variation. (Fuller 1965)

Natural Patterns of Behavior

However tempting such possibilities may seem, identification of the constituent patterns of behavior for any species is, in fact, the first step in carrying on studies in behavioral biology. When Lorenz and Tinbergen established the ethological approach in zoology, they were particularly concerned with those patterns which appeared at birth, thus clearly innate in the animal. In addition, they emphasized the importance of obtaining, as Altmann (1965) did with the rhesus macaques on Cayo Santiago, a complete description of all the patterns of behavior used by the particular species during its entire life cycle. As pointed out in Chapter 1, they called this dictionary of patterns an ethogram. But they insisted that the essential requirement in developing such an ethogram was that these patterns be described under natural conditions in the wild or in situations closely approximating them. They pointed out not only that animals in captivity are not always healthy, but confinement has been shown to produce highly abnormal behavior never observed otherwise.

But these patterns are more than particular modes of behavior; each of them is a fixed action pattern as described in Chapter 1. They may be:

defined as a sequence of coordinated motor actions that appears without the animal having to learn it by the usual learning processes. The animal can perform it without previous exercise and without having seen another species member do it. The fixed action pattern is *constant in form,* which means that the sequence of motor elements never varies (Hess 1962).

Hess goes on to point out that these are not reflexes or chain reflexes. Further, the frequency with which each one is performed depends in part on the elapsed time since it last occurred, in contrast to reflexes which are supposed to be much more automatic.

To illustrate how fixed these patterns are, Hess quotes experiments showing that squirrels raised in isolation and never given objects to handle persist in attempting to bury nuts in a bare floor. They scratch away at the concrete as if they were digging holes in the ground, push the nuts with their noses, and then go through their typical covering up movements (seen wherever squirrels and one's lawn come together), preparing their store for future use. The most surprising finding of the ethologists is how resistant these fixed action patterns are to evolutionary change. Physical characters may appear or disappear, but the behavior patterns are far more resistant. Short-tailed monkeys go through the same balancing movements with their nonexistent tails when running along a branch as their long-tailed relatives though their longtailedness is an old casualty to evolution.

Physiological Basis of Natural Patterns

Not only are these fixed action patterns genetic in origin (though, of course, modifiable by the environmental experiences of the animal), but more and more work is being done to isolate their neuroanatomical bases. Brown and Hunsperger (1965) have called the field, neuroethology, and Hess remarks that ethology is, in effect, behavioral physiology. The former authors have elicited the full range of fixed action patterns of the cat by activating specific neural areas in the brain, those which are used in attack and those which set in motion attempts to escape. As mentioned earlier, the amygdala (part of the Papez circuit), the hypothalamus, and the midbrain (the limbic area) are primarily involved.

By electrical stimulation of the midbrain, for example, the cat hisses, while growling comes from the amygdala, and the hypothalamus, as might be expected, provides a mixed set of reactions depending where one stimulates it. In addition, stimulation of any or all of these areas produces much of the typical threat behavior—laying back the ears, lowering the head, hunching the back, and erection of the hair. Interesting too is the fact that the centers which control the cat's attempt to escape are next to and overlap the threat-producing areas.

Although one might like to assume that the special providence which has selected man for mastery of the universe would also mean that he has no fixed action patterns, they are equally well established. As with laboratory animals, they too can be elicited by electrical (or chemical) stimulation. Their existence was first shown in discoveries by curious brain surgeons that they could get the patient to react in these emotional, fixed action patterns, by stimulating the limbic area. Penfield (1958) in Montreal did some of the most dramatic work in the course of brain surgery and these findings have been followed up in the lower animals on a much more systematic basis than surgeons are free to do on humans.

In a long series of experiments on monkeys, Delgado (1967) implanted electrodes in the various areas of the brain where such emotional behavior is controlled. He then attached a radio receiver to each animal and brought about changes in the interactional patterns and the established dominance hierarchies by radio signals. How far these changes can go can be seen when a subordinate monkey was given a transmitter of its very own. The result was that the boss monkey became the victim of his aggressive attempts. Each time he started an attack, the subordinate (and female) monkey would inhibit his behavior by frantically working her transmitter. Since surgical evidence suggests that the human being is equally vulnerable to the neuroethological control of his fixed action patterns, the potentialities for a "brave new world," if electrode implantation should become the order of the day, are clearly at hand.

After all, the whole gamut of basic emotional patterns (including the sexual ones) are capable of being set in motion with predetermined intensities by electrical or chemical means. Consider each human animal, perhaps not until the next century, busily working his radio-stimulator on those within carrying distance of the radio signal. To have some degree of choice of whom one interacts with and how, one can hope that the electronic engineers will be able to parcel out the broadcast band more minutely than at present. Each person might then hope to have his own particular wavelength, though Big Brother probably would not permit unlisted numbers.

Genetic Aspects of Fixed Action (and Interaction) Patterns

In carrying out behavioral genetic studies, fixed action patterns must first be defined by the actual sequence of muscular patterns occurring. Experiments on the effects of crossing different species of ducks with different fixed action patterns show that the crosses shuffled the constituent patterns. One can see that the first element came from a mallard sire, a second from a ruddy duck and so on. Moreover, by selecting ducks regarded as evolutionarily late and cross-breeding them, ornithologists have been able to reestablish the various motor sequences which are found in evolutionarily older species. Similar studies have been done on other animals.

Further, each fixed action sequence has quantitative properties; that is, one species will take a much shorter time in performing a particular element than another. The portmanteau effect of such variations is evidenced in the different durations each element of the pattern requires and thus the action-inaction sequence is, in fact, the underlying substrate. Even though the combination of such component patterns into longer sequences appears complex, they can be broken down into their specific elements by recording the time duration needed for each to be completed. In these studies, the elements of the interaction pattern provide the constituent genetic framework to be manipulated by cross-breeding. Hence, in principle, the behavioral repertoire of any species and its quantitative properties can be reliably identified from the ethogram. The genotype would then approximate the phenotype which can be directly observed.

As mentioned earlier, few researches on factors having to do with personality and temperament have been carried out by defining the phenotype as a derivative of the ethogram of the species. There are significant and characteristic differences between strains of rats and mice which have been systematically inbred for 20 or more generations—in activity level, aggressiveness and timidity, dominance and initiative. But unsatisfactory operational procedures have been used, yielding measurements not based on unambiguous beginnings and endings (representing fixed action patterns). Thus, the phenotypes contain what may be called "behavioral artifacts"—effects of the apparatus, environmental setting, and the researcher's theories about how animals *ought* to behave. Furthermore, with the exception of activity level studies, using running wheels or counting the number of squares in a grid crossed by the animal to measure distance traveled, most other personality and temperament factors have been evaluated by rating scales. In these, observers interpret what they see in terms of their theoretical notion of "wildness," "timidity," or "fearfulness".

Nevertheless, with all its lack of rigor, the evidence demonstrates that there are significant differences between strains of laboratory animals in a variety of these categories, just as strains of dogs and monkeys not specifically bred to a genetic program differ. It is thus a matter of observation, easily verified intuitively at least, that these differences are inherited. When it comes to establishing the precise properties of the genotype, the happenstance selection of "phenotypes" to work with makes the determination of a genetic model almost impossible. In genetics, where two strains, P1 and P2, are cross-bred (P1 being the parent of one strain and P2 of the other), one can only achieve any beginning comprehension of the ways in which inheritance takes place if the F1 hybrids (that is the first generation) of the two parent stocks in turn produce F2 offspring (second generation) and if backcrosses to each of the parental lines are then produced.

Genes as Limits on Behavior Modifiability

In utilizing genetics in understanding the activity and interaction of individuals, remember that the various experimental and statistical procedures are intended to separate the environmental from the genetic influences. They describe how to test the possibility that a particular genetic hypothesis fits the data accurately. This in no way enables one to assume that environment and heredity are independent of each other. As Sewall Wright points out, the genes are the ultimate physiological and behavioral agents, and the phenotype is the resultant of the interplay of environment and the genotype.

In other words, the genes set the limits for the behavioral capabilities or potentialities of the organism. Whatever the effects of experience (of learning taken in its broadest sense), they must all necessarily occur within those limits which the genetic constitution provides. Environment, therefore, achieves its influences by modifying the expression of particular genes or their combinations in the phenotype. This is by no means restricting. The number of genes in the human is probably quite large. They have multiple functions and, further, vary in their effects by being modified through their "interactions" with adjacent genes. Sometimes the available genes are very resistant to being modified by the environment. When this happens, the genotype does set constraints on the number and kind of possible phenotypes. Only a mutation, altering the genotype, then makes a particular environmental effect possible. The study of physiological (and behavior) genetics, as Ginsberg (1963) has said, "is thus involved in the studies of the capacities of the nervous system, the endocrines, and the way in which all the capacities of the organism behave, including those making possible complexities of group organization, development, and interaction."

One of the great hypotheses in modern genetics may be stated in simplified form by saying that for every gene there is one enzyme. A more precise definition requires one to say that DNA molecules arranged in a specific sequence produce particular proteins from RNA. Enzymes operate through catalytic action (that is, they produce reactions in specific molecules without themselves becoming part of the product) by controlling the rates or velocities of the chemical reactions in the body. Some genes are called structural because their end-results are to be found in physiological and anatomical structures, as the term implies; others are called regulator genes and control the output of the enzyme for which they are specific. Fuller (1964) has pointed out that behavior can probably be regarded as primarily influenced by regulator genes which, for example, would increase or decrease the secretion of a hormone. He then goes on to argue, in the same frame of reference in which this book is written, that genetic studies will have to be carrried out by quantitatively defining the function (mathematical equation) which best describes the data on the rates of behavior change as the environment is modified. By so doing, the trap which all-or-none classification creates for the unwary investigator can be avoided. This means that behavior is no longer to be regarded as if it were a fixed and static quality, like the coat color of the mouse.

In fact, this conception of the mutual dependence of environmental situation and enzymatic activity is inherent in the physiological discussions of biological rhythms; it sets the framework for the shifts in autonomic nervous system operation under various types of stress and the resulting products in the personality and temperament characteristics of the individual. One cannot ignore the genetic substrate since one needs to have some conception of the limits within which environment can have its influence. On the other hand, by stressing the importance of the genotype, there is no reason to think that the human animal is some kind of genetic automaton.

Genetic Potential for Individual Variability

It is conservatively estimated that the number of genes in man is somewhere between 10,000 and 50,000. Without repeating the genetic reasoning, Hirsch (1962) estimated the probabilities that nonidentical twins will be genetically identical as less than one chance in over 64 trillion. Thus, even the traditional method of obtaining a homogenous stock by brother and sister matings of over twenty generations in no sense can be taken to mean that the 21st generation is adequately homogenized. There are many sources of variability, particularly as chromosomes break up and recombine over several generations. Moreover, the phenotypic expression of many genes is strongly influenced by their genetic neighbors, a phenomenon called gene interaction. In consequence, as Hirsch has emphasized, individual differences are fundamental to the genetic constitution of every living thing. Pretending they do not exist will not make them go away. Yet in no sense can genetics be dispensed with. Genes do impose limits or restrictions on what the individual is capable of. The extreme environmentalism of Watsonian behaviorism is as fallacious as its counterpart in rigid advocacy of genetic predestination.

Environmental Differentiation

When the infant animal first sees the light of day (and in fact for many functions in the later stages of its fetal existence), the environment begins to operate on its genetic constitution. Though this is the beginning of learning, this does not mean that "learning theory"—the investigation of the increases or decreases in performance as a function of practice, or the lack of it, under the varying influences of "rewards" and "punishment"—provides a sufficient explanation of the adaptation of the organism as life goes on. For there are many phenomena which are hard to categorize so simply.

If a major series of stresses occur in the first year of life with coincident and extensive autonomic reactions, the equilibrium state of the organism can be shifted to a very different level of autonomic balance. The differential rates of sympathetic and parasympathetic secretion, genetically controlled, are then affected: The environmental influence of the stress significantly modifies the state of the organism. In the usual sense, this kind of modification is not properly labeled, "learning." Lehrman (1962) has proposed abandoning the term as an all-inclusive way of talking about environmental influence. In its place, he suggests that "experiential influences" be used instead. This would avoid the arguments about how "learning theory" should be defined. More usefully, it would emphasize that behavioral and hormonal changes play an important part in shaping the genetic constitution.

Beginnings of Interaction Patterns

The newly born arrives on the scene with a set of inherent biological rhythms, controlling much of his physiological and behavioral performance. As he grows older, these shift at different rates of speed to the circadian patterns of his social and climatic environment. From the moment of birth, interaction takes place. Depending on whether he is human or animal, he slowly or rapidly acquires interactional patterning.

When the mother approaches a high-activity baby, in Escalona's terms, the infant reduces his activity, breathes more slowly and is more relaxed; the low-activity infant, on the contrary, becomes more active and animated, with more tensing of the muscles. The relaxed reaction pattern can be prevented if the mother handles the active baby roughly so that be becomes overexcited. On the other hand, the inactive baby's mother could avoid rousing him or, alternatively, overstimulate him so that his excessive period of action would be followed by a long interval of exhaustion. As Escalona points out, the inactive babies require the initiative of someone else (the mother ordinarily) to be roused to activity and to respond, while the highly active babies act spontaneously and initiate when they see the mother, even when she has not initiated to them first.

From birth, therefore, the child's activity rhythm and its relatively rapid "interactionalizing" not merely set off differential response patterns in the parents but also are the basis for the growth and stabilization of personality traits. But the parents themselves have their own personality and temperamental reactions, and their interplay and potential for complementarity or lack of adjustment are quickly evident. A quiet baby may provide one mother with optimal adjustment, always waiting for the mother to initiate before responding. The hyperactive (and often vocal) child who initiates frequently may, on the other hand, create stress which she is unable to handle. It is remarkable how rapidly parents (and siblings) begin to behave like themselves when they have to adapt to the baby's patterns. They fail to respond to the child and let him "cry it out," or dominate to the point of physical punishment to "make him stop." These and many other patterns are complicated by the degree to which tactile contact is part of the interaction.

The literature of child-rearing places so much responsibility on the mother particularly, and parents generally, for shaping the child in the way he should go that little attention has been paid to the reverse problem—what the child's personality, even at the earliest period, does to the parents. Again the assumption has been, with the strict environmentalists, that the child is an unmarked parchment on which the parents by their every action write out what is the final story. In fact, the child brings a complex genetic constitution to the struggle. Its interactional consequences may elicit severe temperamental reactions in the parents (however much guilt they may feel in consequence). As these in turn begin to produce patterns of reaction to their behavior, the child's future temperamental problems are unwittingly being predetermined.

The Effects of Major Environmental Stress in Monkeys

With rare exceptions, longitudinal studies of the human infant from birth are unavailable, at least as they affect the development of personality and temperament. With the lower animals, however, and with monkeys in particular, the last ten years have seen a remarkable series of studies in the laboratory, reinforced by field investigations in parent-child relationships.

Much of the interest in carrying on these studies is a consequence of the theory of "maternal deprivation" which has become extremely popular as an explanation for various types of psychiatric difficulties. Although Freud's emphasis on the traumatic consequences of inadequate adjustments in early childhood provided a general background, John Bowlby, an English psychoanalyst, is probably primarily responsible for the development of the theory in a usable form. In a series of reviews (1962), he pointed out that loss of the mother before the age of six is far less frequently found in normal than in psychotic patients, or in those who are not psychotic but who are variously labeled sociopaths or psychopaths, that is, individuals with personality or character disorders. The latter typically "act out"; they are aggressive, delinquent, and extremely hard to deal with.

Many of the studies on humans have properly been criticized for various inadequacies in experimental design, as intuitive, retrospective, not experimental. They have led, however, to an important series of laboratory investigations on macaques by Harlow and his associates and, more recently, by Jensen and his group who have tried to describe the interactional events more systematically. Harlow began his work in an attempt to understand the process of "mother love" or, more generally, the development of affectional patterns. In carrying out these researches, neither investigator took into account the kinds of personality and temperament differences which Bridger and Escalona reported for new-born babies. They were content to take all infant monkeys as they came and study them longitudinally over time. Thus, we are no further along in understanding how much different basic activity and reactivity levels are differentially affected by standardized rearing.

Further, the experimental "deprivation" used was far more complete than ordinarily happens in human life. Yet there are parallels in the case histories of many children with psychosis or primary behavior disorders. Their mothers behave in ways similar to those which monkey mothers (disturbed as a result of their upbringing in the laboratory) use with their infants, and the resulting patterns of reaction are comparable. Alteration of the personality patterns from those in normally raised monkeys produce psychotic behaviors exactly like those to be found in any mental hospital. The published descriptions do not provide quantitative data. One cannot, therefore, match patterns of reaction and the specific pattern of stress imposed.

Harlow's initial, and perhaps most famous, studies involved raising infant macaques either on terry-cloth-covered or on bare wire models which, however, provided milk. The baby monkeys universally preferred the soft cloth "mother," to which they could cling over the wire alternatives. In addition, in a variety of tests, he showed that strong attachments were formed to the cloth mothers; even after two years of separation they would rush to the "mothers" and embrace them. The data further demonstrated that actual nursing has little importance in forming and maintaining strong bonds with the "mother." On the contrary, it is physical contact, being able to touch and cling to the mother, which is crucial.

Infants brought up on wire mothers from which they obtained milk "ran wildly about the room, bumping into objects but playing with none; or they ran to some wall or corner of the room, clasped their heads and bodies, and rocked convulsively back and forth." Harlow points out how similar these patterns are to the childhood schizophrenics (sometimes called autistic) found in mental institutions, and to "neglected" children generally. But ultimately, it made no difference whether the monkeys had wire or terry-cloth mothers. All of those separated from their real mothers at birth grew up to be highly abnormal in behavior, even when they were five to seven years old and sexually mature:

> we have seen them sitting in their cages strangely mute, staring fixedly into space, relatively indifferent to people and other monkeys. Some clutch their heads in both hands and rock back and forth—the autistic behavior we have seen in babies raised on wire surrogates. Others, when approached or even left alone, go into violent frenzies of rage, grasping and tearing at their legs with such fury that they sometimes require medical care.

Attempts to pair cloth-raised monkeys with those raised on wire were completely unsuccessful. Equally unsuccessful were attempts to mate an experienced and normal animal of one sex with a laboratory-bred partner, because the latter would not respond to advances or would attack the other animal.

Harlow then raised infants alone with their mothers until they were seven months old. When placed with other animals, they were unable to interact. By the end of the first year, they seemed almost as retarded as the terry-cloth-raised animals. Harlow believes that limiting the infant's interaction to its mother for seven months results in "maternal overprotection" and "infant overattachment," which interfered with the development of patterns of normal interaction with its peers.

He then decided to bring up infant monkeys without their mothers, but with other infants, providing toys and other objects which they could use if they chose to play. These infants grew up and acted normally, whereas the overprotected monkeys as they grew up were extremely aggressive towards other monkeys when and if they interacted at all.

After a series of major struggles to mate some of the female monkeys who had been terry-cloth raised (amusingly and better told in his article), some of them finally became pregnant. Once born, the babies were kept alive only by artificial feeding since the mothers rejected them. As in cases often reported for human infants, the mother was either indifferent and unresponsive to the attempts of the infant to interact, or physically rejected and punished the infant to force it away. By the time the second birth occurred, however, they began to play the mother's role, underlining the often reported problems created for a first child by an inexperienced or unadaptive human mother.

Jensen, following up Harlow's work, maintained mothers and infants in two very different situations. In the first, the environment, space, and access to other animals were severely restricted. The room was soundproof, the cage barren, and there were no climbing facilities. In the second, mother and infant had toys and things to climb on; other animals (and people for that matter) were visible and audible. The restricted infants, like Harlow's, became overattached since, as Jensen points out, there being no other outlet, the interaction was entirely between mother and infant. When the infant became older and his attempts to interact with his mother increased, she punished him to try to make him stop (though interestingly, even when his initiatives decreased, she continued to dominate and punish him). With the "rich" environment, as Jensen calls it, the infant interacted less with the mother. He was freer to get away and play, while in the restricted environment, the mother ordinarily tried to prevent the infant from leaving her.

A Human Parallel of Deprivation Studies

The human similarities of such situations can be indicated by a brief history of an adolescent primary behavior disorder boy, taken from the case records of a state hospital. It is also typical in its inadequacies with regard to chronology and specific descriptions of interactional events.

T. W., a white, Protestant boy, was admitted to the hospital when he was 13. The situations which brought him there included running away from his foster home (his fifth), setting fires, and stealing. He cut a boy's eye by throwing a rock at him and held up three boys of his own age at knife point, tied them to a tree and cut their fingers to "mix their blood with his." His mother was an alcoholic, not wed to the father, and had two boys by her first husband. The oldest, 16 at the time of the patient's admission to the hospital, was taken from the mother and placed in a foster home when the patient was two, and the other brother, first placed in a foster home, was then put in a "school" for delinquent children. T. W. was taken from bar to bar with his mother as a baby, left alone for long periods with little or no food and, when his mother was home, witnessed fights between his father (when he appeared), and his mother's drinking and sexual companions. At one and a half, he was placed in a foster home where he remained until he was three. He was extremely jealous of the foster parents' child and was neglected by them. He stayed in this second home from three to five (his mother died when he was five) and was then shifted to another and then to another because of illness and loss of work by foster parents. In both of these homes he got on well and was attached to his foster parents. The fifth home, where he lived for six years, was extremely disturbing for him. He was beaten by both foster parents, he refused to go to school and tried to run away. They took his spending money (from the agency and his real father who visited him once a month) and assailed his father on his visits.

Children with this kind of background and with "nonpsychotic" emotional problems are so much a matter of course in commitments to correctional institutions or to state hospitals or other treatment agencies that it is not surprising that little attention is paid to obtaining detailed histories of the crises which plagued them in their early years of development. By contrast, great care is lavished on animal studies in the laboratory, but the natural experiments which humans impose on their young are rarely observed. The case history taken by social workers and psychiatrists is too often perfunctory or hurried, with little emphasis on trying to establish the absolute chronology (Saslow and Chapple 1945).

Though many cases are cited to "explain" the maturation of personality and temperament characteristics, the data are rarely, if ever, precise. Because the parent—mother or father—has identifiable patterns and the child (or children) has others, it is assumed that the parent produced the patterns which the child exhibits. Not only does this neglect the effects of the child's presenting personality and temperament when young and as maturation goes on as well as the mutual influences of others in the family constellation but it also usually focuses on intuitively selected events which prior theory argues for, neglecting all others. If the formation of these characteristics is to be thoroughly understood, only longitudinal investigations like those of Escalona are meaningful.

Stages or Critical Periods in Development

All studies of the maturation process of the infant—animal or human—agree that there are stages through which the growth process proceeds, although the degree to which these can be pinpointed as a fixed sequence is debatable. On physiological and biochemical grounds (and, of course, anatomical), it is clear that the animal is physiologically and neurologically immature at birth, and for a considerable period afterwards. Studies of biological rhythms, and their associated autonomic states, demonstrate how these go through a period of development before they finally become stabilized. Similarly, the cultural and experiential environment in which the animal lives shapes and makes habitual a wide variety of physiological and behavioral patterns. On the other hand, the hypothesis that critical periods exist, that is, that there are particular periods when environmental influences have maximum effect, and minimal in between, is much less certain.

Jensen believes there are significant shifts in the interactional pattern of mother and infant macaques at one week and at 16 weeks. At one week, he points out, the mother and infant are almost always in contact. By the fourth month, the mother tends to leave the child, now highly active and able to climb. He calls the process by which this is accomplished by the mother the "progressive detachment-reattachment sequence." After this period, mother and youngster begin to increase their interaction with other animals. Caged by themselves in restricted surroundings, each other their only outlet, the mother's dominance takes the form of repeatedly punishing the infant far more often and for longer periods than in a normal environment.

In humans, particular behavior patterns also appear in the infant and follow a more or less regular schedule. There are individual differences, of course, but still the time of occurrence seems to fall within well-defined ranges. Beginning with Gesell (1928) and brought up, if not to date, at least to popularity by Spock (1957), such information has been a source of eager preoccupation among new mothers, at least in the United States.

As possible evidence of critical periods, Morgan and Ricciuti (1968) found that negative responses to strangers did not become predominant until the infant's 12th month. Lenneburg (1967) has shown that children do not begin to develop speech until they are about 2 years old (when the 7-per-second cycle becomes established). He also holds that somewhere between the ages of 11 and 14, the capacity for language acquisition comes to an end or at least becomes extremely difficult. This period, also the beginning of puberty, is, of course, a critical one since a wide variety of new patterns associated with the acquisition of sexual maturity come into being. In addition, though less well demonstrated, there is considerable reason to believe that the period from birth to three or four years of age (perhaps to five) is one of great susceptibility to maturational shifts and environmental influence.

Human Plasticity Under Environmental Influence

The studies on monkeys and apes and the lower animals have reinforced many of the conclusions now being established for the human young (and for adults), summarized in the old saying, "you can't teach an old dog new tricks." Not only are younger animals more sensitive to physical and chemical changes than older ones, but they are more reactive to behavioral stimuli. The evidence further requires some modification in what is meant by "old" for, as indicated previously, puberty seems to be the point at which significant maturational advances come to an end.

In effect, the genetic constitution, and its modifications through environmental influences at puberty, achieves a stability such that it appears to be highly difficult to bring about further changes in the personality, looked at as an emotional-interactional system. As a consequence, attempts to alter the personality and its associated cognitive processes, if this is the desired end, appear doomed to defeat. This does not mean, however, that modifications in the temperamental patterns of reaction, which are built upon the personality variables, are equally futile. There are a variety of learning or conditioning techniques through which stress reduction can be handled.

This fixation of the personality characteristics may have occurred either as a result of the environment or the genotype or their mutual relationships, though it is usually hard to differentiate the two experimentally in the combined case. Harlow, for example, in his macaque studies found that infants raised in total isolation for 80 days and then placed together were almost completely normal in their peer interaction. Those raised in isolation for six months and then paired did not interact at all. Ginsberg and Allee (1942) staged interaction sessions to try to modify the degree of dominance and submission in two genetically homogeneous mouse strains. By carefully selecting the antagonists and controlling the advantages of the field of battle for the one they wanted to win, they were able to reduce the degree of dominance in the dominant strain but found it much harder to turn the submissive into winners.

Much of what is being done today in terms of personality training or therapy is not directly aimed at these underlying uniformities; more commonly it attempts to alter the severity of some of the temperamental reaction patterns. Even here, the individual must be regarded as an interactional center of a field of force which does not operate *in vacuo*. The "field," which represents his adaptations to the world, is determined in large part by the interactional patterns impinging on him, modified in turn by his own. Thus, the individual personality (including its temperamental reaction patterns) is only a part of a total interactional system. As the system stabilizes over time, and he with it, it becomes more and more difficult to change its component quantitative patterns.

Whatever the point in age—the critical period—which marks the stabilization of these relationships with others, both the personality and the system tend to persist even though individual members may have dropped out and been replaced by others. In other words, beyond this fixating point in human adaptability, the individual tries to maintain the system and the personality balance (or imbalance) by substituting similar personalities wherever possible. From the outside looking in, their acquisition may seem contraindicated, but this hardly interferes with the process. Thus, evaluation of a person's potentiality for change depends on determining the quantitative values of the relationships. This requires data not only on the patterns of interaction constituting them, but how long they, or their equivalents, have been going on in time, how much of the day they take up, and how regular they are from day to day.

Whether for better or for worse, the interplay of the genetic constitution and the interactional environment surrounding it from the very beginning of life does reach a point of no return. However much one might like to say "I would that fate had made me different," the fact is, it did not. Hence, one needs to take stock of the nature of one's interactional system in those moments when emotion is minimal and contemplation possible. One may then have a chance of making environmental choices which force a change in one's interactional system. Thereafter, one has to support such steps by learning to reinforce those interaction patterns which seem profitable and reducing or avoiding those others which perpetuate immobility. Though hard and unpleasant, yet it may still be possible.

Part II

THE DIMENSIONS
OF CULTURE

Introduction to the Cultural Dimensions

The biological dimensions so far discussed give us the basis on which the interactional regularities can be described. When the focus is on the individual, the biological rhythms and their elaborations into integral patterns, physiologically and behaviorally, enable us to take a deterministic point of view towards man. What this means *only* is that the properties of these emotional–interactional patterns are predictable. Yet, as in any beginning science, we are a long way from the mathematical sophistications even of mechanics or electronics.

Our predictions have to assume that the individual is, so to speak, the creation of the interplay of his personality, its temperamental reactions, and the environment within which it moves. Other personalities and all the learned aspects of the cultural situation to which he is continually adapting have to be looked at for their repeating impacts on his equilibrium state as biological man. Such impacts, definable interactionally, can be summated. We can examine, over the day, the varying contributions of particular types of stress. Each has varying degrees of severity, lasting for so many minutes, as do those other intervals when partial complementarity may be identified. Within the 24-hour period, and the days succeeding, we can make useful estimates of the direction and stability of his steady state.

But this, though crucial to one part of our problem—that we can find with reasonable clarity lawful uniformities in the behavior patterns of biological man—tells us nothing about the probabilities that today he will encounter someone whose own interactional patterns are highly disturbing for him. Nor do we know how long this stress will continue nor what possibilities there are for compensatory outlets to intervene. For here the cultural dimensions begin to operate. Culture, the characteristic shaping of particular groups in such a way that they learn and practice common patterns which infinitely vary the underlying interaction (and activity) patterns so far discussed—those carrier waves which organize the biological rhythms—controls these probabilities.

148

Note that we say probabilities. By this we mean that cultural phenomena are not deterministic in the biological sense; rather, the most that can be done in estimating their influence is by treating them as a different order of phenomena, by hypothesis and mathematically. The term probabilistic, in the simplest how-to-do-it sense, means that we shall be concerned with statistical estimates since cultural elements *may or may not* produce predictable results. Thus, the first chapter of this book emphasized that cultural consequences can only be told after the fact. Did the organism respond to the cultural stimulus, for example? Only if it does can we say that it is constraining behavior; only then are limits set within which it is probable (with varying degrees of probability, often capable of quite accurate estimation—and often very high) that specific cultural patterns of behavior will be superimposed on the carrier waves.

On the other hand, within this framework of probability, regularities within the whole array of cultural phenomena can be identified for any human group. Representing logical constructs which can be regarded as dimensions in their influence on interaction, the internal properties of the logical systems composing them may be geometrical, mechanical, or aesthetic. There is great utility in bringing together wide categories of cultural elements and abstracting from them a unifying property. By so doing, they become capable of being treated as independent dimensions, and attain an organizing power. What such dimensions imply, if the abstractive process is done adequately, is that one could construct a culture from their combinations. It is anthropologists who have most closely approached this aim in their studies of communication.

Finally, it must be realized that we are not truly done with biological man. Culture and the cultural dimensions abstracted from it are learned. Its expression is mediated through the central nervous system and, in particular, in the integrating properties of the cortex. Every species, therefore, has its set of limits, which perceptually represent the possible input from the environment and whether the organism can handle these sensory stimuli. Thus, animals unable to synthesize light signals into three-dimensional images differ anatomically and physiologically from those who do.

Much of the discussion in Part II of this book will present comparative material from man and the lower animals. Many examples may have to be only analogies since comparable work is not available for man. They have been selected, however, because it seems possible that similar phenomena could be established for the human if someone looked for them. The best studied and perhaps the most striking (but in no sense the only one) is the subject matter of the first chapter of Part II (Chapter 9)—the ways in which spatial distance is utilized not merely to make interaction possible, but also to set in motion particular emotional–interactional patterns, specifically the initiative and dominance variables.

Constraints of Distance on Interactional Probabilities

The familiar usage of distance as a measure of the degree of separateness of individuals (and places) is so much a part of human language that it is not surprising that it is rarely looked at in isolation. Closeness, togetherness, and distance itself—implying separateness—are ways in which dimensional distance and the interactional characteristics of relationships are interwoven and given common symbols. Yet the dimensions needed to specify relative position on the earth's surface prove useful in helping to understand the events in which all animals take part only if they are described explicitly. Every animal has his species-limited senses. Hence answers to how distant each is, relative to another, differ in their significance if one is talking about moles or eagles, bloodhounds, or human beings.

Except at very short distances, man is little aided by his senses. Like the birds, he is dependent on his sight, but he cannot compete with the eagle or hawk, or soaring man-of-war bird. He must use his ears, but here his performance is also mediocre even though acuity in hearing is reported to be much higher for people living in areas where the noises of modern living are conspicuously absent. No bloodhound he is; his capacity to discriminate at any distance by smell has been lost in his evolutionary past. His sense of touch, as a tactile animal like his primate relatives, is highly developed, but this occurs with physical togetherness during which all the senses reach their peak of discriminative ability.

It is obvious that the sensory repertoire available to a species necessarily sets limits on the distance at which identifiable signals can be received. It provides the boundaries within which individuals will react to one another (given no artificial or technological aids). But these outer limits are of less importance than the intensity and extent of the signal which one individual must produce to reach another. Varying for each of the senses, each depends on geometrical distance apart. Sensory physiologists (and physicians) have long been concerned with establishing the normal ranges and then the degree to which age or disease decreases the individual's sensitivity. The species significance of the sensory repertoire in inhibiting or facilitating interaction has barely been touched upon.

Scales for Biological Distance

Though distance is geometrically defined and measured by the conventional yardsticks of the physical sciences, the effects of distance in biology depend initially on the sensory perceptual properties of the organism. As a consequence, one cannot assume a linear relation between the number of feet or yards separating two people and the significance of a change in distance of, for example, three feet, unless one knows how far apart they were before one or the other moved. If they are only three feet apart and move three feet closer, the ensuing relationship will be very different from what it would be if the starting point was 25 feet. Coming closer by a single yard creates very different probabilities for interaction at the two distances.

Nevertheless, knowing the initial distance does not mean that we can predict that interaction will occur, but merely that it is now much more probable. The mother can walk over and pick up her unmoving and sleeping baby; a man and woman can lie together in bed, touching but not interacting. Apart from sleep, cultural learning or possibly even genetic factors may be involved. Bonnet Macaques (Rosenblum *et al.* 1964) sat in passive contact, huddled together as if sitting for a family photograph in the early 1900's. In contrast, their pigtail relatives, taxonomically very close, sat or stood unmoving within 12 inches of one another, neither touching nor interacting in what Rosenblum calls, "passive proximity." This does not prevent proximity being followed by interaction at other times. However, for these species, the probabilities of interaction when physically in contact or a short distance away are necessarily very much lower than for other monkeys who do not demonstrate such patterns.

At the other end of the distance scale, the probabilities that interaction will or will not occur are strongly affected by the individual's capacity for sensory perception. He has to see the other person who must, in turn, have equivalent visual powers. If he shouts, his voice must carry so the others hear him. Not merely individual limitations and differences in perceptual acuity set bounds on potential interaction, but species restrictions impose significant constraints.

If interaction is to occur, something more than mere reception of a sensory signal must take place. The individual must be able to discriminate between behavioral patterns at whatever distance separates him from another. A shout at night may not be reacted to unless sufficient overtones of the sound enable the hearer to recognize the voice. A distant figure, moving, may be only that to the viewer. Sex, identity, even the direction of the movement may be questionable. Even when the two people move closer, how close do they have to be before some interaction becomes probable? Other factors—the need for interaction, the identity of the persons, cultural requirements of many sorts—compound the probabilities, but at least one can assume that the chances will increase as people move closer together. On *a priori* grounds, and somewhat arbitrarily, it seems reasonable to think of a distance scale with unequal intervals as something like a hyperbola (without infinity at its end). Beyond a given distance, the chances of interaction are very low and roughly equal. They increase curvilinearly as one gets closer.

Within the limits where chance increases, additional probabilities can be identified. So far we have talked only about whether interaction will or will not occur. More important is whether we can estimate the probabilities that particular patterns of interaction will take place. In a crude way, it is obvious that as the distance decreases to a few feet, sustained interaction is far more likely. Common sense is enough to tell us that most interaction occurs within 10 feet, and that certain types of interaction such as loving or fighting reduce such distances drastically.

Hall (1959, 1966) has proposed a scale of distance ranges based on the perceptual discrimination limits of the human sensory apparatus. His efforts have been somewhat overcomplicated by a concern with the *number* of senses—and sensory inputs—involved which, except in closeness, reduce to two: sight and hearing. Touch requires direct contact; therefore tactile interaction (conjoined with other modes) can take place only at zero distance. Smell, except for the recalcitrantly unwashed, is also perceived at minimal distance and, like body heat, may heighten the sensory signals. But interaction is not carried out by humans through chemical, electrical, or temperature intermediaries.

The individual is thus reduced to touch, vision, and hearing, with all three communicative modes involving the "sending and receiving" of interactional patterns. Hall points out that around 25 feet, details of facial expression are hard to see; between 12 and 25 feet, the voice level will have to be raised and more accentuated gestures used. On the other end of the scale, from 0 to 3 feet, though one hears "every sound" the other makes, vision, as in the motion pictures, is largely restricted to the close-up. The entire body and its movements are hard to include in the visual field.

Hall has primarily emphasized the cultural patterning of distance as a significant modality of communication, that is, as a form of language. He advocates the use of the term "proxemics" as the equivalent of linguistics. (To this should be added the term, kinesics, which Birdwhistell (1952) devised to categorize the language of gesture.) Nevertheless, there seems little doubt that a systematic study of distance based on the human limitations of the sensory systems would strongly support the intuitive, though common-sense, ranges which he suggests. What appears to be demonstrable is that the human animal (and all other animals) selects distance ranges for particular types of interactions. Sexual activities, fighting, or child nurturance require actual contact, or a distance range at which touch is potentially possible. Beyond that, a primary factor in how close or how far two individuals position themselves may be the biological properties of what Hediger (1950) called the flight distance—how close the animal would let another approach—based on the autonomic components of the attack-flight system. When Hall described the distance range of 7 to 12 feet as intermediate, in effect he was saying that the individuals could easily move away and thus end the interaction. By coming closer they put themselves in the position where intensive interaction of various types was almost a necessary consequence.

At present, one may use the exact ranges which Hall suggests (0, ½ foot, 1½ feet, 1½ to 2½ feet, 2½ to 4 feet, 4 to 7 feet, 7 to 12 feet, 12 to 25 feet, 25 feet plus), or reduce their number following Kennedy's revision for architectural design purposes (1965), until more precise experimental determinations can be carried out. In any case, the differential size of each interval—each becoming longer, with the "intensity" of the interaction presumed to decrease concomitantly—would indicate that the probability formula for distance as a function of interactional frequency and intensity would be hyperbolic. This means that each of the variables would undergo a logarithmic transformation which would combine the frequency and duration of the contact and the degree of complementarity or its obverse as an estimate of "intensity." The probabilities by which spatial distance becomes dimensional could thus be estimated explicitly.

At this stage of our knowledge, the evidence to back up such a hypothesis is largely restricted to observations of chronic patients in mental hospitals (Chapple et al., 1963)—by no means an adequate substantiation for normal situations. Yet such a formulation provides a more systematic means of testing the significance in probability terms of spatial distance between individuals. One would expect, in differing cultural situations as well as in different animal species, that the parameters which describe the particular quantitative values of each of the variables might well differ. They would thus be useful in distinguishing one from another.

Directional Mechanisms in Spacing

Although animals of different species differ in their capacity to identify, and thus to be able to respond to, different sensory signals, there appear to be quite general uniformities in what happens when one animal becomes aware of another. These underlie the degree of spatial separation they maintain; they set in motion the transformation of distance as mere geometry to distance as a form of biological adaptation. Berlyne (1966), in a review of the evidence, made the point that what had traditionally been called "curiosity" or "exploratory behavior" can better be described in terms of the physiological shifts in autonomic nervous system functions which complex stimuli produce. What they do is to increase the state of arousal through the reticular formation and elicit spontaneous activity or, more accurately, set off the process of entrainment.

He goes on to comment that this physiological process is built on what Pavlov, many years ago, first called the "orientation reflex" (not a reflex in the usual sense). It consists of a combination of body movements and associated physiological states through which the animal focuses its attention after a change in stimulus. Such patterns of orientation vary depending on the species and the type of stimulus. They range from the orientation of body and gaze in interactional situations to the readiness for action when complex stimuli occur, the relevance of which—is he a friend or foe?—is not immediately clear.

But orientation appears to be made up of two components: (a) *direction towards* and (b) *movement towards,* Berlyne, in the article cited, regarded the second as primarily exploratory or investigatory, and dependent on stimulus change. This "movement towards" appears to be complicated by the factors which control the relative spacing of individuals vis-a-vis one another. If two animals of the same species see each other across a field, the probability is high that they will begin to move towards each other. How close they come seems to depend upon their recognition of the potential character of the interaction which might take place. This compulsion to move towards another individual is apparently almost universal—so much so that some investigators have postulated the existence of a social tropism, that is, an innate requirement to orientate towards and move towards the source of a particular type of stimulus. The most common tropism, and easiest to observe, is phototropism, as the moth flutters towards the incandescent light.

The remarkable thing about many such "social" tropisms is the extreme precision with which they are often carried out. Fish who school take up positions at fixed distances from their neighbors and maintain themselves, no matter how many rapid manoeuvers involving changing direction the school carries out under threat of attack. Migrating ducks and geese fly in fixed formations, but they do not "school" when they arrive at their destination. Whatever rationalizations there may be in military "science" for close-order drill and all the variations which delight the audience in military parades and manoeuvers, perhaps this cultural ordering is built on an atavistic necessity derived from the lower animals. In the higher primates—monkeys, apes, and man—both eyes and ears are in the lateral plane; events taking place behind them cannot be localized without the animal turning its head and, ordinarily, its body. Man at least has a broad arc of peripheral vision so that he can march abreast. Whether or not his primate cousins are similarly endowed, they have managed to avoid the joys of close-order drill.

The significance of orientation towards or away from another individual [Berlyne's *type (a)*] has never been investigated systematically. Early studies of nursery school children by Thomas and her associates (1933) demonstrate (what every parent or teacher knows) that the child who does not wish to interact turns away from the group, often facing 180 degrees in the opposite direction. There are several stages of movement *towards* before the child can be considered to be a potential participant in a group, not only moving closer, but orienting trunk and head in the group's direction. Similar studies of schizophrenic patients on a ward for chronic patients dramatize the relevance of orientation (Chapple *et al.,* 1963). So powerful, apparently, is this factor as a first stage in starting interactional contact that many patients will be seen standing facing the wall. If seated, they look away from others who might approach them, or gaze interminably at the floor so eyes will not meet.

Effects of Gaze on Interaction Rhythms

Although the significance of moving towards is only beginning to be investigated, looking towards (gaze) has been shown by a variety of investigators to play an important part in achieving synchronization. In fact, gaze is one of the primary patterns of behavior (in our culture at least) by which individuals signal to each other when they are coming to an end of an action, or want to begin, or are continuing and seek to avoid interruptions which would shorten the full manifestation of their action.

These studies on gaze have been carried out within the last few years by Kendon (1965), Neilsen (1964), and Exline *et al.* (1963). The first two researchers have been primarily concerned with the relevance of gaze for interaction. They have shown that looking away serves to prevent another action being received from the individual with whom he is conversing, while looking towards is the precursor for beginning to act. Thus, as would be expected, in interaction the speaker tends to look away from his partner while the listening member of the pair looks directly at the speaker for relatively long intervals of time, occasionally breaking the gaze by looking away. Kendon points out that ending a speech (not a brief comment) is accompanied by looking towards the listener, associated usually with a postural change of the position of the head or body. Beginning is similarly signaled by looking at, getting the other to look also, and then looking away and immediately starting the speech or gesture to be sure the other will not start before him.

There are significant individual differences in the percentage of time persons look towards or away, correlated with the durations of their actions and silences. Kendon believes that long actions are facilitated in running their full course if one avoids looking at the other person. This enables the individual to concentrate on verbal output, that is, the subject matter of what he has to say. Also, while looking away and talking, he can shift his gaze back towards the partner briefly to elicit a response. He thus achieves an immediate but short dominance interval if he quickly looks away again once the other responds. Actual struggles for dominance in which both persist are marked by both looking at each other. Looking away, in other words, is a signal that a person intends to continue; his brief glances towards the other are both to see that the other is listening (gazing at him) and to maintain momentary dominance. If he should hesitate for a word (intending to continue) while looking at his partner, he can reduce the chances of losing his turn by looking away.

In all these studies of gaze, the investigators make, as is only sensible, the further discrimination of eye-contact. In other words, they try to determine whether the gaze of both persons actually met. Obviously there may be some uncertainty in making the decision operationally since it is possible to look just past the other person, but the reliability of these observations appears to be high. Kendon's data indicate that when two people are interacting, eye-contacts occur between 30 and 60 percent of the total time of the session (the amount and frequency depending on the interaction rhythms), and glances range in duration from one to seven seconds.

Not only does the gaze play an important part in the management of the action-inaction patterns, it is also a significant element in initiative and dominance. In order to initiate action to a person in a group, you look at him. If he looks back and you catch his eye, the probabilities are high that you can begin to interact with him. As everyone soon becomes aware, one can avoid being initiated to by avoiding his eye and watching him through peripheral vision only, thus being able to turn the head or move away just as the gaze begins. These investigators also believe that looking down is an indication of having been dominated, and even that the gaze itself (with or without a "hostile" expression of the face) causes the other to submit.

In apes and monkeys, looking away or, on the contrary, looking directly at another, is an important indication of the nature of the relationship between them. He who is dominant (or wishes to dominate) orients and looks toward his rival. The submissive one faces away and avoids the other's eyes. Both in orientation and in its culmination in the attack and flight patterns of the species, the animals move as well as direct their bodies towards or away from each other. As with humans, the orientation is not only relative to another individual, it is also an orientation towards or away from the apparent path being followed. Thus, if one monkey moves towards food, the subordinate one not merely moves out of the way if necessary, but also looks in the other direction lest there be any implication of challenge.

There is considerable evidence that directing one's gaze toward another, or being gazed at, is associated with emotional states. Not only is this to be found in observing individuals whose interaction is clearly "affectional," but electrophysiological studies have shown that Rhesus monkeys have a marked change in the electrical activity of autonomic centers when they are being looked at. Remarkable changes have also been shown in mute, autistic children, who superficially appear completely unaware of the presence or actions of another person. It can also be shown that gazing at is associated both with dominance situations and with the attraction patterns of boy and girl—further evidence of the ethologist's demonstration that in the lower animals, attack and flight patterns and sexual behavior are closely affiliated.

To gaze, or stare, is to indicate the intention to initiate interaction or to keep it going. To stare at strangers is impolite—a lesson in manners that children learn early. In many cultures, it is an insult (The Evil Eye) which sets off conflict among adults. The *gaze* calls for a response and fluctuates as interaction takes place; the *stare* continues even though the other person does not respond; thus this action does not set interaction in motion. The distinction between the two is, thus, *after the fact* of interaction, though distance plays a part in making a response more or less probable.

Showing how far such patterns might go in some species, Barnett (1967) reported the curious interaction which took place between a strange, wild Norway rat and a male in his own territory. The latter approached the stranger, watching all the while, his teeth chattering and his hair raised. The stranger adopted a defensive posture and throughout the encounter never retaliated. His attacker sniffed him and then moved around his opponent sometimes leaping at him, occasionally, but by no means always, nipping him. After a series of such "mock" attacks, the victim was left stretched out, breathing irregularly and rapidly, and might die within a few days with absolutely *no* evidence of being wounded. In other words, he died from fright.

Barnett's description of the death of the subordinated rat after enduring a prolonged gaze by the dominant animal (and being unable to move during exposure) clearly suggests that the state of fright triggered off the general alarm syndrome with massive consequences on homeostatic mechanisms. Predators are often reported as staring at their prey who become "hypnotized" (in the folk sense of the word). Similar instances have frequently been described among humans when facing their killers; there are dramatic cases of humans dying because of magic, notably in "voodoo death," reviewed by Cannon (1957). Even in presumably pleasant surroundings, at a restaurant for example, the recipient of a prolonged stare becomes uneasy, tries to look away, and occupies himself in "busy" activities, hoping that the next time he steals a look at the starer he will no longer be under surveillance.

Perhaps the impact of the stare is potentiated by the probability of movement towards the victim and the consequent uncertainty as to the nature of the interaction to follow. The drama of "High Noon," imitated in countless western motion pictures, is the long walk of the sheriff and the bad man towards each other—only the slow pace, the stare, and nothing else but the reiterative music. Here the limit of closeness is efficient gun range, but otherwise the increasing closeness and suspense (will one turn away?) are the buildup to the ultimate act of dominance. Speed of movement towards is also a factor in producing reactions in the other individual. In play, young animals rush towards each other, and stop or turn just before coming into contact. Swift movement toward in humans implies either a heightening of aggression or some kind of crisis intervention.

Thus orientation, as direction towards and movement towards, is the underlying component on which the distance scale is built. Without it—if there were no internal requirements to approach or look towards in order to interact—individuals would distribute themselves randomly over the landscape. Interaction would then occur only if they happened to fall over one another in transit. On the contrary, the interplay of the reticular formation and the limbic system sets up the directional properties of the animal's behavior. It provides the needed outlet for its biological rhythms through orientation, whether it takes its form as "curiosity," "exploration," or some equivalent term.

Relationships of Individuals to Space (Territoriality)

Since animals are physiologically required to orient towards others, their relative occupation of space is no mere random matter. Wherever they may locate themselves, this location is partly controlled by those others with whom they react and interact. The requirements of the species (or culture among humans) for sustenance and particular environmental conditions are relevant, as we shall discuss in the chapter following, but it is the orientation process (reflex) which makes each individual aware of the other within his sensory perceptual range. In addition, the particular space which he selects has its own special properties. These play an essential part in maintaining an active neurophysiological state.

Berlyne, in the paper earlier referred to, differentiates between those exploratory responses which are due to uncertainty of information about the environment (including other animals) and what he calls "diversive" exploration. In the former, already discussed as a primary factor in orientation, the individual reacts to and must adjust to the novel stimulus or situation which may involve interaction or, if the stimulus is nonliving, an exploratory investigation. This process, which Berlyne calls "specific," is designed to achieve some type of stable equilibrium even though this may require the individual to undergo the stress of conflict or flight.

On the other hand, a wide variety of studies have demonstrated that the individual, animal or human, requires a continuing stream of information to activate the reticular formation, produce arousal and a high level of autonomic functioning. Where informational input is markedly reduced, severe emotional disturbances result. In the phrase used by Pos and his co-workers at Toronto (1966), an "informational underload" is the common factor in studies of sensory deprivation, isolation, bereavement, and the like. Whether one regards the process of fulfilling these informational needs as primarily a matter of exploratory behavior where the "novelty" and "complexity" of the stimuli are decisive, certainly one can see how a given spatial location, a territory, can provide a continuing set of variations on a familiar theme.

Familiarity as well as novelty and complexity have to be related, otherwise the stimuli are stress-producing and the animal attacks or flees. Berlyne (1960) emphasized that "novelty effects are elicited most strongly by stimuli with an intermediate degree of novelty, like something rather well known, but distinct enough to be 'interesting' " (Marler and Hamilton, 1966). Human parallels are obvious in the effects of such culturally controlled activities as the arts and sports, or, more closely homologous to animals, in the constant effort spent on the house and its surroundings, or the nest or lair. Berlyne calls this property "the quest for intermediate arousal potential" and Schneirla (1959, *inter alia*) has shown how widespread this is in all animal species.

Two factors, therefore, (oversimplifying for purposes of exposition) are thus at work in the individual's identification with a territory. First, there is the internal necessity for reticular arousal which facilitates the free-running states of the biological rhythms. Without such environmental settings within which adequate outlets for spontaneous activity can be obtained, the organism can undergo severe physiological trauma. Reliance on the familiar, safely providing the intermediate states necessary for dynamic equilibrium, in fact enables the organism to function at a level approaching its optimal state. As we shall see later, this identification, in the adaptive sense, with stable environmental contexts, is an important component in the healthy states which possession of a territory affords.

Second, the autonomic-interactional states by which the specific exploratory responses are carried out are the medium through which emotional intensity becomes associated with territory. The literature on territoriality has been unduly focused on defense and attack—the dominance and initiative variables through which interactional adjustment with others becomes stabilized—to the neglect of the territory's intermediate arousal potential. Both have to be taken into account and both are physiologically interdependent.

Possession and Maintenance of Territories

Territoriality is the best known type of spatial organization for man and other animals, and is the easiest to illustrate. It is by no means the simplest. It is a product of the two underlying physiological factors just described. Possession of space *and* maintenance of its separateness from invasion or possession by others are combined through initiative and dominance. Lorenz, in his delightful book, *On Aggression* (1966), points out the apparently universal emotional strength and interactional persistence which the defender brings to such conflicts with an attacker of the same species. Assuming that technological superiority is not present and the individual animals are healthy, even the physical superiority of the attacker is not enough. Both animals have similar systems controlling for attack and flight. It is the invader who loses.

Even in the case of animals whose territory is governed by space only, the hunting ground must not be imagined as a property determined by geographical confines; it is determined by the fact that in every individual the readiness to fight is greatest in the most familiar place, that is, in the middle of its territory. In other words, the threshold value of fight-eliciting stimuli is at its lowest where the animal feels safest, that is, where its readiness to fight is least diminished by its readiness to escape. As the distance from this "headquarters" increases, the readiness to fight decreases proportionately as the surroundings become stranger and more intimidating to the animal. If one plotted the graph of this decrease, the curve would not be equally steep for all directions in space. In fish, the center of whose territory is nearly always on the bottom, the decline in readiness to fight is most marked in the vertical direction because the fish is threatened by special dangers from above.

The territory which an animal apparently possesses is thus only a matter of variations in readiness to fight, depending on the place and on various local factors inhibiting the fighting urge. In nearing the center of the territory the aggressive urge increases in geometrical ratio to the decrease in distance from this center. This increase in aggression is so great that it compensates for all differences ever to be found in adult, sexually mature animals of a species. If we know the territorial centers of two conflicting animals, such as two garden redstarts or two aquarium sticklebacks, all other things being equal, we can predict, from the place of encounter, which one will win: the one that is nearer home.

When the loser flees, the inertia of reaction of both animals leads to that phenomenon which always occurs when a time lag enters into a self-regulating process—to an oscillation. The courage of the fugitive returns as he nears his own headquarters, while that of the pursuer sinks in proportion to the distance covered in enemy territory. Finally the fugitive turns and attacks the former pursuer vigorously and unexpectedly and, as was predictable, he in his turn is beaten and driven away. The whole performance is repeated several times till both fighters come to a standstill at a certain point of balance where they threaten each other without fighting.

The importance of spacing along the distance dimensions and the sense of possession centered on the animal's "headquarters" derive from the emotional aspects of the relationships which acquisition of space entails. Not only does the individual feel able to initiate, and to dominate if necessary, but the habitual reception of stimuli from specific environmental surroundings, and their intermediate arousal potential, makes possible the manifestation of the patterns of activity for which the biological rhythms require a constant outlet. Thus, the experiential influences of possession and defense are reinforced by the emotional-interactional situation accompanying them. The endogenous biological rhythms basic to the individual are activated and sustained through the successful achievement of initiative and dominance.

The maintenance of distance between individuals or groups is, therefore, a balance (sometimes uneasy, as Lorenz's redstarts and sticklebacks illustrate) between conflicting requirements—to avoid or drive away, or to orient and move towards. The controlling factors in achieving this balance are the quantitative patterns of the individual's interaction system. When the behavior of another animal threatens to become stressful, he tries to increase the distance between them, either by flight or by first attacking with the presumed hope that by dominating, he can drive the other away. On the other hand, when stress is minimized and the level of physiological and behavioral adjustment is high, space can be reduced. It is in such circumstances that he can acquire a mate and let her share his territory and personal space.

Yet in many species, as Lorenz shows, even getting a mate involves clear evidence of preliminary conflict. The male often regards the female as another invader. Only after a series of encounters and the proper degree of submissive behavior when she responds to his initiative and allows him to dominate does acceptance take place. Since stability for both members of the pair depends on establishing a complementary relationship, it is not surprising that Lorenz reports, for some species, that if the female does not adapt, she will be driven away or killed. This is particularly true where males and females are not distinguishable by external markings. Being female means acting like one.

Territories Held by Groups

Although many animals establish individual territories, later admitting another as a mate and thus procreating, other species maintain spatial separation initially as a group. In some cases, as with man, this is combined with individual territoriality; in others, it is the group which attacks and defends and by so doing establishes its distance from the others.

Petter (1962) found a remarkable degree of preoccupation with territorial defense among lemur groups. Among them, the availability of opponents is a primary factor in holding the group together and providing them with the necessary outlets for interaction. Madagascar is an island where there are no predators to threaten the lemurs, yet territorial boundaries are of principal concern as indicated by the concentration of groups in small areas. Petter describes the black lemurs, watching for the sight of their neighbors moving near their boundaries. Nothing interferes with this watching, not even their normal habits of feeding. The moment an intruder is spotted, all hands rush to the attack. Ripley (1964) stressed the fact that however peaceful and nonbelligerent the male langurs were within their groups (probably because their dominance positions are long established), their primary occupation was to spot possible invaders, to sound the alarm, and to mobilize the group for defense.

In these species, the group itself defends its territory, though some investigators have been confused by the fact that they have not witnessed

"defense" in the sense of outright combat. Among the lower primates—
monkeys and apes—territoriality has been reported for every species (Carpenter 1959), though not consistently, due to personal definitions of "defense." The howler monkeys when they encounter another group, howl with
vigor and shake the branches of the trees through which they have been
traveling. After this vocal trial for dominance, one or the other group gives
up and moves out of the way of the other. Fang and claw are not in
evidence, but the notion of defence should not be limited so severely.

Among mammals generally, at least among those for whom the sense
of smell is so important (including the lower primates), territories are
marked by scent glands. Dogs, as Lorenz points out, deposit urine and feces
in areas (in suburbia, a succession of trees and shrubs) which they regard as
their property. These are not signals in perpetuity. Cats and other hunting
animals, for example, can determine how long the scent has been deposited,
avoiding those areas where the fresh odor indicates another animal is
around.

Farley Mowat (Never Cry Wolf 1963) described his first field trip as
a naturalist to study the wolves of the Barren Lands of Northern Canada.
In his innocence of the peaceable character and remarkable intelligence of
what he had been told were devouring monsters, he found himself cooped
up in a large territory of a family of wolves when he arrived. Calling upon
his observations of how they maintained the boundaries of their territory,
he decided to emulate them and staked out a three-acre patch around his
cabin for his own. Obviously, he needed to place his mark at convenient
intervals, so summoning up his resources, he proceeded to urinate

> on stones, clumps of moss, and patches of vegetation at intervals of not more
> than fifteen feet around the circumference of my claim. This took most of the
> night and required frequent returns to the tent to consume copious quantities
> of tea; but before dawn brought the hunters home the task was done, and I
> retired somewhat exhausted, to observe results.

When the first wolf appeared and encountered the sign, after a period
of contemplation, he got up and proceeded to mark Mowat's signs all over
again on the *outside* of the territorial boundaries.

> As I watched I saw where I, in my ignorance, had erred. He made his mark
> with such economy that he was able to complete the entire circuit without
> having to reload once, or, to change the simile slightly, he did it all on one
> tank of fuel.

The occasional overlaps of primate bands reported in the literature
appear to be due to the aging of signs left by others. A variety of clues
enable them to judge whether other bands might be encountered or whether
they may proceed safely. Birds, however, like humans, depend on sight and

hearing. With both, individual territoriality is developed to a high degree. Thus, maintenance of territory may be defined by specific boundaries, with invasion and the group reaction to it a mere matter of putting one foot across the Rubicon; or, as with many apes and monkeys, incursion by another group into the space the group is presently occupying sets off the conflict. Field naturalists like to talk of the "home range," to contrast it with the defended group territory—the "turf" of the street corner gangs or the sacred soil of tribes and principalities. In such usage, the home range is differently defined, primarily because the band moves from place to place without boundaries being evident; another band may also use the area not being occupied at a given time by the first. However, if they come into contact, like the howlers, or simple human groups like the Andamanese, the groups are clearly in conflict. One or the other dominates (usually by "peaceful" means) and the other moves away.

Internal Stabilization of Interaction in Group Territoriality

Even in the individual case, where the establishment of a territory is a precursor to admitting a mate to share it, some degree of interactional adjustment must be established (though maladjustment between animal spouses is hardly uncommon). In groups, an equilibrium state becomes more necessary since stability of relationships in terms of who is dominant and who is to take the initiative when other groups appear is a necessary factor in defense. As a consequence, each group develops an essential coherence in that most interaction (other than that of defense and attack) occurs between its members; physical separation from others reinforces its stability.

Even the distinction between the territory and the home range, the latter being considered that area within which the group travels to seek available food, depends on the nature of their interactional systems. Though the ambiguous criterion, defense as physical combat, may be invoked to support the differentiation, the type of environment and its supply of food are more to the point. There are, of course, situations where the frequency and duration of dominance efforts are low, but here what appears to have happened is the prior establishment of relationships. Neither animals nor humans need to fight for dominance each time they encounter one another.

Where the geographical area is too limited for the number of individuals it must contain, where adequate sustenance is low, disturbances of group equilibrium become more frequent. Then individuals begin to fight for territory. The losers not only are unable to obtain mates but ordinarily are driven out to lead a meager and unhealthy life, lacking the physiological stability with which possession of a territory endows the animal. In groups, as space decreases, interactional factors become overriding. If there are personality clashes, less dramatic often than whether the young adult male is contesting for leadership of the group with its old boss, or the eternal female is sought after by rival suitors, conflict or withdrawal occurs, followed by the breaking up of the group into smaller units. Perhaps they will ultimately reorganize in a new interactional system. Experiments have shown that shrinking the space is not the essential factor. Increases in attempts to dominate are primary and controlling.

These internal adjustments, and the need of each individual for orientation vis-a-vis all others, result in the concentration of group members within a space, the boundaries of which are set by the distance scales of the particular species. Thus the distribution of groups is not merely a consequence of ecological factors; the necessity for togetherness and separateness are far more powerful. Simply plot the distribution of settlements in New England; the vast empty areas between them could easily hold an enormous population. Accepting the crowding rate in Harlem, the entire population of the United States, 200 million, could occupy three boroughs of New York City. So, too, the lemurs of Madagascar, for those species where the food they require is not too highly specialized and geographically limited, choose their "settlements" where they can keep a close eye, and indulge in exciting conflict, with each other. Spacing for animals is thus a function of an adequate supply of their fellows; the hermit is as rare among them as among humans.

Personal Space

Many writers like to use the term "personal space." This may be species-specific or idiosyncratic and/or cultural, by which individuals maintain their "distance." Alternatively, it denotes the lack of individual territoriality for a species. Thus, Hall (1959, 1966) has discussed at length the differences between members of different cultures—the North American and the Latins of the Southern Hemisphere. The former, he says, prefer to have several feet between them and those with whom they interact; the Spanish-Americans (and other Mediterranean groups) carry on business conversations a few inches apart or even touching. However perceptive such observations are of culturally induced properties of communication, they do not describe an inevitable and unvarying state where possession of a spatial distance envelope, so to speak, which each carries with him as he moves, substitutes for territoriality.

All such distinctions are to a very large extent dependent upon situational factors. Animals assumed to have only "personal space" can, in laboratory settings, establish territories (for example, with house mice, Anderson *et al.* 1965). Individuals who fight for territories before the beginning of the mating season may, at its end, in conjunction with hormonal factors controlled by long-term rhythms, be content with personal space.

The street groups of Harlem or the North End of Boston furiously defend the street corners and the pavements of their territory. Yet by the time the gang members become adult, married, and parents, they have given up their "turf" and its defense. But other types of territories take over. Let a neighbor dump trash on someone's land, or let it be rumored that zoning laws are to be changed and every member of a suburban community will be up in arms. No wonder that housing restrictions are among the most explosive of all the problems of civil rights.

Personal space is part of a continuum with personal territory, and operates similarly to regulate the occurrence of interaction. It is an expression of the fundamental factors through which all animals adjust their distance and direction to one another. Provide stability of location—and property—which enables the individual to achieve a satisfactory outlet for his daily cycle of activities and interaction, and personal space turns into personal territory. Conversely, in migration or for the human traveler, the motel room, the parking place, and even the table in the dining room take on a territorial coloration.

Though captains and kings are the stuff of history, the possession of land or space within a building which "belongs" to an individual is a primary factor in the human situation. The Englishman's home is his castle, but castles are to be found even in the most *limited* space, Lombard (1955) commented on salesgirls in a department store he studied:

> "Each salesgirl behaved as though it was important to have a location of her own. To be sure, a location of her own meant something different in each of the groups. But in spite of these differences, each girl recognized the rights of other girls to locations of their own."

It might be a particular section of a counter or a table on which clothing was piled, but these spaces and the merchandise found on them made up the territory for each individual salesgirl. For this they would fight bitterly if they were invaded: on this their whole work interaction (and activity) system was emotionally dependent.

Autonomic Disturbances in Crowding (Minimal Distances)

Though orientation necessitates the positioning of individuals at stable intervals on the distance scale, reduction of such distances to a minimum, for animals of the same sex particularly, almost always results in conflict.

Thus crowding of more individuals into a space smaller than it can accommodate (*if* it be remembered that each has to maintain his distance from the others, given the scale of interactional impact) increases the frequency and intensity of struggles for dominance and their emotional concomitants.

Zoologists who have been concerned with the growth of populations have carried out a series of investigations, both in the field and in the laboratory, to try to establish what takes place. Their findings can be illustrated by a quotation from Snyder (1961):

> Present evidence provides unequivocal support for the thesis that the growth of mammalian populations is basically regulated by physiologic, especially endocrine, responses to population density. Included in this thesis is the concept that interactions between mammals in the same population (intraspecific competition, social interaction, etc.) are intensified as density increases. At its lower levels social interaction may promote the breeding and productivity needed to maintain a population or to allow it to grow. But high productivity and a growing population must also increase the level of social interaction, which shifts endocrine mechanisms (raises adrenocorticotrophins and diminishes gonadotrophins) to reduce productivity and increase mortality.

What Snyder is saying is that the more a population increases and the available space for individuals is reduced (a phenomenon referred to as "crowding"), the more fighting takes place for space. In consequence, the adrenal glands and the pituitary produce hormones which decrease fertility (the gonadotrophins) and increase and ultimately exhaust the hormones which fight disease by mobilizing the body against stress (adrenocorticotrophins—ACTH). These studies have been carried out on a wide variety of species. As would be expected, rats and mice, dogs and domestic fowl have been common subjects, but much work has been done on rabbits, field mice, lemmings, woodchucks, deer of various species and, unintentionally, on animals in zoos.

When zoologists first turned their attention to the study of population growth and, in particular, tried to explain the remarkable fluctuations taking place, often within the space of a very few years, they tended to implicate the natural environment. Changes in food supply, in the climate, or the occurrence of epidemic disease (called epizootics for animals) were assumed to be sufficient to cause the differences in numbers of animals. To their suprise they found that a rapid growth or decrease in population occurred independently of such environmental influences. Although many investigators have been concerned with the problem, probably J. J. Christian and his associates (1961), of whom Synder was one, are best known for making explicit the interdependence of interaction and endocrine factors and carrying out careful laboratory studies to supplement their work as field naturalists. Chitty (1967), however, criticized their position, in terms equivalent to those used here, since they minimized the differential effects of personality and its genetic and environmental constituents.

As the population increases, whatever the species being studied, a series of anatomical and physiological changes takes place in the endocrine system. By providing the animals with more food, cover, and other environmental benefits than they could use, and by eliminating animals who might hunt them as prey (easier to do in the laboratory, but possible in natural surroundings), any changes occurring could more easily be attributed to the increased concentration of animals. What the experiments demonstrated was that the debilitation of the pituitary-adrenocortical system was due to the number of interactions (attempts to dominate) between individuals rather than to the density of the population itself.

Bronson and Eleftheriou (1964) showed that putting trained fighter mice together in an open cage for one minute, 1, 2, 4, and 8 times a day for seven days, increased adrenal weight and adrenal and plasma concentration of corticosterone—much more than they could obtain if they put eight mice together for a week. Southwick (1964), in taking into account the differences in the personality characteristics of different strains of mice, found that mice who were "incompatible,"—analogous to complementary in this book—showed no adrenal response when grouped together, but if they were "incompatible," adrenocortical responses were high, thus supporting Chitty's point of view. It is most important to reemphasize that these various studies demonstrate that the endocrine responses occur whether or not there is actual fighting or injury. As Christian and Davis (1964) pointed out in their review, it was the repeated establishment of dominance and the subordinated animals' emotional reactions to the stress of dominance that resulted in endocrine disturbance. The dominant animals showed least endocrine imbalance, the subordinate most. When animals became so submissive and physically debilitated that the dominant no longer interacted with them, they began to show a drop in plasma corticosterone from previously high levels. In the wild, they would die. Only under laboratory conditions could they survive.

There are species differences in the precise nature of the changes which take place, consequent on differences in the interdependence of the various elements of the endocrine system involved in aggressive or dominant behavior. However, the general character of the autonomic changes makes it easy to see why populations decrease as a function of crowding. In the laboratory where controlled experiments are much more feasible, hypertrophy of the adrenals and reduction of the thymus take place in mice with inhibition of growth and delay in sexual maturation. As the population concentration becomes very high, individual sexual development is stopped as the physical size of the sexual organs decrease. In mature females, estrus cycles are prolonged, ovulation and implantation are diminished, and intrauterine mortality of the foetuses (miscarriages) increase. In some species, resorption of the embryo takes place and, where young are born, lactation is inadequate so that the nursling mice are stunted. It has even been found that crowding females before pregnancy leads to permanent behavior disorders in the young.

More generally, from a survival point of view, the young are highly vulnerable to disease at high population densities. They are, after all, subordinated animals. Stress produces more serious disturbances for them than in humans because animals secrete an unusually powerful member of the "ACTH complex" (hydrocortisone) which can directly suppress reproductive function and maturation. Ratcliffe (1961), summarizing some of the consequences at the Philadelphia Zoological Garden, pointed out that young woodchucks became seriously affected by kidney disease (also in the wild) and, for all species of birds and mammals, the frequency and severity of coronary arteriosclerosis increased markedly in spite of a far better and more controlled diet.

Marked differences occur among species in their reactions to crowding. Among the aoudads (Barbary sheep) and tahrs (Himalayan mountain goats), the mothers abandoned all the offspring—about 25 animals. Young kob antelopes and white-tailed deer, on the other hand, were markedly stunted, a condition which could be corrected if the young animals were transferred to isolated pens within two or three months of birth. All species became very susceptible to infectious and contagious diseases when there were too many of them in the zoo. Among rabbits, for example, a highly lethal disease, myxomatosis, spreads like wildfire; interestingly enough, the survival rate was far higher for dominant animals and their descendents. Southwick (1955), carrying out experiments on mice, found that when aggressive encounters in a colony reached a frequency of one per mouse per hour, litter survival became almost zero.

Relatively little attention has been paid to crowding among primates and no laboratory work done. Perhaps the investigators have been too fascinated by attempts at replication of psychiatric disorders in mother-infant studies. Field observations report high infant mortality, including infanticide, in what appear to be crowded groups. Koford (1965), in a two-year study of mortality among the rhesus macaques at Cayo Santiago, demonstrated the high mortality of peripheral males between their fourth and sixth year. These were the adolescent monkeys competing for food at the feeders. He called them "lean and furtive, almost continuously under tension and often wounded." However, no physiological or anatomical studies have been reported from autopsy, though Southwick (1962), discussing the marked population fluctuations among the howlers on Barro Colorado, believed that processes similar to those reported for the lower animals are going on. The extremely high death rate among the Hamadryas baboons at the London Zoological Gardens was primarily a consequence of fighting, but Zuckerman (1932) commented on the unhealthiness and susceptibility to mortality among the subordinate animals.

Crowding among Humans

The human evidence, from the public health point of view, tends to give support to the overriding influence of endocrine imbalance although, again, little systematic experimental work has been done to correlate crowding and struggles for dominance with disease. Not only is there a proper unwillingness to conduct laboratory experiments, but the natural experiments created by slum living and the intense overcrowding found in what are now being called the "ghettos" of the large cities are rarely observed with the techniques of behavioral biology.

On the other hand, reading any newspaper is sufficient to convince one of the degree to which violence and conflict occur in such settings. Public health statistics demonstrate that disease and susceptibility to mortality are concentrated among such crowded groups. It should be remembered that human physiological responses to stress, broadly labeled psychosomatic, are well established. A wide variety of studies have indicated that emotional stress is a component of many diseases, not merely of such publicized disorders as ulcers and coronary heart disease. Gordon and Gordon (1959) in studies of young housewives in New Jersey, described the high frequency of diseases, not only the psychiatric, but also bronchopneumonia, coronaries, ulcers and the like in association with lives in which the women are constantly subordinate, not merely to their husbands, but to their children.

Several studies have shown that "deprivation dwarfism," as stunting of children is now being called, is brought about by highly disturbed interactional situations within the family. In addition, a large proportion of autistic schizophrenic children and the so- called familially retarded, that is, where no organic defects can be established—a group which represents from 75 to 85 percent of all the retarded—are similarly stunted but their dwarfism has not been adequately investigated. A child of eight or nine may look as if he were only three, but will not have the obvious physical abnormalities which mongolism, congenital syphilis, or gene discordancies appear to produce. Powell (1967), who conducted a long term study of 13 dwarfed children at John Hopkins, believed the family situation, rather than the malfunction of the pituitary, was the predominant factor in causing the stunting (although the latter could be produced by autonomic disturbance). Silver and Finklestein (1967) went further in their study of five children (from a group of similarly dwarfed) for whom treatment could be carried out:

Height age was 2½ years retarded in the youngest child, a four-year old girl; 3 years retarded in each of two 4½-year-old children; and 5 years and 7½ years delayed in the oldest, a girl of seven when first seen and a boy of sixteen. Retarded epiphyseal maturation (bone age) was the consistently abnormal laboratory finding.

Behaviorally, these children were either passively withdrawn or highly aggressive. They had voracious appetites with serious behavior difficulties since infancy. Like the white-tailed deer in the Philadelphia zoo, in three of the five cases rehabilitation began when child and mother were separated and the child was placed in a foster home. Appetite decreased to normal levels and despite this, rate of growth was markedly *increased.* Similar studies have been reported from other countries, particularly by Widdowson (1951) in postwar Germany.

Effects of crowding on adults are also evidenced by attempted injury of the child in what is called the "battered-child syndrome" (Helfer and Kempe 1968). Parents, clearly under extreme stress, attack their children, beating them with hammers, kicking and punching them, burning them with electric irons or cigarettes, frequently killing them or causing permanent injury. The similarity to what some species of crowded animals do is very striking.

Crowding, therefore, is a lethal phenomenon, the importance of which, for the human as well as for the animal, is beginning to be realized. It results from the inability of the individual to establish a territory—and stable interactional relations with those around him—through which his equilibrium requirements can be preserved. How severe must be the stresses when a family, even sharing their space with relatives, may be forced to live twelve in a room in the tenements of Harlem or the Bronx. The impact of constant interactional disturbance can only be escaped by fleeing to the streets or to some kind of a job. There is no privacy for the individual under such conditions; privacy means the opportunity *not* to interact when one's internal requirements for rhythmic outlet to interactional stress imposes the need for an interval of time to elapse while being alone. Privacy also means the need to interact *only* with certain people, perhaps just husband and wife, and not to be forced constantly to respond to the initiations and attempts to dominate by others.

The Invasion of Privacy

At the present time, invasion of privacy as a legal concept is increasingly being considered as a fundamental "right" of every human being. The term must be considered to include actual invasion, not merely of the individual's personal space or territory, but also the communication media through which his interaction may be carried on (for example, tapping his telephone or "bugging" his house) and thus robbing him of his potentials for interaction. From what has gone before, "invasion" is a real, not "imaginary" disturbance to the individual's health and well-being.

What is happening is that defense, or territorial maintenance, is no longer possible given electronic intervention, since stabilization of distance through reaching an initiative-dominance balance is ruled out. Thus, perception (evidence) of such privacy invasion requires the individual to orientate towards; his manifest inability to do so is an immediate source of anxiety. Specific exploration, in Berlyne's sense, to restore equilibrium through interactional adjustment is irrelevant. Further, the continuation of such invasions or their repetition minimizes the freedom to achieve a satisfactory state of intermediate arousal potential. The environment (of the house) is no longer familiar and capable of stimulus elaboration. On the contrary, even the complex patterns which are necessary to maintain an adequate informational input are now threatened by the unknown probability that any object or part of the house, formerly an important element in arousal, may be a source of danger.

As a consequence, the autonomic and reticular effects of the invasions of privacy which are associated with crowding continue, in a more serious though less dramatic form, in situations where invasion is carried out through modern technology, psychological as well as technological (Westin 1967). Since even gaze has been shown to have demonstrable electrophysiological effects on the autonomic and reticular functions, experimental demonstration of the full influences of today's varied means of disturbing the individual's territoriality could be easily carried out.

At present, attempts are being made to establish a legal foundation before the courts by treating such invasions within the framework of the rights to property. But the fact that ownership takes its emotional strength from the fundamental (and little understood) necessity of the animal to establish a territory has not been understood. Shifting the argument to the constitutional avenue (in the United States law) of the rights of the individual with regard to factors influencing his health and well-being (both, from the view of modern biology, being aspects of the same phenomenon) one is provided with a much sounder basis for further legal efforts.

Thus, those who advocate broad legal restrictions on the invasion of privacy should examine the fundamental biological properties of the human being for which animal studies have provided an important introduction. In medical literature, the elements are there, but careful studies within the framework of behavioral biology and anthropology could demonstrate that the invasion of privacy is as concrete a wrong in a court of law as the loss of life or limb (Chapple, in preparation).

The Bonds of Distance

The importance of this examination of the autonomic and reticular foundations of the necessity of establishing mutual distance is to emphasize that spatial relations are not mere patterns of convention. Specific distance intervals, on the individual or species scale, determine the probabilities that particular emotional-interactional patterns may occur. Under certain circumstances, as in crowding, the probabilities of conflict and attempts to dominate are so great that lethal consequences will follow. Moreover, the necessity for orientation and the neurophysiological factors involved, set up requirements for *reaction to,* once perception of another has taken place. Direction towards and movement towards are the precursors of interaction and establish the boundaries within which pair and group relationships are formed.

Space, in man and the lower animals, shapes these relationships. The distance scales and their significance are made evident in the way the landscape is utilized, or for humans (and space-oriented birds like the bower birds) in the many ways in which space can be contrived and framed by technology to facilitate or prevent interaction of particular types. Thus distance—vertical or horizontal, encompassing the three dimensions—is transmuted from geometry to biology.

In man, it becomes a major component, or dimension, of culture. The existence of spatial configurations—in architecture, landscaping, and the like—learned and adapted to as part of becoming a member of a society, are also capable of elaboration to influence the interactional probabilities. Among technologically simpler groups, such variations in design are largely traditional. Examination of man-made spaces (and distances held within or outside) demonstrate that space is an important reinforcer of the interaction patterns special to that people. How this occurs is the subject of the chapter following and, throughout, the reader should keep in mind the biological constraints here discussed. Without them, architecture may seem mere aesthetics or formalism. As the foregoing shows, the architect, often unwittingly, has a major influence, the impact of which on the human animal is still too little appreciated.

Chapter 10

The Cultural Dimension
of Space

Although measuring the distance between two or more individuals as a means of estimating the probabilities of their interaction from their biological distance scales might appear a simple process, in practice a variety of complications have to be taken into account. Even on an unencumbered surface, three geometrical dimensions are needed to describe relative location. The earth's surface, however, is rarely as smooth as a ballroom floor, so variations in the landscape have to be considered. In addition, man has varied the topography even further by contriving artificial environments in an almost infinite set of architectural forms. Hence distance cannot always be an absolute measure; it must be subordinated to the shapes of the spaces within which interaction takes place.

Where architecture is involved, and even in the natural environment where physical features intervene, barriers separate space into independent units, like rooms, the walls of which set impenetrable boundaries for the individuals within. However, as every city dweller knows, walls have differential screening potentials for the senses. Vision may be effectively cut off, but sound can penetrate, and even undergo amplification. Measurement of distance stops at the barriers, yet distinctions have to be made between total and partial sensory screening.

In complex architectural structures with many floors and differentiation into wings with minimal connecting passageways, and even in contiguous spaces with doors and windows or other openings arranged to facilitate movement and direction asymetrically, the measurements of distance are, in effect, measures of propinquity. Moreover, in specialized meeting places—

classrooms, churches, courthouses, or factories—vertical heights, and distances thereto, are an important element in controlling the nature of the interactions which can take place, and hence their probabilities. The priest at the altar, the teacher on the dais before the class, the bridge on which the captain of a vessel regulates its passage and the crew illustrate the ways in which vertical distance, often in combination with the horizontal, vary the distance scales.

The Experiential Influences of Space

Within the sensory capacities of individuals of different species, criteria for distinguishing different distance intervals are quickly learned. Based on the yet inadequately explored orientation process, the infant, almost from the moment of birth, begins to associate patterns of interaction and distance intervals. Feeding and nurturing and all its patterned tactile and vocal interaction patterns involve direct contact, the occupance of the same space (or almost the same) as its mother. Growing up requires the separation of infant and mother. In the United States, the infant is kept in a separate sleeping space, his crib; in other cultures or other species, the infant is often carried everywhere by its mother.

In such situations, the infant has to learn to become separate and to remain so without prolonged disturbance, whatever its attempts, by screaming, to reinstate the physical contact. Jensen (1965) described how the macaque mother alternated between pushing its growing infant away and permitting him to return to cling and feed. These alternations in pattern are marked by longer and longer intervals of separation until the young monkey spends most of his time apart from his mother. Coincidentally, interaction with its age mates begins. Among monkeys, far less among humans, tactile contact (and feeding from the breast) continues between the mother and her "grown children" even when they are physically and physiologically adult. For the skeptical, there are cultures like the Eskimo where it has been reported that 21-year old boys refresh themselves with their mother's milk.

As growing up goes on, the individual acquires a far greater repertoire of spaces, and interaction patterns performed within, until a wide variety of spatial situations have become associated with specific interactions. Not only do those involve particular individuals, but the behaviors to be expected from them and to be reciprocated are delineated. Before too long, a relational system develops within accustomed spaces so that the daily round of activity and interaction is distributed between them. Homes, schools, playgrounds, clubs, and the houses of friends make up the geographical or geometrical contexts for outlet for the biological rhythms. Depending on the spatial configuration, probabilities for interaction can be established.

Adaptation to spaces is such a fundamental part of learning to interact with others that its properties and constraints are largely unconscious. Where the behavior is new and very different from prior patterns, as in beginning to perform the rituals of one's church, space is an important element in primary awkwardness. Ordinarily, however, the biological influences of space, or distance from others, is a matter of intuition. Some distinctions are easily acquired: the utility of the car to get the girl friend away from her family, or the danger of the corner on the way home when it is occupied by members of a hostile gang. Sports or learning to hunt or fish serve an equal purpose in many societies. But usually the focus in the learning process is on the environment, man-made or natural. Rarely is space looked at objectively for its potential in facilitating or inhibiting specific patterns of interaction, either by specialists or by the ordinary member of a social group.

The Dimensional Aspects of Spatial Distance

To abstract from the complexities of culture a dimension which can serve as an organizing principle, we need to see how it is interwoven in all types of cultural situations. If the abstractive process is to be successful, its identification and, in a sense, its removal, should demonstrate that it can be used systematically as a building block on which a culture can be built. Since cultures are affairs of human beings (though one can argue that rudimentary cultures are to be found among the lower animal groups), the spatial dimension is necessarily based on the biological distance scales appropriate to them. From one point of view, distance enters every relationship. From moment to moment, each can be given its geometrical (and biological) measurements. Except for the rather ambiguous case of the mother carrying her unborn child, no two persons can totally occupy identical space, so distance has to be recorded in conjunction with what else is going on.

Further, as the preceding chapter has shown, distance is biologically rooted. The distance scales, combining with interaction patterns, are of roughly hyperbolic form (with unequal intervals) based upon sensory limitations and the perceptual input on which they must be based.

The question to be answered is the degree to which the measurement of spatial distance makes its contribution to the interactional probabilities, recognizing that other dimensions have to be included in the final estimate. Granted we are limited by present data. Yet we can examine the variations which space contributes to cultural differentiation and show how reasonable estimates of probabilities can be derived, holding the other cultural dimensions constant as far as possible. Essentially, there are only two of these other dimensions, one of which, the order of sequence in which actions and interactions are performed, is relatively straightforward; the other, communication, is multiple. Compounded by its constituent elements of pitch, intensity, timbre, and symbolic evocativeness, it represents a dimensional system of its own. Both dimensional categories are also biologically grounded as we shall see later on.

The Influence of Physical Environment on Interaction

The easiest beginning to this inquiry is to start with the external environment—the natural landscape—to which a human group must adapt, varying, of course, in the way it does so as a function of its available technology. Obviously, the members of a very simple culture technologically who depend on gathering wild foods and on hunting and fishing are highly influenced by terrain and by fluctuations in the supply of plants and animals. Parenthetically, wherever the term simple culture is used in this book, it means technological simplicity or lack of complexity. Therefore, they are far closer to their animal brethren in being controlled by the space dimension. Yet cultural differences, basically technological, can intervene. Only a very few human groups approach the animal level where each day requires that a new supply of food be obtained. Apart from the occasional instance where the prey is large enough or appetites small enough for something to remain in the cupboard, only the insects parallel the human ability to preserve their food.

But space, and its potentialities for individuals to occupy it and to establish relationships of various types are actually highly differentiated. For animals and the simplest human groups particularly, the natural environment is not composed of general categories of landscape which geographers use for classification of the earth's surface. To a desert dweller, like the nomadic Bedouin of the Arabian Peninsula, the desert is not sand sprinkled with oases, to be driven across in a Land Rover. It is composed of infinite shadings and variations in topography, in potential use and danger for one's camels, and in places to pitch one's tent where one may count on defense against raids from other tribes. In short, it is made up of almost innumerable tiny details, selected by the needs of the culture and the technology upon which it depends. The bulldozer is not available to obliterate landscape and to make the space to be occupied geometrically neat. To look at landscape, therefore, means to look through the eyes of a culture and its technology, as an ecologist would do, to see it in terms of potential usage for those interactions and activities which make up a way of life.

The relevance of such appraisals lies not merely in the capacity of individuals to survive and adapt to their environmental potential to the maximum degree possible; the degree of differentiation necessary for that particular technology to be carried on, as in camel breeding, also sets limits on the number of people who can utilize a given geographical area and thus interact with one another. Of course, if the technology is highly developed, inhospitable environments can be conquered. The almost matter-of-fact acceptance of the notion that man, Russian or American, can establish artificial stations in space or under the sea, or can colonize the moon, Mars, and Venus, is more than a tribute to the vogue of science fiction. Engineering development has been so great that artificial environments can be created almost at will. But the point of such adaptation lies in the term "artificial." To survive, these colonists must be able to adjust to the technological hardware which protects them against the real environments in which they have been placed. Gauges, dials, and computer readouts are the environment—not the bent grass which indicates that a deer has just moved through the rocky terrain, or the ripple on the water that signals a school of herring.

Ironically, these encapsulated cocoons, situated in environments in which man could not survive technologically unaided, even for a moment, bring about an intensity of interaction within a "crowded" space, the implications of which are by no means yet adequately investigated.

In other simpler cultures, extreme environments disperse people, since the size of the home ranges needed to provide the caloric intake may be extremely great. The Polar Eskimo, a hunting and fishing people, live in small communities of a few families, but the hunters may have to travel many miles to obtain food and bring it back. Due to fluctuations in the availability of food, it may be difficult to continue living in any kind of permanent settlement. During the late winter and spring, the ice is a source of seal, since these animals come up through the ice to lie in the sun. During the summer, before new ice forms on the water, hunters can travel in their kayaks, many miles out in the open sea, looking for seal, walrus, and small whales. If game is plentiful, many groups come together; otherwise they live apart. Fluctuations in the food supply have to be counterbalanced by restrictions on population growth—abortions, female infanticide, and the practice of setting the old out to die in bad years. All hunting, fishing, and vegetable-collecting peoples are commonly lumped together by ethnographers under the term "gatherers." Except where the food supply is ample and means of preserving it are available—either naturally or through techniques of smoking or drying, or packing meat in fat as was done in making the pemmican of the Plains Indians of the United States, the size of groups is limited by what their technology can make the landscape yield. But where they live, unless they are truly nomadic, is rarely the consequence of any kind of logistical analysis, conscious or unconscious, of the economic potential of the territory they hold. Far more relevant is the degree to which the permanent settlement chosen (sometimes more than one as in the case of summer and winter villages) provides stability in their interaction patterns both internally and in their relations to other groups.

Among those peoples with relatively simple technology, the number of people remaining together in one spot throughout the year can be highly variable. Only a few families or a single household may be able to obtain enough food by gathering or by agriculture within an area where food can be brought back to the settlement. Yet they may be joined by many others if some particular type of food becomes seasonally plentiful. The Shoshone Indians of the dry lands of the basin-plateau complex of Nevada, Utah, and adjoining regions depended on seeds, grasses, and edible roots until the early fall. If conditions were favorable, vast quantities of pine (pinyon) nuts could be harvested on the mountain slopes—so many that four people could gather 1200 pounds—enough to keep them through the winter. When pine nuts were abundant, other families joined since the sheer weight of the crop was too much to move; the harvesting group built their winter homes together. Ordinarily, some areas bore a heavy crop, others unpredictably would produce nothing, so the erratic nature of the pine nut crop and where it grew determined who would winter together (Steward 1938).

In contrast, in the rich valleys and coast lands of California, Indian groups with similar technology collected great stores of acorns, horse chestnuts, pine nuts, and grass seeds, which they cached and used as needed. Supplemented by small game and, if they lived on the coast, clams and other mollusks, these Indians were almost entirely self-sufficient and rarely moved over more than a 10-mile area. In what are now the agricultural production-line farms on which so much of the fruit and vegetables of the United States are produced, the aboriginal occupants were distributed in small enclaves of many tribes and different languages, each occupying its fertile territory and living in independence from its neighbors.

Along the Northwest Coast of North America, roughly from the State of Washington through British Columbia to Southern Alaska, the enormous supply of salmon made it possible for large villages to be established as permanent settlements along the shore. Since abundant wood could be obtained from the magnificent forests of Douglas fir and other conifers, the Northwest Coast Indians—Nootka, Kwakiutl, Tshimshian, Haida, and Tlingit, to name some of the best studied—built large houses and sea-going canoes and established a highly complex "gathering" culture. In the Great Plains of the United States, with the introduction of the horse, the Indians held tribal buffalo hunts during the summer months. During that time, an ample food supply for the entire year could be acquired by a highly coordinated effort where the entire tribe carried out a "surround," in which they literally surrounded the herd, killing vast numbers of buffalo and preserving the meat for winter months.

Though agriculture is the base on which the most complex societies have been built, again the environment and the techniques available are the controlling factors. In its simplest form—called slash- and-burn, or swidden, agriculture by the ethnographers—part of a forested area is burned over.

The ashes provide fertilizer for a crop which is raised for two or three years. Then another piece of land is selected, the trees cut down, burned, and used for another two or three years. Obviously, technology has to provide cutting instruments to chop down the trees in order to eliminate the much slower technique of killing the trees by girdling and burning them almost one at a time. Depending on the grains available and the resistance of the type of forest to clearing, the whole process can be a matter for an individual family or for large groups combining their efforts.

Only when farming can be carried on in fixed locations where the soil is extremely fertile or is repeatedly enriched by flooding—the Nile in Egypt and the Tigris and Euphrates valleys in Mesopotamia—can high-yield agriculture be practiced. When this occurs and surplus food becomes constantly available, not every one needs to be a farmer on a full-time basis. Craftsmen and other specialists are free to develop and exchange their products for the food that others produce.

Space and the Size of "Groups"

Enough has been said to indicate the nature of the interplay of physical environment, the food supply it provides, and the technology through which these natural resources are exploited. How many mouths can be fed in any given location at any given time may be highly variable or, alternatively, relatively stable. Clearly, these factors set some kinds of limits on the interactional probabilities, but they do so only by restricting population density itself. The number of persons who can be supported by a given environmental-technological complex (and who we shall assume are physically present) is merely the number available who potentially may interact. This is an outside limit, not a statement of actual relationships.

Considerable attention has been devoted to working out formulas by which the number of relationships (of all types, direct and indirect) can be computed, given any number of individuals. The most general statement for all possible relationships is that of Kephart (1950). He provides formulas, among others for calculating the number of set and pair events which can occur in a group of any size, which are extremely useful in dealing with complex systems. Restricting oneself to the number of pairs (dyads in behavioral science terminology) which can be formed from a given number, for example, 10, the expression, $N(N + 1) / 2$ gives the value sought, 10 $\times$ 9/2 = 45, while doubling the number in the group to 20 does far more than double the pairs, that is, it becomes 190. Where more than two people make up the relationships, as in set events, the number rises astronomically.

Consideration of these algebraic accelerations leads the formalists to despair of quantitative analysis. If the number of relationships in even a small group is so vast, how is it possible to make useful statements about a village of a few thousand, let alone the city of New York? Though means by which such complexity can be reduced to manageable proportions are available (Chapple 1941, Chapple and Coon 1942, Chapple and Sayles 1961), the fact is that many of such potential relationships are rarely, if ever, activated even in small groups. Male adults, for example, except the father or consort, are unlikely to interact with infants. The first cultural factor by which the multiplying effect of adding people is reversed derives from the constraints imposed by spatial distance. Though individuals are potentially able to interact according to formula, these interactions must occur in space, and space shapes the probabilities of the patterns of inter-action which may occur. Since each person occupies a location, the number of locations available might be considered very large *if* the individuals were physically in contact. But even packing them in like sardines drastically reduces the number who can be physically next to a single person, and the differential carrying power of speech, if the individuals are all about the same height, is also small.

More important, of course, close tactile association forces interaction patterns with the greatest emotional intensity. Given the personality and temperament characteristics of the constituent individuals, their inter-nal requirements for adjustment and equilibrium will result in an almost automatic trend towards spacing. Only by so doing can the frequencies, durations, and interactional patterns be brought into balance. Given the idiosyncratic needs of each person, distances from one another, close or far, are established and maintained for varying intervals of time throughout the day.

This movement of people to relative distances from one another can easily be demonstrated by observing any gathering where most of those present do not know each other. Like the Japanese paper flower unfolding to unforeseen shape when dropped into the goldfish bowl, collections of individuals rapidly assort themselves into spatial configurations, particu-larly where the area within which they are brought together has minimal natural or man-made barriers. Depending on the daily round of activities— and the interactions necessary to accomplish them—these distances shift. Yet, if photographs of the area and the locations of each person could be made regularly, it would be easy to trace out a repetitive network of inter-actions. The distances framing them would then reveal the influence which the cultural dimension of distance has on human affairs.

Once it is understood that this spacing process is a function of the nature of the interaction which any given personality will have with those others to whom he orientates, it then follows that spatial (and perceptual) limits are set on the number of people who are within interactional distance. As a consequence, the physical space, environmental or man-made, supplements these limits. Beyond that apple tree, over that ridge, or in the next apartment, there is a divide, a boundary, which minimizes the probabilities of interaction across it.

Groups as Spatial and Interactional Units

In subtitling the previous section, deliberate use of quotation marks around the word, group, was intended as emphasis on the ambiguity of its definition. Though numerical statements for algebraic purposes may make it sufficient to say that a given group had 10 members, the quality of "groupness" is omitted. Moreover, available information about a people or an animal species rarely provides much more than arbitrary statements about the size of "groups," again in quotation marks. Thus, for the lower primates, gibbons and orang-utans live in groups of four to six animals, chimpanzees and gorillas, seven to twelve, while baboons and other monkeys may have groups up to 100. Similar statements are often made about humans, particularly those with very simple technologies; alternatively, for animals and humans, calculations are made, based on field surveys, of the population density per square mile. So stated, however, the data are far more ambiguous than they seem since the term, group, or its supporting property of being a "member," is taken for granted.

Hamadryas baboons in Ethiopia habitually forage in small groups with their membership in the teens, *but* at night, hundreds come together in sleeping parties. So what is the size of the group or, when is a group a group—at night or during the day? Is it in the fall when the pinyon nuts have come to fruit, or in the summer when the buffalo come together to breed and can be slaughtered most economically?

If the problem of definition is to be attacked by utilizing the interplay of interaction and the cultural dimensions, then the dimension of distance provides a workable beginning. The first property of a group is that it is made up of individuals who interact with one another in what the sociologists like to call "face-to-face" relationships, *and* these interactions occur within a physical space which is separable from others, even though it may not be fixed and unmovable. Such a group might be a band which travels about its territory (or home range) together, or a village or settlement in which the individual members have permanent or semipermanent residence. For these groups, separateness is spatially defined. There is ascertainable distance between the group members and others, even if they wander about their home range. In a settlement with permanent houses, the boundaries are easy to determine. In addition, interaction between the members of the group takes place with a high and relatively constant frequency. Interaction with those not belonging to the group is erratic or takes place only at occasional periods during the annual cycle and is usually low in frequency.

The band (the term for a migrant group) and the settlement, whether or not it can be dignified by calling it a village, are thus spatially separated. Even where several of them may appear to be cheek by jowl, boundaries exist and can be geometrically (and interactionally) defined.

Internal to such larger spatially and interactionally separated groups, smaller groups exist—like the individual family or household—with similar boundaries. Varying by time of day or by the seasonal shifts which technology and the available food supply impose, these smaller groups, making up those units within which interaction is highest and distance lowest, come together with others. The group, therefore, in this sense, is a product of the cultural dimension of space, built on the human being's interactional properties. Its limits are spatial and interactional; they require definable boundaries or means of demarcating separateness by emphasizing that interaction outside is minimal.* So the tents surround a common fire and the traveling merchants in the Middle East go to their designated quarters in the caravanserai.

Topography, or land usable within the cultural potential, is a prime means by which boundaries are interposed. It creates barriers between one group and another, even though it is a commonplace to say that man can transcend all barriers. So he can, but most groups do become associated with areas in which natural boundaries set a limit to their territory. The Riffians of North Africa, living in their mountain valleys, regard the heights surrounding them as limits. The tribes or clans in the next valley are their enemies, though Riffian too. Even when groups are nomadic, boundaries of the territory are lived *within* that stream, those mountain foothills, or the swamps beyond. When groups split apart, the departing segment searches for a new territory with boundaries which, if fortunate, enclose a replica of the kind of land to which their technology is best adapted.

But boundaries are by no means permanent. As technology changes, the settlement pattern on the land changes with it. Groups break up and reaggregate in new locations with very different territorial boundaries. On the large islands off the Maine Coast, farming formerly was most important. The small communities, even the individual farmsteads, were often in areas of the island where lack of harbors made fishing unimportant. As farming became less and less profitable and lobster fishing far more lucra-

---

*More formally (Chapple et al. 1970) groups can be differentiated by using the following criteria— (1) Interaction measurements of the frequencies and durations of contacts between individuals within the group are high relative to their external contacts. (2) Only a small number of individuals within the group interact in external contacts to any significant degree. (3) A significant number of the contacts to or from persons outside the system fail to set off an internal interactional sequence (in other words, transitiveness does not occur and thus the thresholds at the contact points are high). (4) These interactional criteria are commonly reinforced by spatial separation (and sometimes by cultural sequencing), often within architectural or environmental boundaries, of the members of the group from other groups.

tive, the whole western part of Swan's Island, for example, reverted to woodland, and the use of bigger boats and year-round lobstering made small coves in other sections of the island unusable (Westbrook 1958).

Throughout history, human groups have chosen land both for its potential yield and for its defensibility. Though protection against enemy incursion was greatly facilitated when they learned how to construct walls or palisades or other types of barriers against wild animals or an enemy, almost every group has had to weigh the attractions of a given site for gaining food against the hazards of attack. The settlement on the shore was chosen with its back to the impenetrable forest so that enemies could come only by sea. The village was settled on the heights, with the fields, to which the inhabitants descended to tend their crops, situated below.

Extension of Definition of a Group and Other Cultural Dimensions

Although the dimension of space conjoined with interactional patterns provides a workable definition of a group, the sequence or order in which actions and interactions between individuals are learned and become established routines introduces a second cultural dimension, knitting groups together. Here territoriality is reinforced by conflict or opposition with another group, and the development of political institutions built on these sequences makes possible a larger unit, a tribe, or a kingdom, in which the interactions between disparate groups are mediated through interactions occurring within a hierarchical organization (Chapple and Coon 1942). Fried (1966) has discussed how such conflicts enlarge the group, either by establishing a set of relationships such that one becomes dominant over another, or as a means of uniting separate units to oppose an external threat effectively.

Such extensions of the definition of a group, provided one distinguishes between the various interactional, spatial, and ordinal levels within which interaction occurs at varying probabilities, are entirely proper and capable of discrimination by dimensional criteria. More complex is the problem to which Naroll (1964) addressed himself in a review article commented on by other anthropologists. Beginning with the statistical question, how to establish "ethnic" or "culture-bearing" units, each of which would be homogeneous and comparable with others so that enumeration of their characteristics could be conducted, he became involved with the boundaries which common symbols, artifact procedures, and the like might establish.

In the small group traditionally described by ethnographers, face-to-face interaction, space and territory, sequencing of activities and the institutions built on them, and language form an integral combination for such people as the Hopi of the American Southwest or the Polynesian Island people of Tikopia. But what of the United States or modern Euro-American society or the subcontinent of India split apart between political India and Pakistan? Are these one or many? Where can one cut to make a separation? Asking the question in this form does not make possible an answer, though Naroll and his commentators make clear that the number of categories or factors, analogous to the dimensions here described, can be at least delimited. For our purposes, such questions have to be more narrowly construed, restricting them to problems pertinent to each cultural dimension.

The Interactional Constraints of Architecture

The physical environment, as utilized by the technology available to a culture, does not control the probabilities of interaction occurring with anything like the precision which man-made space and his architectural productions can do. Certainly, the extremes of terrain or food supply, and simple technology, may severely limit the number of people who can form a group. Given the frequency and intensity of attempts by one group to dominate another, features of the landscape serve not only as boundaries but as protective barriers against attack. If these increase, the area of safety (provided food is available) may result in severe crowding of the inhabitants, with all its consequences.

If sources of food are distant, the need to cultivate or hunt on the territorial boundary or to cross its ill-defined periphery may accentuate the need to fight. Even within a group, the subgroup's territorial limits may be more easily invaded, wittingly or not, by neighbors crowded next to them in a mountain village or a narrow harbor on the sea, rather than in the open prairie. Primarily, the physical environment plus technology affects the number of people who can constitute a group; the patterns of interaction which make up the personality and temperamental characteristics of individuals are less obviously controlled.

Man's nearest relatives, the apes and monkeys, have a singular evolutionary blindspot. Unlike many of the lower animals, and even the social insects—ants and termites—they do not take steps to get in out of the rain. Mother grizzly bears dig deep hollows under trees before they have their young, woodchucks dig burrows, beavers build dams with attached houses, and prairie dogs construct elaborate subway tunnels connecting their homes. Man, apparently even in his earliest evolutionary stages, was always associated with caves, particularly during the glacial periods. But chimpanzees and gorillas, who weave a kind of sleeping nest before turning in for the night, patiently sit through downpour after downpour. In fact, Schaller (1964) mentioned that even with trees close by, mountain gorillas would not move even a few feet to avoid a drenching. Though one can argue that their thick matted hair provides a raincoat, shelter-seeking animals are equally well appareled.

The house, hut, or shelter, even a cave, sets physical boundaries for its occupants. In the tropics, it may be open on all sides with only the roof as shelter from sun and wind and rain, yet this covered area separates it from the outside. Additional spaces may be incorporated for family activities, like the porch or veranda for men to lounge on or children to play, but this represents a separate space with its own boundaries as well.

Whatever kind of shelter a people's technology makes possible, its size and shape influence, but do not fix, the number of individuals who can be accommodated within it. In poverty, crowding becomes endemic. A single room or shanty may house a large number of individuals, with only the sidewalk and the street providing more space. Except under these conditions, however, the areas which make up the house and such contiguous units as yards, outdoor hearths, and latrines have to be broken down into personal spaces (or territories) for the individuals occupying them.

An architectural unit can thus be regarded as a set of spaces with geometrical boundaries which can be fixed with relative precision. Spaces are not always, of course, restricted to a single use. They may have multiple purposes. Sometimes they are used for an interval of time during the day (for example, dining room serving as study or playroom) or perhaps only at particular periods within the annual cycle of a group's activities (for example, a school serving as a voting place). These various spaces are, therefore, further defined by the existence of time limits within which specific behaviors and people will be observed.

Among the Swazi, an African Bantu tribe where a man typically has several wives, Kuper (1963) pointed out that each wife had her own enclosure with separate sleeping, cooking, and storage huts shut off from others by a high reed fence. The man was expected to divide his nights equally with his wives, though it was the practice for him to use his mother's hut during the day as his place of operations. Within this family system, sexual interaction of man and wife must be carried on where and when the children were not present. Therefore, the young children slept with their grandmother, adolescent girls moved into huts behind their mothers, and brothers lived in barracks at the entrance of the homestead. Thus, the particular nature of the culture—dependence on the wives for agricultural production while the men looked after the cattle, together with the patterns of separation of *individuals* within the family to prevent, or facilitate, specific patterns of interaction—was framed within the differentiation of space.

The American suburbs are a fruitful source of data on the attempts of builders and architects to match spaces with what they presume are the patterns of interaction which individual personalities require. Take any real estate advertising page and, omitting such panegyrics as "designed with imagination and lived in with love," "oozing with charm," or "heaven for the kids," one finds listed such attractions as spacious living rooms, formal dining rooms, eat-in kitchens, family rooms, playrooms, rumpus rooms— even a mud room—together with studies or studios, master bedrooms and other bedrooms in sufficient number for each child to have his own. In simpler societies, each member of the family may have only a recognized but unmarked place in which to sleep or sit when not outside. By contrast, in the United States, if the family has means, each person's room is furnished to enable it to be used for many activities other than sleeping. As the phrases describing the rooms used in common suggest, the varied cultural activities of family members are concentrated and carried on only in separate rooms.

Reading the ads or, for that matter, visiting houses for rent or for sale demonstrates the remarkable differences in the ways in which the size and shape of available space within any given room influence the kinds of furniture which will fit inside and thus its potential uses by specific members of the family. In addition, the floor plan strongly affects the degree to which privacy can be obtained—it can force interaction to occur under almost every circumstance, or prevent it. The fashion of having living room, dining room, and kitchen as part of a single large space, separated only by counters, often with the door to the outside opening into the kitchen, makes the living room useless for someone who wants to be alone. Togetherness is built-in architecturally. By the time someone's temperamental limits have been breached, the whole family may be at the edge of emotional crises.

Differences in family architecture are found in groups with very simple technologies. The Negritos of the Andaman Islands, to the east of the Indian subcontinent, have a standard hut form. Two tall posts are erected in front and two shorter ones in the rear and rafters are slung across the frame on which mats made of leaves are attached. Each separate hut is occupied by a family, that is, father, mother, children, and any unmarried female relatives. Unmarried men and widowers live in a bachelor's hut of their own. Sometimes two brothers will make a larger hut, actually two individual huts joined together; sometimes, for protection, a family will build two huts face to face. In permanent encampments, a communal hut is often built around an open space. Though on the same model, it is much larger, and each family occupies a special location, marked off from its neighbors by short pieces of wood laid on the floor (Radcliffe-Brown 1922). Even where the "shelters" have no roof, as among some of the Australian groups, families around the campfire separate themselves from one another with branches or stones.

Though a study of house types and associated spaces in many societies indicates that there are fundamental similarities within a particular group, they are, nevertheless, by no means identical. Because a group has not attained the sophistications of the architectural profession does not mean that their houses are produced on a kind of cultural assembly line, each being the replica of the next. If the technology is extremely simple, or if a nomadic technology requires structural simplicity, as in the camel-hair tents of the Bedouin or the tepees of the American Plains, differentiation of space may not be obvious, but their uses, and rights to possession, are as specific as in a ranch-type house.

The Dimensional Uses of Distance

Since spatial distance and the scales derived biologically from its measurements play a significant part in structuring human relationships, each space must be identified and given its probabilistic values. An architectural layout must be prepared for each house, specifying the activities and interactions occurring in its component spaces. Each of its spaces can be treated independently, later to be related to actual observation. Since spaces are made up of distances, the probabilities of particular patterns of interaction occurring within them can be estimated, much as a house hunter does almost unconsciously—"this room is too small for all Johnny's things; I don't like having to eat our meals in one corner of the living room."

Besides the floor plan, therefore (and the elevations if the house is on more than one floor), the furniture and fixtures have to be sketched in in their approximate scale. For example, unless used by a very small child, the bed in an American bedroom will occupy a space at least six feet long and two and a half to three feet wide, while in Japan, where the sleeping mats and wooden pillows are put away during the day, the area provides opportunity for a multiplicity of spaces. Some activities require much more space (and furniture and fixtures) than others. In some American houses, even of the less expensive sort, architects often provide far more kitchen space than the housewife will ever use. Each space, therefore, becomes identified with a single activity or interactional relationship. Some areas have multiple uses and consist of several subspaces, not always geometrical duplicates of one another, since behavior overflows in some patterns across the ordinarily established boundaries.

In the small American bedroom, crowded with essential furniture, all interaction has to occur at the shortest intervals on the distance scale. The physical limitations prevent any separation of two persons by much more than seven feet. Going into the bedroom, therefore, means intense interaction; anything else has to be carried on in some other room or by including the adjoining hall. Propinquity of spaces, whether they are rooms or con-

necting passages, or differentiated areas within one large room, also determines the probabilities. Even if there is a large kitchen area with associated
dining space and a contiguous living room, location of the back door at one
end of the kitchen means that the children, coming in and out in endless
procession, can initiate to mother and interact repeatedly. Only by retreating to the bedroom and closing the door can she reduce the interaction and
minimize the influence of contiguity.

Ironically, given their affluent potential, many well-to-do suburban
dwellers in the United States have accepted an architectural design for their
homes in which privacy is almost unattainable. There are almost no rooms
into which retreat is possible. Kitchen, dining, and living rooms are part of
one large open space. What price the definition and maintenance of territory?
How can the individual control his interactions with others any more
than the Puerto Rican or Negro, literally crowded into a one-room cage in
the slums of New York?

Just as experiments with mice in the laboratory have shown, it is not
the number of individuals per square foot which is the deciding factor, but
the degree to which instability and stress in one's relations to others are
facilitated. Thus, the square foot area available to the housewife in the
upper income suburbs in the United States is very high, yet the emotional
(physiological) consequences from lack of privacy are the inability to develop a system of relationships in which the interactional needs of her personality can obtain a satisfactory outlet.

By contrast, the longer distance intervals also play an important part
in setting probabilistic limits. In societies where architectural elaboration
has resulted in the development of large public buildings, internal spaces
are not only designed to hold great numbers of people, but to reinforce
particular patterns of interaction and inhibit others. By prescribing distances to be traveled, in a church, a court room, or amphitheatre, elaborate
sequences of interaction, notably in rituals and ceremonies, can be more
precisely managed. Ordinarily, all three dimensions are utilized. Architectural space thus controls the movement of individuals, the orders in which
they initiate and interact, following prescribed forms, and the intervals of
time which must elapse (because of the time needed to walk slowly in a
processional, for example) before each new sequence of interaction can
begin.

The great cathedrals of the late Renaissance illustrate, in elaboration
of space and the sheer size of the structure, the segmentation of areas which
can be seen in any traditional church in the United States. Not only are the
distances of the floor surface instrumental in fixing the time needed for the
various stages of the processional, but the vertical heights—not merely the
gradual rise to the level of the altar, but the location of choirs at the end of
the church opposite the pulpit, each elevated above the congregation—serve

to make more effective the order of the interactional sequences between priest, choir and the people below.

Further, the larger the number of persons required to respond in the ritual, the higher the initiator must be above them. Otherwise the angle between each worshiper and the priest would become so slight that cues for responding would not be visible. Even where small groups are sitting in a room, the speaker is more effective and (unless very shy) feels more comfortable if he rises to talk to the others.

So the use of space can also establish the probabilities that particular patterns of interaction (not merely interaction per se) will occur. It is easier to dominate and gain control if one can gain an elevated position with regard to others. It becomes harder to initiate if the distance is great. The suppliant, approaching the chief of state, finds his anxiety and shyness increasing as he walks across the empty space to the great man's desk, since moving towards is, in itself, a reaction to disturbance. Thus, kings and presidents, paramount chiefs and corporation heads, almost inevitably have offices or reception halls whose longitudinal distance is far greater than the outer limit (25 feet) of the interactional distance scale. Variations towards the enormous room or the more intimate, smaller space reflect the personality and temperament properties of the ruler. Dictators like Hitler and Mussolini utilized extreme dimensions to set the stage for the ways they wanted the interaction to occur. Often, however, a series of intermediate rooms must be traversed, at each of which a closed door conceals whether the ruler is just beyond.

Not only is mere size, three-dimensionally, important, but propinquity of rooms or offices, or their separation, sets definable probabilities. In any large institution, governmental or business, the assignment of offices tends to shape the organizational system no matter what the theoretical relations in the formal organization chart are supposed to be. The subordinate whose office adjoins his boss has, by that very fact, a far better chance of building close relations with him than another, of higher rank, located on another floor or in another building. The perceptive observer can often determine the realities of organizational power simply by mapping the location of individual offices. Having to move one's office can thus be an occasion for joy or sorrow. The natural history of such shifts is potent evidence of the rise and fall of executives.

The Organizing Properties of Space

It is so easy to think of social groups as organizational forms with their own identity, independent of the spaces which they use or live in, that a whole literature, in anthropology as well as in sociology, economics, and political science, has grown up trying to reconcile the realities with the concepts. Best evidenced in discussions intended to define the family, similar difficulties arise when other human institutions are considered.

The problems are a consequence of the failure to take into account the cultural dimensions on which human groups are built and, in the case of space, the assumption that the family and the house are, in a sense, equivalent, or rather that the house is a mere carapace for what goes on within it. The facts are otherwise.

When anthropologists first began to try to understand how different family systems came about and, in particular, the rationale behind the ways in which descent and kinship were reckoned, they became aware that the location where a newly married couple took up residence played an important, if undefined, part in the kinship nomenclature. What were loosely called matriarchal or patriarchal groups often had the custom that the mother's or father's house, or community, was the proper place of residence, and inheritance of property often followed one or the other lines. Once looked at, however, exceptions were obvious and soon such terms as patrilineal, patrilocal, unilateral, bilateral—a variety of terms rapidly expanding at the present time—attempt to separate out the constituent components of these family systems without the use of quantitative interaction measures.

Since the minimal family unit of father, mother, and children, called the nuclear or immediate family, appeared to be the means through which continuity of family systems occurred and around which the kinship system seemed to be elaborated, the fact that it also occupied a set of spaces which could be called a household suggested that household and family were interchangeable. Thus, common residence was considered an essential element in the definition of the family in spite of the ease with which one can find, anywhere, numerous examples where families do not form households—the husband may live elsewhere and visit his wife or wives—and, of course, the many households, two men or two women living together, for example, which no one would call a family.

Keesing (1958) and Bohannan (1963) both emphasized the fundamental difference between propinquity and kinship, and Bender (1967) has extended their analysis much further. Though he is concerned with developing a reliable definition of a household in contrast to a family, he makes the point that there are three underlying elements which have to be considered. First, there is coresidence, not in the sense that the individuals are within interactional distance, but that they "live" together, which means that there is proximity in sleeping spaces and, though he does not say it, in a sustained frequency of interaction at minimum distance intervals. Second, he points out that the household involves the performance of "domestic" activities— the cultural sequences of preparation of the food, of maintenance and, if they are present, the care of children. These actions and interactions, to be discussed in the two chapters following, constitute a second cultural dimension. They are learned patterns of ordered actions, carried on either singly or with others, which set quantitative constraints on interactional probabilities. Bender also emphasizes that coresidence can occur with or without domestic activities being carried on. Finally, he emphasizes the absurdity of trying to describe the family, as many authors do, as existing to carry out functions or activities (function is the term used in anthropology, not in the mathematical sense, but as in the phrase, the function of the family is to . . . or the function of the stomach is to promote digestion). The literature is full of statements that the nuclear family can be defined as responsible for regulating sexual activity, reproduction, socialization of the young, and economic efforts. Bender cites examples, which can be multiplied almost indefinitely, where these are carried out through other individuals or institutions. Marriages often do not exist *within* the nuclear family; children are not always brought up by their parents and are often acquired by adoption rather than by reproduction, and economic cooperation is not likely to be an affair of the unit family.

Implicit in this critique, however, is the dimension of communication: the existence of common symbols whose referents are particular patterns of interaction too often taken for granted. The relationships of marriage, of paternity, of togetherness—whatever pattern or systems of patterns (and individuals carrying them out) are differentiated symbolically from what are observationally equivalent (sexual intercourse–marriage, sexual intercourse nonmarriage)—create symbols which set up constraints, the influences of which will be discussed in Chapters 13 and 15.

Similar problems arise in every other type of organization or institution. How does one define the properties of a state, a church, a corporation, or even a social club or secret fraternal order? Each may have some apparent central focus like the nuclear family—the sequencing of work, the conduct of rituals, or the maintenance of territory. But closer examination shows that, as in the case of family and household, they are constructed by the interplay of the cultural dimensions molding the actions and interactions of the individuals within them. These latter, through their embodiment in living individuals and their requirements for interactional outlet, are decisive in shaping the ultimate properties of the structures which result.

Land-Use Architecture

Although houses and buildings generally provide quite manageable spaces to which the distance scales can be assigned, the relationships between such units are also relevant in determining the probabilities of interaction.

Here proximity has to be supplemented by movement towards (sometimes only direction towards when buildings are close by one another). Obviously the ease with which the distance can be traveled makes interaction between some units easier and more frequent than for others.

Even in the simplest societies, camps or villages consist of separate units at varying distances from one another. Sometimes, as with the Andamanese, families occupy their individual places in the communal hut separated by only a few feet from their "next-door" neighbors. On the other hand, as the Andamanese again illustrate, they may occupy individual huts surrounding a dancing ground, with a public cooking place next to the bachelors' hut for the latter to do the communal cooking. When the Omaha Indians of the Great Plains of the United States went on their tribal buffalo hunts, they camped in a circle, each tepee having a fixed relation to its neighbor determined by the membership of its occupants in a specific kinship group (Fletcher and La Flesche 1911). In Greece, by contrast, the fifty or so houses of the village of Vasilika (Friedl 1962) are strung along a ridge, paralleling the main street. Though the two churches, the school, and the two coffeehouses face the street, and the aghora (market place) is situated between the two coffeehouses, the houses either face the street or 180 degrees towards Mt. Parnassus to the northwest. Since most houses have outbuildings scattered around them for storage or latrines and each such complex is surrounded by stone walls or wire fencing, paths wander erratically around neighboring houses with no clear-cut directional trends.

The settlement pattern of a group of people takes on a variety of forms, some laid out by custom with rigid geometrical limits like the camp circle of the Plains or the inner city of Washington designed by L'Enfant; others, like Vasilika, conform closely to the natural features of the landscape, clustering the houses on a rocky ridge so that maximum use can be made of cultivable soil. Actually, there is no useful single term to describe the study of the distribution of house units (and other building forms), either for man or for such lower animals as the prairie dog or the bower bird. The term "landscape architecture" traditionally has been limited to the modification of the features of the land surrounding the buildings. City or regional planning implies the design of something new, not the study of the dimensional relationships which make up the settlement, the town or city and all its spatial parts. Perhaps, with the geographers, one can speak of "land-use patterns," but since every aspect involves buildings, "land-use architecture" may be a better descriptive term.

Analysis of land-use architecture of any group is based upon using similar criteria of spaces (and distances between) that one uses in studying a dwelling or public building. In most instances, distances between separable units are far greater than the ranges within which interaction can be managed except by yodeling or amplifying the voice. However, in small communities, areas such as the aghora in Vasilika or the Andamanese dance ground make contact between members of the community almost inevitable.

Actually most small villages have their houses close together, though this does not mean that interaction will automatically occur. In a settlement pattern like that of the Andamanese, where all the huts face the dance ground and are usually open on all four sides, minimal privacy (the distance where another person's gaze does not invite interaction) is hard to find. In Vasilika, high walls and randomly distributed houses, a few without windows, "successfully limit the ability of members of any village household to see directly just what is happening in more than two or three neighboring households" (Friedl 1962). In New England farming communities where such deprivations were also deeply felt, the curious neighbor often had at hand a sea-going telescope. Privacy, in the more complete sense, assumes that one cannot be seen (or heard) by others. Thus, except within dwellings or in the bushes, a very considerable distance, often more than a mile, is required if one is not to be recognized by postural peculiarities, clothing, or other cues for the astute detective.

In land-use architecture, the distribution of buildings or other man-made or man-modified forms results in even more of a differentiation of types of activity and interaction than is possible within a single building. Churches, schools, fields, and pastures all have their assemblage of spaces which may vary depending upon the degree to which they serve several purposes. In addition, they are connected to one another by roads, paths, or trails which may be clearly demarcated as in present-day United States or may consist of little more than earth which has been tramped down by the footsteps of generations.

Extensions of Land-Use Architecture to the Country and the World

The human geographer, ecologist, or anthropologist can map out the relationships and interdependence of buildings and the individuals using them within a settlement pattern and assign the probabilities that interaction can occur, recognizing that a different order has been introduced by the need to traverse distance. And, of course, in all such studies of distance in any spaces, even the smallest, he is also concerned with observation of the activities and interactions of the constituent individuals to relate their actual frequencies and patternings to his probabilistic estimates. In studying settlements, he can begin to see how the natural environment and its resources (and topographical limitations) are interrelated with the land-use architecture of the group.

The same principles can be extended to the interdependence of communities where the time it takes to travel distance is determined by the stage of technological development of transportation or in the availability of means of communication. Until very recently the distribution of communities in extended land-use architecture resulted from their interdependence because of the need to exchange raw materials or finished goods, to obtain wives or husbands, to raid one another, or to carry on other activities not found in a restricted land-use architectural unit. Specialization grew, as we shall see in the two chapters following, not only within the community but between communities. Their relationships were not merely the reciprocal ones of trading, but of dominance and exploitation through conquest.

Though it is a commonplace to talk of the "pull" of the cities for those living in rural surroundings, it may not be realized that similar "pulls," differing for cultures, have gone on since recorded history. Traders, pilgrims, freebooters, landless men have traveled from place to place, singly or in groups, following the natural confluences of the settlement patterns. Whatever the distances involved, the difficulties of the terrain or the available means of transportation, the trips took time—hours, day, weeks, and years. Even if the automobile on high-speed turnpikes and the jet airplane create an entirely different tempo within which interactional events can now be arranged, it is still true that a significant level of time elapses before either the next activity can be performed or an interactional contact can be initiated to the person towards whom one is traveling. Moreover, the longer the interval of time which elapses before getting from A to B, the greater the chances that other activities and interactions will intervene, interrupt, and possibly deflect the voyager (even across the village square) from his intended haven. So Ulysses took 20 years to return to Penelope, and many a traveler never makes it.

In theory, communication systems such as the telephone or the intercom (apart from written documents) transcend architectural and interactional boundaries. So highly developed is the communication network that one might suppose that the more "primitive" face-to-face interaction is no longer necessary. Certainly, messages can be transmitted from person to person with remarkable speed, but they contribute very imperfectly to the nature of the emotional (and behavioral) adjustment of the individuals concerned. The human animal, like all animals, depends on the nonverbal as well as verbal patterns of interaction (if the sound signals of the lower animals can be classified as verbal) to maintain his equilibrium. From his reactions to the reactions of others in the course of interaction, he is able to establish to some degree the emotional significance of the relationships and their predictability. The information aspects of the messages associated with the inter-action are then "interpreted" from these "data."

The great contribution of modern technology in facilitating interaction is not the telephone—even with the possibility of combining it commer-cially with a television viewer—but the remarkable increase in the fre-quency of travel which the jet airplane makes possible. Statesmen, business executives, as well as smaller fry, are constantly on the move from place to place where relationships involving interpersonal adjustments are at stake. The telephone, whether the message is carried by cable or by radio, is merely a temporary mediator, limited in the length of time it can be used and in the completeness of the interaction which it makes possible. Dis-tance, which prevents face-to-face interaction, is still the barrier to be overcome.

As land-use architectural complexes become more closely interrelated and the means of travel faster, the physical spaces and the distances between, which represent the architectural configuration of an individual, may cover many miles, even the whole globe. The executive of a large oil com-pany, living in a suburb of New York City, may have little or no interaction with any of its inhabitants. Not only are his friends and family distributed widely across the United States, but his organizational life can involve constant travel to Southeast Asia and the Near East, or to Europe, or the oil centers of the Americas.

On the other hand, even for individuals far less traveled, this easier mobility does enable people to escape from the close control of an isolated rural community where the lack of an exit (except a permanent one) forces them to adjust even though the consequences are a serious disturbance to emotional balance. Small towns are frequently looked upon with nostalgia by those no longer living in them. For those who may have once tasted freedom and have been drawn back by interactional forces, the home town can warp the incompatible personality beyond belief. So too can the great cities, or the constant travel between Singapore, Bahrein, Tlemcen, and Tulsa. But cities do have one abiding virtue: the sheer weight of the probabil-ities for encountering complementary personalities is far greater where there are far more people, provided there is a means by which this explora-tion can be focused on the individual's needs.

Not only does distance directly inhibit the expression of certain pat-terns of interaction and facilitate others, but its mere interposition at any sizable interval also means that the likelihood of even coming into contact with a particular person is significantly reduced. History is full of dramatic instances where someone arrived too late—Western movies to the con-trary—and the barriers of the environment are remarkably complicated by architectural forms and by land-use architecture at its present high techno-logical development. Thus, distance apart affects the probabilities that two or more persons can be coincident in space at the same time. Although endless effort is taken in an industrial civilization to overcome these obstacles, the vagaries of transportation failures are all too commonplace. But these accidents are interferences in interactional contacts between persons who are trying to synchronize their movements to meet. How much less likely is it that one person, hero or heroine, will in real life meet that other person? In urban communities, they can live in the same apartment building for years without ever encountering each other.

Potentials of Building and Land-Use Architectures

Architects and urban and regional planners have long been intuitively aware that what they do, among other things, affects the relationships of persons. In varying degrees, the schools which educate them have tried to achieve a balance between the aesthetics of design and their impact on interpersonal adjustment. Too often, for lack of objective tools for interactional analysis, art is the winner. The use of space and the movement of individuals and the activities they are to perform are usually treated as problems in traffic flow and efficient space utilization rather than as problems created by the needs of the human personality. Only in this sense does "form follow function." Some house designs, of course, do result from fairly courageous (but subjective) attempts to diagnose these requirements. In larger buildings, usually only the preferences of the top management are taken into consideration.

There probably exists, to date, only one attempt to combine architectural design and interactional requirements: a research study for a new pediatric hospital as part of the Tufts-New England Medical Center. For almost three years, an anthropologist, Donald A. Kennedy, and an architectural designer, Delbert Highlands (1965), worked in conjunction with the hospital staff in making detailed analyses of the various activities which have to be carried on and the interactional patterns which together make up the work process. Since this is a teaching hospital and not merely a children's hospital separate from a medical school, the design called for consideration of teaching and research facilities as well as diagnostic and treatment areas for patients.

Though the study covers too many factors to be adequately summarized here, it is worth emphasizing that the two men began with the characteristics of the children themselves and the age ranges to be treated. They also realized that continuing relationships of the parents to their children in various settings had to be provided. In addition, they described minutely the ways in which medical technology and differential patterns of treatment for various illnesses prescribed sequences of action between members of the staff. The implications of all these elements aided the definition of the segmentation and combination of spaces required. Even the different amounts of interaction and the relative degree of tactile or visual communication, varying with children of different ages, were taken into account.

As a consequence, their recommendations for ultimate architectural translation of their findings were based on the combined factors of distance scales *and* work flow sequences necessary to the accomplishment of the hospital's activities. As a beginning, the implications of this study for the various forms of architecture are vast, for what they made explicit is the availability of biological yardsticks through which the properties and requirements of the human personality can be built into the design. Granted this was not done as specifically as suggested here, nor did they have the neurophysiological background of the many studies on exploration, curiosity, arousal, as parts of the orientation process, on which I have briefly commented. Yet what they had to say can be put into that framework and, thereby, given a much more solid scientific foundation.

What they imply and what this book's discussion of the constraints of spatial distance tries to outline is that architects, at some future date, will become as much concerned with the physiological and behavioral dimensions of their subject as with the aesthetic. As Suzanne Langer points out, in the first of the three volumes she is writing on *Mind: An Essay on Human Feeling* (Volume I, 1967), "works of art exhibit the morphology of feeling"; therefore, they become effective in the ways in which they organize, at different levels, the constituent emotional states which contribute to the form. In her view, and from the point of view of this book, though art may be regarded as one aspect of mental life, life is not divorced from but grounded upon biological rhythms and their physiological properties.

Architecture, far more than the other arts and almost in contrast, requires a familiarity with the hypothalamic–limbic–reticular system and its specific relevance for the manipulation of space—distances, surfaces, and solids as well as color and shading—in order to combine an emotional–aesthetic and emotional–interactional resultant in the design. Though the first of these fundamental elements is discussed in Dr. Langer's book, approaching it from the point of view of philosophy and moving to the biological, the second, in a parallel way, starts from human interaction and then considers it as part of a total biological system.

Even today, though much research is needed on the orientation process and its perceptual components in order to make more precise the spatial distance scales which interactional intensity can presently define, the means for measuring interaction itself, for determining the probabilities of emotional impact within geometrically defined spaces, are at hand. Surely the consequences of crowding or of isolation are sufficiently evident in the human condition to emphasize the importance of establishing differential criteria, capable of measurement, not only in building design but also in plans for urban reconstitution, too often concealed as slum removal.

It has often been remarked that the cultural patterns of the underprivileged misuse the space provided for them. On the other hand, since these spaces are contrived and built with minimal interactional awareness, it is not to be wondered at that, even if new, the buildings facilitate no interactional reorganization. This cannot be done by architecture alone, but spatial distance is a powerful cultural means, if only one, through which a more adequate adjustment, interactionally and emotionally, can be achieved for those constrained within it.

Chapter 11

Dimensional Constraints
of Cultural Sequences

Ordering or sequencing of human activities and interactions is so inevitable that it is likely to be dismissed without considering its profound implications. Yet the fact that one action follows another and that such sequences of acts have definite and measurable temporal properties suggests that something more than "So what?" should be the proper question. For if a sequence involves more than one person, then the temporal order in which they interact (if interaction is required) is fixed. The first individual who has to act is the initiator and he who responds, if there are others in the chain, in turn initiates to the person next in line.

Even if each one acts only once in such a sequence, the initiative variables are immediately set in motion—the when, and for how long of the initiator, the possible variations in duration of a latency of response, if such occurs, and so on. The order may be the result of endogenous sources, internal to the individual initiating; it can be combined with the movement of an external object—the action involving handing the second person a piece of cake, or imposed by an external, technological process in a work flow which has undergone a division of labor so that two persons are needed to complete the job. A different type occurs when two people sing a duet. Here, the musical composition prescribes an alternating order of action (singing) and of silence while waiting for one's turn.

The all-pervasive character of such ordered sequences, in every cultural setting, depends on the division of labor. This may arise at any time when more than one action has to be performed; in other words, where there is a sequence of steps needed to accomplish a given result. How such divisions of labor arise is a matter for later consideration; here it is sufficient to point out that where they occur, one person occupies the first position, another the second, and so on, to the last. Each of the interactional steps or relationships is, therefore, equivalent to each of the others *except* for its position in the sequence. Each relationship can be further varied by the quantitative values of its component interactional variables. In consequence, each sequence is dimensional in form. It is made up of an ordered array of individuals such that the dimensional distance between two people depends on the number of relational steps between them. One further property of such a sequence is that the dimensional array makes all the persons contained within it mutually dependent on one another *and* imposes also, a separation from all others at its beginning and ending steps.

The Biological Foundations of Sequencing

The actions the human animal performs may appear to be capable of almost infinite variety, but they are more properly regarded as variations on a set of action "themes." These are probably little more in number than the repertoire of fixed action patterns of the nonhuman species. Take walking as an example. Grant that locomotion using the legs involves walking on a level surface, climbing, running, doing the goose-step, dancing in all its forms, and so on. Yet each can be reduced to temporal sequences of contraction and relaxation of the particular muscles used in locomotion—the only way any of these action patterns can be accomplished. Similarly, one can establish other fundamental action patterns—talking, feeding, drinking, fighting, mating, nursing, defecating, and so on. However much the learning process differentiates them, each has a basic core of underlying muscle pattern sequences.

In the human, and in other higher mammals, the capacity to vary the temporal sequencing of the basic action patterns is largely the result of the remarkable development, in these species, of feedback control by which delays or accelerations of the component muscle units can be established. Yet even though differential control is mediated through central nervous system mechanisms, it is limited by the constraints of the human anatomy.

The importance of the action sequence to the organism, at any level of complexity, is obvious enough if one considers what would happen if sequencing did not exist. If definite temporal patterns did not occur, as Marler and Hamilton (1966) pointed out, and different acts occurred at random, the skeletal-muscular system would be in a state of chaos. Far more disordered than any type of muscular dissociation seen in severe neurological disorders, one might find opening the mouth to bite followed by extension of the right leg—the reader's imagination can easily supply far more incongruous sequences.

But these temporal behavior sequences also make up the repertoire or ethogram through which the fundamental biological rhythms are expressed—whether circadian or the faster frequencies. It may seem a commonplace to talk about the rhythms of human activity. The point has long been made that individuals try to adopt an appropriate rhythm for almost every action pattern. Like the rhythmic patterning of such basic behavioral categories as walking, work and play, all types of communication styles built up around the interactional beats are, when one thinks about it, temporally sequenced and organized. Perhaps their omnipresence has caused the lack of careful quantitative studies. Further, to be accurate requires the use of automatic recording devices with enough observers to cover the entire range of behavior patterns over long periods of time, and then there are the complexities of analysis, now manageable with modern computers. In any case, rhythm has not really been seen as integral to *all* aspects of biological inquiry.

Research has also been hampered by the predominant interest in the effects of specific stimuli in eliciting response and, more generally, in studies of learning and conditioning. Yet these temporally patterned sequences were the primary units for such studies since, as Bullock (1961) pointed out, except for such simple actions as blinking the eye (perhaps not even that) or the scratch reflex of a dog, the timing of the ensuing action sequence and, ordinarily, what it was composed of, was endogenously controlled. Bullock thought of the stimulus as a trigger, an extension of the idea of synchronizer, with the rhythm of the actions that followed in the sequence operating independently. He said:

> it seems at present likely that for many relatively complex behavioral actions, the nervous system contains not only genetically determined circuits but also genetically determined physiological properties of their components so that the complete act is represented in coded form and awaits only an adequate trigger, either external or internal.

The Cultural Action Sequence

Where any activity is performed by a single individual, its cultural sequencing effects, in dimensional terms, do not begin unless its consequences, once completed, are to elicit a response from another. Thus the housewife, following the steps outlined in a cookbook for making a chocolate cake, is carrying on a sequence of actions culturally prescribed, each with different movements, different ingredients, different material objects like bowls, measuring spoons, and egg beaters, plus the final timing in the stove. However many steps are involved, she does them herself. Only the completed masterpiece, brought to the dining room table, results in its recipients responding by falling to.

Except for activities where only a single step is needed, the component steps of any cultural sequence can be assigned to more than one person. This is a division of labor, a term which, for the purposes of this book, should rather be called the division of cultural sequences. It prefaces and makes possible the cultural sequencing of individuals in dimensional form. Present-day ethnographic literature is singularly lacking in straightforward description of activities or events, the "who does what, with whom, when, where and how long and how often" which Chapple (1949) called the anthropological criteria for field studies. For this reason, a description by Raymond Firth (1936) of preparing a meal on the Polynesian island of Tikopia in the Pacific Ocean will be used by way of illustration:

> A considerable amount of cooperation takes place among the members of a household at such (a) time, and each plays a part in the division of labour (for example), breadfruit pudding is being prepared in Nukutaukara, the house of Pa Maviva. . . . The breadfruit are roasted on the oven-stones by two women, his married daughters (his wife being dead), while in the dwelling house a son, Rakeimuna, grates coconut and proceeds to express the cream. The breadfruit when cooked are peeled by the women in the oven-house and brought in steaming hot, wrapped in pilaka leaf. The father cuts them up and puts them in a wooden bowl, assisted by one of his daughters, while Mairuja, another son, cuts a pestle and begins to pound the food. After some minutes the father takes a spell at this work, and later the son takes the pestle back, the mashing of the fruit demanding considerable energy. Mairuja calls after a time, "Are the breadfruit ended?" His sister in charge of them answers, "Yes." Then turning to the cream producer, he asks, "Finished or not?" "Wait a while," his brother replies. Soon both jobs are ended, and the men combine, the one squeezing his cream over the pudding while the other continues his pounding. The father meanwhile is tearing up pilaka leaf to hold the portions. A younger son, who has taken no part in the more energetic operations, passes him half a coconut shell, which he covers with banana leaf and then uses as a spoon to scoop out the food. Mairuja, his pounding over, now licks the pestle clean, while the other members of the family hand round portions on their leaf platters. The meal is then begun.

Of course the whole sequence could be carried out by one person, though far more slowly. Yet the division of labor, beginning with the preparation of the breadfruit and coconut through the several stages of the cooking until the meal is ended, not merely involves the performance of specific operations but each of them varies in the length of time required for it to be completed. Further, and the essential characteristic of all types of cultural sequences, each stage has to be finished before the next one is begun.

This does not mean that all cultural sequences are made up of single stages arranged in a linear chain. Several stages may come together (like branches of a tree) to be combined in the stage which follows. These sub-stages are performed at the same point in time in the cultural sequence. Pa Maniva must wait until his daughters bring in the roasted breadfruit; only then can he begin cutting them up. His son, Mairuja, has to wait until the pieces have been put in the wooden bowl by his father and one of his sisters before he can start to pound the food with the pestle he has prepared. In the highly developed technologies of industrial society, the term "work flow" is applied to all such sequences. The term "flow," used for the highly syn-chronized movement of materials or paper (or even people in the hiring sequence of an employment office), provides an image of the direction of a "stream" or "current" moving with varying velocities from its beginning to its end.

Wherever an individual cultural sequence becomes segmented and different persons perform one or more separate steps, the division of labor within the flow sets up requirements for interaction. In particular, a chain of initiatives follows the direction of the flow, with each preceding person initiating to the next one in line. He then begins to act (and thus responds) when something is handed to him or when his predecessor ends his specific operation. It is important to emphasize that the initiative is often reversed. Mairuja, waiting for the breadfruit to be finished, asks his sister if they are done, as a reaction to a delay in the sequence, a latency or lack of response (until he brings it to an end by initiating).

In addition, in most such sequences, the *state of the process* signals to the experienced participant that the next step is ready to begin. The women have learned to take the breadfruit off the fire when it is properly roasted and peel it so that Pa Miniva can work with it. No overt orders (initiative) are thus required. The more efficient and highly synchronized the flow, and the more skillful and highly trained the individuals, the less need for verbal initiative. The members of a work-flow team operation are signaled to act in many ways by the varying states of the process—the color of the iron being heated which tells the smith when he can begin to hammer or forge, the flutter of a sail indicating a shift of wind causing the main sheet man to trim the sail to the precise point when the flutter stops (and other crew members to follow with other operations), the run of a blue marlin towards the sport fishing boat warning the man at the wheel to change his course and the speed with which the boat is traveling.

Miller (1958) proposed that such actions, triggered off by stages in a work-flow sequence, be called "situational interactions," since they may occur without verbal or gestural initiative. Many cultural activities do provide or require an interval of delay before the next person acts because the material being worked on is not quite ready for his action or initiative. Thus, on a sailing vessel in a race, putting the helm over automatically when the wind hauls initiates a chain of actions on the part of the crew. The helmsman definitely takes the initiative under such circumstances, and the crew is expected to handle the sails, trim sheets, and so on—all in silence. Therefore, Pa Maniva's married daughters take the breadfruit off the fire and start to peel by knowing from its appearance and the passage of time that it is done.

In any case, whether it helps the reader to remember that the total context of environment, technology, and the differentiated patterns of a culture may provide noninteractional "situations," there is no question that, both for animals and humans, actions can be triggered off by stimuli derived from the "external environment" in the broadest sense. Dwellers on the Great Plains, seeing a thin funnel-shaped cloud stretching up to the skies in the distance, have signal enough. They do not have to rely on the shouted cry of "tornado!" to get the family into the tornado cellars.

But this does not involve some alternative definition of the initiative variables. The situation, in Miller's sense, is an external stimulus which starts or continues the interaction without prior action on the part of another. A significant change in the process (of weather as far as Kansas is concerned) becomes evident and signals that someone should take the initiative for the next step.

Such cultural-technological situations are often used as legitimizers for taking the initiative or interrupting and dominating. Providing the technological or environmental situation is important enough, breaking in with the message justifies such actions by a subordinate. Hence this is a common ploy for all kinds of personalities, young or old who need attention (interaction). The little boy of fable cried "Wolf," though once too often. If his judgement is wrong (as he found out) and the environmental or technological situation does not call for action by those interrupted or initiated to— apart from their immediate reactions against him—habituation to his incompetence in judgement or prevarication happens quickly. The next time his actions produce no consequences. It is grist to the tellers of tales when such prophets confute the doubters; it is also a source of drama in the temperamental reactions which such situations elicit.

Among humans, such sequences characterize every aspect of culture. Ethnographers—and anthropologists generally—once used the term "material culture" to refer to the objects and techniques of making tools, constructing huts or houses, preserving food—all those sequences which, simple or complex, make up what is called technology. But such a classification is too restrictive. When the priest celebrates mass or a teacher begins a period of classroom instruction, the action sequence may involve objects, even techniques, which have resemblances to those which might be called technological, but are not ordinarily so classified. In fact, there are many sequences made up entirely of actions and interactions in which neither techniques nor objects are to be found. These are also culturally prescribed and usually learned by individuals during their early years of maturation, for example, the stylized behaviors used in greeting a newcomer, or in military drill. Each culture has a multiplicity of patterns in which first one person does something and one or more persons follow this action by another. Whether they be called rituals or manners or even "standard operating procedures," they have in common the cultural sequencing of the actions and interactions of individuals.

Many of these sequences can also be performed by a single individual, typically in technological situations as well as in what have been called ritual techniques (Chapple and Coon 1942). Others, however, compelled by technological limitations, force a division of labor and, commonly, interaction. Building a house of any size, using large logs as the basic material, can be almost impossible for a single individual. An Andamanese hut or an Eskimo snow house can be, but is not often, built by one person if others are around. Managing a huge seine to surround and trap a school of herring is impossible to do alone.

Evolutionary Implications of the Division of Labor

Among the lower primates, division of labor involving technological pursuits is almost completely absent. Chimpanzees and gorillas weave a crude kind of nest for sleeping, but never as a two-man job. Though chimpanzees, as Goodall (1962) described them, availed themselves of simple tools as aids in getting food (or for attack on occasion), this was again an individual pursuit. Termites are a great delicacy for the chimpanzees of the Gombe Stream Reserve. Seeing a termite hole, the chimpanzee scrapes away the thin layer of soil with index finger or thumb, finds a grass stalk or piece of vine about 12 inches long or trims down longer ones if need be, pokes it into the termite hole, leaves it in for a brief moment, pulls it out (the termites grip it with their mandibles) and picks them off with his lips. Goodall reported that chimpanzees had definite preferences for particular vines or grasses, often carrying them over considerable distances to test out likely termite hills and, if they became bent in use, turned them around or broke off the bent portion until they got too short.

If chimpanzees had the propensity for dividing the work which characterizes humans, one can imagine them setting up a work flow sequence like energetic vacationists preparing a campfire for their evening meal. Some chimpanzees would be assigned to examine termite hills and make the holes accessible. Others would be out collecting and shaping stalks of the proper size. The most skillful termite fisherman would be moving from hole to hole, taking the stalks proffered by those preparing them, removing and distributing the haul and, when necessary, requesting new or reshaped stalks from those assigned to stalk collecting.

However fanciful such a picture of a chimpanzee "assembly line," its contrast with the rigorously individualistic reality which Goodall describes emphasizes a point that Kortlandt (1962) has made with considerable persuasiveness. He, too, has studied the chimpanzee in the field; he contrasts their unorganized patterns of technical adjustment with such carnivorous, hunting animals as wolves. Wolves clearly divide responsibilities in hunting (not simply an age or sex differentiation). Some members of the pack lie in wait and others take turns in driving the animal towards those who will do the killing. He believes that animals who must combine to bring down large and fast moving prey through closely synchronized teamwork, with different tasks assigned to different members of the pack, are the precursors of Homo sapiens. He thus supports other human paleontologists who argue for a carnivorous primate, a hunter of large animals—and not their vegetarian cousins still surviving—as the ancestral form in the direct line of evolutionary succession. If only wolves had had hands to work with, how different Red Riding Hood and her adventures would have been!

In contrast to the individualization to which a vegetarian existence habituates both apes and monkeys (occasional instances of the eating of small animals do not alter this essential property), the carnivorous animals, including man, not only have developed a division of labor within at least some of the species, e.g., wolves and lions, but all appear to share the prey with other members of the group. Hence, as Hockett and Ascher (1964) pointed out, among animals who hunted as a group, "Their visual attention must be divided between the motions of the quarry and those of the other participants."

The constraints which the division of labor thus imposes suggest it is a primary factor (though there can be no *one* criterion) in the development of language—of flexible, vocal-auditory communications systems on the basis of which human culture became elaborated. If close coordination of the acts of the members of a group is to be achieved, the messages (verbal and nonverbal) transmitted to others (as in coordinating a group hunt of big game) must be both recognizable and quite varied in their information content. Such messages are too complex and involve too many shadings to be communicated by calls—defined as containing a single and unambiguous signal. Though various linguists and anthropologists interested in the revolution which the appearance of language represents, using Hockett and Ascher's term, have assumed that the manufacture of tools is a primary requirement (including these authors), it seems more likely that the division of labor, and the teamwork enforced by its existence, is a better candidate.

Cultural Sequencing as the Organizing Factor in Teamwork

The necessity for individuals to synchronize their actions and inter-actions within the framework of cultural sequences clearly imposes constraints, not only on *who* will take part, and in what order, but also in the durations of the action step each person performs. As the members of the sequence or flow are able to carry out each step with precision so that the following person can act equally expeditiously, teamwork results. As is obvious, team activities of every cultural type are built upon such divisions of labor. Thus, the dimension of cultural sequencing (called work flow in modern technological situations in business and government and in other institutions where similar technologies are used) is the source on which teamwork is based. Clearly, Pa Maniva's family manifested teamwork in making the breadfruit pudding. It is common usage in the United States and many other countries to regard the concept of teamwork as something far more extensive in its application than to be restricted solely to sports.

Also, the term, as commonly understood, places the leader in a structured context of sequences and minimizes making him all-important. Not that he actually is unimportant as we shall see later; rather, teams (and teamwork) can operate effectively only in terms of the degree to which the individuals constituting them have mastered their part of the work, or game, or ceremony, and the other members of the team are equally skilled and capable of precise synchronization. Here personality and temperament factors become fundamental, particularly where there is a premium on efficient synchronization.

In today's industry, where conveyors or other types of automated systems move the work from one operator to the next, the simple pattern in which one person in the line physically passes the work (and initiates) to his neighbor who responds by taking it, and so on down the line, is not often found. Where this is not the case, the primary sources of emotional–interactional disturbance occur either when the prior operator delays finishing his work, thus holding up the next in line or, alternatively, produces at such a fast rate that those to whom the work goes next cannot keep up. The classic example of such a situation is the sad plight of an inspector in the bank wire test room, described by Roethlisberger and Dixon in their account of the various studies carried on at the Western Electric plant in

Hawthorne, Illinois (1939). Although most of the findings in the book have been popularized and modified by later work, the bank-wire study has never received the attention it deserves. It was the first, and still remains one of the very few, significant anthropological investigations of an industrial organization unit in the literature.

The work-flow was, in essence, very simple. A wireman fastened wires to terminals on a number of banks—frames on which the terminals were serially arranged. A solderman then soldered the wires to the terminals and, once this was completed, an inspector tested the terminals to be sure that the soldering connections were properly done. The production rate depended on each of the three operations being performed at the correct pace, the work flow being complicated by the fact that, apart from the foreman, the department was made up of nine wiremen, three soldermen, and two inspectors. In the many months during which this room was under daily observation, one of the inspectors left and a new man was brought in. He was very slow to learn, clumsy in using the test apparatus and quite unable to keep pace with the wiremen and soldermen in their rate of output.

Using a test set requires knowing how to connect it. For several weeks while he was having trouble, the observer noted that four wiremen were sitting along the radiator watching him (and waiting for him). Whenever a wireman was ready for inspection, he called to the inspector to come over to his bench. Soon they began initiating to him when he was working on someone else's work, then dominating him when he protested, to get him to stop and thus to confuse him. Even when he was able to keep up, they began to play tricks on him, changing the adjustment on the test set when he was not looking in order to slow him down. On occasion, the hapless inspector started to inspect a set before it was ready. As far as one can tell from the incidents reported, he was then dominated by the wireman (or solderman) and told to stop. His only means of reprisal was to start a conversation by making what the observer called a "pompous speech," and even then he was unable to persist against the competition.

Since neither side was able to compel the other to stabilize their rates to achieve a balanced output, the inspector, far more vulnerable to the deliberately erratic shifts in pace forced upon him, took refuge in another chain of contacts (to his supervisors) in an effort to try to force the others not to disturb him so severely. This resulted in the supervisor's supervisor (in the Inspection Department) going to his counterpart in Production, who had wiremen and soldermen under his jurisdiction. In turn, he went to the group's supervisor to relay the complaint which, when delivered, caused an uproar. Shortly thereafter, the inspector was transferred and peace was restored.

By its very simplicity, this case has the great virtue of illustrating the interdependence of each person's rhythm of actions and the emotional–interactional patterns of his relations to others within a given situation.

Here the work flow made necessary the order in which initiative could be taken. On the other hand, both solderman and inspector could detect, from the wireman's progress, when to begin without the latter saying a word.

During the interval of performing the actions making up the operation of wiring, each wireman was trying to stabilize his work rhythm. The universal desire to work at one's *own* pace is based on the differences in tempo which individuals possess and the amount of variation they can manage through the learning and training process. Tempo can be determined both for interaction and for the rapidity with which small or large movements of the various muscle systems can be performed. Breaks in the rhythm caused by erratic flow of materials, by difficulties in using equipment, or in performing the operations (which can be due either to technical problems or lack of skill) require steps, usually interactional, to try to remedy the problem. Even where the trouble is technical, the division of labor again requires that another interactional chain be set in motion. In the event of a single flow like an improper machine adjustment, interaction will occur between the foreman, maintenance man, materials handler, and so on.

Deviations in the rate of flow can be technological in origin or more simply a consequence of the inability of the team members to synchronize. Once they appear, interactional intervention must take place through other cultural sequence or work-flow chains of which the individual whose position dimensionally is the source of trouble is also a part. Such interventions, by the foreman, for example, are again derived from situational evidence— direct observation of the work flow or analysis of individual output and quality records. These, and more generally the interrelations of cultural sequences within any organizational system, are the subject of the chapter following. Here, we must return to the properties of cultural sequences themselves.

Boundaries of Cultural Sequences

By necessity, a single cultural sequence has a beginning and an end. It thus limits the number of people involved. No matter how many internal steps the division of labor provides, at some point the sequence is finished and a discontinuity occurs. This is defined by change in route, tempo, and persons taking part, usually with an appreciable interval of time elapsing before a second chain begins. Whether a copper cooking pot is being produced, finished, and offered for sale, or whether a preliminary rite, anticipatory to the next ceremony in validating a marriage, is ended, an interactional discontinuity, quantitatively defined, takes place.

Within a single sequence then, the individual (or individuals) at the first position initiates to those coming after him. They must respond before completing their stage of action and initiating in turn to those who make up the next link. Where sequences prescribed by a technological process involve the movement of materials, of paper, or of people, the direction of the flow of initiatives and the timing of actions and interactions may be relatively tightly fixed.

The sequence of positions in any flow may vary in number from a minimum of two (i.e., a team of two and thus only one ordinal dimensional unit) to 20, 30, or even more separated steps, particularly in industrial organizations like clothing factories where difficulties in positioning cloth in the sewing machine prevent automation, and the many component parts which go into making a coat lengthen the time required. Yet in each case, short or long, the sequence has its boundaries; there is a first and last position clearly demarcated within it.

Though quickly summarized, it is the temporal factor which provides the primary criteria for discontinuities. However, in highly engineered and automated plants, routing and geographical distance aid in further differentiating the boundaries. Thus, spatial distance very obviously influences the probabilities of interactional boundaries coming into being, and the two cultural dimensions are highly interrelated (as is communication). For purposes of exposition, the other dimensions must be neglected here, and the time elapsing between sequences (and often the tempo internal to each) must be given more explicit consideration.

Cultural sequences, after all, are by no means capable of infinite extension. Whether one is concerned with production (as in the industrial situation), with the care and training of children, the conduct of ritual, or the attack on the enemy, the dimensional character of each is limited by an ending, a completion of the sequence—and the product. The suit is finished and packed for shipment, the child can be sent off to school, the victory or defeat has come to pass, the last act of the ceremony has been performed. But there are much briefer internal time discontinuities. In some instances, the end of the day denotes the ending, in others, the nature of the process.

The discontinuity is further differentiated by changes in tempo. Even though the hurried housewife may have only a brief interval of time between the preparation of a meal and the family's sitting down to dinner, yet the tempo changes. So also does the order in which the individuals are served. The fixed action patterns of eating and their tempos differ from the order in which they were sequenced, assuming they all had a hand in the preparation of the meal. Thus, the discontinuity is also marked by the different order of arrangement (and interaction) if the same people take part in all available sequences. Both tempo and ordering define the break between one sequence and the next.

Ordinarily, the people themselves are different. Time elapses before a new sequence becomes operative and, most important, the tempo of work is significantly altered. Drastically oversimplifying what happens in making clothing industrially, the cloth is cut into component parts in quantity by stacking layer on layer of cloth and cutting through it, but the sewing room personnel work on only one garment (or part) at a time. One cannot sew two garments at the same time in a single sewing machine. Since putting garments together means assembling parts, total assembly cannot occur until all the parts for the garment are ready. The nature of the process naturally builds in ending points where further extension of the sequence is impractical.

The significance of these discontinuities is that they constitute the dimensional limits around which the teamwork pattern is elaborated. As we shall see in the chapter following, these discontinuities set up the constraints which shape and separate organizational units from one another. Within these boundaries, demarcating dimensional arrays of different length, the frequency and duration of their activation vary widely. Presumably Pa Maniva and his family do not make breadfruit pudding every day; perhaps other elements in their cuisine require less teamwork. In most formally organized business and political institutions, the time boundaries during the day are fixed. The work flow repeats itself day after day throughout the year. But many community organizations—boards of charitable societies, clubs, and even some governmental activities—are episodic or, though meeting regularly, do so, perhaps, one evening a month. Further, the requirements for the division of labor vary internally. In some cases, like the housewife preparing the meal, or the secretary of a club running a one-man office, the number of steps may be large, but the division of labor does not exist.

The boundaries delimiting cultural sequences, therefore, mean that within them the probabilities of interaction are higher between their members than with individuals on the other side. Nevertheless, the probabilities decrease as one follows along the chain of people. Except for the person at the beginning and he who brings up the rear, each person has two persons with whom to interact, one who initiates to him and one to whom he initiates along the flow.

Interplay of Spatial Distance and Cultural Sequencing

This dimensional category cannot occur in a vacuum, since interactional probabilities become highly influenced by the spatial distances in the cultural sequence. Two persons might work contiguously in the flow, that is, side by side or facing one another; for technical reasons, the sequence may not be laid out along a straight line. There are innumerable ways in which the dimensions of spatial distance and cultural sequence are interwoven. Wherever distance can be minimized in its influence, interaction probabilities will decrease in each direction starting with a given individual (except the first and last). Hence one's place in the sequence determines both the frequency of interaction and, more important, the likelihood of disturbance because of fluctuations in rate of work completed. Only number one (the wireman in the Western Electric example), starting off at his own pace, has minimal temperamental probabilities (assuming there are no delays from other prior cultural sequences) while the omega worker (the inspector) is most vulnerable to everything that happens before.

These relative positions along the chain, which a single cultural sequence represents, are often referred to in the literature as instances of "social distance." The term is not, however, used in a true dimensional sense; instead it seems to be regarded as a kind of ectoplasm, emotionally endowed, which keeps two persons apart. This lack of precision has seriously hampered the utility of the concept; it stems from the fact that such relationships between two people are not broken down into their cultural sequence components. Rather, it has been assumed that social distance is a simple summated dimension, subjectively experienced by each of the participants. In many cases, it has been confused with spatial distance to try to explain the patterning of distance behaviors between the dominant and those beneath them.

Factors in the Development of the Division of Labor

Reasons for a division of labor occurring among humans are various, but also relatively obvious. They have been commonly discussed since a French anthropologist, Durkheim, in his book of that name (English translation, 1952) first treated them systematically.

Not all flows or sequences, however, are technological; the primary ones arise from properties of the individuals, animal or human. Just as wiremen, soldermen, and inspectors hold their positions in a technological sequence and, by the nature of the technological process, specialize, that is, limit their actions in accord with the job requirements, so the most ancient of all specializations are those dependent upon anatomical and physiological states. Sex and age are the first of the differentiators. In any given species, their biological properties constrain the distribution of the time an individual spends in performing particular action sequences and in interacting with specific other individuals.

The individual's capacities for carrying on certain activities are dependent on his possession of physical strength and dexterity. The human is outstanding by his long period of physical dependence in infancy, and the successive stages of youth reaching their culmination in the late teens. Young men, for example, are regarded as at their strongest and thus are better warriors than those older, even though their senior's experience may make up for it. At the other end of the Seven Ages of Man, the oldster—though the structure of the cultural sequences of his society (as in China until recently) may leave him dominant over the other members of his family—may also be unable to take part in the essential food-obtaining sequences on which the marginal economy of his group depends. Among the Eskimo, he can be left to die if food availability becomes severely limited.

Between male and female, not only does age differentiate but physical strength is less. Woman's biological selection for procreation and the long process required before the human young become independent necessarily restricts her participation in many cultural sequences. Also, having children involves her in those sequences having to do with nursing, food preparation, and the activities which the need for shelter and clothing for herself and her offspring engender. Thus every group, human as well as the lower animals, has a division of labor of some sort between male and female and young and old. Except in man, cultural sequences are minimal, though among the bees and other social insects, "culture" and the division of labor involve endogenous differentiation within the species.

Apart from these age and sex differences, though sometimes depending on them, as in the case of physical strength, the division of labor begins either as a consequence of the size of the task or the number of items to be processed. These may involve raw material, pieces of paper, or people in the varying cultural flows of training, teaching, employing, or treating for illness. In addition, spatial distance may play a part—for example, it is far less cumbersome to prepare metal in ingot form at the mine and only have to transport the relatively purified metal rather than the crude ore to the fabricating center. In many crafts, where the demand for the product is infrequent, one man does all the steps. As more and more requests are received by the craftsman, the less skilled or more laborious steps in the sequence can be parceled out to apprentices.

Outside the technological realm, other factors facilitate the growth of such cultural sequences. Partly these have to do with the interdependence of a complex set of arrays associated with the growth and differentiation of the "dominance hierarchy"—in this context, a dimensional sequence based on initiating in set events—those at the top initiating to all below them, those at the bottom only being able to respond. As more and more people can be taken into such a linear system, more and more intermediate positions have to be established to maintain control over their numbers, a development to be discussed more fully in the next chapter. In turn, such segmentation requires comparable separations in other cultural sequences, particularly the technological, in the army, the temple, or other center of activity. Thus, the division of labor develops and becomes differentiated with the size of the group, the frequency with which initiative for goods and services increases, and the necessity to extend the control of the leader to initiate to more and more people.

The Rise of Specialization

So far, the division of labor has been treated as a series of cultural sequences of work flows where the individuals occupying particular positions in the ordinal array are interchangeable. In fact, of course, and implicit in what has gone before, this is not the case. Not only do anatomical and physiological limitations on participation make a selection process necessary, but people have very different skills and personalities (as well as temperamental characteristics) which make them try to specialize in particular types of cultural sequences and particular positions within them.

That the division of labor gives rise to specialists, full or part-time, is hardly a surprising finding. What is important is that specialists serve as nodal points around which cultural sequences become elaborated. If a society started from scratch, with a moderately well-developed technology and economy, no one would doubt that some persons would prove better at certain activities, and less competent at others. As the cultural sequences became differentiated into several steps and produced products or services beyond the immediate use of the members of the sequence—if Pa Maniva should start up a restaurant for his breadfruit pudding—then the process of exchange would develop. The gradual sorting out of activities into specializations would mean that no one person could depend on his own efforts to supply all his needs, economic, social, or spiritual.

It may be that these skills are distributed relatively equally in every cultural group—though no one knows if this is actually true—yet, in any case, the growth of specialization depends on the possibilities of exchange. Individuals are often assigned by a leader to perform specific activities, not always those for which they are best suited (and specialize in this sense), but ordinarily skills are recognized and specialization grows naturally. In the part-time case, the specialist—the tool maker, the potter, or for that matter, the farmer who needs their products—does not perform all the cultural activities necessary for a living. Where this kind of division of labor does not occur, everyone is self- sufficient—"an island unto himself." If an individual is not skilled, he and his family have to put up with the hut which leaks, the pot that collapses, and the meager food supply he is able to acquire.

Such complete independence (and isolation) appears to be atypical, even in Paleolithic times. Trade in raw materials, particularly for stone used for spear points, arrow heads and scrapers, seems to have been widespread. For most cultures on which ethnographers have reported, some process of exchange appears to have been going on long before the Europeans appeared on the scene. Jasper (a quartz for arrow points) from Lake Superior made its way to New England; the Eskimo got the soapstone from which their oil lamps and cooking vessels were made from a single source, often traveling hundreds of miles to barter for it.

The appearance of specialists, therefore, depends on the existence of a customer. He may not necessarily be one who pays in cash, but one who at least exchanges goods and services (spiritual or material) for what the specialist has to offer. Sometimes the latter may perform all the operations making up the cultural work-flow sequence; sometimes only a few, passing the product on to another specialist for further processing. This linkage of specialists, part-time or full, who in turn may be customers (by acquiring and doing further processing before the final customer comes into the chain) is then a cultural sequence which ties together a series of separate (and separable) cultural sequences into a larger unit.

Since the stability of all types of culture sequences (work flows are the best known examples) depends on the regularity of the interactions and transactions of which they are constituted, the types of specialists will vary as they try to achieve an even balance and equilibrium in the constituent relations making up the sequence. Thus part-time craftsmen, however skilled, may need to farm or practice other occupations, since the frequency with which exchange takes place through their interactional contacts may be low or erratic. This type of adaptation was true of the rural United States until recently, and some few recalcitrant and stiff-necked craftsmen still try to follow it, buoyed up by Thoreau's search for spiritual independence. In many parts of the world, specialists travel to their customers, either to markets within a region or following a definite route, going from one village to another, with wares already made or ready to produce on the spot for the customer's needs.

Considering the evolution of societies and the growth of specialists, it may be worth pointing out that many persons combine more than one specialty. The craftsman not only produces, perhaps performing every step of the sequence by himself or, if demand is high, setting up a division of labor within his family, or by taking on apprentices. He must also be a salesman, whether he sits within his shop waiting for customers or goes out on the road with his handicrafts until they are disposed of. He thus takes part in two cultural sequences (with a discontinuity in between) which are, however, linearly connected. Such combinations are multiplied inordinately by the network of dimensional chains within complex organizations where, as we shall see in Chapter 12, one individual may be involved in a number of quite separate sequences involving different arrangements of members of the organization.

The Interactional Properties of Specialization

As specialists begin to produce for others, they have to perform at least two, and often more, quite different interaction patterns. As craftsmen, they must learn to concentrate on working for long periods by themselves. When they have others assisting them, they must learn to supervise their activities, take the initiative when attention or performance begins to flag, dominate if their assistants disagree. In addition, unless they begin with available raw materials—for instance, the wool from their own sheep, assuming they do not have to act as herders—they must buy materials from other tradesmen and negotiate to obtain the best price possible. Once the product is finished, they must turn into salesmen and, depending on the cultural patterning of such transactions, try to persuade the passerby to buy, bargain for the best price, and play an active, dominant role.

In each of these cultural sequences, the personality characteristics required are different. All, together with technical skill, are rarely possessed by a single individual. As a consequence, where possible, a further division of labor takes place at each of the points where a new sequence is set in motion. In other countries, and in certain types of business in the United States, the division of labor is largely familial. Sons and brothers whose personalities best fit them for particular patterns of interaction specialize as salesman, purchasing agent, foreman, or designer. This type of specialization is, however, dependent on the interplay of all the cultural dimensions. How it operates will be discussed in Chapter 14.

Thus specialization sets constraints on the type of personality able to carry out the cultural sequences. Where the individual specializing is unable to manage all the patterns required for success, his temperamental reactions are easily triggered off. Even if only a single sequence is in question, the personality restrictions may be too great. The boy apprenticed to his father is selected because he is a family member. Inadequate interactional or technical skill can minimize his chances of achieving his appropriate position within the available cultural sequences which this specialty entails.

It should also be emphasized that the division of labor comes about naturally in many interim or part-time activities. Humans, like other animals, rarely like to be alone. Many cultural sequences become established where two or three people aid each other in performing a task. Thus, the need for interaction, for an adequate outlet for the requirements of one's biological rhythms, is not to be minimized in considering how cultural sequences are established. This is particularly true if the process, whatever form it may have, can easily be carried out rhythmically. Though one man with a good axe can cut down a moderate sized tree alone, two men do it faster and gain the interactional outlets which all such team activities make possible. Thus, people search out such opportunities for interplay, today more easily found in sports and games and handicrafts.

Bridging the Discontinuities between Cultural Sequences

The stability of cultural sequences is a product of the repetitive character of the interactions and the boundaries which its discontinuities at start and finish necessarily create. Simplifying the discussion to the single unit sequence (though where more than two people make up the chain, other small flows usually are present), the probabilities and actualities of interaction are high within it, and low at either end. Often this is accentuated by spatial dimensions. After all, making ornaments or copper pots ordinarily occurs within a demarcated set of spaces, specifically the shop.

As a consequence, such cultural sequences tend to promote a state of equilibrium making it hard for its members to leave their cozy interactional nest and initiate new sequences to a customer or other potential recipient. This is partly why service is rarely an attribute of the true craftsman. Yet the reality is the need to carry on an exchange, to give something and, in turn, to receive. To give requires taking the initiative; to receive (in exchange) means that the initiative of one party to the transaction is balanced by the other initiating in turn in a separate event. In some cases, the process of exchange is brief and extremely simple; in others, long complex sequences of interaction, patterned within elaborate cultural frameworks, are necessary and may last for long periods of time.

Many years ago, a French social anthropologist, Marcel Mauss, wrote a short book called *Essai sur le Don* (the American translation was published in 1954). Mauss maintained that the act of giving someone a gift, the word implies that no return was anticipated (and, of course, initiating to the person in so doing), created a disturbance or imbalance in the relationship. The act puts the recipient under an obligation to reciprocate by returning a gift in order to balance accounts. The reciprocal act of initiative restored the equilibrium of the person who had received the gift. Failure to do so was emotionally disturbing; it destroyed any pretense of an equal relationship. Being free to initiate with the individual having to respond at the initiator's will made him subordinate. As pointed out earlier, the consequence of being dominant over another, as field studies of monkeys amply demonstrate, is to be able to initiate, with the dominated individual being conditioned to respond.

Mauss supported his hypothesis with examples from many societies, in particular to explain the wide variety of instances in which gifts are given in increasing frequency and amounts in order to establish the superiority (and order of initiative) of the giver beyond challenge. Examples of this are seen in the potlatch ceremonies on the northwest coast of the United States and Canada. Complicated by elaborate rules for specifying what the recipients were supposed to return, these ceremonies involved giving with the expectation of multifold return, often so much that his rivals in the social swim could never match his openhandedness, and would be ruined if they tried.

Though Mauss did not elaborate, the nature of reciprocity is a quantitative one. A tit-for-tat exchange is the most typical, but relationships vary, depending on relative positions in cultural sequences which affect the number of times X can give Y a gift before Y must reciprocate in kind. Mauss concentrated his attention on the gift *per se,* yet the underlying reality of exchange is the freedom to initiate. The powerful initiate without giving a concrete object, affording the recipient the graces of their interactions. In turn, they receive a sequence of gifts from the lesser fry, who seek to improve their positions in relation to their superiors. Beyond a certain point, depending on the nature of the adjustment, the boss must reciprocate or, if he wishes to preserve his position more cheaply, he must refuse to respond by not accepting the gifts pressed upon him.

The significance of giving, of initiating action across two cultural sequences—particularly where the initiation is the first step in establishing a new relationship—is not limited to a gift in the ordinary sense of the word. Industrialists often talk about "giving" another firm their business. Since they are buying or selling, there is no question of a gift, but the notion that setting up an exchange of goods or services and monies puts the firm under obligation (to some degree at least) is almost automatic.

More broadly, however, the underlying notion of reciprocal initiative lies at the heart of economic transactions. Clearly, the product or service or activity of any sort has to be paid for, whether it is by cash on the barrelhead, "asking them back for dinner after they invited us to such a nice party," or "helping us out when the cellar filled up with water." Maintaining a balance in initiative, its associated interactions, and the goods or services which accompany it, is a fundamental property of the human personality and, from reported evidence, for at least some of the higher mammals. Whether exchange is classified as economic, social, or religious, it is the means through which cultural sequences are linked together across discontinuities. For that matter, exchange also can be a powerful factor within the relationships making up the sequence itself.

From the simplest instance of barter, or the roses bought for the girl friend's birthday, to the complicated transactions of international finance, balancing of initiatives, with an expected value attached, is an essential property of human nature. In complex transactions, where much is at stake—the girl friend or the corporation whose business is being wooed—gifts, entertainment, and all sorts of services are the coin of the realm. At the end, the hope is that the exchange relationship will be consummated and that the desired payoff will occur. So Mauss, without any knowledge of behavioral biology, put his finger on a crucial problem. Until there is reciprocal initiative, the display, the suggested sale, and the favors done are potential gifts whose acceptance upsets the balance (though instituting interaction) until an equivalent sum or gift cancels the obligation.

Dimensional Consequences

The cultural sequence, however extended in number of steps and positions of the individuals of which it is constituted, is the building block out of which more complex systems of human relationships are constructed. Varied by its necessary occurrence in space, and thus by the dimensions of spatial distance, it provides the framework for human institutions in conjunction with the third of the cultural dimensions or dimensional systems—communicative symbols. Yet it can easily be separated from other dimensions. The complex network of relationships built upon it can be unraveled through direct observation so that the interactional probabilities may be estimated. Within such a framework, the next step can then be taken—namely the description of the quantitative properties of the interactions which these probabilities set up.

As the constraints of cultural sequences become transformed into organizational systems, they become more impervious to change than the dimensions of space and communication. In anthropological terms, these are the structures which guide human affairs. The institutions built upon them, particularly in the sequences of supervision and rule, tend to persist in a stable form even though the words used to symbolize them change, or the geometrical distances within which they occur are significantly altered. Governmental structures last over centuries, even though the labels applied to them and the territories they hold may be very different. Bureaucracy continues, no matter who the ruler or what his banners say. Although new brooms and concepts may promise change, it is rare when bureaucracy (and its equivalents in other institutions) fails to win the final battle.

Chapter 12

The Organization of Institutions

The behavioral anthropologist's need to tackle the enormous range in the size of human institutions, from small Bushmen bands in the Kalahari desert, rarely numbering more than 25 people, to the American Telephone and Telegraph Company, Standard Oil Company of New Jersey, the Federal Government of the United States, or the Roman Catholic Church, poses unusual problems. Other disciplines, such as sociology, economics, and political science, ordinarily concentrate on only one type of organization, often only those to be found within a single culture. More daringly, the anthropologist looks for organizing principles across the board. Can he in fact find means of bringing order into comparative chaos? Are there even ways of extending the analysis across species? For behavioral biology cannot abdicate at the door of the modern corporation nor exclude those uniformities identifiable at least down to the lower primates.

The sweep of inquiry so stated may appear unmanageable. It is not too hard to consider jumping backwards, so to speak, from Bushmen to chimpanzees or baboons; yet the organization man, and the institutions within which he acts and interacts, seems laughably different. To undertake such an analysis does *not* mean that one should caricature the corporate executive, with the reality of the ape peeping through the rags of his cultural elaboration. To do so is to minimize man's special capacity for using that part of the brain—the cortex—which differentiates him from all other animals. (The possibility that the porpoise could be a rival because of the

221

size of his brain and its cortical development can be tabled until his enthusiastic supporters adduce more evidence.)

One need not belabor the importance of the human cortex. It is indeed remarkable in its capacities for learning complex patterns of physical movements and communication configurations. Philosophers too often have placed "mind" on a pedestal for all to worship (replacing poor Eve whose mind they consider subordinate to her flesh). Such adulation, however, ignores the biological similarities of subcortical areas within the mammalian order. Since these are the primary source of emotional–interactional patterns which delineate the shape of human nature, mind has to take its chances within the organism. There, reduced in ego, its integration with the lower centers is becoming increasingly demonstrated. Since the limbic complex, when stress occurs, too easily overrides its cognitive controls, man and woman (as equals) are now free to climb onto their separate pedestals, or stay more firmly on the ground.

Some Problems of Labeling

In the study of human institutions, labels, as always, create misunderstandings. A distinction between structure and function is prevalent in social anthropology, sociology, and related disciplines, though borrowed from biology and earlier commented on in a different context. In the years when this usage was common in biology, attention was concentrated on the too solid stability of anatomy as the point of departure. Its image was rather like throwing the switch to set the electric trains in motion. Once the parts began to move, function became manifest. Function in this sense was both the activity and the purpose—"a function of the family is to socialize the child." So family structure referred to its organization on some kind of general principles, while family function was what it presumably did.

This view assumes that structure was, in fact, like anatomy—hard bones, gristle, flesh, tissue, blood—displayed for all to see on that long white table in the dissecting room. The difficulties which such a dichotomy created became obvious once functions (or structures for that matter) were looked at closely. Today, the dynamic point of view has become prevalent, yet the tendency is still strong, though often unconscious, to think of relationships within institutions as rigid bonds or connections rather than made up of fluctuating, quantitative interactional states which direct observation demonstrates. The fields of force are not independent of the magnets which produce them. Hence social structure, as used here, is a dynamic state, the properties of which can be quantitatively described.

A further area of confusion lies in the use of the term "institution" and, for that matter, contrasting it with "organization." In some academic disciplines, organization is current and institution avoided, but this can vary not merely within and between the human sciences, but from country to country. Another complication is introduced, paralleling the structure–function quarrel, by a duality in the definition of institution. In this book again, organization (or one could alternatively use social organization in its fairly well accepted meaning) is equivalent to institution. For many writers, however, the term, institution, refers to a cultural pattern, often to a cultural sequence. Thus, people speak of marriage as an institution, of the institution of prayer, or the Yankee institution (or custom) of having hot-buttered rum after skiing.

The Organizing Properties of Interaction Patterns

The elements of "social" organization, the structuring of the relationships of individuals, are rarely looked at from the point of view of direct observation. The pervasive influence of symbols is so great that generalized, and often philosophically derived, labels are used to categorize these relationships. Terms like solidarity, cooperation, power, authority, superordination, subordination, and alienation are only a few; the list is interminable. As a consequence, relationships between people are categorized by these labels almost by default, with no concentrated attempt to peer beneath the term to see what criteria exist to identify it and differentiate it from others.

The problem of operational definition is most evident in trying to see how individuals are ordered in their relationships to one another. If one observes several of them in interaction (even before beginning to use measurement) and separates out who is interacting with whom as carefully as possible, it is immediately obvious that almost all the interaction is between pairs, often with frequent switching of the partners. Far less common, under ordinary conditions, are those situations where more than two individuals appear to be involved.

Considering such pair relationships in a group of individuals where the frequency of interaction is high, and everyone can be observed, presumably every potential pair can interact if they remain together long enough. Though one person may take the initiative to another more frequently in repeated events, yet trying to line the pairs up directionally to isolate any internal organization proves futile. First, there are no "all-or-none" initiative–response relations. Excluding infants in their mothers' arms, even the smallest child is likely to initiate to the oldest person if he gets within range. As periods of observation are repeated, the researcher ends up with percentage figures for each relationship. Trying to plot such a network on paper makes its structural properties appear almost random. Yet we know they are not—that order, even bureaucratic rigidity, is more likely.

Suppose the individuals are interacting within what we would without rigor label an organization—a factory, church, or government bureau. When we trace out their relationships, step by step, from one cultural sequence unit to all those others interactionally linked to it, circularity (and frustration for the investigator) is the immediate consequence. Everyone occasionally seems to interact with everyone else. (Be it remembered that we are restricting our observations to interaction, so cultural classification by way of spatial dimensions, types of techniques practiced, symbols of all sorts including signs on the office door indicating positional rank, is excluded.) One can, of course, abandon the pursuit of an organizing interactional principle and use traditional cultural labels to categorize the relationships. Or one can measure all the interaction that occurs and see what to make of it.

In so doing, the interaction variables, even in pair events, are clearly involved. Within the organizational framework to which the cultural dimensions contribute such important constraints, certain individuals do dominate others, are free to take the initiative, do have a captive audience for their activity rates, and so on. But these, although indicative of directional organization, are not in themselves sufficient if limited to pair interaction. Something more is needed if individuals are to be organized vis-a-vis one another.

What makes the difference is what Chapple (1940) called set, or group, events (see Chapter 3). These alternate but equivalent terms simply mean that there are directional interactions where more than two individuals are involved. Though a minimum of three people is required, the maximum can be the hundreds of thousands assembled in great meetings staged by powerful rulers. In these interactions, one person (though it could be several as in the theatre or in ritual) takes the initiative; the others respond, approximately simultaneously. Or one person interrupts and outacts all the others, after which he controls the initiative. More commonly, but not necessarily, dominance is established in pair events before the "leader" achieves the freedom to initiate and to be sure the others will respond.

All kinds of cultural settings (and institutions) provide examples of set events—the army or any military organization, the church in the conduct of its ritual and ceremonies, the teacher starting off the daily class, or the public speaker in any forum. That set events occur, and in some situations of command do so with high frequency, is obvious enough once the criteria are pointed out. Less apparent, however, is how they become the basis for organization and why their quantitative properties provide the dynamics for the structure of institutions.

In one sense, the solution is a simple one. If one person initiates and several others respond, in *that* interaction sequence their interaction rhythms have become synchronized with one another, even though there may not be perfect synchronization with the initiator. So doing, their *orientation system* is no longer random (or at least distributed between pairs). All have to assume a direction towards (and often, as in military drill or in ritual, a movement towards) the individual initiating the set event. When set events become repetitive and the group initiated to responds in unison, they share a common rhythm. In so doing, one can assume that they undergo reticular arousal and the autonomic concomitants of synchronous interaction. It is well known from practical experience that once such group response patterns are established, they generate a powerful influence on the emotional states of the individuals participating.

Thus set events organize by conditioning people to a common relationship to one or more others. Since they are directional, they produce what might be called a polarity in interactional patterns. Individuals learn from earliest training to respond, not merely in one to one relationships, but in one to many. Once these are established, the order is rarely broken. If tried, it is a visible attempt to displace the initiator and take over his or her position (a violation of "discipline"). This does not exclude these responders from initiating individually in pair events to the set event initiator. Johnny can ask the teacher a question; he had better not try to get the class to respond to his action in competition with her.

Set events easily fall into ordered sequences where the initiator to one group may join with that group as a responder if another person comes into the situation. Best illustrated by the military (or the church), the platoon leader issues orders to his men, but when a superior officer takes over, both the platoon leader and his men respond in unison to the command to march initiated by their superior. Thus, set events themselves combine into arrays or cultural sequences having a beginning position with an initiator to whom all respond, and so on down the line to a final group who, in that array at least, responds to everyone and never initiates in set events to those before them. These arrays are called sets (Chapple 1940).

Parallels among The Lower Primates

In the many field studies of apes and monkeys which have been carried out to date, it is quite evident that set events do occur and do structure the relationships of the members of the group internally, as well as their relations to other groups. Yet overconcern with recording the communicative aspects of expressive behavior superimposed upon the interaction patterns (and, of course, the lack of use of interaction measurement) enables us ordinarily only to infer that set events are taking place, or are referred to as leadership patterns are summarized.

Rowell (1967), comparing the "interactions" of wild and caged baboon groups, found no straight-line "dominance hierarchy" in her wild group in Uganda. This is in contrast to reports by Hall and DeVore (1965) for Nairobi National Park. She said, however:

> "Interaction," in the limited sense used here, does not reflect the immense amount of cooperation between males in a group. This took the form of paying attention to each other's interactions with the "environment." If juveniles registered alarm or excitement the nearest male would investigate the cause and notify the others of his assessment of its importance. Thus the males provided a continuous intensive policing of the environment for the troop.

In her excellent studies of the langurs of Ceylon, Ripley (1967) described a variety of situations which clearly consisted of set events. One of the most interesting was the performance by males, and females without infants, of what she called a "display jump," brought about by hearing the sound of a neighboring troop. The animals, in response, jumped between branches and trees in a stiff, heavy manner, often landing on dry branches and breaking them (which they would otherwise avoid), whooping all the while. She emphasized that they both began and stopped these displays as if at a signal. Further, these langurs, peaceable enough within their own group, had a penchant for attacking other groups. Like their human relatives, they went forth to attack, often putting the enemy to rout by rushing at them or actually fighting—wrestling and pulling tails until one or the other group retreated. Every morning, furthermore, males (which ones or how many is not stated in the published material and no doubt hard to determine) climbed to the tops of tall tamarind trees, 100 or more feet high, and whooped simultaneously, to be answered by whoops from other groups.

Within other species of apes and monkeys, set events are also repeatedly reported, often as instances of the "dominance hierarchy"—their frequency obviously affected by the number of animals and their age and sex. As stated earlier, dominance has been a catchall term. No clear distinction is made between its occurrence in pair or group situations. Carpenter (1942) called an individual "dominant over another when it has priority in feeding, sexual, and locomotor behavior," that is, in its initiative and "when it is superior in aggressiveness and in group control to another or other individuals," which can mean either dominance interactionally defined or initiating in set events. He then proceeds to count the frequencies of occurrence of all such categories in the relationships of rhesus monkeys on Cayo Santiago, expressing their relative positions in a linear chain for the seven adult males in the group he was studying.

Initiative is operationally defined as acting first (priority in activities in Carpenter's statement given above). Thus, if it is reported that the "dominant" or "alpha" animal (the Greek alphabet is used as a ranking order in animal studies, representing the extent of the dominance hierarchy) moves and the others follow or scuttle out of his way, he has initiated and not dominated.

Dominance attempts, after all, occur only when the orders of priority in acting have not been learned; where young juveniles infringe on the space occupied by their elders, or where competition for the right to initiate to others is at issue. Nor will each animal (or human) always try to take the initiative even if his position entitles him to. For here we see the extensions of set events into sequences which I have called sets. For example, Ripley (1967) described one encounter where the Alpha and Beta males withdrew from conflict after briefly responding, leaving Gamma to carry on the fight.

Koford (1962) commented that the leader of a rhesus macaque group on Cayo Santiago only initiated when two or more animals were squabbling or when the group had to defend its young. In the first situation, the leader was clearly ready to persist in his attempt to dominate until they stopped, in case the mere act of moving towards them failed to have its usual results; in the latter, he led the defense against the opponents. Even in two groups on the island, individual differences in personality were obvious. One leader moved to the feeder when food was put in it and permitted no other animal to approach until he had finished. In another group, the leader ate in close physical contact with various females.

Although the Reynolds' describe large groups of chimpanzees coming together in night-long "rock and roll" performances, the group size among the great apes are usually too small for anything more than a simple sequence of a male, one or two subordinate females and younger males, and juveniles. Among baboons, however, DeVore (1965) described patterns of interactions which suggested more complicated interactional sequences of set events. Though they had one animal who acted as a leader when danger approached, he had observed what he called a "central hierarchy"—a group of adult males who cooperated in maintaining the order of command (and dominance where necessary) over the other animals, both males and females. The leader was superior to these others, and took the initiative in total group situations. For example, if the group encountered a predator like a leopard, he went off to find a safe route to bypass the danger, came back to the troop and led it along the alternate path. In other instances, he acted with his cohorts or let them act, much as if together they constituted the higher management of the troop.

Although set events are far more ordered in their sequencing than pair events, among the lower animals they are the consequences of the natural patterns of moving from one place to another, defending territories, managing the young, or obtaining sex. They are facilitated by physical and personality differences and by differential skills which certainly do exist among them. Most important, they can be quantitatively defined. In every group there appears to be several such sets—ordered sequences of set events in which the membership in a class of responders (or initiators) is well established by the frequencies with which they occur.

In humans, this structuring is highly developed, among the lower animals to a far lesser degree. Further, there are many opportunities for embryonic sets to start, by accident or design, only to be strangled by the dominance patterns of the set members. An infant, squealing wildly as it falls from a tree, can cause the whole group to respond by rushing to its aid. Presumably this does not occur too often, though crying "Wolf!" is the proverbial means of getting one's betters to reverse their relative positions (in that one set event, at least). In the common run of the mill situations occurring in every group, the hand of calamity descends to emphasize to the young that his elders are not to be disturbed unduly.

Sets and the Dimension of Spatial Distance

The earliest development in human history of multiple sets may well have been the consequence of spatial distance and the numbers of individuals contained within it. Human perceptual limits embodied in the distance scales require some linear organization of relationships if any sizeable number of individuals is to move and be directed over the terrain. In migrations or warfare, a single leader can coordinate and synchronize the actions of a small number of men. For larger groups, human history (and everyday experience) demonstrates that these biological limitations on ability to coordinate groups can only be overcome by developing sets (the hierarchy of command) through which each small group and its leader are in turn subject to the initiative of "higher" leaders. In final form, a linear, cultural sequence is established in which the commander can initiate through the descending ranks of the set as if he were the leader of a single, small group.

Wherever distance intervenes, the discontinuities (since both spatial distance and cultural sequencing are intertwined) have to be bridged. To accomplish this, one individual has to initiate to spatially and sequentially separated units. The effects of distance are obvious and need not be elaborated on here, although its influence must again be examined as we look at more complex organizations. It is worth remembering that from the earliest times attempts were made to bridge such distances through sound or visual signals. Solving the problem of managing set events across distance has been an important technological concern for man.

In historical accounts, the king addresses his troops, gives the order to unfurl the banners, to sound the trumpets, and beat the kettledrums. A classic illustration of this is the rallying call of King Henry V to his men before the Battle of Agincourt:

> Follow your spirit; and upon this charge, Cry God for Henry, England, and St. George!

Music too, in its most common form, became associated with the ordering and reinforcing of set events and the development of synchronous responses among its members. Moreover, the sounds and visual signals were also intended to alert the enemy and cause him to respond—in the days of chivalry by taking the field—or to overpower him with such concerted noise that he would surrender or run away.

Sets and the Dimension of Cultural Sequencing

The division of labor and the rise of specialists (and specialization) necessarily result in the development of interactionally well-defined cultural sequences with an equilibrium of their own. In the preceding chapter, it was implicit (though obvious) that such ordered arrays of people are rarely built up on pair relationships in complex cultures. Such sequences do occur in very small groups, but ordinarily several people occupy a single position. They are, therefore, liable to respond in set events and, more generally, to become members of a set. Thus, Pa Maniva did initiate to the *two* women roasting and peeling the breadfruit; a wireman could initiate to more than a single solderman, and so on.

The addition of individuals, one or many, to any single position in a cultural sequence almost inevitably results in set events. They will also occur if the cultural sequence is made up of several linked pairs, i.e., is more than minimal in length, a pair or dyad of two persons only. Thus, the lead man in a sequence may frequently initiate to the others following. If he stops, thereby bringing the others to a stop in some technological processes (even highly skilled ones like glass blowing), his next action, with or without words, signals the others to get into their relative positions again.

Lest it be forgotten, cultural sequences are in no sense limited to technological activities. Though the parade ground has been used to illustrate a highly formalized and ritualized set, the sequences followed by its members are learned. They involve a complex configuration of postural movements and communication patterns, shaped, as every cultural sequence must be, by spatial distance. In industrial settings (more properly in technological situations since "industrial" implies an institution as well as specific types of cultural activities common to governments, churches, and so on), the customary label for cultural sequences is "work flow." Since the term is such a useful one, it should be pointed out that this book's usage differs from that in industrial engineering (the work-flow design specialty). Industrial engineers include each operation as a work-flow step, even if several of these are performed by the same person, or even where no human is involved, as in the work-flow design of a continuous strip steel mill.

In highly developed technological systems like manufacturing, the flow is rarely a single linear system. Rather, at various stages in the process, there may be a number of flows converging on one another. These are integrated into a single flow, then disperse in separate channels, only to come together again. Thus, where the primary flow is a factory assembly operation, there are subassemblies feeding the main line at appropriate places, for example, in the conversion of raw materials to parts which are then used to build up subassemblies. At the end of such lines, as in an automobile plant, there are separate routes for the assemblies to follow if different models need separate painting or finishing which require different methods or materials. Even on Tikopia, the prepared breadfruit and the coconut cream are combined by pounding in order to produce the pudding.

Formal Definition of an Interactional Set

Before we concern ourselves with the ways in which cultural sequences (and sets) are interdependent and form the basis for organizational structure, it is time to state formally how an interactional set is defined. A set consists of an ordered sequence of group events such that every individual is either a member of a class who always takes the initiative in set events to the other members of a set, or he is a member of a class who always respond together with others in such group events, or he may belong to an intermediate class who respond to the initiations of the first class, but on the other hand initiate to those at the end of the sequence. Many well-structured sets are made up of only two classes: the initiators and those who respond. Thus by observation, one can establish a set, in all cultures, where females initiate to males, and in another, its alternate. These sets are manifested not only informally in the family but in highly organized form in ritual and ceremony.

As societies grow larger, and technology and spatial distance become increasingly diversified, a large series of intermediate classes develop—the "hierarchy" of common usage. However, the division of labor also produces similar complex sets. Thus, the assembly lines in a clothing factory, referred to in Chapter 11, are highly differentiated. Membership in a set does not mean that an individual at the bottom or, alternatively, in the end position cannot initiate to those on top (or at the beginning). He can, but this must occur in pair events; otherwise, by going against the direction of the flow of initiators, he is trying, even if feebly, to establish a counterbalancing set.

It is important to realize that set "structure" is established through observation, even though the number of events, in very large organizations, initiated by the top to the hundreds of thousands at the bottom may be very infrequent. Nevertheless, at adjacent classes and usually including the next below and the one above, every effort is made to reinforce the ordering of relationships. If this begins to break down, if the central and superior class or individual is unable to manage such initiations *and* get those below him to respond, he, and the organization, is in trouble and likely to split apart.

Variation (or manipulation) of the quantitative flow of set events along an interactional set, particularly in the hierarchical set through which the individuals are coordinated and led (or ruled), provides remarkable examples of the way that power is seized and held. A dissident satrap, hoping to free himself from his subordinate position and either take over from the ruler or become independent, tries to maneuver himself into a position where he can avoid responding with his peers to initiations from the top. If he can do this, and get away with it, in other words, if the hierarch does not realize that he must take up the challenge and force his unruly subordinate to accept his position and respond when initiated to, he has lost his power or is on the road to doing so. This means that he must be prepared to go to any lengths to dominate. These realities are known by men of power, often unconsciously; much of the "political" maneuvering on which reporters or historians comment is designed to maintain position or grasp power from a competitor, whatever the communication rationalizations.

Similar processes can be seen in other sets. In manufacturing, a department organized around a single work flow (or even a series of linked sequences) can obtain a powerful position vis-a-vis departments following them in the sequencing by the way they control the flow of work. Shifting the rates of production or their tempo, withholding finished parts, forcing the next department into a state of disturbance, even bringing a prior work-flow unit to its heels by refusing to take work or insistently demanding it will give a department unusual power. Clearly, such arrogations need to be supplemented by the supervisory set controlling the technological sequences in the department. Often these shifts in power occur directly at the work-flow set with its supervision having to follow the "troops" no matter how much their superiors in the hierarchical set try to bring such group behavior to an end.

Countervailing Sets

Sets are not limited to the hierarchy of command and work flow, or its equivalents in other institutional settings like the rituals of the church. Most organizations include countervailing sets through which compensatory adjustments in interaction are brought about. These are of the greatest interest in understanding the dynamics of institutions and how particular relationships become predominant and shape the ongoing interactions within the system. These constraints are best illustrated and most studied within the family structure in different cultures. Yet other sets are perhaps easier by way of brief example.

An important type is found in industry and business, with the rise of the union, and increasingly in governmental institutions. Initially, this is a set which forces management into a position of being on the bottom rung. Though other sets develop to form the labor organization itself—the division of labor creates a need for officers, clerical sequencing and ensuing sets and, sometimes, even a "union" set of its own—this directional set is the heart of the compensatory process. Many cultural factors play a part in stabilizing this countervailing system, particularly in the ways the logics and the language of the law have been extended to define the nature of expected and stable relationships. This has been facilitated by sheer growth in size and consequent vulnerability of large organizations in contrast to small ones.

But the union's set dynamics stem from the necessity for the workers to compensate for disturbances to their rhythms and patterns of interaction (Chapple 1942, and Chapple and Sayles 1961). Wages have always been assumed the basic issue, since the union member must achieve stability as a provider for his family and the other institutions in which he interacts. Yet far more crucial, and far less publicly understood, are those factors which control how he shall spend his time, at what rate he shall work, when he may rest, the temperament of the foreman—all bundled up in labor terminology under the phrase "working conditions." This is where one cuts to the heart. Often it is these issues, all-pervasive but hard to identify in bargaining terms, which give the labor leader seeking a contract the same sense of helplessness as the aging warlord.

Interactional Properties of Sets

When groups of people are under observation, the frequency of set events is often very low and their durations brief. On the other hand, someone with high dominance can easily increase the set events and reduce the ordinary pair interaction prevalent in most small groups. Watch some determined returned traveler forcing his audience to accept and respond as he "shares" his experiences on his Grace Line tour of South America. Most humans, given half a chance, like to initiate to an admiring group and will go on talking until defeated by competition or the obvious glaze of nonresponse.

In many human activities, the responders are drilled until their response patterns are executed with precise duration and perfect synchronization. Apart from the military services where raw recruits are "licked" into shape, educational patterns of all varieties are imposed on the youngest (and each year thereafter) so that "classroom discipline" can be maintained by teachers. Whether the full patterning of set events is demanded at first, as in many cultures, or a degree of permissiveness eases the adjustment and the transition of the pupil to appropriate behavior, the end result, here and in many other contexts, is schooling to obey in the broadest sense.

In crises for the group, set events are the rule. Almost anyone can sound the alarm. Thereafter, sets become activated and group events frequent and sustained unless no set exists and someone must take over through sheer force of personality. On the other hand, when emergencies are not occurring, but coordination is required, all kinds of temperamental and personality limitations begin to interfere. Capacity to get responses from groups in set events is much more vulnerable to emotional–interactional patterns than most types of interaction with a single other person.

One has the impression that a particular temperamental reaction, say shyness, is multiplied (certainly increased) by the number of people facing the potential initiator. Part of the stress is the prior anxiety that his attempted action will be met by nonresponse. With so many present, the chances of success can appear to be minimal. Even seasoned performers experience this feeling. Going on stage is terrifying. Doing so and finding the audience does respond, no matter how badly one thinks one did, is the only therapy.

In more complex affairs, where dissident groups are present, the management of power, or gaining access to it, depends in large part on well-established and prior interaction with at least the key individuals to be initiated to. Often the dominant in pair interaction is likely to succumb easily in groups. Ability to initiate to one other person is very different from having to obtain response from a group.

The interplay of pair and set events must, therefore, be looked at conjointly. One reinforces the other, but the set event (or more properly the interactional set within which it occurs) provides the direction and limits on who will interact with whom, and who may initiate even (though not always) in pair events. Albert (1964) describing the elaborate etiquette followed in Burundi by individuals in particular relationships (patterns widespread in other cultures) said:

> In the old days, age-mates greeted each other in a lengthy ceremony of sung greetings, embraces and stylized gestures; children knelt before parents or grandparents to pay respect and to receive blessings; feudal inferiors greeting a superior proceeded through the numerous steps of an elaborate assurance of affection and respect that involved verbal formulas accompanied by touching the superior with both hands literally from head to foot.

Even today, specific postures are maintained in any interactional situation in which gifts or favors are petitioned for. Not only are the various elements of speech, gesture, and posture patterned in a highly formal manner, but the other cultural dimensions are interwoven with this ritualization of speaking.

> The order in which individuals speak in a group is strictly determined by seniority of rank. If the eldest present is lower in social rank than some other individual, age gives way before social status. Thus a nephew may be older than his uncle but the uncle is of higher rank and will speak before him. A prince or chief may be younger than others present, but speaks first because of his higher rank. There are no recorded instances of confusion or conflict in the matter of determining order of precedence, even in very large groups.
>
> In public, the rule for servants, females, and other inferiors is to speak when spoken to but otherwise to maintain silence. Nevertheless, the pattern is so arranged that younger or socially inferior persons are in due course able to express their views.

The imposition of cultural sequencing on the patterns of interaction, superseding what might be thought of as the natural order of give-and-take more common in western society, is further extended by spatial as well as cultural sequencing patterns.

> The inferior walks behind the superior, drinks and eats after the superior has begun or only after he has finished. If the superior is of princely rank, nobody may be present during mealtimes, the taster remaining but his back to his master. The inferior talks only after the superior has spoken. He inclines his

head in respect, and the body, too, must signal humility, obedience, and respect.

It should be clear that stable sets depend on the unhampered flow of set events, initiated by the proper individuals and responded to in turn by those who are expected to. The emphasis on training implies and, in fact, is associated with the determination by the trainer (or the superior individual in a set) to dominate and force the others to respond. Thus set events are ordinarily a consequence of prior interactions and the establishment by the supervisor, for example, of his "authority."

In training manuals for foremen, for executives, for school teachers, and in folk discussions about managing people, the point is repeatedly made that you have to "get the jump on them"—not let "them" think they can disregard your directions. In a more sophisticated discussion, but with an equally simple admonition, Mr. Justice Holmes said of the law that "its ultimate sanction is force." This does not mean that one necessarily has to use violence; what it does mean is that only by exercising dominance (or being ready to) can one take over the control of the interaction. Even partly successful attempts by others to dominate when someone tries to initiate can easily destroy an entire organizational system.

Much of the concern with developing more effective means of communication—insofar as this implies that specific actions are to result—has been concentrated on how the communicator or persuador is to manage the single someone on the other side of the desk. Techniques of handling groups are often relegated to the sidelines as improper, or "political" or evidence of unseeming ambition. "Understanding," through counseling or role playing, whatever the present fashion, is no substitute for life in groups, and adjustment thereto. Here again, the individual's personality and his capacity for managing stress are primary. Perhaps the current distaste for managing derives from an increasing acceptance of temperamental reactions in the young, nourished by the dictum that "you should be yourself," without considering the many patterns which each individual possesses among which he still has the opportunity and the responsibility to choose.

Complementarity in Group Events

With the exception of the highly trained performances of cultural sequences (and the sets which they involve), complementarity is not easy to achieve in set events. Pair events are much more frequent, their durations much longer, and give greater scope for attempts to synchronize. In groups, the many personalities involved, the often brief durations of set events, make it hard to provide full outlet for one's basal biological rhythms with a high degree of synchrony. On the other hand, some personalities come alive only in public speaking. Adjustment in group situations is an uneasy process. The initiator must constantly be watching for cues which indicate that the interaction may be getting out of hand and know how to act to maintain control.

Further, in observing groups, one should not confuse sequential interaction where *A* speaks, *B* says something, followed by *C* as instances of set events. These sequential chains may be highly synchronized, but they are very different in form. The major problem in understanding how groups are managed is that absolute reliance on the clock is essential. Though many investigators have made valiant efforts to try to describe what goes on in groups, particularly among apes and monkeys—less often in humans—the lack of accurate time measurements of the interaction make it inevitable that the group dynamics are never quite clear.

The Growth of Organizational Structures

Within a single organization, proliferation of structure comes about primarily by linking cultural subsequences together. In industry, for instance in automobile manufacturing, the final assembly line is fed by subassemblies, ordinarily with discontinuities separating them from the ultimate manufacturing area where the whole automobile first appears as a completed object. Prior to the subassemblies, however, are units, often entirely separate organizations, making components which are acquired by the manufacturer of cars by purchase from other companies, or produced within the organization. In other words, the increase in volume and the subdivision of jobs into smaller units, sometimes involving only one operation, is paralleled by the division, at each of the points of discontinuity, of the constituent sequences into separable institutions which still have to be conjoined through set extensions.

As new subflows or sequences prove to be necessary as the technology becomes more complex, the hierarchical sets erected on each must coordinate and ultimately integrate them into a single system in which, as management theorists like to put it, the "chain of command" is clearly defined. Remarkable difficulties arise, however, when this integration is attempted. Leaders of the separable "subinstitutional" units increase their interactions to maintain their positions as the alpha animals in their set. They compete in trying to extend their "span of control" to take in more subsequences. The stresses which personality differences and interactional skills introduce need no elaboration, as novels, case books, and organization studies amply testify.

But the "executive jungle," at least at the organizational level, is easily penetrated if the work-flow sequences are identified and hierarchical structure designed to bridge the subsequences. How important work-flow sequences prove to be in modern industry in shaping the total organizational structure has been well demonstrated in England by Woodward and her associates, in her book, Industrial Organization: Theory and Practice (1965). In studies of 100 industrial firms, she was able to show that the basic differences in their hierarchical (management or dominance) structure were due to the nature of the production process.

> In firms where large batch production [author's note: where a large number of units of whatever was being manufactured had to be finished before a new or slightly different product could be started, in contrast to production of single units] had been superseded by continuous-flow production, the command hierarchy had lengthened, the span of control of the chief executive had widened, and the ratio of managers and supervisors to total personnel had increased.

Thus, organizational structures are limited by the nature of the constituent work flows or cultural sequences, and the degree to which discontinuities can be bridged by interaction following along the chains of relationships set in motion by the cultural framework. Whatever the symbolic or linguistic relationships of the organization chart, like the kinship terminology of the ethnographers, these subsequences—what Chapple and Sayles (1961) called "unit work flows"—tend to develop their own autonomy unless bridged through continuous flow techniques, often computer managed. Otherwise, coordination can occur only by increasing the frequency of set events and establishing dominance throughout the hierarchical set, thereby forcing the constituent individuals to respond to the initiated directions of their supervisors.

At some point, the single organization, however small or large and complex it may be, has to relate to other organizations. For here the major discontinuities intervene, the product has to be sold, the boundaries adjudicated, and the rituals brought into line. Organizations, like the solitary craftsman, bridge the discontinuity when their members initiate across the barrier to those of another organizational system. Whether the cultural sequence is in business or industry, is political or religious, the problems of initiating a relationship and maintaining it are essentially similar.

In quite different cultures, similar processes are at work. Although not described in interactional terms (and interpretation is, therefore, necessary to estimate the interactional referents underlying the description), Goldschmidt and his associates in the *Culture and Ecology Project* (1965) have been interested in such problems. In one of their papers, Conant (1965) has summarized the factors at work in differentiating the organizational structure of the Pokot people of west central Kenya. The Pokot use a word, "korot," to describe a topographical unit which may be the sloping buttress of a mountain wall or a lesser slope in the plains. They also use the same word for the social unit, for the area of settlement and cultivation, and for the primary location for grazing their cattle.

Among the farmers, particularly in the mountain and hill areas, the greater intensity with which farming can be done results in greater stability in relationships within their topographical korok. By solidifying kin group relationships, this stability results in a tighter integration (as against other koroks) and, in so doing, strengthens the necessity to obtain wives from outside groups. In contrast, the pastoralists, though locating their main homesteads in the center of a topographical korok, range their cattle over several. The greater instability and scattering of the pastoralists increase the chances of finding wives within the topographical unit and reduce the strength of the kin group boundaries and the necessity for korok exogamy (marrying outside the group). Conant says:

> These differences between korok which are predominately herding or those which are predominately farming in their subsistence techniques manifest themselves despite the proximity of the one to the other. Pokot herders and farmers are seldom more than a day's march from each other; they inter-marry, they exchange subsistence produce, they share common rituals. And yet, profound differences in settlement patterns, affinal relations, and local councils occur and occur regularly. The regularity with which these differ-ences occur, despite the interdependence of farmer and herder, adds consid-erable force to the view of a subsistence technique as an intervening variable, conditioning much else in the cultural behavior of the Pokot.

In this brief example, processes similar to those reported by Wood-ward for English industrial firms are going on. The Pokot illustrate how the interplay of the cultural sequencing of subsistence and the dimension of spatial distance differentiated the social structure. They also show how significant differences in discontinuities, and the capacity to bridge them, affect the nature of the family structure as well as the definition and preemi-nence of territoriality within two groups.

Implications of Quantitative Differences between Sets within an Institution

Industry, government, the schools—any institution one might select—provide examples of the ways in which the quantitative properties of their constituent sets relative to one another shape the structure (and the emotional–interactional properties) of the organization. The family, as an institution, is the most interesting, because it is the most personal. Further, it is the focus of many social anthropological studies carried out in cultures all over the world. As the primary interactional system through which personality and temperament characteristics are developed and the basic biological rhythms given cultural form, family analysis can bring home to the reader, for whom the complex hierarchies of large corporations may be a mystery, the way cultural sequences and their sets operate.

The simplicity of sets (and the set events which give them structure) within the family should not be regarded as evidence of their relative impotence. In the United States, the familiar constituents of a household are the members of the nuclear family—father, mother, and children. Yet this does not mean that the family stops there. Families often have additional relatives living with them; on the other hand, in the so-called ghetto areas of the cities (and by no means rare in towns and countryside in the Caribbean and elsewhere), the basic nurturant unit of mother and children, the fundamental biological dependency, is most common. Often, the mother's mother or a sister lives with them; males are episodic, with minimal involvement with the children. Even though the number of people is so limited, the differential effects of age and sex, and the division of labor built upon them, mean that set events do occur, from parents to children, males to females, females to males and, lastly, from the children (ordinarily with a much lower frequency) to their parents. The cultural sequences constraining these set events are those necessary in carrying out the domestic tasks. In addition, they include controlling the activities of the children and teaching them to accept the initiated directions of the parents. Except in Victorian days and before, the kind of patterning of interaction described by Albert for the Burundi, previously quoted, has disappeared. Though it is rumored that the oldest existing cuneiform tablet found in Mesopotamia contains the lament of a Sumerian father that the young no longer respect their parents, there is reason to believe that such heretical behavior is now more common among present-day American families.

Even in complete, suburban middle-class nuclear families, the father, for five days at least, leaves early in the morning, returning in the early evening. Completeness, therefore, does not imply continuity of presence and interaction. In other societies, for example, the polygynous peoples of Africa, husbands live apart from their wives and their crop of children. Fortes (1947) described Ashanti children bringing pots of cooked food from their houses to their father's dwelling and, in those groups practicing polyandry in other parts of the world—a form of marriage in which one woman had several husbands—these might live separately, awaiting her beck and call. Conversely, there are families, as in China, where all the male offspring of the oldest male, together with their wives and children, often comprising five generations, live in a single great household around a central courtyard with many rooms.

In various parts of the world, therefore, the interplay of spatial distance, its constraints strengthened by architectural form, and the cultural sequences associated with coresidence, domestic tasks, marriage, and the care of the children, define different coliving units. In addition, in cultures where the division of labor and the complexity of economic institutions are much simpler than in the United States, the members of the family (in this case more than the household) take part in securing food and in producing objects for use or sale. Thus, family becomes an "economic institution" also. Domestic activities, together with the carrying out of the technological sequences through which the family maintains itself as a group, are parceled out along the lines of sex and age. Every society has man's work and women's work, some things to be done by children, and some by the old.

In considering how family systems develop and become differentiated, there are two processes operating. The first, and least discussed in modern literature, is the way in which spatial distance and cultural sequencing impose constraints on the interaction, constraints which apply both to the frequency and duration of contacts between individuals in the family and to the patterns of interaction which make up these contacts. Actually, this process is no great mystery. Chapple and Coon (1942) pointed out how environment, the techniques available to the culture for getting food and producing goods, as well as the possible need to wage war in order to maintain territorial cohesion of the group, could all be shown to bear directly on the distribution of interactions within the nuclear family.

The Bedouin of Northern Arabia are camel nomads, living under desert conditions. Because of the meagreness of available pasture and water, they are constantly on the move within the sparse limits of very large territories. Camels are their major source of revenue. In consequence, Bedouin are always interested in adding to their herds at the expense of their neighbors. Raids between tribal units, both to acquire camels and to redress any imbalance in reciprocity in the perennial feuds existing between them, are constantly occurring. So warfare and camel herding, where even the young boys can aid their fathers, are the prime cultural sequences.

The emergency nature of such raids, and the necessity to become skilled in camel care and in fighting, separated out the males as a unit, so much so that set events of males to females (even of small boys to their mothers and other female relatives) are well established. This is not the place to discuss how the cultural sequences, reinforced by spatial distance, increase the frequencies and durations of both set and pair events along one set, minimizing others. Other examples are cited in the reference previously given.

Directional Shifts in Family Organization through Preponderant Sets

What needs to be considered now is the second element in structuring the family (or other institutions). Here a quantitative predominance of one set modifies the frequencies of the others; it creates patterns of behavior towards classes of family members which may then be extended outside, first to a large family as a complex of relationships, and then to other institutions. Hsu (1965) has been particularly concerned with what he calls the "dominant" relationships. In several papers besides the above, and in a symposium with a number of other social anthropologists interested in this problem, he has tried to make explicit how such preponderances operate.

He makes clear the significance of this kind of structuring of the nuclear family in developing idiosyncratic personality patterns in interaction terms, commenting that out of what he defines as the eight basic relationships in the nuclear family—father–son, mother–son, father–daughter, mother–daughter, husband–wife, brother–brother, sister–sister, and brother–sister—most cultural groups have one (or a limited number) in which a preponderance of the interaction takes place. He uses the term "attributes" to mean characteristic patterns of interaction. In his hypothesis, and in the discussions by others, it becomes clear that it is difficult to try to describe in qualitative terms the variations which quantitative data of frequencies, durations, and the component interaction variables would afford unambiguously. Some of the issues are, at bottom, semantic; others are due to restricting the consideration to pair rather than including set events and sets.

Beyond that, however, Hsu points out, as Chapple and Coon did explicitly in interaction terms, that as one relationship becomes preponderant, others are necessarily minimized. In the Bedouin case, the high degree of interaction between father and sons reduces the amount of interaction which can take place with the women. In fact, the patterning of the spatial distances between males and females and the separation of "male" cultural sequences from those carried on by the females is given explicit demonstration by the division of the tent into two sections, separated by a curtain. In addition, the young men early become equal in usefulness and fighting ability to their fathers and older relatives. As this happens, the directional properties of a dominance relationship of the father to his sons is reduced. The nature of the fighting puts a premium on the older teen-ager or the young man in his early twenties. Beyond that, he is past his peak as a warrior.

Posing the problem in interaction terms, we should remember that each individual requires a constant amount of interaction, derived from the limitations of the circadian expenditure of activity and interaction. Thus, for given family types, the dynamics of displacement can be calculated as one relationship (or more) increases in the frequency and duration of its contacts and the emotional–interactional patterns of which these contacts are comprised. In particular cases of nuclear families to whose behavior interaction measurement is being applied, this can be varied by idiosyncratic personality and temperament patterns. Nevertheless, as in any study, if a sufficient sample of families is measured, the ranges, means, and variances can be determined and a reliable description for a cultural group provided by factoring out the idiosyncratic.

The extension of the particular personality and temperamental patterns which a given nuclear family structure produces to other institutional settings probably needs little discussion. Where individuals become conditioned to particular patterns of interaction, focused on age–sex categories (or relationships), they tend to repeat the same patterns in what they regard as equivalent situations, for reasons to be commented on later. Albert's discussion of Burundi styles of interaction and the cultural sequences developed around them illustrates how the same patterns are used in the family, in the political hierarchy, and so on. In addition, the dynamics bringing about Burundi need to develop manipulative techniques for those in power appears to derive from the ambiguities of their position in sets and the rapid fluctuations in chances to achieve and sustain complementarity which is part of the structuring of their particular type of nuclear family.

It is a common observation, not limited to those with psychiatric sophistication, that people behave in many situations as they do in their families. The executive who reacts temperamentally towards his superior officer and to the world as he did (or does) to his father, or the young man who is unconsciously searching for a young woman who will enable him to enjoy long intervals of complementarity and thus be equivalent to his mother may never shed their family shackles, but they, and many other variations on this theme, are the stuff on which popular literature is built.

There is thus a major uniformity, a point made both by Hsu and by Chapple and Coon in different terminology. Beyond the shaping of the personality, large institutions are also shaped in the ways in which the interaction patterns are carried out; these, in turn, derive from or at least are reinforced by family dynamics. Many people, not only the social anthropologists, have emphasized how in religious institutions, particularly in Christian denominations, different patterns of relationships of priests and followers, and the symbolic statements by which these relationships are defined, express different family patterns. Similar processes go on in other institutions, including the economic.

Probabilities of Interaction within Institutions

Organizations of every type—familial, religious, political, associational as well as economic—are built upon multiples of cultural sequences. Hence, the probabilities that individuals will interact depend on the quantitative properties of the linkages in sets as well as the number of dimensional steps (relationships) separating them. The executive head of a large department may be many steps away from his messenger boy along the hierarchical set where the primary cultural sequence consists of transmitting administrative instructions. The latter may initiate frequently in another set by bringing mail, memos, and reports from other departments directly to him. Though widely separate in one, the two are adjoining in another.

Starting from any person, therefore, one can trace the number of steps in a network of interrelated cultural sequences and the sets underlying them which separate him from every other individual in the organization. If the structure is looked at as abstracted from the spatial dimensions within which it necessarily must operate, unless the chain of classes or ranks in a set extends beyond a few sequential linkages, the probabilities of interacting become minimal. The cat may look at the Queen, but is not likely to become involved in affairs of state.

Other dimensions do intervene, of course, notably proximity in space. The consequence is that widely separated individuals may potentially have almost as high an interactional frequency as those who occupy the same position in a work flow sequence. On the other hand, physical separation, in different buildings or different floors, or even in some other part of the country, introduces discontinuities within sets which are hard to bridge. One cannot assume that a given institution, even a family system, is necessarily manifesting a high frequency of interaction within its nuclear families if, as in the case of West African groups, the household (the true nucleus, so to speak) only sees the father on occasion. And, if the mother is no longer attractive physically or emotionally, he may come into sight only on ceremonial occasions.

In what has been said so far, the primary focus has been on the ways in which the dimensions of spatial distance and cultural sequencing, built up on the patterns of interaction occurring between the two or more people present, combine to organize human institutions. For the purpose of exposition, the dimension of communication has been kept out of the discussion, although it has been implicit throughout. Thus, Hsu's summary listing of the eight basic relationships mentions father, mother, husband, wife who, in the nuclear family at least, reduce to two individuals. Moreover, the cultural sequences themselves are very often communicational. They may simply involve postures, movements, words, and phrases which individuals learn to use in regulating their interactions with others, as the Burundi example so well illustrates.

The large institutions of the present day could not exist without the mediation of the communication dimension, for the sets which organize them and tie them together, distributed as they often are in the far parts of the globe, depend on the capacity of humans to react to symbols. These symbols are highly differentiated. The process of ascertaining precisely what they refer to and their mutual relationships, though complicated, is essential to understanding culture in its full scope. So it is time to face up to the spate of speech which differentiates man from the lower animals, at the same time remembering that communication is not his private property. Thus, we again return to behavioral biology in terms of which man "communicates." In so doing, we shall see how its constraints affect the subtle quantitative variations of the interaction patterns themselves.

Chapter 13

Constraints
of Communication Patterning

Language (or more broadly, communication) is the mediator through which man's other cultural achievements have been made possible. Resulting from the cortical efflorescence which differentiates man from all other animals, it provides the means by which the perceptual world, internal and external, is interconnected and can be labeled so information can be transferred from one individual to another. Yet, from the point of view of behavioral anthropology, the logics of language are not really relevant in themselves. Or rather, they concern us only as one more cultural dimension, like spatial distance and cultural sequencing. Dimensions are not part of the emotional–interactional system of the individual; they provide the boundary conditions within which it operates.

Dimensionally, communication is more complex, since one can isolate a group of subdimensions affecting different interactional patterns. The probabilistic framework which these set up depends on the degree and manner in which they impose specific constraints. Questions of accuracy of information transfer (involving cognitive as distinct from the emotional–interactional process) in a particular cultural setting are outside the realm of behavioral anthropology. Moreover, language (or communication) is to be understood as that complex of speech, gesture, and posture occurring in, and further differentiated by, the dimensions of spatial distance and cultural sequencing. Verbal *and* nonverbal, linguistics and meta-linguistics, the total communicative response is the medium, framed by the necessities of the interaction rhythms. To simplify the presentation of how communication affects the interaction probabilities, we shall attempt to hold the other cultural dimensions constant.

Given the individual personalities, caught up in their continuing need to interact and the differential consequences of complementarity and asynchrony, what straight-jackets or flexible barriers do language interpose? Two broad categories will concern us:

1) those deriving from the biological properties of communication— (a) fluctuations in intensity or amplitude of sound or movement, (b) changes in intonation or pitch, (c) in timbre, and (d) articulation rates (of minor influence and not treated here);

2) the symbols—words, phrases, gestures, or postures or material objects, spatial distance and cultural sequences which evoke responses (or prevent them) in the interactional patterns of the listener.

Both categories have their roots in biology, the first directly, the second through the learning process.

In what is to follow, one must not forget that communication patterning is superimposed on the underlying interaction itself. The latter provides the carrier waves which set the beats, determine the rhythms, and are the organizing principle on which language in its broadest sense is elaborated. Language, of course, has its own regularities, but if we are to understand its dimensional impacts, we have to realize that the beginnings and endings of actions set limits on the amount of communication which any given duration can contain. On the other hand, some cutting and shaping of action durations take place through the constraints which a given statement or sequence of statements requires if it is to be fully expressed. The interplay is complex but, in what follows, it is hoped that the nature of this mutual dependence will be clear.

Biological Properties of Communication

The limits of this book make it impossible to describe in any detail the biological foundations of language. In any case, Lenneberg, in his book with that title (1967), has done a first-class job though, in his words, it is essentially a "theoretical treatise." As he demonstrates, speech (voice) has its biological components, and we can thus begin by considering what kinds of measurements can be made on the language patterning contained within any action. In effect, we need to ask how these variables provide dimensional character and constraints on the differential effects of two actions whose duration and position in an interactional sequence are, by assumption, equivalent.

It is well known that the variables making up human speech can be measured. Potentially then, they represent true dimensions in the scientific sense. However, although spectrographic recordings of speech can be obtained—with adequate funds, perhaps continuously—no one as yet knows how these data can be effectively analyzed and interrelated with the underlying interaction rhythm. Beyond that, of course, other than through schematic representations, the expressive movements of gesture and posture, including gaze, are far more recalcitrant to recording systems.

These latter elements of communication require such laborious and time-consuming procedures that experimentalists can only dream of reducing the nonspeech patterns to potential order. This is not to decry the efforts of Birdwhistell (1952) and Scheflen (1965) in kinesics and Hall (1966) in proxemics who have tried to bring about some such reduction. But their concern is primarily with the information-carrying aspects, not with gestural and spatial elements as measurable variables.

In spoken language, measurement is possible, and one can see, in theory, how similar criteria might be extended to expressive movement. Excluding distance, which has a quantitative dimension of its own, one has to begin with motor events, that is, with the contraction and relaxation of muscles in fixed action patterns. In speech, the syllable appears to be the fastest physiologically separable unit with an articulation rate of approximately 6 per second. It is based, or activated, by what Stetson (1951) called a "breath pulse." The anatomical, neurological, and physiological complexities of what goes on in speech are well summarized by Lenneberg. How complex the process is is indicated by the fact that over 100 muscles are involved and must be controlled by the central nervous system. Which ones come into operation at a particular time depends on their position in bringing the phoneme into being (the linguistic elements of syllables). These vary in being activated depending on which phonemes precede and follow them.

However fixed this basic rhythm of articulation is (it appears to have very little variation across individuals or cultures), its periodicity is only the substructure on which interaction patterns are constructed. More interesting, and important, is the fact that when speech begins, the dynamics of breathing undergo a major change. In contrast to what happens if, when silent, we try to breath rapidly (hyperventilating) with giddiness and other central nervous system effects occurring, breath patterns during speech are remarkably adaptive. The physiological shifts which go on can continue interminably as in a "long-winded" speech. As commented on in Chapter 4, physiological (emotional) stress produces changes in respiration rates; although they may not alter the articulation rate (though little is known here), they do directly influence interaction durations.

But breathing has another, and more important, consequence in establishing a dimension, the significance of which is straightforward. Lenneberg points out that the degree of loudness is determined by the amount of air available. Since it is clear that loudness or softness of sound is a dimension influencing response, shifts in respiration rate (including depth of breathing) due to autonomic changes are the source through which the modulations in amplitude accompanying action are brought about.

A)   Subdimension of Loudness or Amplitude

Though it might be assumed that continuous measurement of amplitude of voice could be managed concurrently with duration of actions, the problem is complicated by two factors.

(1)   Apart from the expense of accurate recording, each phoneme carries with it its own idiosyncratic degree of amplitude. Hence what phonemes are used by the speaker and in what order vary the degree of loudness measured.

(2)   More important, no one has yet worked out a scale of loudness in terms of its interactional consequences, that is, to establish that just so much of an increase (or decrease) will modify the expected interactional response as measured in durations.

We know, from empirical observation, that the amplitude of sound in most conversations appears to fall within rather constant limits. Only if there is a major deviation beyond such limits do we look to see whether it has a differential impact on interaction. Unfortunately for analysis, apart from the phonemic amplitude problems, each person has his own average loudness level (and range limits) to which the other person ordinarily adapts so that no absolute measures can be relied on. Moreover, as discussed in Chapter 9, the dimension of spatial distance directly affects the amplitude; the farther away, the louder one has to speak.

Provided these factors are taken into account, we can set up limits for each individual, presumably at different distance intervals. These constitute an amplitude band whose width indicates the expected variability under basal conditions. Whenever significant deviations in amplitude occur outside these limits, we can assign a scaled value of dimensional impact. By calculating a series of intervals or ranges outside this "normal" band, a scale of deviations (one for increased and one for decreased amplitude) can be established as the hardness scale in mineralogy or the Beaufort scale for ocean weather. Measurements provide the basis for these interval scales (they might differ for loudness and softness), but only extended experiments can fix the size of the intervals with precision and determine whether the scale units are equal in width (linear) or logarithmic or whatever. Until such studies are carried out, only a qualitative judgment can be made and existing techniques have little value in interaction measurement.

B)   The Subdimension of Intonation or Pitch

To complicate the problem of utilizing loudness, at least two other subdimensions of speech interfere. The first is intonation or pitch. The latter term is more common to music; one might hope that the musical scale could be taken over for dimensional purposes, yet it is unlikely that B# in the middle octave has a different impact on interaction than A flat even in an octave above. In language, pitch primarily refers to the ways in which a pattern of intonation is utilized to elicit or inhibit a response from another person. Using a particular tonal sequence can indicate a question—in grammar this is called the interrogative—and the pitch contour here is very different than in a simple declaratory statement, even though both have the same action duration. To complicate matters further, there are many tonal languages where the meaning of the word shifts with the tone level adopted (including English to some degree). These might be manageable if some preliminary, workable scale were available for intonation itself. In addition, gesture is a common supplement; raising the eyebrows is a gestural interrogation.

Pitch, therefore, in its interactional impact is little explored although it appears possible to classify pitch contours (with amplitude held constant) much as suggested for amplitude itself. In other words, a set of limits could be determined experimentally and deviations therefrom ranged on a continuous scale.

C)   The Subdimension of Timbre

A category with less easily perceived differential effects on interaction is the tonal quality of the voice—its timbre. However one might measure it dimensionally and determine its scale of biological influence, individuals differ remarkably among themselves in timbre. In turn, for a given individual, the occurrence of stress reactions varies the timbre significantly. Such an observation is, of course, highly empirical. Again, we are at present dependent, as with intonation, on relatively crude and partially intuitive discriminations. Yet timbre is a well-defined (and measurable) property of musical instruments and voice. The question is: How to develop a scale of quantitative effects?

Timbre is the occurrence of vibrations at varying frequencies at a single pitch. Voices with this kind of tonal quality have more capacity to evoke responses than those flat monotonal speakers who linger on a single note (a simple note in musical terms). In gesture, timbre has its parallel (but no equivalent term) in what are referred to as free expressive movements, an accolade to bestow on a ballet dancer. One can easily establish a scale ranging from single to complex vibrations (measurement is not too hard), but its intervals, and biological influences, can only be guessed at.

Each of these subdimensions, however precisely they can be recorded and utilized, fluctuate with time and emotional situations. It is just this capacity to vary that produces their effects. Otherwise, whatever their level on the ultimately-to-be-developed scales, if their values are repetitive and fall within narrow limits, the initial impact will be quickly habituated to by other people and lose its effect. For each of these subdimensions, empirical observation also suggests that there are individuals whose loudness, intonation, and timbre vary with some kind of periodicity within a sequence of actions. These fluctuations seem independent of shifts associated with emotional–interactional changes or those directly concerned with eliciting an immediate response of a particular type in the next unit, as in the pitch contour of interrogation.

The significance of these subdimensions is that their properties supplement or inhibit the influence of the durations themselves. A loud shout is clearly likely to increase the probability of a response. If done concurrently with an interruption, dominance may be that much more easily established. Intonation and timbre have similar properties. However, it is important to remember that all three subdimensions influence interaction only by setting probabilities. A loud voice *may* make dominance more likely to be won; a rich tonal quality *may* produce more and longer responses; intonation *may* shift a long action to a brief one if the individual responding tries to answer the question. On the other hand, such is the preponderance of the interaction rhythms that no perceptible change in rates may be detected. As stated earlier, the cultural dimensions define probabilities; they do not have the predictable regularities of the biological rhythms of the individual.

Evocative Properties of Symbols

The content of any communicative interval, whether it be speech and gesture alone or elaborated by expressive movements in space and cultural sequencing, is made up of separable units—words, phrases, sentences—limiting this discussion, for ease of exposition, to language itself. These larger units are built up from a set of elementary ones—the phonemes, although Lamb (1964) has argued that the phoneme itself can be reduced to what he calls a phonon, analogous to a meson or proton in physics. In any case, it is generally agreed that there are four levels or strata on which language is built, each with its elementary unit, each having a composite relational unit which manages the transition from one level to the next higher one. These strata begin with the phonemic, proceed to the morphemic, then to the lexemic (from word), and finally to the sememic (roughly grammatical class).

Lamb, taking his two highest strata, the lexemic and sememic, illustrates what they mean with an example:

> that the word *can*, as in *he can go*, is lexemically different from *be able to,* as in he *will be able to go,* but sememically these are one and the same unit.

In other words, the sememic level describes those structural elements of meaning which are interchangeable. In effect, Lamb is saying that one can use the same building blocks from the sememic level down and thus reduce the analytical procedures for grammatical classes, phrases, words, and syllables, to a common framework.

Although this brief statement by no means states his argument adequately or the parallelisms between his position and others in the field, it does make the point that in ethno- or psycholinguistics, a consistent logic has been developed for dealing with the formal properties of language. But beyond these four levels which together make up the structure of language, there is a fifth level—the amorphous area of semantics. This is the province of meaning, where the structural properties of language, in units of varying complexity, make possible information transfer and/or have emotional impact on both speaker and listener.

Lamb illustrates how semantics differ from the formal properties of language by the differential meanings in four sememes, "big rock," "big sister," "big fool," and "he's a big man in our town." Since each is very different in meaning, the sememe, "big" has a wide variety of meanings depending on context, and hence no uniformity can be established. It is with the semantic aspects of communication that we are concerned since, in a far more complicated and difficult way, they too provide dimensional constraints on interaction.

Before we consider how symbols take on meaning, and their differential influence, it may be helpful to anticipate the discussion by commenting on how they work. Since we assume from common knowledge that symbols evoke responses in a listener—for instance the cry of "Fire!", or "I love you," there is little need to add examples—then the spacing of symbols both within an action and in conjunction with the beat can set up or accentuate rhythms on their own. One must hasten to add, *if* the other person responds to the symbols.

Thus when the other person (or in groups, the audience) does respond, the speaker dominates. By remaining in control, he is able to continue the duration of his action at his own rhythm. In addition, if evocative symbols are properly spaced, the individual tempos of the responders are activated. With a large group, the effective speaker gradually synchronizes these individual tempos of response to a single unifying beat. So, if symbols, within their appropriate interaction setting, are properly spaced, the speaker is able to shift the adjustment of the group. He can determine when it is safe to pause, when to expect a response, and when to resume, without fear of losing his audience.

To do this, symbols cannot be scattered randomly across the interaction. There is a logic in speaking, whether to an individual or a group. It requires one to program the symbols as well as the interaction to fit the needs of the audience. And they vary. The sermon, the political speech, the reassurance of a physician, the protestations of a lover, the maintenance or restoration of discipline in any group setting, all require careful planning of symbolic as well as interactional sequences.

Everyone knows that a public speaker is expected to warm up his audience by telling a few jokes. The purpose, of course, implicitly or explicitly, is to get them to begin to respond, hopefully in unison. But another purpose is also served; such stories are ordinarily told at different tempos, beginning with a shorter beat, then gradually lengthening as the speaker gets serious. The successful speaker knows he must introduce variations in tempo, doing this by varying the evocative quality of the symbol. Shift gears—do not be serious all the time—are cautions given the tyro.

History has recorded the rhetorical performances of famous preachers—and dictators like Hitler—who could dominate an enormous throng, getting them to respond at such a regular and accelerating beat that the rhythms took over and the resulting behavior of the group was hypnotic in its automatism. The speeches, usually successful (but incomprehensible to the student of history who reads them), were preceded by elaborate "warm up" periods to increase the state of arousal of the audience before the main talk began. So too, the design of religious services—the interspersion of prayer, hymns, responsive readings, and the sermon—was directed towards accomplishing this arousal, perhaps half-consciously and by trial and error as to what succeeded best.

Underlying such performances are the interaction patterns of those taking part. If the speaker lets his interaction rhythms and those of his audience get away from his control, the spell is broken. However high the emotional level of the symbols, they no longer have the same impact. In fact, their repetition at cross-synchrony to the interaction rhythms can destroy their effectiveness. If the audience does not dwindle away and disappear, it may turn on the speaker and dominate him, destroying his position of authority by shouting slogan-symbols back.

The Formation of Symbols

Though the previous section illustrates, in general, how symbols can be evocative in the course of interaction, it does not provide us with any specific means of estimating which ones will do so or to what degree. We now have to turn to the process of symbolization itself to see how symbols become established and how they acquire this property of evocation. This question can be restated in a slightly different way, since eliciting a response assumes an emotional–interactional property. What we need to know is why this symbol did so and not that; further, why it was this symbol in this particular sequence of other symbols and the interactions underlying them?

To answer these questions requires a brief and oversimplified excursion into how learning takes place although, in the sense to be considered here, learning is limited to symbolization. The Russian physiologist, Pavlov, is often considered (not quite properly) the source and origin of it all. Pavlov was interested in understanding the ways in which animals could be conditioned: that is, how they learned to discriminate between various stimuli, and how the "teaching" process came about. At the period when his work was first becoming known in English-speaking countries (and in some quarters even today), his apparent restriction of explanatory hypothesis to the influences of external stimuli was the source of great enthusiasm among "behaviorists" like Watson in the United States. A continuing conflict then began in biological and psychological circles between those who felt that the organism was entirely a creature of its conditioning and those, now in ever-increasing numbers, who maintained that endogenous factors are equally relevant. Pavlov himself was not on the side of the behaviorists since he showed that animals with different personality patterns (temperaments or humors in the ancient sense) reacted differently in his experiments. Actually, behavioral biology has long since moved apart from this battle, but dissension still lingers on in the field of psychology which is, as Beach (1965) pointed out, the science of learning.

Pavlov's studies of what he called the "conditioned reflex" began by using the reflex act of salivation. He showed that if a stimulus like ringing a bell—which might become a sign or symbol—was presented to a dog at the same time as another stimulus which had previously made the dog salivate, like a piece of meat, then sounding a bell and presenting the meat resulted, after a few trials, in the dog "learning" to salivate when only the bell was rung. Ringing the bell *after* waving the meat in the dog's face did not work. The sequence had to be followed rigorously.

Much of Pavlov's work was devoted to investigating the fineness of the discriminations animals could learn. For example, they can discriminate between the sound of a metronome beating 104 times a minute and one beating 100 times a minute. Many types of incongruous responses were established—a dog wagging his tail and showing signs of "joy" when burned. Pavlov also investigated how long a training process was needed (number of events, effects of variations in intervals between sequences, and so on), and how the conditioning pattern could be extinguished by providing the stimulus of the bell without "reinforcing" it with a piece of meat. Of special interest in his studies of extinction was his discovery that a pattern could be reactivated if "sufficient" time elapsed before the stimulus was tried again.

The dog's discriminations are merely indicative of mammalian capacity to learn to differentiate subtle shadings in temporal characteristics in interaction and in selecting, as we shall see, all kinds of variegation in perceptual stimuli as symbols. More important was the development of quantitative studies of conditioning, an important concern of present-day psychology, which led to the testing of schedules or programs by which learning could be facilitated or retarded.

If Pavlov in his laboratory (and countless investigators afterwards) could condition the animal to learn, then it appeared likely that the environment which greeted the new-born baby could do likewise. Without trying to sketch a developmental history, two processes of learning are at work:

(1)   The infant learns to interact, to impose beginnings and endings on the bursts of activity set off by his own internal rhythms through the conditioning presence of those around him;

(2)   He learns to distinguish perceptual configurations—shapes, individuals, colors—and to recognize words which adults associate with them. As his capacity for acquiring language reaches maturation, he begins to use symbols in an adult way.

The first of these processes involves the autonomics-skeletal nervous systems with their mediation through the controlling limbic- hypothalamic-reticular centers. The cortex is, of course, involved as discriminative patterns of muscular movement (through external stimuli) are activated. Yet the whole process is far more complex (and total) than accounts of ordinary learning imply since so much of it is due to the interplay between internal rhythms and the external world. Moreover, it is subvocal (more properly subverbal), since language is still minimally associated with it.

At the same time, it is perceptual—internally and externally—since events or interactional contacts between mother and other members of the family occur. These are associated with the internal requirements of food and tactile sensation, discomfort, anxiety, or fear and rage. These events, in which the infant acts and interacts and is thus responding, may be regarded as parallel to the substructures which Pavlov used to hook his stimuli onto in carrying out his conditioning process. Not that babies do not salivate, but restriction of conditioning to the "reflex" (which Pavlov abandoned in his later work) confuses the issue. There have been some sad consequences in lengthy exercises in dialectics to distinguish one kind of "learning" from another, and all from Pavlov's.

Derivation of Symbols from Contexts of Situation

If the world be looked at as the laboratory in which the individual is being studied, or at least that segment of real estate within his distance scales, then emotional–interactional events become the experimental variables, and the contexts of physical and cultural surroundings provide the raw material—the ringing of the bell—which become the symbols. Malinowski (1927) used the term "context of situation" for the human activities and the surrounding environmental and cultural elements. Chapple (1940) defined this term more specifically by limiting each context of situation to one interactional event, so that human affairs consisted of a sequence of interactions, each with its associated context of situation. Looked at in this view, the conditioning or learning process in its more general sense was sequenced in time and involved discrete interactional events (experiments). The secondary stimulus which became the sign or symbol was not decided on for experimental purposes by Mother Nature; like Pavlov's bell it was selected out of the context of situation by the act of repetition in a sequence of interactional contacts.

Biological Factors in Symbol Selection

Studies of animals (and humans) have demonstrated that each species seems to have particular predilections for particular perceptual configurations or stimulus complexes. Presumably this is a consequence of the evolutionary history of the species; in any case, there is a filtering (using the zoologist's term) which highlights some properties of the external environment and minimizes others. Marler and Hamilton (1966) pointed out that when some external situation which required rapid adaptation on the part of the individual arose:

> animals evolve mechanisms for responsiveness to some abstracted property of that situation. The essential quality of this sign stimulus or stimulus complex is that it is shared by all situations in which the response is appropriate.

How specific the stimulus has to be depends on the number of factors, but seems to be a consequence of the impact of natural selection over the history of the species. Once the species begins to choose particular stimulus-complex properties, natural selection then continues the process by refining the characteristics for the species which emphasize that particular trend towards filtering. These fall within the great class of recognition symbols (or signs)—the plumage of the male grouse or the variegated color (and shape) patterns of tropical fish.

Although insects and some birds require precise synchronization of their calls, individual recognition among birds and the primates is also clearly dependent on visual cues. Among primates, the ways in which eyes, brows, mouth, ears, body, limbs, and tail (and movements thereof) combine enable their cohorts to recognize who is coming into interactional distance. But in addition, there are preferences for colors, shapes, and forms. Yellow, orange, and red colors are highly conspicuous to man and many other vertebrates, and commonly selected as distinguished signs. In addition, certain kinds of spatial patterns, particularly broken and concentric designs, are intriguing to human babies and, inexplicably, to bees. (Fantz 1961, 1965, in Marler and Hamilton 1966).

Marler and Hamilton comment on the extremes of plumage ornamentation and sexual dimorphism among humming birds, birds of paradise, certain shorebirds, and so on. In these species:

> instead of there being a durable pair bond, the contact between male and female is brief. The males display, females visit them, and copulation occurs. The females then leave to lay eggs and raise young on their own. The brevity of the pair bond allows little opportunity for the correction of errors. This has presumably placed special emphasis on the plumage characteristics that are attractive to the female, resulting in distinctive plumage patterns and displays.

Obviously, where recognition must be done quickly and the relationship is brief, cues for recognition must be highly pronounced. Human parallels occur in many cultures; perhaps today, in Western societies, the passion for high fashion in which a woman (or man) indulges is inversely correlated with her (or his) affectional staying power!

In humans, filtering derives its stimulus complexes from cultural contexts, but the general description of the process which Marler and Hamilton (1966) gave is applicable.

> Confronted with a critical situation to which a response must be given, animals evolve mechanisms for responsiveness to some abstracted property of that situation. The essential quality of this sign stimulus or stimulus complex is that it is shared by all situations in which the response is appropriate. . . . The degree of specificity of an effective stimulus will vary widely in relation to

several factors. If a narrow range is appropriate, responsiveness will be restricted to highly specific stimuli. ... If the receptors are inadequate, particularly at a distance, there is likely to be a sequence of stimulus–response relationships, unspecific at first but becoming more specific in subsequent steps. In other circumstances there may be a chain of stimuli and responses with a specific stimulus early in the sequence. ... A degree of filtering of the incoming situation is thus universal, varying in its refinement according to what we presume to be the dictates of natural selection.

Thus colors, shapes or sounds, in relatively simple patterns and combinations, can stand for the particular contexts of situation within which interactional (and emotional) experiences take place. The policeman's peremptory blowing of his whistle, bringing the hurrying motorist to a sudden stop, is a stimulus with a narrow acoustical range. It requires few contexts of situation to establish a profound sympathetic nervous system reaction pattern, the relative distribution of adrenalin and noradrenalin of fear and anger—varying due to the individual temperament. The shape of the cross for members of the Christian faith, or the crescent for Moslems, needs only to be sketched in visual form to serve as a preliminary signal of particular contexts to come. Colors (particularly black and white, red, green, yellow, ordinarily the bright colors of opposing hues), associated with a wide variety of shapes and forms, take on similar meanings in every culture.

If reinforcement does not occur through repetitive interaction and its component autonomic elements within these contexts, what Pavlov calls "extinction," and biologists refer to as "habituation," takes place. Though one may quibble about what differences, if any, can be established between the definitions of these two terms, what happens is that animals (and humans) become used to (habituated to) the occurrence of stimuli if no alarming or other emotional responses are associated with them.

Further, habituation makes possible a greater refinement in discriminatory power between elements of the context. A filtering out of nonessential elements can occur or, conversely, more elements may be needed as symbols to produce the appropriate response. Young animals typically give escape responses to many kinds of unspecific stimuli but, with experience, the innocuous or ineffective ones are recognized and habituated to. So the motorist learns that police whistles are sometimes to be found in the hands of small boys; hence visual evidence of a police car or a blue uniform is needed to supplement the sign-stimulus of its piercing sound.

Two processes, then, take place within the general framework of conditioning or learning. First, there is the increasing specificity of a symbol. This may be aided by its association with other symbols which delimit the context in which the response is to occur. Without these associated elements, the response is not produced. Alternatively, there may be greater particularization of the symbol-stimulus itself, that is, only this particular cross made of ivory, with these particular color shadings, shaped just so . . . produces the response of the true believer. And secondly, generalization of symbols takes place over a wide variety of contexts; again all crosses are genuflected to, and the color black warns of mourning.

It should be apparent that these two processes depend on what occurs in the emotional–interational events making up the contexts of situation from which the symbols are selected. Where repetition brings about finer and finer discriminations in order to separate a particular emotional state from others which differ in greater or lesser degree from it, then emblemization (filtering, in zoology) takes place. Marcel Proust in *Remembrances of Things Past,* describes how the orchid, cattleya, which Odette wore when they first made love became for him (and for her much more briefly) the symbol of their relationship, while the special crumbly taste of the teacakes, the madeleines, could bring forth powerful feelings associated with his visits to the Guermantes. For him, the special differences in his relationship to Odette and the effects of her personality upon him made it impossible for the symbol to be generalized. Cattleyas, or orchids generally, did not become symbolic of other amours. In contrast, as psychiatrists have shown with what often appears to be unimaginative repetition, particular objects may become the necessary symbol for reinforcement to take place in all sexual encounters—a condition the literature refers to as fetishism. Whatever the aberration, in posture, clothing or objects present, the sign-stimulus of the particular fetish or fetishistic practice makes all sexual partners equivalent to one another.

The Cumulative Properties of Symbols

The process by which a given object—flower, teacake, crucifix—or words or gestures associated with it, becomes a symbol endowed with emotional relevance for an individual, is relatively straightforward, though the rationale for the linkage may be obscured or "repressed" through emotional conflict. The assemblage of such symbols and their mutual relationships for any given individual can be extraordinarily complicated, given the number of events (and contexts of situation) making up his life. A single relationship is made up of enormous numbers of interactional events, from the moment when the two individuals first meet until the present. How much vaster is the totality for the individual in all the interactions, brief or long, making up his life.

If one were trying to study the process over time, one would have to include all the cultural elements making up the contexts of situation. This would require not merely a continuous sound motion-picture recording of what happened (with maximum fidelity to record "everything"), but also some way of including the impact of the weather, the temperature of the room, the odors, all the stimuli, internal and external, which even sound film is helpless to depict.

Out of such contexts surrounding single events, symbols would begin to be differentiated, whether they were objects or particular words which referred to a particular relationship and its interactional properties. Though the cattleya blossom represented one type of context in which Proust as hero and Odette as antihero experienced each other, the tortuous and ambiguous nature of their total relationship required far more complex efforts on his part to give them symbolic as well as a kind of natural history expression. On the other hand, after the interval of "I love you" to what might be its antithesis of hate and grief, the terms themselves became associated with other people. "Love" for Proust involved a whole series of relationships, heterosexual and homosexual, maternal and filial, social climbing and dependent.

Hence the analysis of the meaning of one single symbol (love) requires a hierarchical order built upon series after series of interactional events as the constituent units on which it is based. And beyond the simple statement that "I love Odette" or "I hated my father," there is the tendency to generalize love or hate, and project them on the universe, a process described as "reification" or "hypostatization."

To determine the meaning in behavioral anthropology terms, to establish the emotional power of any symbol, one has to identify the contexts in which the particular symbol occurs. Malinowski pointed out that this may require the collection of a thousand statements for complete and accurate definition.

It is the ethnographer's dilemma that man is a verbal animal. If he should feel compelled to record the words as they came spilling out and code all aspects of the nonverbal material besides, he would soon decide to give up. Estimate an average output at 200 words a minute, assume that some of his subjects are high activity personalities in the interaction measurement sense, with long units of speech quite typical, and little opportunity for their listeners to get a word in edgewise. Give the subject eight hours of sleep (perhaps a little high but it makes the figuring easier), allow his several audiences the chance to talk somewhat over 5 percent of the time themselves; by simple arithmetic, the daily output of words alone reaches 180,000. And then, there are 365 days in the year, for how many years . . . and this is for only one individual in the group! (In case the reader is curious, the annual output would be 65,700,000 words, ignoring the endless redundancies of repetition.)

No wonder the ethnographer tries to turn off this flood by cross-examination, perhaps no longer taking a set of questions into the field as the old field manual, "Notes and Queries on Anthropology." recommended, but finding the queries in the culture being studied. So doing, as Frake (1964) commented, one returned, not with a description of a "complete culture," but rather with descriptions of particular cultural manifestations:

> Metzger and Williams, for example, emerged from one field session with descriptions of firewood, terms of personal reference, curers, weddings. Conklin has described ethnobotanical systems, agriculture, betel chewing, pottery, verbal play, color, kinship, and water.

(Frake believes that this procedure of breaking the culture into "domains" will "reveal the kinds of ranges of patterns in the culture for construing the world.")

To develop a semantics of personality, the problem is definitely unmanageable. Only slightly less so is this true for the ethnography of communication. Here, even without Frake's stated limitations, the concentration on cultural properties, that is, those which might be regarded as common across the members of a group and their *particular* background, makes the going somewhat easier. It is fortunate that habituation (or extinction) does take place in the human animal. For reasons too complex to be dealt with here, symbols lose their power and meaning; and others take their place, newly linked to the emotional–interactional substratum.

If one is only concerned with determining the dimensional impact of symbols, such precision in definition of meaning is unnecessary. What is needed is an ordering of symbols in a form which enables us to categorize their probable constraints on interaction. This excursion into the cultural aspects of symbolism should clarify the nature of the problems we face in such an ordering.

A Rudimentary Scale of Symbolic Impact

At the level of the observable interactional event and its context of situation, we are, for the purposes of exposition, able to give an extensionalized description of what we see and hear. By extensionalized, we mean the assignment of separate labels to the elements we have differentiated during observation, without now imputing any meaning to our labels other than that through their means we keep each element separate from each other. At this level of abstraction (Chapple and Coon 1942), often called first-order abstraction, a pedestrian and extremely detailed account results. In the conditioning experiment of the dog, the sight of the meat would be a first-order abstraction.

But once interactional events repeat themselves, that is, the same two people, say, interact again, common elements in the two events can be categorized and given a label selected out of the two contexts. As categorization begins, a second order of abstraction (from both contexts) takes place. If, in the next event, a third person takes part, the interactional category has broadened and the level of complexity becomes greater.

Shifting from such sterile examples to more common interactional situations, a progression is clearly evidenced when the symbol refers to a particular event between two people, to a relationship made up of many events, say of man and wife, to their relationships to one or more children (as parents), their mutual relations as a "family," their relations in turn with other individuals, their "relatives," and thus to the whole "family," and so to larger clusters until one symbol is used for the entire group, however large—"we, the people."

As symbols include more of the emotional–interactional contexts of the individuals using them, their evocative significance increases. By using levels of abstraction as a basis, a rudimentary scale for determining symbolic power can be derived. Each step to greater inclusiveness is one interval greater, however crude one may have to be in estimating the differential influence of that particular interval. These scales are not, however, limited to the example cited above, since a single relationship may have equally definite gradations of symbolic reference. "When we went to Atlantic City," "When we were living on Magnolia Street," and "Our whole life together," enable one to make such rough categorizations of levels of evocativeness. In Chapter 15, where the dimensional complexities of symbolic patterns—in organizations and the like—and the ways in which they set constraints on interaction are to be considered, such scales will become a little more general in application.

But symbols do not operate in isolation. The probabilities that they will evoke a response depend on their relative position in the interactional sequence. Just as a symbol can affect the interaction, so conversely its position in the interaction can determine whether it will impose any constraint at all. And, since this is a matter of probability, the test is, of course, did or did not any appreciable change occur? This is, of course, measurable, but a full consideration requires some comment on the mutual relationships between the two.

Symbolic Influences on Interaction

Although one can hypothecate that the more complex the emotional–interactional patterns to which a symbol refers, the greater the likelihood (probability) that a reaction will take place, mediated by the symbol's influence, there are complications. The major one is the fact that symbols are the prime content of interactional sequences; hence one has to "sterilize" the interaction to see how that influence operates by itself. In doing so, it is almost impossible not to make some interactional assumptions. In what follows, this will be minimized as much as possible.

Let us select a traveler returning from an extensive sight-seeing tour through Europe with Baedeker in hand and total recall. Here surely is grist for his high level of activity, with built-in audiences as he and his wife entertain their friends for dinner. At a pause in his discourse, an alert guest picks up a cue, left carelessly by the speaker, and starts off on his own (quite logically, of course) telling of *his* trip to a quite different part of the world which our hero has never visited. He has two alternatives: one, semantic, the other interactional. Either he can wait patiently and try to switch the topic back when his guest stops for a response or, using dominance, he can interrupt and try to persist long enough to reestablish control to salvage his yearnings for self-expression.

Obviously, the nature of the topic plays a part in the degree to which it can be used satisfactorily by high-activity people. Some provide a much longer series of intervals of continuous exposition than others. Moreover, the level of abstraction plays a part also, although it runs the risk of reducing the impact of symbols if the description is too much at the first-order level. The traveler who describes each action and event in relentless sequence can talk forever. Yet the lack of variation in the communication dimensions (for the moment limiting them to symbols) reduces the frequency with which response (and momentary dominance) can be obtained.

Earlier, the importance of spacing symbols to establish a rhythm of response has been commented on, though the problem is again complicated by interactional properties. Long-winded individuals can compel a forced response by low order symbols and a shift in gaze direction. This signals the need for response, but control is established by looking quickly away after securing it. But the symbols cannot be metered out in too rigid a fashion since the challenge is to find the rhythm (tempo of response) at which the audience (single or otherwise) responds best. Moreover, symbols have to be varied in their emotional complexity. God, the Flag, Motherhood, and such other sure-fire symbols, attributed (unkindly) to public speakers as a class, should never follow each other without alleviation, any more than tempos, pauses, and other interactional devices can be unvaried. Otherwise, the speech is caricature, and not reality.

In addition, and an important aspect of language management, grammatical structure plays a significant part combined both with the choice of symbols and the subdimensions through which varying patterns of emphasis are communicated. Asking a question, for example, or making a comment designed to encourage the speaker to continue at his basal rate or to approach it can inhibit him because of the limited extent of the topical material needed for the response or, conversely, can facilitate a long, free-running action.

The technical properties of this process have been worked out intensively in interviewing, counseling, and therapy—a variety of interactional patterns or forms whose significance will be commented on in Chapter 14. This can be viewed purely linguistically (omitting the impact of the interaction variables) in the type of interviewing to which the term "nondirective" was first applied by Rogers (1942) and standardized by Chapple (1953) and his associates over many years. Here, three criteria are essential, if the content—the symbols and their grammatical contexts—is not to impose constraints. Failure to follow these rules cuts short free-running actions and may even result in monosyllabic responses.

In the first of these, the interviewer frames his question or comment, designed to start the individual off again when he has stopped his action, by using approximately the same words with which he ended. Only the implication of interrogation, with minimal intonation shifts, alters the sememic structure. This will be followed (or preceded) by a question or request for continuation which cannot be given a specific answer; the purpose of the question is indeterminate or indirect (nondirective)—for instance, "what happened next?" This cannot be answered by a phrase which closes the response and provides no freedom to continue in any chain of symbolic "free association" the individual pleases to use. Thus, if one asks someone when he was born and he answers with his birth date, this ends the topic (though high-activity persons may be forced by their interaction rhythms to continue without any logical connection between the answer and the next topic they introduce). Finally, interviewers watch the level of abstraction of the symbols used by the individual to whom they are talking. If they want him to become more or less "specific," they shift levels of abstraction in their questions or comments by only one step or interval at a time. Too great a shift in levels again acts as a brake on the action patterns.

The significance of mentioning this kind of procedure is not to provide a "complete" guide to interviewing (used among other things to aid in establishing basal levels), but rather to illustrate that the semantic pattern can cut short the interaction unwittingly. On the other hand, as mentioned above, you never can tell. There are people who go on and on no matter how incongruous the symbolic match turns out to be.

The Impact of Language on Interaction

Deficiencies in language fluency are so obvious in their effects on interaction that it is surprising so little precise observation has been carried on. What happens is well illustrated in a study by Ervin-Tripp (1964) in which she compared the results of interviewing Japanese women married to Americans and living in the United States, either using a Caucasian–American interviewer or a Japanese. The women were forced into an abnormal situation when they were asked to speak English with another Japanese woman, since they would not normally do so. The effects on the style of English were clear when the two situations were compared. With the Japanese listener, there was much more disruption of English syntax, more intrusion of Japanese words, and *briefer speech* (italics author's). Though this study did not compare the interaction patterns of the women, speaking Japanese versus English, other studies have shown that except where the speaker is equally fluent in both, the interaction patterns differ as one would expect.

Language differences, of course, are major sources of barriers between groups, but where several are available (true languages or distinct dialects), there tends to be a division of usage depending on the nature of the relationships. There are two ways of looking at such examples: first, the use of the dialect occurs only in conjunction with particular patterns of interaction; therefore, when used, the cultural conditioning elicits those patterns, and prevents others from occurring. Conversely, one can take the alternate view and say that, as the interaction shifts, so does the language. Examples of this are common, ranging from the shifts in parts of speech from the formal to the familiar, to the actual alternation of intervals of different languages, or symbols derived from them, as the interaction patterns change.

Gumperz (1964) compared two cultures where this was the case. In the village of Hemnes in Southern Norway where he worked, people used the local dialect, not only among themselves, but often with people in the city, rather than using one of the two standard literary languages. In Khalapur in northern India, the local vernacular was spoken within its bounds but, in more formal relationships within the community and in their relations to people outside, particularly in the city, Hindi was the official language and used insofar as possible. Actually, in Khalapur, linguistic variability was even greater. There were three local untouchable groups, each with its own dialect, who lived in segregation, while another speech variety was used for interaction with merchants in the local bazaar, or with wandering performers and priests.

Gumperz distinguishes between those formal patterns of interaction in which what is said and done is rather highly specified (which he calls transactional)—for instance, a job interview or a religious service—and what he calls "personal interaction." This latter type, in the context of the present discussion, should more properly be called "personal communication," thus distinguishing its interactional patterning from the content of the language employed. The occurrence of such shifts, which he calls switching, in language style and interaction, is quite common. In Khalapur, those situations which he calls "personal" evidence more shifting between dialects and Hindi, and the topics discussed have great variety; in the transactional case, interactional restrictions of the situations limit the variability, both in use of language and in its style.

Gumperz comments on the:

> commonly agreed-on conventions which serve to categorize speech forms as informal, technical, vulgar, literary, humorous, etc. To be sure, such conventions are subject to considerably greater variations than grammatical restraints, but wherever they are well established, the style of a message also gives advance information about its content. When we hear, "Mr. President, Ladies and Gentlemen," we suspect that we are in for something like a formal address or political speech... Speech styles provide advance information about the nature of messages and speed up communication in somewhat the same way that titles and tables of content help in reading a book. The social etiquette of language choice is learned along with grammatical rules and once internalized it becomes part of our linguistic equipment. Conversely, stylistic choice becomes a problem when we are away from our accustomed social surroundings. Expressions which are customary in our own group might easily offend our interlocutor and jeopardize our mutual relationships by mislabeling messages.

Though style, in Gumperz's sense, is an easily distinguishable element in speech in every culture, its properties, linguistically, have been little studied. We know what the language content is going to be once we hear the opening bars; we also expect the interaction patterns to follow particular rhythms and fluctuations in quantitative patterning, varied in a familiar way, not merely by the symbols chosen, but by the flourishes with which the subdimensions of loudness, intonation, and timbre are worked into the combined sequences. It is interesting to wonder, cross-culturally, whether there are uniformities in speech styles for particular patterns of interaction; in other words, how different is the semantic and symbolic composition, and the interactional rhythms underlying them, among Hindi, Norwegians, and Americans when the cultural equivalents of "Mr. President, Ladies and Gentlemen..." are set in motion. Perhaps there are physiological–interactional invariants common to the species; at least, it is a question worth considering.

Personality and Temperamental Limitations on Symbolic Efficacy

The art of public speaking or, for that matter, any type of performance where language is, in its broadest sense, the means of eliciting responses within some kind of interactional patterning and design, is so evidently dependent on timing that too often it is taken for granted. Yet the differences in personality and temperamental reactions described in Part I of this book clearly set very specific limits on the durations of each action and, obviously, on the number of words that can be crowded within it. Someone with a low-activity level, whose durations are very short, cannot string out a long story. Either he has to be brief (that virtue so often honored in the breech) and succinct or, each time he stops, run the risk of losing the topic to his listener.

If the interval of action is short because it is set in motion by a temperamental reaction to stress, not only will the speaker be brief in the same way, but the adrenergic pattern, as its intensity increases, selects out symbols the emotional content and level of abstraction of which become high. On the other hand, though illustrating the point by one pattern of overreaction only, the press of speech, when cholinergic reactions are elicited, so loads the action with symbolic material, as one emotional context after another goes on proliferating, that both the symbols *and* the interaction are joint evidence of the severe reaction to stress.

Thus, the observer (and listener) can utilize interaction measurement and the scaled intervals of the several communication dimensions to characterize the temperamental reaction occurring. It is through such means that symbolic content can be associated with particular quantitative patterns, a technique used as an aid in exposition in Part I in describing how the emotional reactions to stress can be categorized. Here, however, the symbols are cut to length (or more accurately, to number) by the interaction rhythm. Even the dimensional intervals of all the categories of communication are evoked and carried along by the strength of the autonomic reaction.

The ways in which emotional reactions override whatever constraints language might impose are too common to require much discussion. In severe emotional states, judgment—the capacity to think logically, and to control one's adjustments to others—becomes inhibited. But interaction plays an important part in much less stormy situations. For the impact of symbols, as mentioned earlier, is highly affected by the timing of the actions in which they occur. This is again a commonplace, but it is worth considering just how precise such timing can actually be.

Perhaps the best description of this process has been given by Mark Twain, commenting on the factors which made his telling a story to a given audience successful or a consummate failure. As is well known, he was a most successful lecturer and performer, and wrote his own copy. What he has to say in this excerpt from his memoirs can be supported by any competent actor:

> When a man is reading from a book on the platform, he soon realizes that there is one powerful gun in his battery of artifice that he can't work with an

effect proportionate to its caliber: that is the *pause*—that impressive silence, that geometrically progressive silence which often achieves a desired effect when no combination of words, however felicitous, could accomplish it. The pause is not of much use to the man who is reading from a book because he cannot know what the exact length of it ought to be; he is not the one to determine the measurement—the audience must do that for him. He must perceive by their faces when the pause has reached the proper length, but his eyes are not on the faces, they are on the book; therefore he must determine the proper length of the pause by guess; he cannot guess with exactness and nothing but exactness, absolute exactness, will answer.

The man who recites without the book has all the advantage; when he comes to an old familiar remark in his tale which he has uttered nightly for a hundred nights—a remark preceded or followed by a pause—the faces of the audience tell him when to end the pause. For one audience the pause will be short, for another a little longer, for another a shade longer still; the performer must vary the length of the pause to suit the shades of differences between audiences. These variations of measurement are so slight, so delicate, that they may almost be compared with the shadings achieved by Pratt and Whitney's ingenious machine which measures the five-millionth part of an inch. An audience is that machine's twin; it can measure a pause down to that vanishing fraction.

I used to play with the pause as other children play with a toy. In my recitals when I went reading around the world for the benefit of Mr. Webster's creditors, I had three or four pieces in which the pauses performed an important part, and I used to lengthen them or shorten them according to the requirements of the case, and I got much pleasure out of the pause when it was accurately measured, and a certain discomfort when it wasn't. In the Negro ghost story of "The Golden Arm" one of these pauses occurs just in front of the closing remark. Whenever I got the pause the right length, the remark that followed it was sure of a satisfactorily startling effect, but if the length of the pause was wrong by the five-millionth of an inch, the audience had had time in that infinitesimal fraction of a moment to wake up from its deep concentration in the grisly tale and foresee the climax, and be prepared for it before it burst upon them—and it fell flat.

Chapter 14

Cultural Elaboration
of Interaction Forms (Roles)

Human interaction in the raw—an interval of time cut randomly from a continuing stream of words and gestures, postures and movements—may appear unshaped by culture. Even the rhythms are likely to be masked, roiled by the "noise" of frequent asynchronies, capable of disclosure only by precise interaction measurements. Though one knows that all its elements are learned and culturally derived, dimensional organization is hardly obvious.

Clearly, however, any selected sample will vary in the likelihood that evidence of its source will be manifest. In the United States perhaps, this seeming cultural randomness may be more common; among other peoples—though often such statements have to be qualified by adding, "in the good old days"—precise patterning of interaction by the cultural dimensions occurs with a high frequency. Albert (1964), in her description of the Burundi already quoted, describes the precision with which superiors and inferiors handle their spatial distance, the sequencing of actions through which initiative is controlled, and the care with which the subdimensions of communication are arranged. This is a learning and teaching process:

> The ideal of good breeding and aristocracy, *imfura,* includes "speaking well" as one of its principal elements. From about the tenth year, boys in the upper social strata are given formal speech training. The "curriculum" includes composition of impromptu speeches appropriate in relations with superiors in age and status; formulas for petitioning a superior for a gift; composition of

Amazina, praise-poems; quick-witted, self-defensive rhetoric intended to deflect an accusation or the anger of a superior. Correct formulas for addressing social inferiors, for funeral orations, for rendering judgment in a dispute, or for serving as an intermediary between an inferior petitioner and one's feudal superior are learned in the course of time as, with increasing age and mastery, each type of activity becomes appropriate. Training includes mastery of a suitable, elegant vocabulary, of tone of voice and its modulation, of graceful gestures with hand and spear, of general posture and appropriate bodily displacements, of control of eye-contacts, especially with inferiors, and above all, of speedy summoning of appropriate and effective verbal response in the dynamics of interpersonal relations.

Albert goes on to emphasize the consequences of ineptitude, whether from lack of inherent skill, emotional blocks or upsets, or sheer failure to do one's homework. There are:

high-born men who speak badly.... Failure to speak clearly and well, clumsy and wild gestures and allowing emotions to show, earn such unfortunates the epithet "muhutu," peasant, whose socially stereotyped speech pattern they employ for want of the power to do better.

But this is "etiquette." Many older middle-class American parents may sigh with envy at the sound of such a curriculum; yet in an egalitarian democratic society where children are perhaps more equal than others, surely such emphasis on styling of the elements of the interaction patterns is inappropriate. No need to cite in opposition the enormous sale of books of etiquette or the perusal of daily newspaper columns. For what the Burundi illustrate (or the more formal and elegant manners of our forebears) are the ways in which the patterns of interaction of individuals are shaped by the cultural dimensions, often unwittingly—by the situations within which the individuals adjust to one another.

Among the Burundi, the young of the upper ranks of the hierarchy were trained. This training was reinforced by the dire necessity to practice these patterns in their interactions with superiors. Otherwise, because of serious instabilities in maintaining relative position in the hierarchical set, inadequate adjustment, or implications thereof through language itself, was:

marked by the rapidity with which heavy punishments can be inflicted by those superior in the hierarchy if they are displeased. Only rarely is a statement so innocent that it is not necessary to consider the possibility that it will bring trouble.

In the United States, held by many as a culture far less concerned than others with the propriety of rank and situation—with the forms of interaction comprising etiquette considered subsidiary—the same processes are at work. The cultural dimensions do, in fact, continuously organize the patterns of interactions conjointly; they intersect, so to speak, and, through the variations in the ways they combine, structure the situations in which people interact.

Roles and Interaction Forms

Beginnings and endings of interactional contacts are an obvious illustration—the visitor to an executive's office, opening the door and walking a few feet, the executive then rising from his desk, walking around it to shake hands and make appropriate remarks, indicating the chair where the visitor should sit, the sequence is all too familiar. But even within the contact, the nature of the interaction varies depending on the requirements of the situation. The visitor may be a troubled subordinate, a salesman from a major supplier or a union official. Though one might try to categorize the whole contact (or for that matter the continuing relationship) as a single unit—what the sociologist likes to call a role (the role of the salesman or the customer, the union leader, the executive)—this obscures the cultural and interactional realities.

Actually, the unit elements of sequential interaction, shaped by the intersecting cultural dimensions, can be separated out and identified. They represent what can properly be called *interaction forms,* like musical forms; even one contact may be made up of several. Not only are they learned informally or through formal instruction, but they structure the interaction to achieve (like the young Burundi) a semblance of complementarity, for example, by controlling the timing and rhythms of the interaction. They do this by requiring cultural patterns to be followed which have that property. By conditioning the suppliant to use appropriate language for praise and felicitation, thus specifying the durations of each action, by prescribing the distances to be assumed at each stage in the sequence, by determining the order of actions when gifts are to be presented and to be received, definable constraints are imposed on the interaction. At the same time, this interaction form itself can become a symbol. The performance of the form then reinforces its symbolic contexts.

These interaction forms, moreover, can be described by precise interaction measurements, supplemented by recording the dimensional steps through which the constraints are mediated on their constituent scales. They differ, also, from "raw" interaction, idiosyncratic to the individual. Not that this is not culturally shaped; yet in contrast to the interaction form, its patterns constitute the manifestations of the personality and its temperamental reactions to stress or complementarity. Though some people become so highly conditioned that performance of the interaction form comes naturally—psychologists like to speak of "role" behavior being "internalized"—actually, this "naturalness" derives from the similarity of the interaction form and their own basic rhythms. By contrast, for many, like those inadequate "high-born" Burundi, interaction forms are incompatible—hard to learn and even more difficult to attempt. Since they are essential ingredients of any culture, however, their significance needs to be thoroughly understood. (I should add, by the way, that this concept of the interaction form and even the term itself, long predated my coming across Dr. Langer's book and her parallel development of the concept of forms in art and nature as felt acts or units of activity—combined emotional–interactional elements. Her discussion beautifully amplifies aspects of this book which can only be touched on in passing, in particular, the aesthetics of forms and their human significance.)

Dimensional Elements of Interaction Forms

A teacher in a classroom must be able to see and be seen by the members of his class; hence, except for small groups, he stands on a dais elevated above the floor level of the rest of the room. He must not be too far away or he will have to raise his voice. Proceeding with the teaching requires at least some sequencing of set events, certainly to begin and end the class. Clearly, teaching cannot be accomplished in monosyllables. To explain the significance of Henry the Fourth or the meaning of elliptic functions, words in quantity (thereby requiring longer durations of action) are a necessity. The subject matter, the clarity of exposition, and the ability of the class to grasp the intellectual content may, of course, vary these durations. Briefer amounts of exposition can be followed by actions which require responses to indicate comprehension for some groups of students, or more sustained and continuous lecturing for others.

Such patterns of interaction, culturally shaped by the dimensional elements of the contexts of situation constituting them—in this instance those of the teacher—are often referred to in social science literature as "roles." The term, borrowed from the theater, implies unintentionally that playing a part can be assumed or dropped at the individual's convenience, depending no doubt upon the exigencies of cultural casting. But Shakespeare and others after him did not so intend. . . .

All the world's a stage
And all the men and women merely players.
They have their exits and their entrances;
And one man in his time plays many parts.
His acts being seven ages.

A teacher who is unable to talk without stopping for his 50-minute hour, or who finds his material inappropriate, requires some other technique than giving a lecture if he is to teach. Alternative means exist. He may use the case or Socratic method, he can require student recitations, or he can shorten the need to talk by giving written tests. His role is still that of teacher, but the interactional forms required by the method he selects are very different, even without taking into account possible personality limitations.

Limitations of Role as a Descriptive Concept

The concept of a role is utilized by social scientists to do away with the necessity to base analysis on individual personalities. Granted that mothers have idiosyncratic differences—the personality peeping through—nevertheless it is held that the role of mother can be separated from individual mothers and that cultures and societies can be regarded as made up of role relationships. But the mother is also a wife; thus roles have to be split into smaller segments. And mother–wife may be President of the Women's Club (another role). Soon one finds that most people, depending on their relative positions within the interactional sets which make up their organizational life, constitute collectivities of roles. What are the criteria for telling when she is wife, when mother, when president, in the contexts of situations making up her daily life?

The vast literature on roles has served a useful purpose in pointing out that cultural situations require different patterns of interaction. Where it founders is in its emphasis on eliminating the individual personality in the presumed interests of simplicity. One does not observe roles, but people acting and interacting within specific contexts of situation culturally defined. The role of "mother" requires symbols at such high levels of abstraction from the operations of interaction measurement (and of cultural dimensions) that one is forced to minimize the realities of observation in order to create one stereotype for an entire society. Should one then try to find the individual who typifies all the symbolic elements of the stereotype? For all the literary impact of Morte d' Arthur, one is hard put to believe that Sir Galahad would ever have been considered chivalric reality in the jungle universe of the knights of the Dark Ages.

One could, of course, use the term "subroles" as Bohannon (1963) did when he realized the difficulties created by the all-inclusive term. But even this does not avoid the complexities of summarizing a whole series of separable patterns of interaction, structured by learned patterns and built on cultural dimensions, under a single heading. The role of mother, or the "role relationship" of mother to child, assumes there is a something—a kind of behavior and associated symbols—which represents, presumably, "mothering," as opposed to all those other patterns of interaction in which mother and child are to be observed—teaching, disciplining, or doctoring. For once the role is differentiated into activities and techniques (and all the interaction patterns underlying them), then one finds similar patterns in other roles, the teacher, the doctor, and so on.

By avoiding the confusions of inclusiveness which such otherwise appealing terms create, it becomes possible to identify the interaction forms occurring within a group. One can then establish how they are used in various institutions and relationships. Moreover, since they pattern the interaction by imposing constraints (which are probabilistic), one can examine instances of repeated use in different situations to achieve—such is cultural traditionalism—similar interactional consequences. So if the interaction form of something which could be called "mothering" is isolated, then the recommendation made seriously by some psychiatrists that attendants in mental hospitals be trained to adopt the "mothering" role would not appear so absurd—to the attendants hearing it, particularly if the label were changed.

Since multiple (and very different) interaction forms are too often classified under the same label—an obvious candidate in American society is the term "salesman"—the vagueness of attempts to generalize from the "role" to the personality needed for compatibility within its requirements could be avoided. There are as many different kinds of doctors or salesmen or mothers in the nature of their specialization as patients, customers, or children with whom they have to cope. Within each specialty, a variety of situations arises which have to be dealt with differently, that is, by using interaction forms appropriate to them.

Development of Interaction Forms

Though culture is mediated through the learned habits of the individual, their constituent ingredients, insofar as they depend on his biological properties, are relatively limited. Thus the fixed action patterns and their physiological components appear numerous only because culture, built out of the complexities which the human cortex makes possible, varies to a remarkable degree in the timing and precise coordination of these patterns. The term, culture, as used here, is merely shorthand for the sum of all the elements making up the learned repertoire of a group and their dimensional elaboration. Yet it can be looked at in two ways which are interconnected. In the first of these, the learned patterns constrain the emotional–interactional sequences, setting probabilistic limits on the individuals involved through the operation of the cultural dimensions. Second, and perhaps too often regarded as primary, the learned patterns have cultural logics of their own; it is through them that the cultural dimensions are altered to bring about cultural change.

Such changes can be major (and multiple) like the technological revolutions marking the course of human history. Though they influence the development of interaction forms, their effects are long-term and more encompassing, shifting the organizational systems themselves. But these are built out of the manifold short-term changes resulting from successive stages of modification of a cultural process or technique. A baseball player learning to pitch is acquiring a particular technique; a public speaker soon realizes that some ways of keeping an audience responsive are better than others; a mother learns, too often the hard way, that there are alternative methods of handling her infant by such empirical tests as which produce squalls or which result in coos. But these do not have to be discovered *de novo,* by each mother, each pitcher, or each after-dinner speaker. For within the resources of a given culture, there are rules, procedures, and traditions which presume to assist the new learner.

Some of these cultural forms are technical or cognitive—how to calculate a square root, how to adjust a lathe, how to fly an airplane, or how to read a foreign language. Others are interactional. They consist of styles or patterns of managing particular types of situations which have emerged through the process of cultural evolution. A vast body of "knowledge" exists—aphorisms, proverbs, and folklore generally, with kernels of more accurate prescription. It can be called upon to aid the mother with her child, to aid the speaker confronted by a bored and inattentive audience, and even the pitcher with a particularly difficult batter. One learns that if one follows a particular interaction pattern, supplemented by specific culturally derived actions defined by the three dimensions, a desired interactional result will be accomplished.

It is important to realize, for all cultures, that in spite of the lack of precision in formulation, this cultural patterning of interaction does work more often than not. The child gurgles with joy; the audience wakes up and reacts appropriately to the speaker. And the reasons for these successes lie in the interactional properties of the personality. By prescribing the contexts of situation within which the interaction takes place and, crudely perhaps, how the interaction should be managed, interactional effectiveness is enhanced since the cultural dimensions set up limits both minimally and maximally on the quantitative patterns of interaction. Within the culture, most personalities can operate within such limits or, at least, the interaction forms can be performed without too great disharmony.

As new situations arise—as cultures change even to minor degrees— new trial-and-effort attempts are made to find new solutions or to modify old ones used in other contexts. Over time, therefore, changes take place in interaction forms. Sometimes they are rapidly applied to a variety of institutional situations, sometimes one pattern becomes differentiated into a large number in order to deal with the differences in situations which have evolved. Whatever happens, however, each culture possesses a repertoire which constitutes its store of adaptations internal to the group as well as to the outside. If transitional stages in the evolution of such forms cannot be developed, that is, if they fail to meet new situations which involve too radical a change, then the culture breaks down in its capacity to organize interaction patterns. What results, as in many detribalized groups in Africa, for example (or in the "ghetto" areas of the United States), are idiosyncratic dimensional patterns developed *ad hoc* within small, disarticulate groups of people.

Significant Types of Interaction Forms

In the United States, there has been a remarkable growth of interest in developing interaction forms as techniques for dealing with "the emotionally disturbed," for selling, for business management, or for teaching and training. Each of these areas has many practitioners and is, of course, financially remunerative. Hence, how-to-do-it books have naturally multiplied, together with special courses, schools, and all the panoply of higher education. In addition, a number of investigations have been carried out, some with greater precision than others, which have begun to provide useful data on the interaction forms involved. These studies can be differentiated into two categories:

(1)   Those in which the natural situations are observed and analyzed to isolate their uniformities and the criteria which distinguish them from others, and

(2)   those in which interaction forms have been created deliberately and presumably tested for their efficacy.

Of course, (2) ordinarily follows a considerable amount of work in (1), but it is useful to separate them.

A)   Interviewing—Symbols and Interaction

Interviewing as an interaction form was initially developed for psychiatric purposes, both as a means of obtaining "relevant" information about a patient and as a technique of psychotherapy. When used as a means of inquiry, it may become similar to interrogation. This, as the art of cross-examination shows, has a long and independent history in the law. The interview—the term now includes a wide variety of forms—has spread to all kinds of organizational settings. It is used in personnel employment, in guidance, in schools, in counseling (as a semitherapeutic procedure) in social work, in business and, of course, in truncated form, in market surveys and public opinion polls. It has even been expanded from its original two-person or dyadic form to group situations, where several interviewers interact with one or more persons, or one interviewer manages a group.

Although more investigatory effort has been devoted to interviewing than to any other interaction form, the rules and techniques available have typically confounded content (the symbolic elements of the communication process) and interaction patterns. Moreover, the emphasis has remained predominantly on the subjective interpretations of the interviewer—he is to feel, to be aware, to be sensitive to. There has been too little attempt to specify either the interaction patterns to be followed or the words and gestures which should be used. Suggestions range from such vague statements as "be sure to put the subject (patient or job applicant) at his ease," "listen in a patient and friendly manner," and more elaborately, in Kahn and Cannell's words (1957):

> perceptions and sensitivities must be oriented towards the maintenance and enhancement of the relationship between himself and the respondent, and towards the fullness and adequacy of the responses in relation to his interviewing objectives.

The concern with the problems of symbolism began with Freud and has been pursued with enthusiasm, though with few evidences of rigor, by psychoanalysts generally (Glover 1952). Yet the most important contribution to the control of interview content was made by Rogers (1942) when he defined what he called the "nondirective method" in psychotherapy (also employed by Freudians less systematically). Though there is argument about the degree to which he is solely responsible for making this technique explicit (Roethlisberger and Dixon 1939), his work has resulted in wide acceptance. Briefly, he emphasized the importance of letting the subject (client, in his terms) select the topics to be discussed and for the interviewer (or therapist) to use responses which encourage the individual to go on. He was to avoid assiduously statements which require a direct answer and might thus bias or interfere with the subject's chain of associations. In psychoanalysis, of course, the method of free association is used with similar intent, but Rogers differs in his comparative abstention from interpretations of meaning. Chapple (1953), subsidiary to his development of standardized (or programmed) interaction interviews, set more rigorous limits on both the verbal and nonverbal content patterns. He required both to be regarded as actions, their communicational subdimensions—loudness intonation, timbre—and their expressive movement analogues to be held within limits, while the symbols used by the interviewer were to be derived from what the person has just said.

Rogers and his associates in psychology (and psychoanalysts and psychiatrists in addition) concentrated their attention on psychotherapy. It is this particular subclass of interaction form—within the more general class, interviewing—on which much effort has been expended in preparing instructional materials such as hi-fi records and associated texts, and sound motion pictures now available on the market. Scheflen (1965) has developed what he calls "Context Analysis," recording words and gestures in a sequential lexical and kinesic transcript, to try to obtain a "complete" communication interpretation. "Complete" is the goal; Scheflen would not claim that this has yet been achieved.

By way of contrast, Chapple's development of a series of interaction forms for interviewing, the so-called standardized diagnostic interview being the best known (Chapple 1953, Matarazzo 1957, 1958), was a consequence of the application of interaction measurements to ongoing interaction. From observations of interviews and nonpsychiatrically oriented interactions by psychiatrists, he isolated the constituent interaction variables. As Part I of this book indicates, he has shown how any combination of such patterns, given varying quantitative values, enables one to design interview forms to fit specific needs (Chapple 1970b). His concern with content was a consequence of the necessity for obtaining high reliability, since communication patterning, as a major cultural dimension, influences the interaction itself.

Although the design of any type of interview interaction form can now be worked out (and in some areas, this is being done), a complete compendium of such forms is a long way in the future. The reasons are simple. Granted that one can now specify (and program) the quantitative values of each of the interaction variables as they come up sequentially in the interview, with all possible alternate choices equally prescribed for shifts in the subject's pattern; granted also that the complex of communication dimensions can be structured so that the interviewer operates within predetermined limits. One thing only is still missing. To design an interview requires one to ask: design for what?

The design can be looked at as an experiment and, in fact, is one. But only by repeated experiments can uniformities be uncovered. One has to show that, given this individual's initial interactional condition and these changes in it required (say therapeutically), *this* sequence of interview forms should be used for this individual, and *not* that. Such knowledge slowly accumulates; it cannot be looked at as independent of the situation within which the individual lives, his total system of relations—in dynamic equilibrium or in an unstable state. Although changes can be clearly demonstrated within interviews, carry-over of these changes to other interactional situations is usually what is needed. This may be difficult to achieve if the stresses which the situation exerts on the individual are too great.

The large group of interview interaction forms available are by no means limited to those intended to reduce emotional stress or to enable a person to achieve an adequate outlet for his biological rhythms, but none of them require control of (or are strongly influenced by) the noncommunication dimensions. Though spatial distance and cultural sequencing can sometimes become important modifiers, particularly where the interactional sets have patterned·the hierarchical relations of individuals, these are more easily controllable by interview design, with exceptions like survey interviewing. The interplay of communication dimensions and interaction remains primary.

B)   Selling: Constraints of Space, Sequencing, and Communication on Interaction

From a cultural point of view, one of the most interesting interaction forms is the selling transaction, too often neglected by ethnographers, perhaps because of its implications of crass materialism. Though the interaction patterns involved are remarkably varied, the denouement, in most cultures at least, is the accomplishment of exchange in which the seller receives money for his part of the event. The "salesman" who persuades a major airline to purchase jet passenger airplanes from his firm rather than another is not removed from a street pitchman selling dolls at a theatre exit merely by the number of dollars involved. His "transaction" requires innumerable meetings in which many members of the company's organization take part. On the side of the purchaser, an evaluation has to be made not merely of the technical and economic advantages, but of its impacts on such relationships as to banks, insurance companies, or other sources of finance, as well as to the federal government and governments overseas. These are great (and extended) performances, using a complex set of selling forms. There are many varieties of these to be found in the business world.

More familiar are the salesmen who call on wholesale or retail firms, endeavoring to develop a steady and continuing outlet for their merchandise. They are in marked contrast to the salesmen who sell directly to the customer, like peddlers of insurance, encyclopedias, cosmetics, or the ubiquitous Fuller brushes. In the first case, the pattern of selling itself must always be bent towards considering not merely what the customer will buy today, but what he might buy tomorrow; in the second, selling is much more likely to be a "one-shot" deal; much greater pressure (dominance) is used to make the sale.

Though the stereotype in American society has always been that a salesman can sell anything, the fact is that this is not the case. Even within the apparently limited confines of a department store, types of selling are widely different. The work done by Chapple and his associates over many years illustrates not only that these differences are culturally derived but also that a particular personality type can succeed at one and fail at another because the interaction form in the first deviates too widely from his basic interaction patterns.

Consider the physical appearance of a department store. As everyone is aware, some merchandise is sold from counters with the salesperson behind, some from tables at various places within a department, spatially separated from others, and some from open areas where the objects to be sold—furniture, rugs, or major appliances are displayed side by side or in some spatially patterned relation to one another. In departments selling clothing, the suits, dresses, or whatever may be hanging from racks in the open (inexpensive to moderately priced merchandise), or they may be concealed so that the salesperson has to go and get samples of what might be of interest to the customer (high-fashion merchandise). Some types of clothing require trying on in the garment fitting room. Items like millinery may be tried on in the open before a mirror, while others can be taken home when the sale is made without trying them on.

If one observes a series of selling transactions in different departments by reasonably competent salespeople—those who sell a high percentage of the customers with whom they begin a contact—the differences in the patterns of interaction are very evident. Consider the spatial element. The customer comes directly to a counter, the merchandise is displayed immediately underneath the case or kept in drawers or on shelves. The number of choices is limited as to size, color, and type of material and the information is quickly communicated. The transaction is, therefore, ordinarily brief in duration, yet it varies depending on whether one asks for a man's shirt, a bottle of cleaning fluid, or a package of cigarettes.

Counter departments ordinarily are high volume, hence a number of customers may besiege the salesperson. The greater her ability to manage transactions with several people and do it quickly, the better her performance. The tempo is quick, the amount of palaver needed for each customer is brief, *but* the capacity to be flexible enough and quick enough to handle many people on days of sales or before major gift-buying holidays like Easter or Christmas is essential.

By contrast, consider a salesperson selling high-fashion (and expensive) dresses. The customer comes into the department, is approached (initiated to) by one of the staff, often is asked to sit down while the problem of what the customer is looking for is discussed and the transaction begins. In the low- to medium-priced selling of dresses, on the other hand, the salesperson goes to the racks, brings several choices back, shows them to the customer, gets indications of interest, and goes back again; the transaction is made up of brief interactions interspersed with trips to get more possibilities. In high fashion, the salesperson spends much more time talking about the style and material and its relation to the already existing wardrobe, often trying to get the customer to talk at some length about the "fashion image" she hopes to achieve. The salesperson waits patiently for an opening. When indications of serious interest appear, she begins to sell *that* dress at some length and with enough dominance to get a positive decision. This selling continues in the fitting room. In fact it may be concentrated there while the customer inspects herself in the mirrors. By contrast, the medium- and low-priced salesgirl depends on the volume of dresses produced and her capacity to build a transaction out of a series of alternate interactions and visits to the racks or stockroom for what she hopes may prove attractive.

In a series of intensive studies of interaction patterns, both of salespersons and the selling transactions, Chapple and his associates demonstrated that there are seven basic interaction forms in department store selling (incidentally differing substantially from other types of selling). By conducting experiments of transferring top salespersons from one type of selling to another, they found that the personality patterns were not compatible. Previously outstanding performers became only average. They also predicted, with remarkable success on a blindfold basis, the performance of persons placed in particular types of selling—again through interaction measurement of their standardized type of interview.

In one such study, with a total of 115 cases placed in various selling departments by the personnel office of a large department store, performance was determined by calculating the average daily sales for each individual. Since the departments differed widely in the dollar figures a salesperson was able to attain due to the differences in volume and price of the merchandise—furniture by contrast with handkerchiefs—dollar ranges were set up for good, above average, average, and poor performance. Remember that each of these individuals was placed in a department on the assumption that he or she would succeed. Blindfold predictions showed that evaluation through interaction measurement of standardized interviews correctly selected 96.8 percent of the good, 84.5 percent of the above average, only 61.5 percent of the average (as would be expected), and 97.7 percent of the poor (who were expected to do well by the employment department). The significance of these findings is unlikely to revolutionize selection. Most retail establishments are not interested in taking the amount of time an interview requires to select and place salespeople. What is relevant is that spatial distance, cultural sequencing, and the symbolic elements of the customer–salesperson communication pattern combine to produce these different interaction forms which set very precise requirements on individual personalities. Some people have the personality characteristics (the particular quantitative values of their interaction variables) which enable them to do well; others, misplaced, do badly and drop out unless they can be transferred to a selling situation which fits them better. Interestingly enough also, studies have shown that the amount of training and even knowledge of the merchandise is uncorrelated with performance, though it should be added that interactional training was never attempted in these experiments.

C)   Teaching Requirements and Set Events

Teaching as an interaction form, as suggested earlier, has a wide variety of distinguishable forms, although far less is known about it on an interactional basis. Teacher's manuals are fertile sources for the beginnings of research but again lack specificity in how the teacher is to behave. Yet the properties of teaching as an interaction form differ significantly from those previously discussed because they involve the management of groups and, therefore, the interdependence of set and pair events. (Some teaching is individualized, that is, in pair relations, but this begins to move into the kinds of situations which interviewing symbolizes). A few directions from any manual on how to begin a class suggest the differences:

> (1) Be there first, before any pupil arrives. (2) See that the room is in good order. (3) As the pupils enter, be at the door; direct the pupils to their seats. Insist tactfully, but firmly, "No talk, please." (4) When all or most have arrived, close the door. (5) Tell the class what they are to do (and so on).

Apart from all the detail which any teacher must cover to satisfy the bureaucratic needs of the organization, the manuals go on to describe how the teacher should behave,

> Act as if you expect pupils to be orderly ... have everyone's attention before you start talking, speak quietly, don't talk too much and if problems of group misbehavior arise, don't wait until a class is out of hand. When pupils become restless, change your activity, your approach or your tempo, focus on individual culprits, keep your temper, avoid making threats ... when a pupil is committing a minor infraction, try stopping and looking directly at him, don't argue...

The list goes on with the assumption that somehow the teacher will be able to disentangle content and interaction by observation of "successful" others during a training period or merely as a result of, often, bitter experience.

When it comes to the teaching itself, the instructions become vaguer:

> Make provision for active participation of the greatest number of pupils, make the entire period stimulating and challenging...

These kinds of suggestions to the teacher need little comment. It is clear that the age of the children and the nature of the curriculum, or rather of the particular subject being taught, modify the patterns which the individual children present.

With so much emphasis on education in the United States, it is surprising that so few direct observational studies have been conducted on teaching. Burnett (1965) recorded the durations and frequencies of interactional contacts in individual classrooms and showed that significant quantitative differences associated with estimates of success existed between teachers. However, there has been little emphasis on the analysis of the teaching process in its various interaction forms except on a philosophical basis. How should a teacher, given a particular subject and a particular age group with all its members' idiosyncratic differences, carry on the teaching process to obtain maximal results tested by whatever standards of cognitive achievement?

In fact, for all the emphasis on the logics of communication, very little is known about the interdependence of the interaction form and the symbolic material which is to be learned. Learning studies by psychologists, though suggestive in laboratory situations, are hardly applicable in the classroom because the interactional variables of teacher and pupils are constantly in motion. They are controlled only by the happenstance of a teacher's personality, and rely on traditional rules for interacting when "misbehavior" occurs whose scientific basis is nonexistent. Emotional stress is constantly appearing, interfering with the learning process. What is needed is an explicit analysis of their mutual relationships.

D)   Management: A Composite of Interaction Forms

A remarkable number of books and articles concerned with the art of managing or supervising, and training programs which try to implement them, appear in the United States. Management, as Chapple and Sayles (1961) and Sayles (1964) have pointed out, is made up of a series of different interaction forms which vary in the frequency with which they occur, the length of time they last and, most important, in the percentage of time during the working day which they occupy. In other words, the job of the manager or supervisor is not made up predominantly of a single interaction form, like the salesman, teacher, or interviewer, but of many. (Even in these types, other interaction forms may occur which occupy a relatively small amount of time—the teacher talking to parents, the salesman in his relation to the plant or stockroom personnel, the interviewer to other members of the patient or subject's interactional systems.)

But the manager or executive, as Chapple and Sayles point out:

> makes inquiries, interviews, trains, negotiates, sells, makes speeches, conducts meetings, and transmits information. Also, and this is sometimes overemphasized, he supervises. But supervision is not a single pattern of interaction, it is (also) a combination of many distinct activities. Subordinates are given orders

that result, at least in part, from the time the supervisor spends working on reports, schedules, etc. If the orders involve getting his foremen to take corrective action, for example, it is not just a matter of making a concise request. He has to learn the reasons for deviations, perhaps by interviews, decide whether any changes in scheduling or operations are necessary, and then persist in getting over his point of view to make sure that changes in his subordinates' behavior is forthcoming. Under the general area of supervision, he also acts as a trouble shooter. If one of his foremen needs help, he may have to intervene with another superintendent, another foreman, or an engineer. He delegates responsibility to his subordinates and may want verbal reports on what has been accomplished.

Chapple and Sayles go on to break down jobs of various executives into these "administrative patterns" or interaction forms. They describe (in words) the interaction patterns required and the total weekly time for each in sample companies, showing how each executive's job differs in its constituent cultural sequencings or work flows and their quantitative distribution. Each of these interaction forms (administrative patterns), whether it be to negotiate, train, supervise or trouble-shoot has, in addition, been defined in terms of the measured values of its interaction variables. As in studies of salespeople, comparisons have been made between the personality characteristics of individuals and the interaction forms they are expected to carry out. Webber (1964), utilizing some of Chapple's data on corporations, showed that discrepancies between the job requirements and the patterns of interaction in a series of 50 executives indicate again (as in selling) that successful performance of any particular interaction form is dependent on the possession by the executive of the appropriate interactional capacity.

In contrast to other interaction forms which represent the major requirement of the individual's performance (like selling or teaching), the number of different forms which an executive is required to carry out serves a protective function for him in many organizations. As is to be expected, people do those things which they find easy to do, obtaining satisfactions from them; they avoid the others which they dislike. Through this, the individual executive can change the organizational pattern of his job; for example, by spending the majority of his time handling paper work or sitting in long, drawn-out negotiations so that he can avoid having to train his subordinates or "sell" the services of his staff department to a line unit.

Incompatibility of Interaction Forms and Personalities

Thus, interaction forms are by no means always (or often) compatible with the individual's personality requirements. Put someone in a job situation where, to succeed, he must take the initiative many times a day to potential customers although his capacity to initiate is very low. Disharmony results. Perhaps he can convince himself and his superiors that activities not requiring initiative are more valuable; if he cannot manage such a safe haven, he is immediately subject to multiple stresses. His habitual pattern of adjustment (letting others initiate to him) is disturbed; his emotional–temperamental reactions are liable to decrease (rather than increase) his capacity for initiating (or maneuvering himself into situations where others will initiate to him). In addition, he becomes the subject of aggressive behavior or dominance, with the threat of being fired. Thus, any complementary relationships he has established on the job are imperiled, as is the cultural necessity of the paycheck through which he manages the exchange transactions facilitating his interactional stability at home.

Lack of complementarity between the interaction rhythms of the personality and the interaction forms imposed by the situations arising in the external world has, therefore, serious impact. Obviously, minor deviations are not significant, since most people have the capacity for some degree of flexibility. But given any major quantitative disparity, the result is stress since the cultural dimensions which shape the inharmonious interaction forms compel asynchrony. The severity of the stress results not so much from maladjustment to *one* individual, but to the necessity for adapting to a succession of stressful situations and individuals, any one of which, alone, might not be a significant source of disturbance. Thus, the incompatibility of interaction form and interactional capacity is cumulative. The cultural requirements cause the repetition.

In complex societies, the performance of interaction forms typically is imposed over long periods of the day. The salesgirl at the hosiery counter is located in a fixed place. The sequence of the transaction may vary depending on the customer, but it is relatively uniform. It involves showing and mentioning price, color, and style variations in the merchandise. If the sale is made, she has to wrap the purchase, take the cash and ring up a sale on the register, make change, or fill out a charge slip with the needed identification. No matter how many customers arrive at her station and how fast, whether they initiate to her or she to them, she must adjust to many different types of personalities—apart from the adjustments to other members of the department, to stock boys, buyers, floor supervisors, and the rest of the organization whose interactions impinge on her. All these relationships make up the conditions (and the system) within which the repetition of the interaction form takes place.

If the salesgirl's tempo is fast, if she can continue to initiate and talk easily and freely to the customer, if she is flexible enough to adapt to the varieties of people who appear at her counter and able to dominate enough to get the customer to buy, the performance of this particular interaction form over and over again is easy and provides a satisfactory outlet for her personality needs. Variations on the familiar form and successful adaptations to the difficult customer provide her with a significant increase in her need for intermediate arousal potential. Interest and excitement heighten the performance. If there are few customers and sales are slow, the reduction in the pace of contacts may be tiring unless her fellow salesgirls are compatible; if the counter is swamped (as at a sale), her inability to manage enough time to complete the interaction form because of importunities by newly arriving customers may be disturbing.

Unfortunately for the customer, there are many salespeople in stores whose personalities (and temperamental reactions to the stresses set off by repeated contacts, even if no *one* customer is "impossible") are clearly unfitted to perform the particular interaction form required. To maintain a modicum of equilibrium, they become skilled in avoiding the customer's eye or questions, ignoring them by failing to respond.

Such obvious incongruity between the constraints of the interaction form, which require repeating an interactional performance within reasonable quantitative limits, and the personality of the individual is rarely a matter of a single interaction variable. Ordinarily the form is made up by the interplay of a number of variables and dimensional properties. When this is the case, it is often possible for an individual to adopt an alternate pattern to carry out the interaction form. The salesgirl who finds it difficult to initiate contacts can maneuver herself into a position (spatially) where it is hard for the customer not to initiate to her. The teacher does not have to rely on the lecture as *the* educational form. The executive, lacking the persistence to achieve dominance, may avoid the argument and, utilizing his initiative, come back repeatedly on successive days to try to get his point across. (For fuller discussion, see Chapple and Sayles 1961.)

Natural Selection of Personalities within Cultures

The compatibility of personalities and the interaction forms which fit their basic rhythms must, of course, occur with sufficient frequency to enable them to be performed. Otherwise, those particular forms would soon disappear if the available personalities could not adapt easily and if the form did not provide them with adequate emotional–interactional outlets. So strong can this compatibility be through cultural natural selection, that those who were unable to fit the situation go elsewhere. Thus, the situation selects appropriate personalities, whether accentuated by genotypic flow towards appropriate patterns or by modifications through early experience culturally structured. As a consequence, it is reasonable to believe that the cultural dimensions and their interaction forms can create a high degree of personality uniformity.

One of the most explicit and interesting analyses of just this kind of situation is to be found in Miller's description (1955) of the concept of authority among the Fox Indians, a Central Algonkian tribe who lived around the western Great Lakes in the 17th century. The early Europeans coming into the area were surprised (and shocked) by the fact that no one, not even the elected Head of Warriors, had any authority to give an order to anyone. Their independence of one another was unchecked; anything resembling an order was rejected immediately. Miller contrasts this with the interaction forms found in European society then, and even today, with their emphasis on the dominance (and initiative rights in consequence) which existed between lord or superior and follower. He points out that, in a wide variety of organizations, the hierarchical pattern involves specific interaction forms, "roles" in his terms, for the superior or superordinate and the subordinate. As he sees the factors which brought this about:

> In the first place, the *range* of activities involving coordinated action was quite limited. Only about five or six such activities (the war party, religious ceremonial, council meeting, some group games) were frequently recurrent; the total number of recurrent collective activities did not exceed ten or twelve. Second, the *size* of the group participating in such activities was limited. The war party consisted of about five to fifteen men; the religious ceremony involved fifteen to forty participants. Only very infrequently were larger groups involved in a coordinated enterprise. Third, since the rate of social change in Fox society was slow, the procedure of such activities was familiar to all participants. They had observed or taken part in them since early childhood; each knew his own part and how it fitted in with the parts of others; the activities changed little from year to year. Fourth, the "division of labor" in Fox society was neither complex nor ramified. There were few real specialists, no secret or esoteric groups of craftsmen; in important coordinated activities such as ceremonials and council meetings, the whole range of the population—all age groups and both sexes—was customarily participant.

In addition, Miller emphasizes the brevity with which most positions were assumed: The war leader was only chosen for the duration of the expedition. Anyone was free to join or not and to accept or disregard suggestions; at all levels in other types of group activities, particularly in the tribal council, decisions had to be by unanimous consent. The pattern of behavior to be assumed on every occasion was known from early childhood. Suggestions of acting outside these interaction forms (and their contexts of situation) were regarded as implying inadequacy. Further, the culture itself was based on the tracking and killing of wild game by hunters who usually went off alone for long periods. From their earliest years, children were sent into the woods to fast as well as to go on long expeditions by themselves. Since so many of the patterns of behavior were individual with minimal temporal constraints, combat between individuals established no permanent dominance relationship. Not merely in everyday situations, but in the symbolic statements of the supernatural world, to be defeated today was no sign that tomorrow the tables would not be turned.

The contrast between the Fox and the French explorers of the 17th century and the society from which they came is an example of the incongruity of interaction forms and the personalities associated with them. Miller was interested in this point because the French seriously considered organizing companies of Indians as militiamen. They discarded the idea due to the incompatibility of Fox patterns of interaction and those required by military sequencing. But the case also illustrates how differences in the cultures themselves and the interaction forms required appear to operate as selective factors in shaping the personality patterns of the individuals in the group (a majority of them at least).

As a consequence, though there seems to be no testimony from the Fox as to what they thought about the French, the latter, and the English later on, regarded them as self-willed and insubordinate, quick to resent any attempt to dominate them. Thus, they would accept only a limited number of interaction forms (their own), and attempts to impose others met with violent reactions of resentment.

Although Miller could make no statistical estimate of such a distribution among the Fox, it is fairly safe to assume that a majority of the male warriors tended to fall within certain limits in their interactional variables. These clearly differed from many of the French and English who came in contact with them. Such distributions, by their statistical nature, represent the frequency of occurrence of particular ranges of given interaction variables. This does not mean that all (or even almost all) individuals are so distributed. Categorizing a culture in this regard is complicated by the variety of interaction variables which define both personality and temperament characteristics; hence a statistical definition of population similarities and differences has to be multivariate; only now, with modern computers, does it become relatively easy to estimate.

Nevertheless, although interaction measurements have not been applied to tribal or other ethnic groups, studies of large institutions have shown that there are significant differences between the populations who are attracted to and remain in one kind of organizational institution or another. Chapple (1954) described highly significant differences between the interaction patterns of department store salespeople and executives and the personnel of manufacturing organizations or government bureaus:

In a random sample of 260 department store employees, slightly over 30 percent showed a significant occurrence of persistence, whereas in 500 individuals selected at random in a government agency, significant degrees of this trait were found in only five percent of the sample. In the same way, only seven and one-half percent of the sample of 500 people in a government agency showed any indication of that type of emotional reaction to nonresponse which, when extreme, leads to a long outburst, while 23 percent of department store employees showed this characteristic.

Some of this difference, no doubt, comes from the differential rates of attraction which the symbolic "images" exert on different types of personalities, though there is inadequate evidence on this score. On the other hand, there is extensive evidence that even for people who, as the psychologists say, "are highly motivated" to work in a department store, such "dedication" is not enough. Without the necessary interaction patterns—those which make for successful adaptation to the cultural situations which retail selling requires—they are unable to succeed. Most, in studies of hundreds of cases, simply quit, "dissatisfied." Some were so poor that, even with severe shortages of potential replacements, they had to be let go.

Implications of Cultural Diversity for Personality

Differences in the distribution of personality patterns in a given culture are not the sole factor to be considered. Interaction forms depend upon the particular combinations which the cultural dimensions set up. As a result, since cultures are often undergoing change, one must not expect to find too close a parallelism. A major problem in many cultures today is just this incongruity. As modern industrial technology is adopted in a country, a new set of interaction forms (or roles) becomes necessary. The individuals available to learn and practice them often have incompatible personalities. Such incongruities are a major plague in the so-called underdeveloped countries. So the Fox of earlier days would be completely unable to work today in a factory setting, as their Winnebago relatives presently do.

Although the problem for the individual is to find a compatible complex of interaction forms within which his interactional requirements can be satisfied, for the group there is little existing evidence to suggest that this will be facilitated by a shift in the frequencies of types of personality as the culture shifts. In the long run, perhaps one might make such an assumption but, so far at least, there are no signs of cultural engineering for the automated and computerized age.

Yet there is no question that a far more accurate process of defining interaction forms, fitting the needs of individual personalities, is possible. Since the interplay of genetic and environmental factors affecting the interaction patterns is fortunately so complex, it is highly dubious that any group in the immediate future will begin to produce personalities tailored to fit industrial civilization, as studies of simpler groups by cultural anthropologists might seem to imply. Natural selection in society does go on; yet the requirements for different types of personalities and the cognitive skills associated with them are so great, and the sheer number of varieties so large, that it is probable that a much greater variety of personalities can be utilized.

As science acquires greater skill in aiding individuals to handle the stresses of interactional life, many of its so-called mentally ill and mentally retarded can achieve their true potential. Necessarily, this will mean that a wider range of personalities will be available. In spite of the apparent incongruities of modern life, this, rather than the stereotyping of personalities, is what the future holds. Differences in personality are not necessarily a consequence of that long-past, simple, rural society. If ethnographers and anthropologists are to be believed, the deviant is much more likely to be cast out or killed in such cultural situations. Whether preservation of variability is "good" or "bad," at least the increasing complexity of culture and the variations in interaction forms resulting will make such variability and flexibility a necessity.

Multiple Uses of Single Interaction Forms

Every group has its repertoire of interaction forms built out of the cultural dimensions and their interplay. The contexts of situation—the cultural content—may vary enormously. Among the nomadic Bedouin of the Arabian desert, the preparation and serving of their bitter coffee in tiny cups not only define relationships—the members of the family, the proper gestures to guests, and to people of higher rank—but elaborate patterning occurs in the order of serving—whether one receives the cup or passes it to another, all the niceties of appropriate adjustment. Beyond that, the coffee fire and coffee gatherings are associated with all the tribal business, including its government.

This kind of economy in usage of interaction forms is typical of every society. A form becomes established, like the handshake of greeting in the United States; it becomes an essential component of a wide variety of cultural settings. From greeting, it extends to membership—The Right Hand of Fellowship in Protestant churches—to contractual agreements where the shaking of hands is commonly used to indicate that the negotiating parties have agreed—there are many variants in the use of this pattern and its associated interaction.

Sometimes a single interaction form may be used for almost all important relationships like the drinking of coffee among the Bedouin. When this occurs, as with these desert nomads, the interaction form becomes capable of a high degree of elaboration. The more skilled one is in using it to achieve one's interactional and cultural purposes, the greater the esthetic variations of its form.

Frake (1964), in describing "How to ask for a drink in Subanun" (an agricultural people on the island of Mindanao in the Philippines), illustrates this well, even apart from any intrinsic interest in the subject. Drinking, it should be hastily added, in Subanun at least, is not just concerned with getting drunk. Rather, as Frake says, it is the method by which one gets ahead socially. From what he has to say, one can easily see how the inter-action patterns and the patterns of speech which reinforce them are closely integrated.

Drinking in Subanun is a competition whose purpose is to arrange to get more to drink than the others. To do this, however, is not a matter of sheer speed in getting the liquor down. Each drinker has a turn, and (to simplify Frake's amusing and highly relevant article) the amount one gets to drink at each turn one is afforded depends on the length of time one talks and, decisively, on one's skill in eliciting verbal responses from the others by the effectiveness of one's use of the communication dimensions. If this works successfully, the drinker is encouraged to continue drinking and talking, and becomes entitled to take another turn after gracefully handing over the beer to the next in line. The contest begins with a brief first round when each one tastes, asking permission with the appropriate phrasing. Thereafter, each turn becomes longer and involves comments on the virtues of the beer and the performance of the other drinkers. Interaction is con-trolled by the necessity to keep a mental record of the consumption of the others, and to be sure, on each turn within each round, to equal their consumption. Ability to keep on going thus depends on being able to sus-tain a continuous unit of interaction, much like any persistent after-dinner speaker in the United States. The only inhibiting factor, from Frake's ac-count, is the need to be so skilled in one's verbal art that others respond appropriately, thus maintaining one's dominance (presumably gracefully). Frake's article does not say whether the drinker, trying to extend his turn, can continue talking (and drinking) against any persistent attempt by one or more of the others to interrupt and take over.

Within this framework of stylized interaction—powerfully assisted by alcohol—most Subanun affairs are accomplished. Settling grievances by negotiation, managing business of various sorts and, through repeated trials, achieving a preponderant position in the leadership of the group, all depend on one's capacity to keep acting and to keep drinking. Perhaps the cocktail rite, so common an interactional lubricant in the United States, could evolve in this direction except for the differential impact of Subanun beer versus the Martini.

Cultural Maximizing of Interactional Probabilities

Since interaction forms are compounded of the several cultural dimensions, coincident intervals at the high end of their scales strengthen the probabilities of the occurrence of particular interaction patterns. Thus two people, sitting close together and engaged in some sort of work flow where one helps the other and where the symbols used have high intensity, experience a reinforcement which can extend to the interaction form of patterned counseling. Inadequate data are at hand to answer the question as to the degree which such equivalent dimensional intervals in combination increase the probabilities. It is more likely that the variance decreases, that is, the chances that interaction will or will not take place. There is a greater likelihood that it will fall within narrower limits on its continuum.

Moreover, when several dimensions combine in contexts of situations, the interactional probabilities are compounded by the particular scale intervals of each within which the participants are constrained. In some instances, they will have opposing effects; for example, a high value on one—in cultural sequencing (say, being in the next position)—is associated with wide spatial separation. On the other hand, if the scale intervals are all in the same direction, then the probabilities will increase as some cumulative property of the scale values. One is tempted to consider these as multiples, for all dimensional combinations. The fact is, we do not know how they are compounded; only that probabilities of interactions do increase significantly in such combinations.

In addition, the contributions of each cultural dimension in reinforcing the probabilities that the interaction form will be managed effectively are an important part of the folk knowledge of a group, as well as the subject of technical inquiry. Not only are the cultural conditions for success the subject of concern, but every effort is made to facilitate successful performance of the interaction form by proper arrangements. Notice the care with which the properties (in the theatrical sense) set the stage for an important public speaker—the dais properly covered with carpeting, the rostrum with a reading light, a pitcher of water and glass within easy reach, the tested sound system, the appropriate backdrop of flags or other symbolic objects, the careful seating arrangements for important organizational representatives as well as audience—this listing should make the point quite obvious.

Moreover, the space itself is designed to structure the performance of specific interaction forms. Much architectural discussion is devoted to the esthetic and symbolic aspects of such spaces as well as their effectiveness for their intended purposes. Consciously or unconsciously, those concerned with the performance of interaction forms by themselves or by others endeavour to maximize the contexts of situation which enhance them while minimizing distractions. The obvious rationale is to increase the likelihood that the interaction form will come off successfully. Thus, much of culture is focused on such problems, not only architecturally, but in the development of techniques and procedures and the physical means of accomplishing them, through which all the dimensions make specific contributions to the stability of the interaction form.

Beyond this, of course, performance must be learned. All societies emphasize the importance of training or teaching their members the precise patterns of interaction and their associated cultural elements which serve to frame them in contexts which can be repeated with precision. Military drill is an obvious form where endless repetition to reinforce the performance of the form, even after being learned, is an apparent necessity. But all interaction forms require practice. This may be done within the framework of organization sets with hierarchical impact, or acquired in the normal course of growing up within less formal situations.

More important, interaction forms are performed with far greater precision within some institutional contexts than they are in others. Where this occurs, the probabilities that the particular interaction form will *not* be followed accurately become almost minimal. In other words, at certain points in the flow of events making up the life of a people, the cultural dimensions can so increase the probabilities that the interaction patterns to be followed by designated people do, in fact, occur, not that their chances are only a fractional percent out of 100.

These interaction forms are ordinarily referred to as rituals and ceremonies and, many years ago, were called ritual techniques by Chapple and Coon (1942). But ritual is too limited a term to include all types of maximized performance. Although military drill, on certain special occasions, is thought of as ceremonial, its rationale is also regarded as a practical necessity if men are to be maneuvered in battle. The performing arts—dance, theatre, musical recitals—are both esthetic and interactional (if these can so easily be differentiated). They, too, require specific performance even though idiosyncratic differences in tempo and expressive movement can also be detected, although no more so than in a priest celebrating Mass. So too, in sports and games, precision accompanies competition, though the disparities of reaction to the opposing side within the context of the game introduces greater variations than in the arts, rites, or military drill.

At this point, we need to ask how interaction forms are selected out of particular contexts rather than others, and why the same interaction form is used in a variety of situations, and, for that matter, how it is differentiated from its other uses by the precision with which it is carried out. To understand the process, we have to return to our biological foundations, to the means through which the emotional–interactional patterns become associated with culture and its dimensional constraints. But this must include the process of symbolization, for, as will become clear in the next chapter, the interaction forms and the dimensional elements which shape them become integrated into the communication dimensions. They become symbols whose efficacy is reinforced in the course of their performance.

Cultural Dimensions and Interactional Crises

The consequences of man as animal are perhaps best seen in the ways in which his culture and, in particular, the dimensions of communication are biologically (emotionally) affected and possessed. Remarkable as is his capacity to use his conceptual powers and frame them in language, at the same time these symbols become vulnerable to the Old Adam within. In strong emotional reactions, his autonomic–interactional systems short-circuit logic. More important, because more pervasive, they also endow the symbols he uses for rational purposes with the consequences of his emotional–interactional experiences. From first-order abstractions on up to the highest levels through which complex situations are brought together under a common symbol, he is influenced by every temperamental nuance with others. The symbols he uses in referring to these relationships have emotional and dimensional impact; it is this which affects the probabilities of response.

Suzanne Langer very properly makes the point that concepts generally, and art forms in particular, are built upon biological rhythms and the autonomic variants through which they obtain their effects. More directly for our purposes, it is important to emphasize the emotional components of the interaction forms. This is no mere dichotomy; these components are decisive because they are an integral part of any observable pattern of skeletal muscle actions. The visible component is comparable to the above water mass of the iceberg. Its structure and magnitude lie below the surface of the skin.

Yet something more happens through the influence of these interaction forms than their obvious utility in organizing patterns of interaction—constrained by the cultural dimensions—through which relationships with others can be handled. They facilitate the acting out of particular types of adjustment—complementarity, dominance and subordination, alleviation of emotional stress, or building transactional relationships. More than that, they become most necessary and most carefully performed where significant changes in interaction patterns are anticipated or have occurred, and where the stability of the system—its equilibrium properties, individual or group—is endangered.

These changes are inevitably associated with stress. This is not the single instance of asynchrony—the latency, the attempted dominance—but its continuous repetition. Sometimes these consist of significant quantitative increases or decreases in interactional relationships to certain others, or major readjustments where new individuals or groups must be adjusted to. Often such states of stress are a consequence of changes in the dimensional intervals separating or bringing together individuals, where one or more interaction forms have had to be ended and new ones begun.

Such continuous or repeated states of stress are called crises. They can be divided into two categories:

(1)   The first type of crisis results from changes in the interactions of individuals with one another consequent on a change in *their* interactions to some one person. These are commonly called the life crises—birth, marriage, illness, or death are the most obvious—but they include the changes occurring if one begins to interact in a new institution (going to school or joining a club) or leaving an old one (retirement or separation.)

(2)   The other type of crisis is one which requires a shift in interaction forms and, ordinarily for the participants, starting new ones. For instance, cultural contexts require that work be ended and members of the family come together, that all the members of the Tribal Council leave their other affairs behind and begin their juridical and governing duties, or that the entire population—village or tribe—meet to prepare for new activities like the beginning of planting or the tribal hunt. These are the institutional crises. They may involve one institution only, a part of one, or many, in which case they are often called communal.

Interactions occurring during such crises can be described entirely by the use of the quantitative measurements necessary for the analysis of systems—individual or group. The constituent interaction forms through which these changes are to be controlled with the greatest interactional effectiveness are called rites, rituals, or ceremonies. They operate either to reestablish equilibrium or to reorganize the system of relations so that a new one becomes possible. Van Gennep (1909) first made a systematic study of them in his book *The Rites of Passage* (English translation, 1960). Chapple and Coon (1942) further differentiated these rites, showing that those which mediate the changes due to the life crises, the rites of passage, should be distinguished from those associated with the institutional crises. They called these the rites of intensification.

When interaction forms become utilized as the ingredients of these rites, they shift their dimensional qualities. However separable they are into their constituent distances, sequences, and symbolic components, the total contexts of situation within which they occur take on a further dimensional quality on the symbolic scale. Accuracy in conducting the interaction forms becomes reinforced by the major reactions derived from the autonomic states aroused by the crises whose interactional patterns they endeavour to control. Clearly, rites differ in the intensity of their emotional properties, yet almost universally variation in performance becomes significantly reduced. One can say that, as ritualization increases, the probabilities that the interactions will take place according to pattern also increase.

The performance of the rite or its component interaction forms reinforces its value on the symbolic interval scales derived from the levels of abstraction identified in the culture. Far more complex than any Pavlovian model, the greater the frequency of performance and the extent to which emotional–interactional patterns are included within it, the more precise and fixed will be the performance of the ritualized form. Feedback also operates so that variations in cultural elements, in temporal characteristics, and in membership—in those who participate—modify both the performance and its symbolic intensity. How this comes about is far less difficult to understand than this introduction perhaps suggests.

The Life Crises

People differ considerably in the magnitude of their temperamental reactions to interactional stress. Yet most of them are affected by bereavement or separation or by having to rearrange their lives (and old relationships) when it becomes necessary to adjust to new persons. The death of someone close results not only in immediate autonomic disturbance but also removes an essential interactional outlet. Hence grief, with all its potentially long-lasting emotional–interactional disturbances to the bereaved's basic biological rhythms, is set in motion. Replacement of the lost interaction to its former levels of complementarity or stabilized temperamental interplay is required. Success in substitution depends on the quantitative values of the new relationships and their approximation to the old.

Although death has a finality which separation does not quite possess, the latter's consequences are similar. Such deprivation often occurs combined with beginning to interact with persons who are complete strangers or known only within a limited interactional pattern. Thus the Chinese bride, leaving her family in an arranged marriage, may never have seen the groom and certainly not the members of his family with whom she now must live. Her separation from her own family (at least in the old days) is rigidly enforced, with limited and occasional visits. The new interaction forms she must perform, "her role," requires her not only to be subordinate to her husband and gratify his needs, but she is also under the rigid authoritarian control of her mother-in-law. The husband, on the other hand, in acquiring a wife, may only incur a slight addition to his other interactions. If he becomes emotionally involved with her, he runs the risk of reducing the amount and pattern of his interactions with his family; marriage in such a case, might, in the future, become a source of serious stress for him. On the other hand, his relationship to her may involve only that minimum contact to father sons, to honor the ancestors, and continue the family name.

Even in societies like that of the United States where marriage is ordinarily a continuation of an already existing "affectional" relationship, where bride and groom set up a separate household, and where their families do not establish formal economic bonds through exchange of money and property in conjunction with marriage, changes in interaction patterns cannot be avoided. Necessarily, the newly wed must adjust to the total personality and temperamental susceptibilities of each other, rather than the complementarity maintained during courting. But coresidence, domestic cultural sequencing, and perhaps even the beginning of employment produce an increase in their interaction. Inevitably, this reduces the time spent with their former friends and relatives. Yet each soon discovers that the people in these old relationships seek to maintain their former interactional patterns; many an outburst will result in consequence.

The birth of a child is similarly a source of stress and crisis, declining perhaps as the number of births substantially increases and the older children take on responsibility. Apart from the danger to the mother's life and the risk that the marriage relationship might be ended, the child will maintain or extend the parental or generational set. In many societies, the sex of the child is thus a further risk; a girl baby may be quietly eliminated. More generally, the addition of the infant shifts the interaction patterns already existing in the nuclear family. If it is the first, the mother cannot avoid reducing her interactions with her husband significantly. As the child grows older, the husband must compete for her attentions. If there are other children, their relations to each other and to their parents will shift with much storm and stress and many emotional outbursts—a common topic for those who dispense advice on "family problems."

Illness, whether the sick person is hospitalized or moved apart from other family members, is a partial separation. It ordinarily requires a rear-rangement of interactions as those who care for the patient focus on him and reduce their interactions with others. Changes in the sick person's capacity to interact are equally evident, either through increasing lassitude and pain or through his demands for attention and response. With greater sophistication in medicine, the emotional stresses associated with physical illness or injury are being taken seriously. Hospitalization (creating separate-ness in intense relationships) is now looked at as a serious emotional problem both for children and for adults.

Aside from these primary crises, there are many other categories of great importance resulting from the maturation process. The beginning of formal training in the interaction forms associated with adulthood—going to school or, as part of the initiation process in many tribes, moving into the men's house, forces a significant change in interaction within the family and in free interaction with one's age mates. In some groups, the young person is physically removed from his family, sometimes for several years. In others, as in the United States, the removal is perhaps only for a large part of each day. In all, however, he becomes subjected and forced to learn how to interact within a hierarchical system with definite (and often severe) restrictions on his freedom to behave as he did formerly. Such changes in relationships occur in all sorts of institutions—joining a club or secret so-ciety, becoming a member of a church, or getting a job. Within an institu-tion, progressions within the sets (transfers or promotions, for example) establish significant alterations in rank or position, and hence in interactions.

Conversely, leaving the institution or the position attained also in-volves the loss of well-established and interactionally satisfying outlets. Of-ten, these may constitute the major part of the individual's affective inter-actions in his present life situation. Little wonder, in the United States, that retirement (forced or not) is coming to be regarded as a major cause of premature mortality. Whatever the advertisements may say about living in Florida on $300 a month, the reality can mean that the individual has "nothing" left. Severe autonomic disturbances are the consequence.

The Rites of Passage

Though these crises differ in their quantitative properties and their emotional significance for any particular individual, they constitute major disturbances of equilibrium in the systems where they occur. Compensatory interactions take place in each individual affected, the type and severity depending on his idiosyncratic temperamental reactions. How transitive human interaction is is evidenced as each person endeavours to accomodate himself to the others, and the whole system which they constitute together becomes unstable. Each reaction sets off another (in another person); this in turn entrains another until the interaction patterns relating them become highly asynchronous.

But countercurrents are set in motion since each constituent rhythm tries to reestablish itself, and the less severely disturbed individuals begin to return to their basal patterns. Beyond that, however, the cultural dimensions have evolved interaction forms, the performance of which simulates some approximation of what the system requires if equilibrium is to be reestablished. Quantitative analysis of these rites has not as yet been carried on, yet there exist in the literature highly specific descriptions of such rites for many cultures (Turner 1967). These are often so detailed that the interplay of the cultural dimensions within each successive context of situation (and the interaction forms themselves) can be easily understood.

Both Van Gennep, and Chapple and Coon, emphasized, in different terminology, that the differential distribution of interaction forms within any given ritual and the frequency and elaboration of their performance depend on the degree to which the institution undergoing disturbance has already built into its system of sets "automatic" mechanisms for stabilizing the institution without the performance of a rite. For example, where a marriage is based on a contractual relationship between families such that a breakup (through death of the wife provided by one family) would upset a complex network of relationships, the family may automatically produce a substitute (possibly a younger sister) with little or no ceremony. For similar reasons, parts of rituals may be "aborted" or reduced to minimal length; others, within the relatively uniform sequencing which all rites follow, may be significantly lengthened.

To understand the process, it is necessary to look closely at the sequencing of these rituals. Their general framework was originally worked out by Van Gennep, and restated in interactional terms by Chapple and Coon. Van Gennep showed that all rituals or ceremonies could be broken down into three stages, each involving one or more ritual sequences which occur consecutively, always in the same order. The terms he applied, in French, are *separation, marge,* and *aggregation,* which can be translated as separation, transition, and incorporation.

In the first stage, separation, the individual and group involved in the crisis reduce their interactions in other institutional relationships; often there will be a complete cessation so that the participants are literally separated. The interaction forms making up this ritual stage serve to reinforce their patterns of interactions with each other, depending on the varying degrees of separation quantitatively defined.

In the second stage, transition, new interaction forms are learned and

As Turner explained, is learning in this period is accomplished thru the use of myth.

practiced, symbolically at least, with the new individuals. Familiar ones now requiring alteration are rearranged through interaction forms to compensate for the changes the crisis has brought about. Some, like the initiation ceremonies, are made up of many long and involved rituals and sequences; the training period may last several years. In others, as in mourning, abstention from "normal" activities, wearing of identifying symbols in dress, and the repetitive performance of subsidiary interaction forms, can also be long drawn out. Coincident with the transitional rites, all kinds of devices are used to heighten the emotional and autonomic effects—fasting, purgation, infinite repetition of postures or phrases, prayer, repeated self-punishment, self-torture, continuous wailing, and the acting out of grief.

The third stage, incorporation, requires the reintroduction of the separated individuals through "programmed" interactions with the members of the group from whom they have been separated during the rite. The resumption of "normal" activities will be symbolized by a ritual, say of eating a food forbidden to them, or by starting to perform the interaction forms (the roles) of a new office or position. Once these introductory interaction forms have been acted out, the crises are over, whatever the emotional state of the individuals undergoing them.

This three stage process which all rites follow is interactionally easy to separate into its component stages. Within each stage a series of subsidiary rites are practiced, each following the same sequence but with a briefer duration of performance. Thus, in the initiation ceremonies, whether they involve the means through which the young boys (and often girls) learn the interaction forms necessary to achieve adulthood or the elaborate rituals by which the heir to the throne takes on the full requirements of kingship when the period of mourning has come to an end, many subrituals have to be performed. Each is equally divisible into three stages, and so on down until the ultimate component contexts of situation and their interaction forms can be isolated. These are the basic ingredients out of which larger ritual sequences are compounded.

Ritualization

Even in a largely secular society like that of the United States, most people participate in and have experienced such rites—in churches, schools, fraternal organizations, and in business where the crises are celebrated, but often without "religious" implications. Consideration of any of these rites or ceremonies will indicate how easily each stage can be identified. Detailed examples are available in any ethnographic account, and in Chapple and Coon's chapter on the rites of passage. They need not be cited here since the important thing for us to consider is their interactional influences.

In simple hunting and gathering groups, and even among those portions of European or American culture where belief in the symbols and the interaction forms which represent them is intense, the sanctions which accompany their correct performance (even their performance at all) derive from the autonomic stages set in motion by the crisis. This does not mean that the nonbeliever may not also suffer similar and extreme emotional reactions of fear or anger, with all the variegations which the temperamental patterns can induce. For him, however, the symbols and the interaction forms are no longer part of the same contexts of situation, reinforced over his life by the interplay of the cultural dimensions.

The Indians of the Great Plains of the United States, during the early part of the 19th century, lived in a culture in which all males, at the beginnings of adolescence, fasted alone far away from the camp, usually for four days. In doing so, they expected to achieve a vision of a supernatural being who would select a special object as his symbol (totem is not quite appropriate as a term) and endow him with his or a derived power. Whatever it was, it was an emblem derived from the cultural contexts of his tribe. It became the focus around which his ritual life centered within the more general rituals of the group.

The symbol yielded through the vision quest or the sacredness with which particular elements of the symbolic world became endowed, for individuals in other cultures had a common selection process. The interaction forms and their associated symbols were derived from those particular contexts of situation in which intense patterns of emotional–interactional behavior were manifest. Their activation and concentrated emotions were based on the sensory-physiological mechanisms described in Chapter 13. Once one looks at the symbols of a particular group (or individual) and the ritual techniques associated with them, and sees how the sequencing of the rites reinforces their significance, it is clear that it is the recurrent element in the contexts of situation which is selected out through the filtering process. A particular symbol or symbolic object becomes endowed with the emotional states associated with the interaction patterns.

Normally, these ritualized forms are derived from very simple and common technological or environmental elements of the culture. To illustrate, the eating of a meal together is probably universal. Beginning as a daily practice (being biologically necessary at least to eat), the ordering of interaction through cultural sequencing associated with preparing, serving, and eating food (the food ordinarily being that which represents a major collective effort to produce, whether bread or buffalo) becomes ritualized in the ceremonial meal. All kinds of elaborations in sequencing, in the objects used (often special to such rituals), are evident, but their basis is obvious, however sacred the rite for the participants.

Performance of the interaction form in its ritual contexts is essential for reinforcement. Otherwise, it can be extinguished. Although the particular crisis and the rite associated with it may be infrequent, the reinforcement is maintained by the regularity of repetition of equivalent contexts in other types of crises. If this begins to become intermittent, if only at occasional points in the intersection of the cultural dimensions do the same contexts repeat, symbols become separated from their contexts and the symbolic network of faith becomes ruptured.

Sometimes this is due to the speed with which contexts change, thereby preventing filtering from coming about; sometimes, in cultural change, contextual and interactional bridges become too difficult to establish between the old symbols and their new contexts. New interaction forms (and symbols) arise when the whole basis on which a society is organized changes radically—from agriculture, for example, to industrial technology. The sewing of the seed, the first crops, and the harvest are far removed from automobile manufacturing. The needs are still there, but the new means developed to manage them lack interactional interdependence and symbolic equivalences.

The Rites of Passage Today

One can ask whether the rituals themselves, in new form or old, will be necessary in a world where medicine has eliminated most major infectious diseases, has lengthened the expected age of life, reduced the risk of childbirth significantly, and thus partly sterilized the life crises. In fact, the better-phrased question is: Will man, the human animal, under the combined mediation of medicine, technology, economics, and the whole cognitive system by which he sets forth to stabilize his world against adversity, actually succeed? Will he no longer be afraid, lonely, or grieve? Will he be angry or hate? In short, will he react to the people within the world around him emotionally as in the past and, if he does, will tranquillizers or psychotherapy be enough?

One can, of course, argue that the physician plays an important part in the management of the life crises themselves. Much of what is being developed under the name of therapy, administrative medicine and the like is ritual in disguise, not to denigrate its rational significance also. In addition, a wide variety of specialists have sprung up—lawyers, personnel men, counselors, social workers—a division of labor so extensive that almost any aspect of an individual's problem in meeting change will have a specialist available to aid in dealing with it.

But actually, almost unnoticed, another development is taking place. New interaction forms are beginning to appear to deal with the primary problems of those who must live in a technological and corporate civilization. Examination of any large governmental or business organization will reveal that a wide variety of practices, carried on by specialists, are coming into existence to manage the process of passage from one state of interaction to another. Specialized training courses, meetings, methods of induction into new positions all serve (usually unconsciously) to regularize the stages of separation, transition, and incorporation which vertical or lateral movement within an organizational framework necessitates. Trice and his associates (1968) have commented on the necessity to look at this whole "training" movement in terms of its ritual significance to the individual, not as a set of techniques whose rational, as opposed to emotive, value is predominant.

Similar movements are occurring within the family, in the schools and in the community. Given the complexity (and rapidity) of the changes underway in the United States, perhaps a significantly increased stabilization of symbols and interaction forms is by no means as delayed as it might seem. For example, whatever the rational significance of psychotherapy and counseling and all their variants, no one will deny, least of all their practitioners, that belief and faith (emotional states) play an important part in making them effective. Even scientific evaluation of drug effects is plagued by the fact that roughly one-half of their users improve when given a placebo (a fake pill made up to look like the real thing).

But the world of psychotherapy does more. Its techniques (interaction forms) are widely recommended for handling all kinds of interpersonal situations—parents to children, boss to employee, priest or minister to parishioner; in medicine generally, outside of psychiatry, even in the relationship of physician and patient. Beyond that, symbols derived from its contexts are becoming an increasing part of the communication universe—"understanding," "insight," "adjustment," "acceptance," "confrontation"—the list is endless. Not only are these symbols being projected onto the structure of society, they are being absorbed into the dialectics of theology and metaphysics. This we shall return to, but first we need to examine those crises affecting an institution or community.

Institutional or Communal Crises

A) The Internal Crises

The crises arising in groups appear very dissimilar to the life crises of the individual since they are not often the consequence of disaster or the danger of attack. Most of them, however minor they may appear and how small the participating group, occur regularly, predictably, during the day, the week, the month, or year or even at much longer intervals. Often the term, ceremonial cycle, is applied to them. In Christianity, for example, the great rituals build up to their peaks at Christmas and Easter. Similar sequences are characteristic of other cultures.

Consider the custom of saying grace before meals. This is a ritual associated with an institutional crisis, ordinarily within the family. Superficially, it may appear incongruous to apply the term, crisis, with all its overtones of emergency, to a group of people assembled to eat a common meal. Yet it is a good case to begin with if we are to understand crises in the institutional sense.

What happens is quickly told. For an appreciable interval of time before the meal is to begin, members of the family have been engaged in other activities (and interaction forms), adults working, older children being taught to learn new patterns, women in the kitchen preparing the meal, and younger children playing outside. These cultural sequences and their associated interaction forms may take place in other institutions (in more complex societies) or almost entirely within the family as an institutional system itself. These now end; the family members come together and begin their interactions as a group, no longer pursuing their separate ways. The previous interaction patterns stop, the individuals combine in different relationships (within the family sets). They begin to interact within the cultural sequencing and the interaction forms established around the meal. After they finish, the interaction patterns within this system come to an end. The members disperse, often to renew the activities interrupted by the meal.

What are the stresses? First, however familiar the personalities involved may be, the change from one situation to another requires a change in interaction pattern, and a readjustment to a new situation. Second, the transitive properties of human beings make possible the carry-over of temperamental reactions into (and biasing) the new adjustments required. If this should happen, the family's approximation to complementarity will be disturbed (apart from its effects on their digestion). Finally, the interaction patterns within the family are reinforced through the cultural sequencing and interaction forms which the meal specifies. This has emotional benefits as the members return to or begin new relationships (with food and drink as an essential mediator physiologically).

So stated, the potentialities of stress are evident although the presence or absence of an obvious ritual (saying grace) is another matter. Yet even when not present, people change or straighten out their clothing, wash perfunctorily or carefully, sit in specified spaces, wait while particular persons initiate in serving, control the order of their beginning to eat, and depart only when one or all are finished. These are clearly defined interaction forms, often highly ritualized, whether or not they are accompanied by the use of verbal symbolism when the prescribed initiatives are taken.

Typically, therefore, institutional and communal crises enforce a transformation of relationships. Their interaction forms and accompanying contexts of situation require quantitative changes in the interaction. Between some persons it will be increased or begun anew; with others, it will be decreased or temporarily ended. A significant element is the formal acting out of set events. The crisis itself elicits them. Their ritualization reinforces and reaffirms the sets on which the institution is based. Though a family meal (the example could have been of a common meal of a much larger institution—the ruler in his great hall surrounded by courtiers) might seem trivial, it illustrates the nature of the institutional crises and the interaction forms which emerge as etiquette, manners, or as formal rites.

Many institutional crises, great or small, take place because of the internal rhythms of a society and its organizational systems, and may be so subcategorized. Whether the family eats together, once, twice, or three times a day, meals follow a regular round, a calendric cycle (if calendar can be extended to the internal divisions of the day). So, too, for the congregation assembling weekly on its holy days or the club or association at its monthly meeting; institutional calendars in every society comprise a complex temporal pattern. These crises are a consequence of the need for reestablishing relationships and reinforcing them. If they are delayed too long, other interactions can become too emotionally significant, superseding those still unperformed. Remember, too, that the outlets, through the interaction forms special to them, channel the interaction to maintain not only the organizational equilibrium, but that of the participating individuals. Without reinforcement, these interactions can be extinguished if others are available.

Each personality achieves its stability through its system of relationships. These relationships necessarily are institutional. Cliques, gangs or—in pairing—best friends or lovers, though appearing unstructured, link institutions and are embryonic institutions in the process of formation—only potential, since they can, of course, break up before this happens. Hence the individuals making up each institution, varying in the degree to which its internal interactions are most necessary for them, need to interact recurrently. Without this, the institution will decay (quantitatively as well as in its cultural and interactional elaborations). Members drop out, fewer and fewer are left to celebrate its interactional forms. As this happens, these people as a group, like each as an individual, experience the emotions of loss, of separation, and of disequilibrium.

Each gathering together of the institutional members is accompanied by the increasing intensity of the crisis of noninteraction since the last time they met. When they meet, the number of people coming together, the success with which the interaction forms are performed, and the emotional–interactional patterns elicited are crucial in reestablishing equilibrium and bridging the gap until the next scheduled meeting is held. Where highly elaborate rituals, to which each individual has been conditioned, provide the contexts of situation, the cultural dimensions have been sufficiently ritualized within the symbolic scales to carry the interaction along. By contrast, in the secular world, enormous effort and ingenuity in framing the interaction forms must be expended by those controlling such meetings to make sure that they are "really" successful.

B)   The External Crises

Outside these calendric cycles of institutional crises internal to each system, the society is also subject to *external* crises deriving from the interplay of environment and the technological adaptations available within the culture to utilize it—hunting, gathering particular foods, and agriculture. These are supplemented by those crises due to conflicts, potential or otherwise, with other groups. Since their magnitude and intensity are dependent on factors over which the group may have relatively little control, they are more disturbing and potentially far more dangerous. Moreover, they may be stretched out over long periods of time, creating recurrent or continuing states of uncertainty, with fluctuations towards or away from a final reestablishment of equilibrium.

Though farming, in this era of complex machines, chemical fertilizers, and all the panoply of technical and scientific services provided by departments of agriculture, might appear to be equivalent to a factory operation, crops still fail, ravaging insects refuse to accept their toxicological fate, wind and hail are still unmanageable; science shows no signs of producing that gentle rain from heaven at the agriculturalists' beck and call. How much less predictable are the efforts of farmers in every other culture! Gathering the foods which the earth produces without tillage, hunting, and fishing are even more chancy. In the latter, the dangers which face the men who go to sea are as beyond belief today as they have ever been.

As a consequence, depending on technology and the cultural sequencing developed out of it, each stage in the process, where a clear discontinuity marking a beginning and ending occurs, is a crisis, though all may combine into a more massive crisis whose beginning and ending stretch over weeks or months. One need not elaborate the obvious stages in agriculture; for example, as winter begins to pass and spring (or its climatic analogues) urges the husbandmen to prepare the fallow fields for planting. From the crop's beginning until the final harvest, each family and the whole community centers its life and future on the fields. The crises associated with the process not merely compel new patterns of activity and interaction but are hurried by the external needs of growing plants and by the weather, which are the ultimate control.

Crises resulting from attack or defense similarly need little elaboration. Though the decision to go forth on a war party or a more extensive military venture is, to some extent, more easily planned for, the process of preparation requires the men involved to separate themselves from their other institutional relationships. Moreover, those staying behind, as well as those who are to fight, well know that death, serious injury, or captivity may be the consequence.

Attacks by outsiders, other tribes, or feuding families involve immediate danger for all since, even in the simplest societies, not only the warriors are legitimate game. Even if noncombatants are spared, houses, food, and property may go up in smoke and whatever is valuable appropriated. Mobilization, by the threat of attack or its actual occurrence, disturbs all and is the strongest of unifiers. It intensifies the emotional–interactional patterns of conflict (and their autonomic consequences of fear and anger); it facilitates the synchronization of responses to the repeated initiatives of their leaders. During the struggle, life crises occur and, afterward, rites of passage as well as of intensification are necessary mediators to reestablish the equilibrium of the group.

The Rites of Intensification

Exactly as in the rites of passage, the three-fold division of cultural sequencing holds for the rites of intensification: separation, either of the participants from others (if all are not included), the ending of other interaction forms and the relationships built upon them. Sometimes the prior states themselves are dramatized. They build up intensity of one type of interaction only to shift radically to the new. The celebration of Carnival in many Christian countries immediately before the beginning of Lent—the period of fasting, prayer, and intense performance of rituals leading up to Easter—prefaces one rite of intensification with another where freedom for complete complementarity through Saturnalia provides maximum outlet for all. Transition, the second stage, requires the performance of the interaction forms through which the group structure is made explicit and reinforced; finally, incorporation takes place where group interaction reaches its optimal level of intensity through increasing the precision of the set events which unify and polarize the individuals in their institutional relationships until "the people speak with one voice."

Essential to these rites is the systematic utilization of the component contexts of situations of even the smallest constituent groups and the interaction forms which they perform. So the family commonly serves as the model for the larger system. The roles performed by its members become the symbols for the relationships between the leaders of the larger group and its members. The church is the house of the Lord (and of the people), the priest is father, the parishioners are children. The rites of intensification in Christianity provide a particularly clear illustration of this entire process, but no more so than those found in other very different cultures.

Among the Omaha, a Siouxan people of the Great Plains of the United States (analyzed in interactional terms by Chapple and Coon 1942) the great tribal rites of intensification took place at the time of the annual buffalo hunt when everyone came together. During the winter, individual families went off on their own, often the men to hunt and the women remaining behind in their villages; in the spring, since the Omaha were also agricultural, care of the gardens after planting was a necessity. By summer, when the buffalo herded together and horses could travel easily, the tribe moved as a unit, setting up their tepees in a camp circle, each family, each clan or subclan to which they belonged, and the two major divisions of the tribe, had their fixed positions. The camp circle was the tribe (the tepee, of course, also being circular); the positions of the clans within it were regarded as equivalent to the positions traditionally assigned to members of the family within the tepee.

The great ceremonies performed at this time began when the initial decision was made to begin the hunt. They built up from the first surround when the total tribe cut off part of a buffalo herd and encircled it until the fourth and last surround was finished and sufficient meat had been obtained for the ensuing winter. Without repeating the description and its analysis here, in essence it consisted of the performance of set events involving more and more of the tribe. At its peak, the entire tribe participated in their proper family and kin affiliations, spatially separated, with the contexts built up on the sequencing of activities and interaction forms of raising corn, killing and preparing the buffalo, and defending the tribe from its symbolized enemies.

Ritualization

The symbolic impact of the rites of passage and intensification needs to be understood, particularly since so many of the most sacred rituals reported by ethnographers appear to be little more than the repetition of interaction forms and their contexts, derived from the cultural dimensions which set up their constraints on everyday life. This is familiar enough in Christianity (without concerning oneself with theological interpretations) in the act of partaking in Holy Communion, the symbolic incorporation of the group in the body of Christ (the Church), just as the Omaha in their ceremony of the Sacred Pole (symbolizing the individual tepee, its household, and the whole tribe) sent, from each family, a special cut of the buffalo for preparation of the fatty mixture used to anoint the Sacred Pole and constructed its "tent" with one pole from every tepee in the tribe.

The emotional significance of the Omaha's rites are particularly clear if one reads the classic monograph by Alice Fletcher and Frank LaFlesche (son of the Head Chief of the Omaha), since this is, in effect, a description by believers. But the process by which this is built up, outlined in the analysis by Chapple and Coon, involves a more complex society (and thus a more elaborate set of rituals) than can be dealt with here. On the other hand, these authors have also utilized a much simpler case, that of the very simple negrito peoples of the Andaman Islands south of the Indian subcontinent, initially described and analyzed by the British anthropologist Radcliffe-Brown (1922). Its virtue is that it represents the first systematic attempt to demonstrate how symbols, derived from contexts of situation as a consequence of cultural sequencing, develop strong emotional significance.

> Among the Andaman Islanders, hibiscus fiber is used for making the rope with which turtle nets are made, and which also serves for the lines of turtle harpoons and for hawsers to attach a canoe either to a stone serving as an anchor or to a tree. No other fiber is used for these purposes. Therefore, in a series of contexts of situation in which the Andaman Islanders are hunting the turtle (one of the two principal sources of meat, the other being the wild pig), with a number of men paddling canoes in pursuit of one of these animals, the complex series of interactions which take place during the turtle hunt ... three or four men paddling a canoe, and sometimes the combined efforts of two canoes, is associated with the use of hibiscus fiber. ... It is, therefore, not surprising as Radcliffe-Brown has pointed out, that in the initiation ceremony of the boys about to become adult in which the initiate begins, after a long period of abstention, to eat turtle meat once again, he is surrounded with hibiscus leaves. When he starts to eat, he cannot use his fingers but has to use a skewer of hibiscus wood. Moreover, hibiscus fiber is used in an amulet to protect a man from the dangers of the sea. Thus even when a man is not fishing for turtle, the presence of the hibiscus fiber in the amulet symbolizes all the previous events in which the individual has taken part at sea.

This uniformity in using hibiscus in the series of contexts concerned with the hunting of the sea turtle, an enterprise not only involving interaction vis-a-vis the crew of the canoe, but also the dangers of the sea itself, simplifies the analysis of the filtering process; that is, they used only one material for the rope, for the spear, and for other ritual-related purposes.

The repetitive influence of the contexts of situation in which emotional-interactional events take place endow the elements making up the context, the objects (or any kind of sign stimulus) with the intense properties of those particular emotional states. Thus, the power of the amulet or talisman is derived from its association with the physiological states which the interaction produces. As the conditioned response pattern is built up, the amulet elicits that response in the individual conditioned to it, always providing that reinforcement takes place at appropriate intervals by repetition within the total context of situations with which it is associated.

This does not limit the institutional or communal reach of symbolization, since higher order abstractions, relating a whole group of lower order contexts, ordinarily occur. The kinds of specific contexts which the hibiscus symbolizes in this example become generalized because of the similarities between its contexts, emotionally (and interactionally), and those of others through the process of equivalation (Chapple 1940). In simpler terms, one can say that those contexts of situations where emotional-interactional patterns are approximately equal (quantitatively and autonomically) become associated cortically through the impact of the lower centers. The symbols, objects, and environmental conditions which make them up then become interchangeable. Chapple and Coon point out, following Fletcher and La-Flesche that, among the Omaha, the relative decline in importance of corn, as the tribe became adapted to a full-fledged buffalo economy, resulted in the rituals associated with corn shifting their position. They were now performed within the buffalo rituals and, even more relevant, they became equivalent as alternate foods at the sacred feast preceding the buffalo hunt. Further, the myths explaining the rites shifted. The buffalo were said to have intervened supernaturally, bringing maize to the Omaha, though the fact is that the historical order of use was the opposite.

The importance of equivalation, of the generalization of contexts with high emotional intensity across various institutions and interaction forms within a society, is well and simply described by Radcliffe-Brown. Again using Chapple and Coon's analysis:

> In the Andaman Islands, Radcliffe-Brown has shown how the word "ot-ki-mil" (literally, "hot") has come to symbolize a number of situations which involve many different individuals in a community, all of whom are undergoing certain characteristic changes in their relations to one another. The term "ot-kimil" is used to describe the state of an individual who is ill, or who is passing through his initiation rites, the stage of individuals in a community during a typhoon period, the condition of individuals after eating certain foods, and the state of persons who have lost a relative. It is also used to designate a person who has just joined in a dance.
>
> Each of these situations has in common the fact that it represents a change in the interaction rates of the individuals. In the initiation ceremonies, the youth who has been forbidden to eat any of the important foods of the Andamanese is, as Radcliffe-Brown points out, unable to take part in the activities of the group when a pig or turtle is being consumed, therefore he is unable to interact with the other individuals during these meals, which are periods of great enthusiasm and excitement.
>
> During the period of heavy storms, life in an Andamanese village is distinctly hazardous. The high winds and lightning send a veritable shower of

branches and falling trees upon the Andamanese, whose only refuge often is to wade into the water and stand there until the storm is over. During such a period, the whole ordinary routine of existence is upset. The state of individuals after a crisis such as a death, or being lost in a forest, is also an obvious disturbance of the habitual relations of an individual. The only case which is not quite so dramatic is the state of "ot-kimil" derived from eating certain foods. Here, however, there is an equally clear, if less obvious change, in the interaction rate. Hunting the pig or the turtle involves long sustained interactions of a group of men. When they eat the food and dance in the evening, they are interacting no longer with men only but with the members of their family, women and children. Moreover, this interaction during the feast and dance takes place at a high rate, and changes, therefore, markedly.

It is important to note that the Andamanese do not consider themselves to be in a state of "ot-kimil" after eating all foods; it is only those which involve the sustained interaction of the men in a cooperative technique that are held responsible for this condition. Thus when the Andaman Islander says that he is in a state of "ot-kimil," he is referring to a condition of changed interaction rates, which he experiences subjectively in the heightened activity of his autonomic nervous system, and which brings about a specific emotional state. When he tells the investigator about this condition, his description of the similarity in his feelings on different occasions, that is, the physiological events of which he is aware, and also his statement as to the precise events in which he experiences these feelings, indicate that these changes are brought about by the similar disturbances in his interaction rate, and thus the equivalence in disturbance, i.e., in referents, is symbolically represented by the use of a single symbol.

Here closely following the work of Durkheim, the French social anthropologist, Radcliffe-Brown, using his own field material, isolated a series of contexts of situation, all equivalent in the emotional states which they generated, but involving different types of events in the lives of the Andamanese—from hunting the wild pig or the sea turtle, to being initiated into manhood, to experiencing someone being ill or dying or lost in the forest, to having the group threatened by violent tropical storms. As Durkheim had originally shown in his *Elementary Forms of the Religious Life* (1912), though not in the terms used in this book, the uniformity of the contexts of situations and the interaction crises which they represent has resulted, in every culture, in the definition of a generalized emotional state of power and of intense autonomic reaction in the contexts with which it is associated. *Ot-kimil* for the Andamanese, *mana* for the Polynesians, *wakonda* or *manitou* among the American Indians, and, without becoming involved in theological disputation, the major religions have equivalent terms like the *Holy Spirit, baraka* among the Mohammedans, and so on.

The significance of what Radcliffe-Brown accomplished in 1922 is worth emphasizing since it is probable that his contributions to the understanding of the cultural dimensions of symbolism are the most important part of his work. This is particularly ironic since he explicitly stated on several occasions that he regarded cultural phenomena as of little importance in social anthropology (White 1966).

Nevertheless, he made explicit the mechanisms on which the symbols and rituals are built. This has been amplified by Malinowski's analysis (1927) of the meaning of language and how symbols are filtered out of contexts of situations, and Chapple's examination in 1940 of the specific ways in which interaction patterning controls the process. It is, of course, evident that not all emotional-interactional contexts are equivalent. On the contrary, they may be remarkably disparate and opposed since, in fact, they are dependent on the temperamental reactions, their autonomic components, and the institutional structure through which the personality variables operate.

Thus the states of power, the concatenations of symbols, are commonly dichotomized—not merely good and evil, but war and peace, male and female, land and sea, those who belong and those outside. As a consequence, symbols and their contexts and the interaction forms which utilize them can be separated into antagonistic configurations and systems. To strengthen this separateness, many of the subrites within the major rites are devoted—particularly in managing the first stage of separation—to the performance of forms which reinforce one side of the dichotomy, maleness, for example, or peace. Every effort is made to prevent contamination by opposing elements. So elaborate linkages of objects, colors, and patterns of expressive movement and speech become the symbolic configuration, each element of which is identified with one condition or its opposite (Turner 1967).

Beyond this, the institutions themselves develop their own configurations. Here symbolic hierarchy is evident and the symbols become the integrators of the independent systems. Each institution, coordinated through the hierarchical set itself, develops symbols which refer to all the interactions which take place within it. The contexts of situation in which the American flag plays a part from the earliest experiences of the child in school, in military life, and in its association with rituals and ceremonies of all sorts make it a symbol for the whole political structure of this society. Just as the ancient Jews carried the Ark of the Covenant containing the Tables of the Law, every group has a common symbol or group of symbols which represent its unity.

Idiosyncratic Aspects of Symbols

Given two people whose personalities are such that they are unable always to adjust to each other within their equilibrium limits, the temperamental reactions which ensue carry with them sympathetic nervous system disturbances. Before too long, in successive meetings, the fact that one grows increasingly unresponsive and the other, driven by this lack of response, grows tense and initiates quickly and frequently, becomes symbolized not merely by words to describe the antipathy—unsympathetic or sulky for the first, and pushy for the second—but other aspects of the context, physical appearance and subjects talked about, are selected out as symbols of disturbance. On such foundations, often intensified within family interaction to a very high degree, equivalence of individuals can quickly be built; "He reminds me of my father," "All Jews (or Negroes, Unitarians, or women) are like that"—the opportunities for equivalation and projection are commonplace. Individuals, groups, organizations and occupations, relative positions in interactional sets—and all the cultural forms associated—are brought together under common symbols. Thus, the paranoid individual finds the whole world, and the heavens too, spying on him and persecuting him. If each interactional situation has elements of nonresponse, as they almost always do, then the paranoid's conception of reality is reinforced by their recurrence, caused unwittingly by other persons.

Although the paranoid in our midst represents an extreme case (the nonhospitalized ones, of course), such idiosyncratic differences in which the symbols and the interaction patterns are equivalent are the basis on which individuals cohere, form groups and, perhaps ultimately, ongoing institutions. Alternatively, these idiosyncratic personality and temperament characteristics result in people trying to separate themselves from others. As a consequence, the symbols formerly held in common either take on new meanings or there is a search, unconsciously, for new symbols and interaction forms to become the banners around which new relationships can be crystallized.

Symbolic Equivalence and Interaction

The historian of culture, or the ethnographer describing the universe of a given group, can provide hundreds of illustrations of the ways in which symbols acquire, change, or lose their emotional meaning. Too often the fact is recorded; the changes in the interactional patterns responsible are glossed over or ignored. Groups of people whose interactions with one another are highly complementary build their symbolism from technology and linguistics to refer to these interactions. By so doing, they make explicit their differentiation from those others with whom they do not interact or with whom their relationships involve overt or latent conflict. Thus the cultural content, in ritual and theology, of each emerging sect becomes the means by which the interactional states of the individual members are symbolized. By the constraints which it imposes, it helps to reinforce these interactions within the framework of the cultural dimensions. If particular words or postures symbolize particular patterns of interaction, if these are reinforced through spatially differentiated cultural sequences, then the interacting individuals take part in context after context of situation with expected emotional components. Others are unable to take part unless their emotional-interactional patterns are similar. Assuming reinforcement takes place at necessary intervals, the symbols increase their dimensional efficacy. Rites of intensification then emerge or are borrowed and modified from those already practiced in the culture. The power of the communication dimensions lies in the fact that above a particular level of abstraction, the emotional states short-circuit the "rational." The higher the level on the symbolic interval scale, the easier it is to assume that the symbol is the prime mover. In fact, schismatic influences are first set in motion and, only after the group begins to split apart, do symbolic and ritual differences begin to develop.

The history of Christianity is a paramount but not very edifying example. Over and over again groups who attempt to differentiate themselves from the total church by utilizing new symbolic and ritual sequence combinations to demarcate their particular emerging sect from others appear. Shall baptism be total or partial? Are not infants predestined to damnation? And is not the bread and wine physically transmuted to flesh and blood? Viewed logically, the incredible and bloody conflicts over ritual niceties, over nuances of interpretation of the symbolic carapace of Christianity, seem unbelievable to the nonparticipants of today. But every time and every place in human history has its own verbalisms to mask its interactional conflicts. The 20th century is proving no exception.

Biological Properties of Rites and Symbols

There is a common tendency in ethnographic discussions to assume that individuals participating in rituals hold to a common interpretation of their meaning. This would imply that a poor farmer, following the rites to the letter, is on a par with the High Priest of a cult or great religion. Somehow, though limited in vocabulary, he has the same conceptual framework. No one can seriously maintain that the Pope, or any member of the Roman curia, defines the Trinity in the way some Irish countryman might. Only a superficial knowledge of church history tells one that major differences in interpretation have been maintained between the elect, apart from those who at the moment are considered heretic. In fact, the remarkable quality of all rites is the high precision achieved in carrying out the interaction forms and the equally high variability in meanings attributed to the symbols (in the broadest sense) of which their contexts are composed. This may appear a paradox since historians of culture tend to unify a system of beliefs in order to differentiate it from others. They then easily pass into the fallacy of regarding their intellectual constructs as one logically consistent configuration held by all. Granted they realize that the logics are not those of the logician; rather that the assumptions, however arbitrary to the rational mind, have a system to them.

The result is that attempts are made to differentiate those symbols which trigger off an action in an interaction sequence from those which are primarily carriers of complex cultural meanings. Here, as Fernandez (1965) comments in an excellent paper, one has to try to define symbols, signals, and signs in terms of their operative impact on behavior. Not only does such discussion confuse the biological issues, but the next step, as he points out, involves talking about sign-symbols and similar combinations. Without returning to our earlier discussion of symbolism, it is worth emphasizing that trying to make such distinctions is only useful in comparing individuals. For one person, as Fernandez emphasizes, the symbol is simply a signal like a red light at the corner; for another, the same red light (though he too may put on the brakes) has implications of authority, even of police brutality (the last conceit is mine).

The important thing about such idiosyncratic differences on the intellectual or "interpretive" side is that each of these two persons *responds* to the symbol. Each discriminates its order of dimensional magnitude and recognizes its differential importance on the interval scale on which it is arranged. Fernandez comments, in his study of a reformative cult among the Fang in the Gabon in Africa, that there is little discussion of cultural meanings except by the cult leader. Attempts to raise such questions are overtly discouraged since they are correctly perceived by cult leaders as a threat to their cult. Given free rein, they can easily lead to an attempt to set up a new group, a trend paralleled in every hierarchical religion, particularly within Christianity. The only permissable interest in symbolic meaning is to learn the leader's latest pronouncements. To be the recipient of "wisdom" (and the responder) is tolerable and necessary. Adopting another interaction form might affect the ritual. In other words, only the leaders may use ideology since this is how they maintain their hierarchical position.

Many ethnologists hold that symbols are cognitive, and signs emotive. Such definitions create even greater difficulties since all sign–symbol–signals contain common elements. They are ways of referring to *reactions to* which are made up of both autonomic and cortical states. To assume otherwise would mean that human beings manage their world with brains split completely between the cerebral cortex and the hypothalamic-limbic-reticular systems.

Moreover, the biological definitions of signs and signals are further limited by their communication properties in producing skeletal-muscular reactions. They also specify particular types of sensory input. Their structural constituents may consist of a single tonal frequency or a particular color pattern which elicits recognition from the other sex. To use such terms in the ethnological literature would require the assumption that the "cultural" should be differentiated from the "social" (or interactional). One need not elaborate that within the framework of behavioral biology and anthropology, such distinctions between signs, signals, and symbols are unnecessary.

If we reemphasize the position that ritual serves to reduce the variability and thus increases the probabilities that particular interaction patterns will be followed (Fernandez calls ritual a "more tightly patterned and repetitive form of nonrandom behavior" then Fernandez's further point on "meaning" seems quite relevant:

> The principle that can be suggested at this point is that the more rigorously regularized social interaction becomes, the more highly trained the participants in carrying out an increasingly alternative free interaction (ritual in the terms of this book), the greater possibility there is that the symbolic dimension of this interaction should have variable interpretation.

The increased precision with which interaction forms are performed in ritual is vastly facilitated by the rigor with which the participants are trained, but this precision is interactional. It requires a closer synchronization than ordinary and accurate temporal programming and rhythmic regularity—the organizing principle of all interaction (and language, as Lenneberg shows). Moreover, the interaction forms are made up of and structured by the cultural dimensions. What has to be done, what objects used, what movements and words expressed, what distances covered, and what sequencing of the correlative actions of the participants provide the constraints, the limits, or boundaries for the interaction.

Deviations from this sequencing are asynchronous and induce emotional stress. Stumbling on the beat, missing the cue, mishandling a ritual object—whatever the disparity between form and performance—contribute to disturbance. Moreover, participants in ritual commonly have lowered thresholds to the perception and incidence of stress. Here, as the situation itself increases the excitement through autonomic influences by the buildup of interactional intensity, much smaller quantitative values of asynchrony can become stressful and reacted to accordingly. In addition, the symbolic dimension to which the individuals have been conditioned compels intense reactions through the superposition of its intervals of heightened emotionality upon the basic biological rhythms through which all emotion is mediated.

In most cultures, a variety of techniques are used to intensify and stereotype the interaction forms—fasting, purgation, repetitive prayers or chants, hypnotic sequences, incense, drugs, alcohol, music with its primary emphasis on the beat, and expressive movement, whether it be called dance or prolonged gymnastic gyrations. Even if such techniques are not used, the need for precise behavior creates anxiety in performance, and the emotional–interactional components of the symbols produce a state of heightened awareness. They lower the threshold for perception of the cues of the interactional process.

All of these influences are accentuated by the stages of the rite. Separation requires giving up the emotional properties afforded by many of the individuals with whom one interacts each day. Also, the activities associated with these interactions must stop. Further, change is involved as one begins to increase interaction with those people participating to whom one is now limited. At transition, new interaction forms must be performed, ordinarily under supervision, with every means used to entrain and enforce correct performance of the patterns. And at the end, when incorporation takes place, one must begin to interact in the institutions from which one has been absent.

In each of these stages, temperamental reactions are inevitable. They include the loss of important complementary relationships, having to interact with individuals who are disturbing, the awkwardness and shyness of dealing with new people, being dominated or having to respond continuously to initiatives from many people (as in hazing in college fraternities or the army). It is easy to see then that, apart from the rituals themselves and the symbolic interval scales with their own impacts contained within them, all kinds of emotional currents are set in motion.

Beyond this, in the rites of passage and, in a less obvious and dramatic sense, in rites of intensification, performance of the rites, in almost every society, is obligatory. Not only must one be present, but one is required to act out the interaction forms. Thus the bereaved, however much they may be overcome by grief and try to withdraw from interaction with others, are forced to go through the rituals. Perhaps they must act out their grief, keening as among the Irish, throwing themselves about wildly, slashing their flesh, scarifying their wounds, or sitting up with the dead, and greeting friends and distant relatives. Whatever their idiosyncratic tendencies, the participants must carry out the interaction forms even if, as has often been observed, they have to be dragged through the motions by others.

It seems quite evident, but little studied systematically, that the rites have evolved, in part at least, as structural means through which equilibrium, in all its complex emotional—interaction patterns, is reestablished. In the case of death or separation, the rites of passage in many societies enable individuals to abreact, act out their grief; in so doing, they discharge the emotional tensions which the sympathetic nervous system has built up. Adrenalin, noradrenalin, and other hormones are used up and further secretions brought to an end. The management of grief, in psychiatric practice, means utilizing the therapeutic interview to try to obtain the pouring out of emotional–interactional energy similar to that which the rite is able to do. Many depressions are a consequence of repressed (unacted out) grief. So similar techniques are used to try to reestablish equilibrium after the long past crisis has systematically distorted the temperamental patterns.

Although death (or separation) are important threats to emotional stability, other life crises can be equally disturbing through different autonomic–interactional mediators. Each can have serious stress potentials (differing by society and, of course, idiosyncratically) not only for the person directly concerned but for those closely associated with him or her. The approach of birth may not be as stressful to the mother as to the father, since she, by contrast, is usually the center of attention. In some societies he, too, withdraws from his ordinary activities and may even take to his bed. After the birth of the child, he may go through a rite of incorporation. The crisis and its ceremony for the father, the "couvade," has its parallels among people far removed from such cultures as those of the Solomon Islands. In the United States, couvade reactions, morning sickness, and similar manifestations are well established for a surprising number of fathers but there are no rituals, only tranquilizers, by which they are supposedly controlled.

In all these rites, and the contexts of situation from which they are built up, the emotional properties of the symbols are an obvious and predominant element. As outlined earlier, it is possible to range them on a rough interval scale, based on the levels of abstraction which they represent. It is assumed that the symbol whose emotional–interactional referents are most inclusive undergoes a kind of additive process. By cumulating the emotions with which it is associated, its impact in obtaining a response will be greater than a symbol which refers only to a single interactional event (and thus is on the first level of abstraction).

A single event can have been particularly traumatic for that individual at that time. If this is the case, one would suspect that it symbolized a whole series of past traumatic events whose existence had been forgotten or repressed. But one cannot try, in most instances, to develop an idiosyncratic symbolic scale for each person. For ordinary purposes of estimating symbolic constraints, this would be impractical. Yet in the management of people, the skillful person tries to utilize those symbols (together with patterns of interaction) which he suspects are best suited to establish a proper rhythm of response in the individual he hopes to persuade or cozen.

More generally, a speaker or other practitioner of the art of influencing people uses fairly well-established levels of abstraction within the culture. He runs up and down the scale of abstraction levels, now brandishing a high-level symbol—"God," "the German people," "the Red barbarians seeking to destroy us"—now shifting to the more homely examples which are closer to the actual contexts of situation within which the audience interacts. Further, he varies the contexts and the symbols. Where possible, he selects them from such opposed emotional states as love and hate or attack and counterattack. Ordinarily, the buildup takes place by moving to higher and higher levels of abstraction; by so doing, he includes more and more emotional contexts until everyone in the audience is presumably responding in unison. In general, one can establish such scales, remembering always that their influence is determined after the fact (did they or did they not respond) and that ritual contexts are far more effective because of the automatism of the conditioned rhythmic patterns of which they are constituted.

Chapter 16

Rituals, Symbols, and The "Secular Society"

The almost unbelievable growth of technology in modern society, the proliferation of cultural sequencing and of organizational complexity, appears to many students to have brought to an end the power of the ritual world. Whether or not one's tastes run to religiosity, one cannot help admit that the old interaction forms of the rites of passage and intensification have lost or are losing much of their emotional force. Yet the crises of life are still there and still as important as they were to people in a more believing era. Furthermore, the communal crises, for all those bold predictions of a planned and controlled society, have an uncanny way of persisting through a technological haze.

What has happened is that countries like the United States (and all the others as they, too, presumably achieve industrialization) lose the old gods and the old beliefs which essentially were grounded on an agricultural economy. Some of the ceremonial peaks like those of Christmas and, to a lesser extent, of Easter continue. A shift in their underlying foundations in the social system which have not yet undergone all the changes which appear in store for them depends on changes in cultural sequencing and the rituals and symbols which make them up.

Still, much of what is taking place today in the United States, and in other technologically advanced countries, suggests that the quest for replacement is intensifying. Its urgency for the young, in particular, is becoming more acute. On the other hand, preoccupation with the cognitive world, the attempt to develop some highly rational schema through which ultimate "understanding" can be achieved, is definitely confusing the issue (and the search). Fernandez (1965) very acutely pointed out that:

> The prospect of men both acting together socially and thinking together culturally in entire mutuality cannot fail to inspire, but it cannot cause us to forget the degree to which men value acting together and distrust thinking together about the meaning of that action. It cannot cause us to forget that the gutfeeling or moral community created by coordinated interaction such as ritual may be actually threatened by an attempt to achieve moral community on the cultural level where the symbolic dimensions of interaction must be made explicit.

Today, the symptomatic evidences of this search for the "gutfeeling or moral community" are all around us, possibly more acutely than in the past. Of course, conflict between generations as the young reach adolescence and early adulthood is a perennial theme in cultural history. At this point in time, however, the controls (through which the young are conditioned at an early age to respond to the "discipline" of set events) have become fragmented, even if they have not entirely broken down. The reduction of family structure to nuclear units, the accomodations which the schools have had to make to opposition to authority and, perhaps most important, the wide acceptance and utilization of such paired interaction forms as interviewing and counseling make it less likely that, as in the past, after the revolt the young will rejoin the establishment.

Beyond this, however, the increasing complexities and rigidities of institutional structure restrict free movement. Not merely is there no West to go to, in Horace Greeley's sense, but the interaction forms required within all types of large organizations are highly differentiated and formalized (even if not yet ritualized). In addition, the rewards (and the sanctions) in theory at least, are given for performing them accurately and acceptingly. The organization man is by no means as rigid as the stereotype. Like the Roman Catholic Church of the Italian Renaissance, remarkable deviations in personalities occur and perform successfully. There are perhaps no Borgias, but the historian of industrial civilization will find it easy to point to their equivalents.

From the outside, however, the impression is of monolithic "role" specification. Thus, one common label for youth's present disease is that they suffer from "role anxiety." Yet this is mere fashion. Afraid they may well be. Perhaps their personality requirements cannot be met within the institutional setting. In consequence, their lives will go on and on with continuous disharmony between the situations imposed by the cultural dimensions and their emotional–interactional needs. But this is projection, not reality. Even if there are some exceptions, the remarkable proliferation of interaction forms (and roles) today makes it improbable that effective institutional outlets are not available for almost everyone.

How does one find them? To a considerable extent, the prior conditions for selection are at issue. All too obvious are the necessities for specific educational achievements, appropriate dress, speech, posture and appearance, religious affiliation, sex, skin color, and all the rest which imply to the keepers of the institutional gates (the employment departments) that their interaction forms will be appropriately carried out. To a large extent, these barriers are institutionalized. Schools, craft unions, and professional associations maintain their institutional unity by increasing the internal interactions within the structured sets and the cultural contexts which stabilize them. In the author's lifetime, educational achievement as a badge of entry has shifted from the high-school diploma, to a bachelor's degree, then to the M.A. and its variants. Now even the janitor will probably be required to have a Ph.D.

But all this is peripheral to the main issue. What is really being sought, often in the most bizarre forms, is a new symbolic universe with rituals which are instrumental in that all can participate. In these contexts, the interaction will achieve the highest emotional levels of complementarity, supplemented by the underlying stratum of its opposites, the stresses which need to be overcome. Most directly, this is the crisis within which the black people of this country find themselves. The various Afro-American Christian churches have in the past provided a ritual framework perhaps only today to be found in the Pentecostal churches. Now these traditional churches of the Negroes have become close approximations to those of the white middle class, equally lacking in ritual and symbolic targeting.

As a consequence, there has been an upsurging of attempts to develop interaction forms and contexts of situation to express and channel the powerful emotions which a new and potentially far more adequate equilibrium state appears to make possible. If found, then all can interact—to begin with each other—under the rubric of Black Power. Thus, a total communal and institutional life would come into being. Continuous subordination in the set events of caste to their white initiators who so long have maintained these caste relationships through institutional means of achieving dominance would come to an end. Whether in the long run black people believe they can remain sectarian is inconsequential since all the institutional networks will pull the other way.

The emphasis on blackness, on Africa and the history of tribes and empires, the incongruous concern with Islam (the religion of those Arab slave traders who still sell Negroes into bondage in Saudi Arabia and other Arab countries and the Arabic-African lingua franca, Swahili), however touching, is secondary. For out of this search will also come quite usable interaction forms built on the contexts of situation of their strong contribution to the rich culture of music and expressive movement now existing in the United States.

In striking contrast is the muddled search of middle-class white young people for "love," the "hippies," the "flower people," congregating like schools of herring in the more permissive sections of large metropolitan centers. Seeking the emotional experience which, in the bygone days of fundamentalist and revivalistic Christianity, would have been available to them within the churches or through traveling evangelists, they now try to achieve such states through marihuana and other drugs, through unrestricted sex in all possible variants, and through dalliance with the much talked about but little practiced Oriental religions—Zen Buddhism being the most popular.

The primary crisis in such a quest is a complete separation from home, family, and community. Following the inevitable sequence, this is followed by their participation in an erratically ritualized state of transition with its heightened emotional condition. In addition, perhaps without conscious awareness of the symbolism, the contexts of familial and community interaction forms are reversed by avoidance of bathing, nonshaving among the males, wearing disintegrate clothing, and the adoption of garments, jewelry, and other objects to symbolize the complete breakdown of sex role differentiation. For the occasional personality seeking to initiate, "exhibitionistic" patterns are performed; at least they would be so regarded back home.

However much this inchoate striving for rituals and symbols and intensification of emotional–interactional states provides temporary surcease, the problem extends throughout modern industrial society. Not as various political theorists hold, because this is a natural consequence (and evil) of technological civilization, to be countered by some new political and economic organization of the sources of power. On the contrary, the problem lies much deeper; the outlines of the ultimate solution should be apparent from what has gone before.

The Shape of Things to Come

The major religions available to industrial culture are all primarily built on the constraints of agriculture (and pastoralism) and the environment affecting it. Their symbols and rituals have, therefore, developed a major disconformity from the interaction forms of which they are constituted, supplemented by the strong emphasis, in each of them, on abstention, withdrawal—the individual's search for *his* religion's variant on perfection as the preferred interaction pattern. In addition, the composition of the contexts (agricultural and pastoral) from which the symbols have been filtered out are structured, particularly within Christianity, on the family as an institution, and the church as its communal expression.

Yet the family, with all its emphasis on the control of sex and the procreation of children, is no longer the primary structural building block of society. Not that it is necessarily going to disappear; rather that the institutional forces which utilized the biological continuity of generations as the organizing principle for the parental hierarchy *and for technology,* the set of relationships which can extend over five generations in the human, have lost their interactional coherence through the impact of fundamental changes in spatial distance and cultural sequencing. The separation of the sexes and the dangers to maleness of the female element (and less important quantitatively, its converse) are becoming minimized.

Further, the essential interaction forms of withdrawal from the world and abnegation of all affectional relationships are becoming almost incongruous in the present culture. Increasingly, the doer, the intervenor, provides the fundamental pattern to be emulated. Withdrawal has become equivalent (in large part) to being mentally ill. Traditional religions have given some small recognition to the activist's role—even in Buddhism, once the Bodhisattva has achieved Nirvana, he may (but rarely does) return to aid his people since he can now act freely, being no longer bound to the Wheel of Illusion.

Stirrings like existentialism have become popular, not only in religion but in psychiatry and less formal disciplines. Here confusions still exist between acting for acting's sake (for the internal needs of the personality) and acting as *inter*action. As these evolve, however, there are indications that adjustment and complementarity are in some sense presumed its consequences; at least "the other" person is necessary for any individual's emotional completeness. And this is not the relationship of acting towards (in charity, for example) for one's *own* benefit, through initiative and dominance, as in Christianity. Curiously, this kind of complementary patterning did occur among the early Christians. For them, until the hierarchy took over, agape, the love feast, was the highest ritual form. This emphasis on working at what is here called complementarity was a recurrent theme in many heretical movements, at least until the slaughter of the Albigensians in the 13th century.

One can only speculate on the next state of symbolic and ritual crystallization, and how soon it will appear. Yet on this, one can be dogmatic. However different the rituals and interaction forms turn out to be from "traditional religion," the demands of the human condition will begin to reshape the cultural dimensions to provide effective emotional outlet for the fundamental crises of existence, both for the individual and the group.

Man is quite clearly capable of incredibly abstract, cognitive mastery of the universe. He will, no doubt, achieve a complete and scientific understanding of his own behavior (to which this book may make some small contribution). Yet understanding is not enough. One cannot sterilize the autonomic nervous system by intellectual efforts.

For man, like all animals, is a creature of his physiological requirements. He gains his satisfactions through them. Perhaps in the infinite future or on some planet far removed from Earth, mutant species will appear with only a cortex, a living moving computer for cognitive apotheosis. Until such time, man will continue to hate and love, to be afraid, to react with all the intense emotions of which he is capable. And until he disappears forever as a species, he will still need the aid of cultural patterning to channel and control the over-powering forces which his biological inheritance has given him. There is no choice and, for this, perhaps, we may be grateful.

Bibliography

Abruzzi, Adam, *Work Measurement: New Principles and Procedures.* New York: Columbia University Press, 1952. *(See p. 21.)*

Albert, Ethel M., " 'Rhetoric', 'Logic', and 'Poetics' in Burundi: Culture Patterning of Speech Behavior," *Amer. Anthro.,* vol. 66, no. 6, pt. 2, pp. 35–54, 1964. *(See pp. 234, 268.)*

Altmann, Stuart A., "Sociobiology of Rhesus Monkeys," *J. Theor. Biol.,* vol. 8, no. 3, pp. 490–522, 1965. *(See p. 132.)*

——, "The Structure of Primate Social Communication," in *Social Communication Among the Primates,* Stuart A. Altmann, Ed. Chicago, Ill.: Chicago University Press, 1967, chap. 17, pp. 325–362. *(See p. 6.)*

Anderson, Paul K., *et al.,* "Mus Musculus: Experimental Induction of Territory Formation," *Science,* vol. 145, pp. 1753–1755, 1965. *(See p. 166.)*

Andrew, Richard J., "The Origin and Evolution of the Calls and Facial Expressions of the Primates," *Behaviour,* vol. 20, pts. 1 and 2, pp. 1–109, 1963. *(See p. 7.)*

Ardrey, Robert, *African Genesis.* New York: Atheneum, 1961. *(See p. 11.)*

——, *The Territorial Imperative.* New York: Atheneum, 1966. *(See p. 11.)*

Aschoff, Jurgen, "Exogenous and Endogenous Components in Circadian Rhythms," in *Cold Spring Harbor Symposia on Quantitative Biology.* New York: Long Island Biological Association, chap. 25, pp. 11–28, 1960. *(See p. 25.)*

——, "Circadian Rhythms in Man," *Science,* vol. 148, pp. 1427–1432, 1965. *(See pp. 26, 27, 29.)*

Barnett, S. A., "Rats," *Animal Behavior,* vol. 12, pp. 2–3, 1967. *(See p. 157.)*

Beach, Frank A., *Sex and Behavior.* New York: Wiley, 1965. *(See p. 253.)*

Bender, Donald R., "A Refinement of the Concept of Household: Families, Co-Residence, and Domestic Functions," *Amer. Anthro.,* vol. 69, no. 5, pp. 493–506, 1967. *(See p. 191.)*

Berlyne, Daniel E., *Conflict, Arousal and Curiosity.* New York: McGraw-Hill, 1960. *(See p. 159.)*

——, "Conflict and Arousal," *Sci. Amer.,* vol. 215, no. 2, pp. 82–87, 1966. *(See p. 154.)*

——, "Curiosity and Exploration," *Science,* vol. 153, pp. 25–39, 1966. *(See p. 101.)*

——, "Novelty, Arousal, and the Reinforcement of Diversive Exploration in the Rat," *J. Comp. and Physiol. Psychol.,* vol. 62, no. 2, pp. 222–226, 1966. *(See p. 159.)*

Birdwhistell, R. L., *Introduction to Kinesics.* Louisville, Ky.: University of Louisville Press, 1952. *(See pp. 153, 247.)*

Bohannon, Paul, *Social Anthropology.* New York: Holt, Rinehart and Winston, 1963. *(See p. 191.)*

Bowlby, Edward J., "Childhood Bereavement and Psychiatric Illness," in *Aspects of Psychiatric Research,* D. Richter, Ed. London: Oxford University Press, 1962, pp. 262–293. *(See pp. 95, 140.)*

Brazier, M. A. B., "Long-Persisting Electrical Traces in the Brain of Man and Their Possible Relationship to Higher Nervous Activity," *The Moscow Colloquium on Electroencephalography: EEG J. Supplement,* H. H. Jasper and G. D. Smirnov, Eds., vol. 13, pp. 347–358, 1960. *(See p. 39.)*

Bridger, Wagner, *et al.,* "The Effectiveness of Various Soothing Techniques on Human Neonates," *Psychosom. Med.,* vol. 28, no. 4, pp. 316–332, 1966. *(See p. 34.)*

——, "Behavioral Inhibition in Neonates Produced by Auditory Stimuli," *Child Develop.,* vol. 36, no. 3, pp. 639–645, 1966. *(See p. 42.)*

Broadhurst, P. L., "Determinants of Emotionality in the Rat." I. "Situational Factors," *Brit. J. Psychol.,* vol. 48, pp. 1–12, 1957. II. "Antecedent Factors," *Brit. J. Psychol.,* vol. 49, pp. 12–20, 1958a. III. "Strain Differences," *J. Comp. Physiol. Psychol.,* vol. 51, pp. 55–59, 1958b. *(See pp. 35, 131.)*

Brody, Elizabeth G., "The Genetic Basis of Spontaneous Activity in the Albino Rat," *J. Comp. Psychol.,* vol. 17, pp. 1–24, 1942. *(See pp. 35, 131.)*

Bronson, Franklin H., and Basil Eleftheriou, "Adrenal Response to Fighting in Mice: Separation of Physical and Psychological Causes," *Science,* vol. 147, pp. 627–628, 1965. *(See p. 168.)*

Brown, J. L., and R. W. Hunsperger, "Neuroethology and the Motivation of Agonistic Behavior," in *Readings in Animal Behavior,* Thomas McGill, Ed. New York: Holt, Rinehart and Winston, 1963, pp. 148–161. *(See pp. 65, 133.)*

Bullock, Theodore H., "The origins of patterned nervous discharge," *Behavior,* vol. 17, pp. 48–59, 1961. *(See p. 202.)*

Bunning, Erwin, "Biological Clocks," in *Cold Spring Harbor Symposia on Quantitative Biology.* New York: Long Island Biological Association, 1960, vol. 25, pp. 1–9. *(See p. x.)*

Burnett, Jaquetta, unpublished doctoral dissertation, Columbia University, 1965. *(See p. 282.)*

Cannon, Walter B., *Bodily Changes in Fear, Hunger, Pain and Rage,* 2nd ed., Boston, Mass.: Branford, 1953. *(See p. 75.)*

——, "Voodoo Death," *Psychosom. Med.,* vol. 19, pp. 182–190, 1957. *(See p. 158.)*

Carpenter, C. R., "A Field Study of the Behavior and Social Relations of Howling Monkeys," *Comp. Psychol. Monogr.,* vol. 10, no. 48, pp. 1–168, 1934. *(See pp. 35, 54.)*

——, "Sexual Behavior of Free-Ranging Rhesus Monkeys," *J. Comp. Psychol.,* vol. 33, pp. 113–162, 1942. *(See p. 226.)*

——, "Territoriality: A Review of Concepts and Problems," in *Behavior and Evolution,* A. Roe and G. G. Simpson, Eds. New Haven, Conn.: Yale University Press, 1959. *(See p. 163.)*

Chapple, Eliot D. "Measuring Human Relations: An Introduction to the Study of the Interaction of Individuals," *Gen. Psychol. Monogr.,* vol. 23, pp. 3–147, 1940. *(See pp. 3, 55, 92, 121, 224, 225, 255, 310, 312 . . .)*

Chapple, E. D., and Erich Lindemann, "Clinical Implications of Measurements of Interaction Rates in Psychiatric Patients," *Appl. Anthro.,* vol. 1, pp. 1–10, 1941. *(See p. 46.)*

Chapple, E. D., and Carleton S. Coon, *Principles of Anthropology.* New York: Holt, Rinehart and Winston, 1942. *(See pp. 92, 181, 184, 206, 240, 262, 292, 296, 308 . . .)*

Chapple, Eliot D., "The Analysis of Industrial Morale," *J. Ind. Hyg. and Toxicol.,* vol. 24, no. 7, pp. 163–172, 1942. *(See p. 232.)*

——, *The Interaction Chronograph: Its Evolution and Present Application.* New York: American Management Association, 1949. *(See p. 203.)*

——, "The Standard Experimental (Stress) Interview As Used in Interaction Chronograph Investigations," *Hum. Org.,* vol. 12, pp. 23–32, 1953. *(See pp. 44, 263, 276.)*

——, "Contributions of Anthropology to Institutional Psychiatry," *Hum. Org.*, vol. 13, no. 2, pp. 11–15, 1954. *(See p. 287.)*

Chapple, Eliot D., and L. R. Sayles, *The Measure of Management.* New York: Macmillan, 1961. *(See pp. 6, 181, 232, 237, 282, 285.)*

Chapple, Eliot D., A. S. Chamberlain, A. H. Esser, and N. S. Kline, "Measurement of the Activity Patterns of Schizophrenic Patients," *J. Nerv. Ment. Dis.*, vol. 137, pp. 258–267, 1963. *(See pp. 6, 153, 155.)*

Chapple, Eliot D., "Toward a Mathematical Model of Interaction: Some Preliminary Considerations," in *Explorations in Mathematical Anthropology*, Paul Kay, Ed. Cambridge, Mass.: M.I.T. Press, to be published 1970a. *(See p. 23.)*

——, "Experimental Production of Transients in Human Interaction," pending publication, 1970b. *(See pp. 81, 89, 111, 277.)*

Chapple, E. D., *et al.* "Principles of Programmed Interaction Therapy" (in preparation 1970). *(See p. 114.)*

Chapple, E. D., *et al.* "An Ecological System Model for Studying Change in Individuals and Groups" (in preparation 1970d). *(See p. 183.)*

——, "Multimodal Distributions of Interaction Values" (in preparation 1970e). *(See p. 38.)*

Chesterfield, Lord, *Letters to His Son by the Earl of Chesterfield: Letter CXXX.* London: Tudor Publishing Co., 1751. *(See p. 39.)*

Chitty, Dennis, "The Natural Selection of Self-Regulatory Behavior in Animal Populations," *Proc. Ecol. Soc.*, pp. 51–78, 1967. *(See p. 167.)*

Christian, John J., "Phenomena Associated with Population Density," *Proc. Natl. Acad. Sci.*, vol. 47, pp. 428–449, 1961. *(See p. 167.)*

Christian, John J., and David E. Davis, "Social and Endocrine Factors as Integrated in the Regulation of Growth of Mammalial Populations," *Science*, vol. 146, pp. 1550–1560, 1964. *(See p. 167.)*

Cobb, Stanley, *Foundations of Neuropsychiatry*, 6th ed. Baltimore, Md.: Williams and Wilkins, 1958. *(See p. 66.)*

——, "Some Clinical Changes in Behavior Accompanying Endocrine Disorder," *J. Nerv. Ment. Dis.*, vol. 130, pp. 97–106, 1960. *(See p. 75.)*

Conant, Francis P., "Korok: A Variable Unit of Physical and Social Space Among the Pokot of East Africa," *Amer. Anthro.*, vol. 67, pp. 429–434, 1965. *(See p. 237.)*

Darling, F. Fraser, *A Herd of Red Deer.* London: Oxford University Press, 1937. *(See p. 6.)*

Darwin, Charles, *The Expression of Emotions in Man and Animals.* Chicago, Ill.: University of Chicago Press, 1965. *(See p. 4.)*

DeCoursey, Patricia J., "Phase Control of Activity in a Rodent," *Cold Spring Harbor Symposia on Quantitative Biology.* New York: Long Island Biological Association, 1960, chap. 25, pp. 45–55. *(See p. 35.)*

Delgado, Jose M. R. "Social Rank and Radio Stimulated Aggressiveness in Monkeys," *J. Nerv. Ment. Dis.*, vol. 144, no. 5, pp. 383–390, 1967. *(See p. 134.)*

DeVore, Irven, "Baboon Ecology," in *Primate Behavior*, Irven DeVore, Ed. New York: Holt, Rinehart and Winston, 1965, pp. 20–52. *(See p. 227.)*

Durkheim, Emile, *Elementary Forms of the Religious Life.* Glencoe, Ill.: Free Press (English translation, 1954). *(See p. 311.)*

——, *The Division of Labor in Society* (Eng. trans.). New York: Macmillan, 1952. *(See p. 213.)*

Eayrs, J. T., "Spontaneous Activity in the Rat," *Brit. J. Anim. Behav.*, vol. 2, pp. 25–30, 1956. *(See p. 131.)*

Ervin-Tripp, Susan, "An Analysis of the Interaction of Language, Topic, and Listener," *Amer. Anthro.*, vol. 66, no. 6, pt. 2, pp. 86–102, 1964. *(See p. 263.)*

Escalona, Sibylle K., "Some Determinants of Individual Differences," *Trans. N.Y. Acad. Sci.*, vol. 27, pp. 802–816, 1965. *(See pp. 34, 42.)*

Exline, Ralph V., *et al.*, "Exploration in the Process of Person Perception: Visual Interaction in Relation to Competition, Sex and the Need for Affiliation," *J. Personality*, vol. 31, pp. 1–20, 1963. *(See p. 156.)*

Falconer, Douglas S. *Introduction to Quantitative Genetics.* New York: Ronald Press, 1960. *(See p. 129.)*

Fantz, R. L., "Visual Perception From Birth as Shown by Pattern Selectivity," *Ann. N.Y. Acad. Sci.*, vol. 118, no. 21, pp. 793–814, 1965. *(See p. 256.)*

Fernandez, James W., "Symbolic Consensus in a Fang Reformative Cult," *Amer. Anthro.*, vol. 67, no. 4, pp. 902–928, 1965. *(See pp. 315, 321.)*

Firth, Raymond, *We the Tikopia*, 2nd ed. New York: Barnes and Noble, 1957. *(See p. 203.)*

Fletcher, Alice, and Francis La Flesche, "The Omaha Tribe," *BAE Washington, Annual Report*, no. 27, 1911. *(See pp. 193, 309.)*

Fortes, Meyer, R. W. Steel, and P. Ady, "Ashanti Survey, 1945–1946: An Experiment in Social Research," *Geog. J.*, vol. 60, 1947. *(See p. 239.)*

Frake, Charles O., "How to Ask for a Drink in Subanun," *Amer. Anthro.*, vol. 66, no. 6, pt. 2, pp. 127–131, 1964. *(See pp. 260, 290.)*

Fried, Morton, "On the Concepts of 'Tribe and Tribal Society'," *Trans. N.Y. Acad. Sci.*, vol. 28, pp. 527–540, 1966. *(See p. 184.)*

Friedl, Ernestine, *Vasilika, A Village in Modern Greece.* New York: Holt, Rinehart and Winston, 1962. *(See pp. 193, 194.)*

Fuller, John L., and W. Robert Thompson, *Behavior Genetics.* New York: Wiley, 1960. *(See p. ix.)*

Fuller, John L., "Physiological and Population Aspects of Behavior Genetics," *Amer. Zool.*, vol. 4, no. 2, pp. 101–109, 1964. *(See p. 137.)*

——, "Conference on Neurological Mutant Mice," *Bio. Sci.,* vol. 802, 1965. *(See p. 132.)*

Gesell, Arnold, *Infancy and Human Growth.* New York: Macmillan, 1928. *(See p. 144.)*

Ginsberg, Benson E., and W. C. Allee, "Some Effects of Conditioning on Social Dominance and Subordination in Inbred Strains of Mice," *Physiol. Zool.,* vol. 15, pp. 485–506, 1942. *(See p. 145.)*

Ginsberg, Benson E., "Discussion (of Scott and Fuller Paper on 'Behavior Differences')," in *Methodology in Mammalian Genetics,* Walter J. Burdette, Ed. San Franciso, Calif.: Holden-Day, 1963, pp. 293–296. *(See p. 136.)*

Glover, Edward, *The Technique of Psycho-Analysis.* New York: International Universities Press, 1958. *(See p. 276.)*

Goffman, Erving, "The Neglected Situation," *Amer. Anthro.,* vol. 66, no. 6, pt. 2, pp. 133–136, 1964. *(See p. 15.)*

Goldman-Eisler, Frieda, "On the Variability of the Speed of Talking and on its Relations to the Length of Utterances in Conversation," *Brit. J. Psychol.,* vol. 45, pp. 94–107, 1954. *(See p. 21.)*

——, "Speech and Thought," *Discovery,* April 1962. *(See p. 105.)*

Goldschmidt, Walter, P. Porter, S. Oliver, F. Conant, E. Winans, and R. Edgerton, "Variation and Adaptability of Culture: A Symposium," *Amer. Anthro.,* vol. 67, no. 2, pp. 402–447, 1965. *(See p. 237.)*

Goodall, J. van Lawick, "Relatives of Man," *Ann. N.Y. Acad. Sci.,* vol. 102, pt. 2, pp. 455–467, 1962. *(See p. 206.)*

——, "Chimpanzees in the Gombe Stream Reserve," in *Primate Behavior,* Irven DeVore, Ed. New York: Holt, Rinehart and Winston, 1965, pp. 425–473. *(See p. 35.)*

Goodenough, Ward H., "Residence Rules," *Southwest J. Anthro.,* vol. 12, pp. 22–37, 1956. *(See p. 15.)*

——, "Cultural Anthropology and Linguistics," in *Report of Seventh Annual Meeting on Linquistics and Language Study, Series on Language and Linquistics No. 9,* Paul Garvin, Ed. Washington, D.C.: Georgetown University Press, 1957. *(See p. 15.)*

Gordon, Richard F., and Katherine K. Gordon, "Psychiatric Problems of a Rapidly Growing Suburb," *Arch. Neurol. Psychiat.,* vol. 79, pp. 543–548, 1958. *(See p. 170.)*

Grinker, Roy R., and John P. Spiegel, *War Neuroses in North Africa.* New York: Macy, 1943. *(See p. 94.)*

Gumperz, John J., "Linguistic and Social Interaction in Two Communities," *Amer. Anthro.* vol. 66, no. 6, pt. 2, pp. 137–153, 1964. *(See p. 264.)*

Halberg, Franz, "Temporal Coordination of Physiologic Function," in *Cold Spring Harbor Symposia on Quantitative Biology.* New York: Long

Island Biological Association, 1960, chap. 25, pp. 229–310. *(See pp. 152, 165.)*

Hall, Edward T., *The Silent Language.* New York: Doubleday, 1959. *(See pp. 152, 165.)*

——, *The Hidden Dimension.* New York: Doubleday, 1966. *(See pp. 18, 152, 165, 247.)*

Hamilton, W. J., *Textbook of Human Anatomy,* W. J. Hamilton, Ed. New York: St. Martin's Press, 1958. *(See p. 63.)*

Harlow, Harry E., "The Development of Affectional Patterns in Primates," in *Determinants of Infant Behavior,* B. M. Foss, Ed. New York: Wiley, 1962. *(See pp. ix, 141.)*

Hediger, H., *Wild Animals in Captivity.* London: Butterworth, 1950. *(See p. 153.)*

Helfer, Ray E., and C. Henry Kempe, Eds., *The Battered Child.* Chicago, Ill.: University of Chicago Press, 1968. *(See p. 171.)*

Hellbrugge, Theodore, "The Development of Circadian Rhythms in Infants," in *Cold Spring Harbor Symposia on Quantitative Biology.* New York: Long Island Biological Association, 1960, vol. 25, pp. 311–323. *(See pp. 31, 42.)*

——, "Circadian Periodicity of Physiological Functions in Different Stages of Infancy and Childhood," *Ann. N.Y. Acad. Sci.,* vol. 117, pp. 361–373, 1964. *(See pp. 31, 42.)*

Hess, Eckhard H., "Ethology: An Approach Toward the Complete Analysis of Behavior," in *New Directions in Psychology I. New York: Holt, Rinehart and Winston, 1962, pp. 159–266. (See p. 133.)*

Hinde, Robert A., *Animal Behavior.* New York: McGraw-Hill, 1966. *(See p. 22.)*

Hirsch, Jerry, "Breeding Analysis of Natural Units in Behavior Genetics," *Amer. Zool.,* vol. 4, no. 2, pp. 139–145, 1962. *(See p. 137.)*

Hockett, Charles F., and Robert Ascher, "The Human Revolution," *Curr. Anthro.,* vol. 5, no. 3, 1964. *(See p. 207.)*

Hsu, Francis L. K., "The Effect of Dominant Kinship Relations on Kin and Non-Kin Behavior," *Amer. Anthro.,* vol. 67, no. 3, pp. 638–661, 1965. *(See p. 241.)*

Hudgins, C. B., and R. V. Stetson, "Relative Speed of Articulatory Movements," *Arch. Ne'erl. Phonet. Exper.,* vol. 13, pp. 85–94, 1937. *(See pp. 21, 37.)*

Huggins, A. W. F., "Distortion of the Temporal Patterns of Speech: Interruption and Alternation," unpublished doctoral dissertation, Harvard University, 1963. *(See p. 21.)*

Hymes, Dell, "Introduction: Toward Ethnographies of Communication," *Amer. Anthro.,* vol. 66, no. 6, pt. 2, pp. 1–33, 1964. *(See p. 14.)*

——, "Directions in (Ethno-) Linguistic Theory," *Amer. Anthro.,* vol. 66, no. 3, pt. 2, pp. 6–56, 1964. *(See p. xiii.)*

Irwin, Orvis C., "The Activities of Newborn Infants," *Genet. Psychol. Monogr.,* vol. 8, pp. 1–92, 1930. *(See pp. 33, 42.)*

Jennings, H. S., *The Biological Basis of Human Nature.* New York: W. W. Norton. *(See p. 4.)*

Jensen, Gordon D., and Ruth A. Bobbitt, "Effects of the Early Environment on Interaction Development," in *Child Development,* N. Wagner, Ed. New York: Random House, 1965. *(See p. 175.)*

Kahn, R. L., and C. F. Cannell, *Dynamics of Interviewing.* New York: Wiley, 1957. *(See p. 256.)*

Kaufman, Charles I., and Leonard Rosenblum, "Variations in Infant Development and Response to Maternal Loss in Monkeys," *Amer. J. Orthopsychiat.,* vol. 38, no. 3, pp. 418–426, 1968. *(See p. 84.)*

Kavanau, J. Lee, "The Study of Social Interaction Between Small Animals," *Anim. Behav.,* vol. 11, no. 4, 1963. *(See p. 131.)*

Keesing, Felix, *Cultural Anthropology: Science of Custom.* New York: Rinehart, 1958. *(See p. 191.)*

Kendon, Adam, "Temporal Aspects of the Social Performance in Two-Person Encounters," unpublished doctoral dissertation, Oxford, 1963. *(See p. 46.)*

——, "Some Functions of Gaze Direction in Social Interaction," *Acta. Psychol.,* vol. 26, pp. 22–63, 1965. *(See p. 156.)*

Kennedy, Donald A., M. B. Kreidberg, H. H. Field, D. Highlands, and Geneva Katz, *Problems of Pediatric Hospital Design.* Boston, Mass.: Tufts-New England Medical Center, 1965. *(See pp. 153, 197.)*

Kephart, William M., "A Quantitative Analysis of Intra-group Relationships," *Amer. J. Sociol.,* vol. 55, no. 6, pp. 544–549, 1950. *(See p. 180.)*

Kleitman, Nathan, "A Brief Activity Cycle in Man," presented at the 5th Conference on Sociological and Biological Rhythms, Stockholm, Sweden, 1955. *(See p. 34.)*

——, *Sleep and Wakefulness.* Chicago, Ill.: University of Chicago Press, 1963. *(See p. 108.)*

Koch, Sigmund, *et al., Psychology,* Vol. 13, Sigmund Koch, Ed. New York: McGraw-Hill, 1959. *(See p. 22.)*

Koford, Carl B., "Group Relations in an Island Colony of Rhesus Monkeys," in *Primate Social Behavior,* C. H. Southwick, Ed. Princeton, N.Y.: D. Van Nostrand, 1963, pp. 136–152. *(See pp. 55, 122, 169, 227.)*

Kortland, Adriaan, "Chimpanzees in the Wild," *Sci. Amer.,* vol. 206, no. 5, pp. 128–138, 1962. *(See p. 207.)*

Kuper, Hilda, *Swazi: A South African Kingdom.* New York: Holt, Rinehart and Winston, 1963. *(See p. 186.)*

Lamb, Sidney M., "The Sememic Approach to Structural Semantics," *Amer. Anthro.,* vol. 66, no. 3, pt. 2, pp. 57–58, 1964. *(See p. 250.)*

Langer, Suzanne, *Mind: An Essay on Human Feeling,* vol. 1. Baltimore, Md.: Johns Hopkins Press, 1967. *(See p. 198.)*

Lehrman, D. S., "Interaction of Hormonal and Experiential Influences on Development of Behavior," in *Roots of Behavior,* Eugene Bliss, Ed. New York: Hueber, 1962. *(See p. 138.)*

Lenneberg, Eric H., *Biological Foundations of Language.* New York: Wiley, 1967. *(See pp. xii, 5, 21, 23, 37, 144, 246.)*

Lindemann, Erich, "Symptomatology and Management of Acute Grief," *Amer. J. Psychiat.,* vol. 101, no. 2, pp. 141–148, 1944. *(See p. 92.)*

Lindemann, Erich, and J. E. Finesinger, "The Relation of Drug-Induced Mental Change to Psychoanalytical Therapy," *Bull. WHO,* vol. 21, pp. 517–526, 1959. *(See p. 94.)*

Lobban, Mary C., "The Entrainment of Circadian Rhythms in Man," *Cold Spring Harbor Symposia on Quantitative Biology.* New York: Long Island Biological Association, 1960, vol. 25, pp. 325–332. *(See p. 28.)*

Lombard, George F. F., *Behavior in Selling Groups: A Case Study of Interpersonal Relations in a Department Store.* Boston, Mass.: Harvard University Press, 1955. *(See p. 166.)*

Lorenz, Konrad, *King Solomon's Ring.* New York: Thomas Crowell, 1952. *(See p. 127.)*

——, *On Aggression* (Eng. trans.), Marjorie Kerr Wolf, Tr. New York: Harcourt, Brace and World, 1966. *(See p. 160.)*

Ludwig, A. M., and A. J. Marx, "Influencing Techniques of Chronic Schizophrenics," *Arch. Gen. Psychiat.,* vol. 18, pp. 681–688, 1968. *(See p. 114.)*

Malinowski, B., *Argonauts of the Western Pacific.* London: Routledge, 1922. *(See p. 2.)*

——, "The Problem of Meaning in Primitive Language (Appendix I,) in *The Meaning of Meaning.* New York: Harcourt, Brace and World, 1927. *(See pp. 255, 312.)*

Marler, Peter, "Communication in Monkeys and Apes," in *Primate Behavior,* Irven DeVore, Ed. New York: Holt, Rinehart and Winston, chap. 16, pp. 544–584, 1965. *(See p. 7.)*

Marler, Peter, and W. J. Hamilton, III, *Mechanisms of Animal Behavior.* New York: Wiley, 1966. *(See pp. 5, 159, 200, 255, 256.)*

Marx, Otto, "The History of the Biological Foundations of Language" (Appendix B), in *Biological Foundations of Language,* Eric Lenneberg. New York: Wiley, 1967. *(See p. 21.)*

Masters, W. H., and V. E. Johnson, "The Sexual Response Cycles of the Human Male and Female: Comparative Anatomy and Physiology," in *Sex and Behavior,* F. A. Beach, Ed. New York: Wiley, 1965, pp. 512–534. *(See p. 75.)*

Matarazzo, Joseph, "A Technique for Studying Changes in Interview Behavior," in *Research in Psychotherapy.* Washington, D.C.: American Psychological Association, 1957. *(See p. 277.)*

Mather, K., *Biometrical Genetics.* London: Methuen, 1949. *(See p. 129.)*

Mauss, Marcel, *The Gift* (Eng. trans.). Chicago, Ill.: Free Press, 1954. *(See p. 218.)*

Medawar, Sir Peter, "A Biological Retrospect," *Nature,* vol. 207, pp. 1327–1330, 1965. *(See p. 3.)*

Miller, F. B., "Situational Interaction—A Worthwhile Concept?" *Hum. Org.,* vol. 17, no. 4, pp. 37–47, 1958. *(See p. 204.)*

Miller, W. B., "Two Concepts of Authority," *Amer. Anthro.,* vol. 57, no. 2, pt. 1, pp. 271–289, 1955. *(See p. 286.)*

Morgan, G., and H. N. Ricciuti, "Infants' Responses to Strangers During First Year," in *Determinants of Behavior,* B. M. Foss, Ed. New York: Wiley, 1968. *(See p. 144.)*

Mowat, Farley, *Never Cry Wolf.* Boston, Mass.: Atlantic Monthly Press (Little, Brown), 1963. *(See p. 163.)*

Naroll, Raoul, "On Ethnic Unit Classification," *Curr. Anthro.,* vol. 5, no. 4, pp. 283–312, 1964. *(See p. 184.)*

Neilsen, G., *Studies in Self-Confrontation.* Copenhagen: Munksgaard, 1964. *(See p. 156.)*

Opler, M. E., "The Human Being in Culture Theory," *Amer. Anthro.,* vol. 66, no. 3, pp. 507–528, 1964. *(See p. 14.)*

Orbach, J., and A. Kling, "The Stump-Tailed Macaque: A Docile Monkey," *Anim. Behav.,* vol. 12, pp. 2–3, 1964. *(See p. 130.)*

Osmund, H. F., "Function as the Basis of Psychiatric Ward Design," *Ment. Hosp. (Architectural Supplement),* pp. 23–29, 1957. *(See p. xiv.)*

Parmelee, A. H., *et al.,* "Sleep Patterns in Infancy," *Acta Paediat.,* vol. 50, p. 160, 1961. *(See p. 32.)*

Penfield, Wilder, "The Role of the Temporal Cortex in Recall of Past Experience and Interaction of the Present," in *Neurological Basis of Behavior,* G. E. Wolstenolme and C. M. O'Connor, Eds. London: Churchill, 1958, pp. 140–174. *(See p. 134.)*

Peterson, G., and I. Lehiste, "Duration of Syllable Nuclei in English," *J. Acoust. Soc. Amer.,* vol. 32, pp. 693–703, 1960. *(See p. 21.)*

Petter, J. J., "Ecological and Behavioral Studies of Madagascar Lemurs in the Field," *Ann. N.Y. Acad. Sci.,* vol. 102, no. 2, pp. 267–281, 1962. *(See p. 162.)*

Pittendrigh, C. S., "Circadian Rhythms and the Circadian Organization of Living Systems," *Cold Spring Harbor Symposia on Quantitative Biology.* New York: Long Island Biological Association, 1960, vol. 25, pp. 159–181. *(See p. 25.)*

Pos, Robert, and Peter Brawley, "The Informational Underload (Sensory Deprivation) Model in Contemporary Psychiatry," *Canad. Psychiat. Assoc. J.,* vol. 12, pp. 105–124, 1967. *(See p. 159.)*

Pospisil, Leopold, "A Formal Analysis of Substantive Law: Kapauku Papuan Laws of Land Tenure," *Amer. Anthro.,* vol. 67, no. 5, pt. 2, pp. 186–214, 1965. *(See p. 15.)*

Powell, G. F., "Emotional Deprivation and Growth Retardation Simulating Idiopathic Hypopituitarism: A Clinical Evaluation of the Syndrome," *New Eng. J. Med.,* vol. 276, no. 23, pp. 1272–1278, 1967. *(See p. 170.)*

Radcliffe-Brown, A. R., *The Andaman Islanders.* Boston, Mass.: Cambridge University Press, 1922. *(See pp. 187, 309.)*

Ratcliffe, H. L., "Phenomena Associated with Population Density," *Proc. Natl. Acad. Sci.,* vol. 47, pp. 428–449, 1961. *(See p. 169.)*

Redlich, F. C., and D. X. Freedman, *The Theory and Practice of Psychiatry.* New York: Basic Books, 1966. *(See p. 73.)*

Reynolds, V., and F. Reynolds, "Chimpanzees in the Budango Forest," in *Primate Behavior,* Irven DeVore, Ed. New York: Holt, Rinehart and Winston, 1965, pp. 368–424. *(See p. 227.)*

Ricciuti, Henry, "Social and Emotional Behavior in Infancy: Some Developmental Issues and Problems," *Merrill-Palmer Quart.,* vol. 14, no. 1, pp. 82–100, 1968. *(See p. 144.)*

Richter, C. P., *Biological Clocks in Medicine and Psychiatry.* Springfield, Ill.: Charles C Thomas, 1965. *(See p. 36.)*

Ripley, Suzanne, "Intertroop Encounters Among Ceylon Gray Langures," in *Social Communication Among Primates,* Stuart A. Altmann, Ed. Chicago, Ill.: University of Chicago Press, 1964, pp. 237–253. *(See p. 162.)*

Roberts, J. M., *Zuni Daily Life.* New York: Toplinger, 1965. *(See p. 36.)*

Roethlisberger, F. H., and W. Dickson, *Management and the Worker.* Cambridge, Mass.: Harvard University Press, 1939. *(See pp. 208, 276.)*

Rogers, C. R., *Counseling and Psychotherapy.* Boston, Mass.: Houghton Mifflin, 1942. *(See pp. 44, 263, 276.)*

Ronken, H. C., and P. R. Lawrence, *Administering Changes: A Case Study of Human Relations in a Factory.* Cambridge, Mass.: Harvard University Press, 1952. *(See p. 122.)*

Rosenblum, L. A., et al., "Individual Distance in Two Species of Macaque," *Anim. Behav.,* vol. 12, pp. 338–342, 1964. *(See pp. 130, 181.)*

Rowell, Thelma, "Female Reproduction Cycles and the Behavior of Baboons and Rhesus Macaques," in *Social Communication Among Primates,* Stuart A. Altmann, Ed. Chicago, Ill.: University of Chicago
Press, 1967. *(See p. 226.)*

Rundquist, E. A., "Inheritance of Spontaneous Activity in Rats," *J. Comp.
Psychol.,* vol. 16, pp. 415–438, 1933. *(See pp. 34, 131.)*

Sade, Donald S., "Determinants of Dominance in a Group of Free-Ranging
Rhesus Monkeys," in *Social Communication Among Primates,* Stuart
A. Altmann, Ed. Chicago, Ill.: University of Chicago Press, 1967, pp.
99–114. *(See p. 55.)*

Sargant, William W., *Battle for the Mind.* New York: Doubleday, 1957.
(See pp. 38, 94.)

Saslow, George, and E. D. Chapple, "A New Life History Form, with
Instructions for its Use," *Appl. Anthro.,* vol. 4, no. 1, pp. 1–19, 1945.
(See pp. 121, 143.)

Sayles, Leonard R., *Managerial Behavior.* New York: McGraw-Hill, 1964.
(See p. 282.)

Schaller, George B., *The Mountain Gorilla: Ecology and Behavior.* Chicago,
Ill.: University of Chicago Press, 1963. *(See p. 55.)*

——, *The Year of the Gorilla.* Chicago, Ill.: University of Chicago Press,
1964. *(See pp. 16, 35, 117.)*

Scheflen, Albert E., *Stream and Structure of Communicational Behavior.*
Philadelphia, Pa.: Eastern Pennsylvania Psychiatric Institute, 1965.
(See pp. 247, 277.)

Schneirla, Theodore, *et al.,* "An Evolutionary and Developmental Theory
of Biphasic Processes Underlying Approach and Withdrawal," in
Nebraska Symposium on Motivation, M. R. Jones, Ed. Lincoln, Nebr.:
University of Nebraska Press, 1959. *(See p. 160.)*

Scott, J. P., and J. L. Fuller, *Genetics of the Social Behavior of the Dog.*
Chicago, Ill.: University of Chicago Press, 1965. *(See p. 130.)*

Selye, Hans, *The Stress of Life.* New York: McGraw-Hill, 1956. *(See
p. 69.)*

Shannon, C. E., and Warren Weaver, *A Mathematical Theory of Communication.* Urbana, Ill.: University of Illinois Press, 1949. *(See p. xiii.)*

Silver, H. K., and Marcia Finklestein, "Deprivation Dwarfism," *J. Pediat.,*
vol. 70, no. 3, pp. 317–324, 1966. *(See p. 170.)*

Snyder, R. L., "Evolution and Integration of Mechanisms That Regulate
Population Growth," *Proc. Natl. Acad. Sci.,* vol. 47, pp. 1540–1549,
1961. *(See p. 167.)*

Spock, Benjamin, *Baby and Child Care.* Philadelphia, Pa.: Duell, Sloan and
Pierce, 1957. *(See p. 144.)*

Southwick, Charles H., "Regulatory Mechanisms of House Mouse Populations: Social Behavior Affecting Litter Survival," *Ecology,* vol. 36, pp. 627–634, 1955. *(See p. 169.)*

——, "Patterns of Intergroup Social Behavior in Primates, with Special Reference to Rhesus and Howling Monkeys," *Ann. N.Y. Acad. Sci.,* vol. 102, no. 2, pp. 456–454, 1962. *(See p. 169.)*

——, "Peromyscus leucopus: An Interesting Subject for studies of Social Induced Stress Responses," *Science,* vol. 143, pp. 55–56, 1964. *(See p. 168.)*

Stabenau, J. R., W. Pollin, L. Mosher, and J. Turpin, "Life History Differences in Identical Twins Discordant for Schizophrenia," *Amer. J. Orthopsychiat.,* vol. 36, no. 3, pp. 492–509, 1966. *(See p. 95.)*

Stephens, Grover C., "Circadian Melanophore Rhythms of the Fiddler Crab," *Ann. N.Y. Acad. Sci.,* vol. 98, pp. 926–939, 1962. *(See p. 28.)*

Stetson, R. H., *Motor Phonetics: A Study of Speech Movements In Action,* 2nd ed. Amsterdam: North Holland Publ. Co., 1951. *(See p. 247.)*

Steward, Julian H., "Basin-Plateau Aboriginal Sociopolitical Groups," Smithsonian Institution, Bureau of American Ethnology, Washington, D.C., Bull no. 20. *(See p. 179.)*

Stier, T. J. B., "Spontaneous Activity in Mice," *J. Gen. Psychol.,* vol. 4, pp. 67–101, 1930. *(See pp. 34, 42.)*

Strughold, Hubertus, "Day-Night Cycling in Atmospheric Space Flight, and Other Celestial Bodies," *Ann. N.Y. Acad. Sci.,* vol. 98, no. 4, pp. 1109–1115, 1962. *(See p. x.)*

Struthsaker, T. T., "Auditory Communication Among Vervet Monkeys," in *Social Communications Among Primates,* Stuart A. Altmann, Ed. Chicago, Ill.: University of Chicago Press, 1967. *(See p. 7.)*

Sturtevant, W. C., "Studies in Ethnoscience," *Amer. Anthro.,* vol. 66, no. 2, pt. 3, pp. 99–131, 1964. *(See p. 14.)*

Thomas, Dorothy, *et al., Observational Studies of Social Behavior: vol. 1: Social Behavior Patterns.* New Haven, Conn.: Institute of Human Relations, Yale University, 1933. *(See p. 155.)*

Tinbergen, Nikolas, "The Hierarchical Organization of Nervous Mechanisms," in *Society for Experimental Biology: Physiological Mechanisms in Animal Behavior.* New York: Academic Press, 1951, pp. 305–312. *(See p. viii.)*

Tolman, Edward, *Psychology,* vol. 2, Sigmund Koch, Ed. New York: McGraw-Hill, 1959. *(See p. 22.)*

Trice, Harrison, James Belasco, and Joseph Alutto, "The Role of Ceremony in Organizational Behavior," *Ind. Lab. Rel. Rev.,* vol. 23, no. 1, pp. 40–51, 1969. *(See p. 303.)*

Turner, Victor, *The Forest of Symbols.* Ithaca, N.Y.: Cornell University Press, 1967. *(See p. 299.)*

Twain, Mark, *Mark Twain in Eruption,* Bernard DeVoto, Ed. New York: Harper, 1940, pp. 225–226. *(See p. 266.)*

Van Gennep, Arnold, *The Rites of Passage* (Eng. trans.), Monika Vizedom and Gabrielle Cafee, Trs. Chicago, Ill.: University of Chicago Press, 1960. *(See p. 296.)*

Watson, J. B., *Behaviorism.* New York: Norton, 1925. *(See p. 128.)*

Webber, Ross, "The Perception of Interactions by Superior-Subordinate Pairs," unpublished doctoral dissertation, University of Pennsylvania, School of Finance and Commerce, 1966. *(See p. 283.)*

Westbrook, Percy, *Biography of an Island.* New York: Yoseloff, 1958. *(See p. 183.)*

Westin, Alan, *Privacy and Freedom.* New York: Atheneum, 1967. *(See p. 172.)*

White, Leslie, "The Social Organization of Ethnological Theory," *Rice University Studies,* vol. 52, p. 4, 1966. *(See p. 312.)*

Whitehead, A. N., *An Introduction to Mathematics.* London: Oxford University Press, 1925. *(See p. 111.)*

Whitehead, Thomas N., *The Industrial Worker.* Cambridge, Mass.: Harvard University Press, 1938. *(See p. 21.)*

Whyte, William F., *Street Corner Society.* Chicago, Ill.: University of Chicago Press, 1943. *(See p. 54.)*

Widdowson, E. M., "Mental Contentment and Physical Growth," *Lancet,* vol. 260, pp. 1316–1318, 1951. *(See p. 171.)*

Woodward, Joan, *Industrial Organization: Theory and Practice.* London: Oxford University Press, 1965. *(See p. 237.)*

Wright, Sewall, "The Genetics of Quantitative Variability," in *Quantitative Inheritance,* E. C. R. Reeve and C. H. Waddington, Eds. London: Her Majesty's Stationery Office, 1952. *(See p. 129.)*

Wurtman, Richard, and Julius Axelrod, "The Pineal Gland," *Sci. Amer.,* vol. 213, pp. 50–60, 1965. *(See p. 29.)*

Wynne-Edwards, V. C., *Animal Dispersion in Relation to Social Behavior.* New York: Hafner, 1962. *(See p. x.)*

Zuckerman, Sir Solly, *The Social Life of Monkeys and Apes.* London: Routledge, 1932. *(See p. 170.)*

Index